Where Histories Meet

BIGHORN

Where Histories Meet

*Indigenous and Settler Encounters
in the Toronto Area*

VICTORIA FREEMAN

© 2025 Victoria Freeman

LCR Publishing Services
An imprint of University of Calgary Press
2500 University Drive NW
Calgary, Alberta
Canada T2N 1N4
press.ucalgary.ca

All rights reserved.

This book is available in an Open Access digital format published under a CC-BY-NCND 4.0 Creative Commons license. The publisher should be contacted for any commercial use which falls outside the terms of that license.

No AI Training: Without in any way limiting the author's and publisher's exclusive rights under copyright, any use of this publication to "train" generative artificial intelligence (AI) technologies to generate text is expressly prohibited. The author reserves all rights to license uses of this work for generative AI training and development of machine learning language models.

LIBRARY AND ARCHIVES CANADA CATALOGUING IN PUBLICATION

Title: Where histories meet : Indigenous and settler encounters in the Toronto area / Victoria Freeman.
Names: Freeman, Victoria (Victoria Jane), author
Description: Includes bibliographical references and index.
Identifiers: Canadiana (print) 20250217686 | Canadiana (ebook) 20250217694 | ISBN 9781773856438 (softcover) | ISBN 9781773856421 (hardcover) | ISBN 9781773856445 (open access PDF) | ISBN 9781773856452 (PDF) | ISBN 9781773856469 (EPUB)
Subjects: LCSH: Indigenous peoples—Ontario—Toronto—History—19th century. | LCSH: Indigenous peoples—Ontario—Toronto—Social conditions—19th century. | LCSH: Colonists—Ontario—Toronto—History—19th century. | LCSH: Colonists—Ontario—Toronto—Social conditions—19th century. | LCSH: Toronto (Ont.)—Ethnic relations—History—19th century. | LCSH: Toronto (Ont.)—Race relations—History—19th century. | LCSH: Toronto (Ont.)—History—19th century.
Classification: LCC E78.O5 F744 2025 | DDC 971.3/5400497—dc23

The University of Calgary Press acknowledges the support of the Government of Alberta through the Alberta Media Fund for our publications. We acknowledge the financial support of the Government of Canada. We acknowledge the financial support of the Canada Council for the Arts for our publishing program.

This book draws on research supported by the Social Sciences and Humanities Research Council. We acknowledge the support of York University Faculty of Liberal Arts and Professional Studies and Office of the Vice-President Research & Innovation, University of Toronto Libraries, and Toronto and Region Conservation Authority via the Federal Economic Development Agency for Southern Ontario for this research.

  Canada Council for the Arts   Conseil des Arts du Canada

The manufacturer's authorized representative in the EU for product safety is Mare Nostrum Group B.V., Mauritskade 21D, 1091 GC Amsterdam, The Netherlands. Email: gpsr@mare-nostrum.co.uk

Copyediting by Lesley Erickson
Cover art: Wampum illustrations by Kaia'tanoron Dumoulin Bush. Map detail from "A Map of the Province of Upper Canada Describing All the New Settlements, Townships," Sir David William Smyth, 1800.
Cover design, page design, and typesetting by Melina Cusano

They really need to understand that we have been here since the beginning of time, and our stories tell us we'll be here to the end.

—Sherry Lawson, Chippewas of Rama

And I just kind of came back [from Black Creek Pioneer Village] and told my mom about these pioneers, and she said, "Our people were the pioneers, honey. Just in a different sense."

—Kelly LaRocca, Mississaugas of Scugog Island

Contents

Maps | ix
Relationship Charts | x
Introduction: Where Histories Meet | 1

PART ONE: THE TORONTO CARRYING PLACE | 11

    1 Toronto's Indigenous Name | 13
    2 Deep Time in the Humber River Watershed | 23
    3 Trade and Colonial Rivalries | 41

PART TWO: FOUNDING YORK | 49

    4 Early British Treaties | 51
    5 Turning Indigenous Territory into Private Property | 61
    6 Indigenous-Settler Encounters | 69
    7 Settlers on Indigenous Lands | 77

PART THREE: CHANGING RELATIONSHIPS | 91

    8 The War of 1812 and Its Aftermath | 93
    9 The Postwar Fur Trade along Yonge Street | 107
    10 Deforestation, Farming, and Milling | 119

PART FOUR: THE CIVILIZATIONAL AGENDA | 129

    11 Indigenous Christianity | 131
    12 Yonge Street Camp Meetings | 143
    13 The Credit Mission | 157
    14 The Coldwater and the Narrows Settlement | 165
    15 "Progress," Setbacks, and Strategies for Self-Sufficiency | 179

PART FIVE: AGENCY IN TIMES OF STRUGGLE | 185
    16 The Quest for Secure Land Tenure | 187
    17 Defending the Crown | 199
    18 Surviving, Rebuilding, Adapting, Resisting | 211
    19 From Civilization to Assimilation | 223
    20 Black Wampum | 235

PART SIX: NEW STRATEGIES FOR DARK TIMES | 247
    21 The Indian Act and the Great Council Fire | 249
    22 After 1876 | 263

    Conclusion: Confronting History, (Re)making History | 285
    Acknowledgements | 297
    Selected Bibliography | 299
    Map Credits | 309
    Notes | 311
    Index | 341

Maps

Geographic focus of *Where Histories Meet* | xi
Toronto Carrying Place portage routes, by Jean-Baptiste-Louis Franquelin, 1688 | 15
Toronto Carrying-Place Trail (east and west) | 16
John Graves Simcoe's 1793 journey to Matchedash Bay | 18
Historical Wendat and adjacent Iroquoian societies | 25
Haudenosaunee villages on the north shore of Lake Ontario, late seventeenth century | 29
Humber and Black Creek watersheds | 30
Historical Wendat, Seneca, and Mississauga villages on the Humber River | 31
Mississauga routes into southern Ontario | 33
Anishinaabe place names, south-central Ontario | 34
Regional Anishinaabe Council Fires | 38
The Humber route of the Toronto Carrying-Place Trail | 42
Fur trade from the Humber River to French and English trading posts and centres | 43
Lands granted to the Six Nations through the Haldimand Proclamation of 1784 | 53
British land purchase strategy, 1783–88 | 54
Land ceded in 1805 Treaty 13 according to a 1911 map | 74
Treaty 13 boundaries superimposed on a modern road map | 75
Detail from "A Map of the Province of Upper Canada," 1800 | 80
Early settlers near The Village at Black Creek | 84
Indigenous engagement in selected battles in the War of 1812 | 94
The Mississaugas and Chippewas at the Battle of York, 1813 | 97
Anishinaabe land treaties, by date | 100
Mississaugas of the Credit land treaties, 1781–1820 | 101
Regional fur trade via Newmarket and Holland Landing | 108
Mills in the Greater Toronto Area, 1859–60 | 122
The King's Mill on the Humber River, 1793 | 124
Indigenous attendance at Yonge St. Methodist gatherings | 146

Peter Jones' missionary travels and fundraising tours | 154
Credit Mission and land cessions on the Credit River | 158
Chippewa family traditional hunting territories as described in 1923 | 166
The Coldwater and Narrows Reserve (1830–36) and present-day First Nations | 170
Chippewa and settler villages at Orillia, 1836 | 175
Saugeen "Indian Territories," 1844 | 192
Lots purchased for the Chippewas of Rama Reserve | 205
Mississaugas of Scugog Island Reserve, 1844 | 218
Reduction of Six Nations lands and Mississauga relocation to New Credit | 232
Participating communities at the Grand General Council, 1870–1906 | 252

Relationship Charts

Chiefs of Lakes Huron and Simcoe in the seventeenth, eighteenth, and mid-nineteenth centuries | 19
Mississauga relations of Augustus Jones | 64
Haudenosaunee relations of Augustus Jones | 65
Relations of Thayendanegea / Joseph Brant | 67
The Fishers and related families | 85
Borland & Roe, Newmarket fur traders, and their connections | 111
Peter and William Robinson, fur traders of Newmarket and Holland Landing | 114
Dr. Peter Edmund Jones' family tree | 272
Dr. Oronhyatekha's family tree | 273

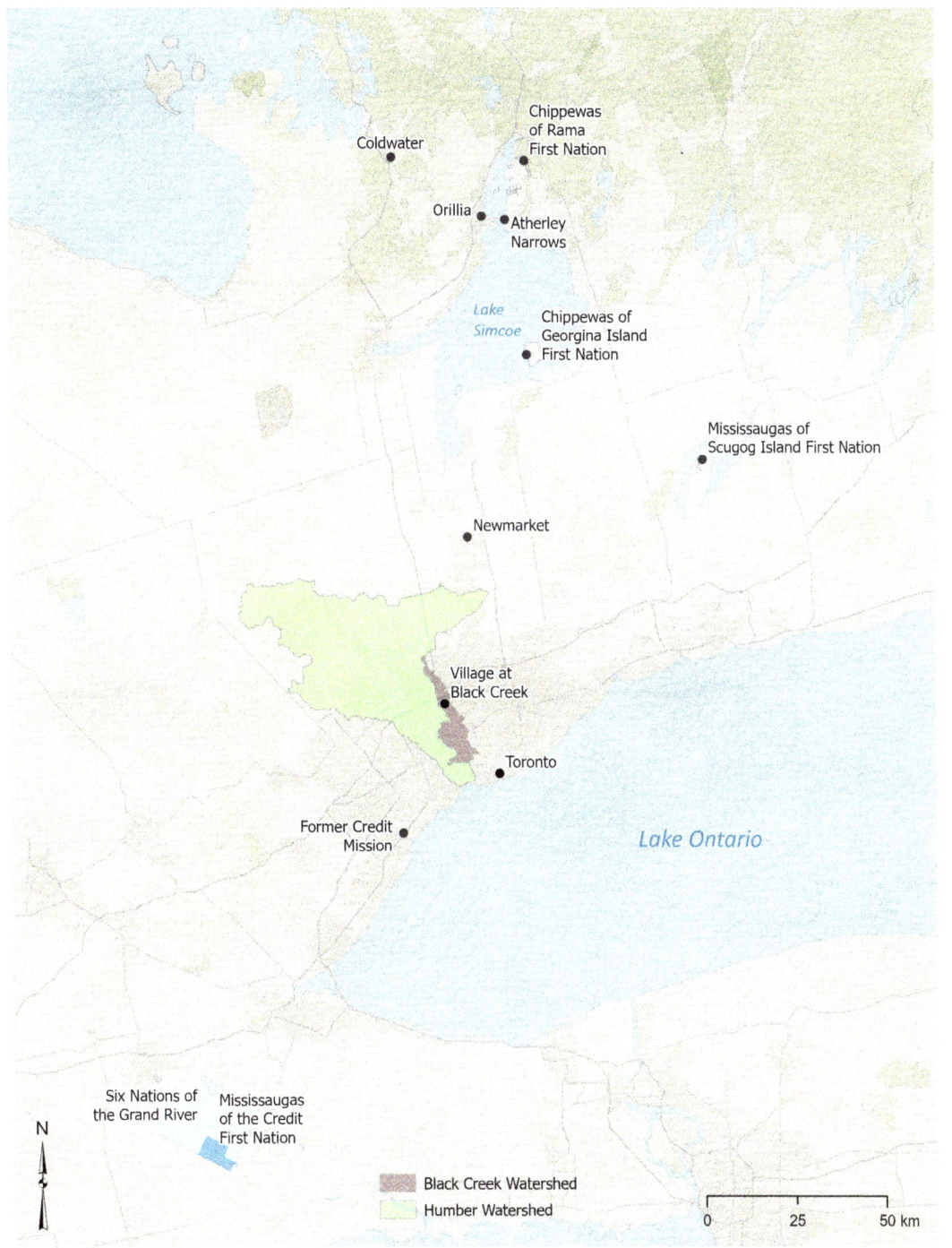

The geographic focus of *Where Histories Meet*

Introduction: Where Histories Meet

You look up "pioneer," it has three different definitions of it. Every one of them says "the first people in to open up an area and welcome the other people in"—that would make us the pioneers . . . And we weren't lost, and they weren't opening up anything. We were here. They were pushing us out of the way. There was nothing to open. We were already open for business.

—Sherry Lawson, Chippewas of Rama[1]

Like similar "pioneer villages" in Canada, the Toronto heritage site known until recently as Black Creek Pioneer Village is not an actual historical village: it was created in the 1960s to tell a particular story. Built around Elizabeth (née Fisher) and Daniel Stong's settler farm, the village consists of buildings transported from other villages and hamlets in southern Ontario to create an image—actually, an idealized version—of nineteenth-century settler village life. For decades this "living history" museum on the city's northern edge, owned and operated by Toronto and Region Conservation Authority, has been a popular destination for tourists and Torontonians alike. Today, as it gradually recovers from pandemic lockdowns, it hosts educational sessions for more than 25,000 schoolchildren and sees about 115,000 visitors annually.[2]

Although the Village's creators vividly represented many aspects of life in a southern Ontario hamlet, they had a significant, telling blind spot: they didn't consider the context and meaning of "settlement" in a land that already had Indigenous laws, Nations, cultural practices, worldviews, and history. Nor did they acknowledge that settlers had interacted with local Indigenous populations or caused massive environmental transformations that greatly impacted the ability of Indigenous peoples to be self-sufficient. In fact, they didn't acknowledge the link between the settlers' arrival and the dispossession of Indigenous peoples at all. A visitor to the Village might be forgiven for thinking that no one had ever lived on these lands before settlers arrived. The Village offered a sanitized version of local history, a bucolic vision of successful settler colonialism that lauded the "pioneers." This version of history dominated most local histories—and much Canadian history writing—until recently.

The Village at Black Creek (formerly Black Creek Pioneer Village) | Photo courtesy of Toronto and Region Conservation Authority

This book originated in a research project titled Changing the Narrative: Reconnecting Indigenous and Settler Histories at Black Creek Pioneer Village, which was sparked by the recognition that the old narrative needed revision. Although the push for change came from many directions, including from staff at the village, *kiskisiwin | remembering*, a punchy six-minute video by Métis-Cree author Jesse Thistle and documentary filmmaker Martha Stiegman concisely made the case.[3]

Led by Jennifer Bonnell and Alan Corbiere of the York University History Department, the Changing the Narrative project addressed the lack of Indigenous content, context, and perspective in The Village installations and interpretation. York University, Black Creek Pioneer Village / Toronto and Region Conservation Authority, and the University of Toronto's Map and Data Library collaborated with the five First Nations closest to Toronto: the Mississaugas of the Credit, Mississaugas of Scugog Island, Chippewas of Rama, Chippewas of Georgina Island, and the Six Nations of the Grand River. In one of its first acts, the research committee of First Nations representatives strongly recommended that the name of the site be changed. In 2024, it was officially renamed The Village at Black Creek—the more inclusive name used throughout this book.

As the principal researcher for the Changing the Narrative project, I explored the interconnected histories of Indigenous and settler peoples, particularly on Toronto's northern and western periphery closest to The Village at Black Creek. Because the Village was said to represent nineteenth-century village life, especially in the 1860s, I focused on the period between 1787, when the British first attempted to purchase land at Toronto, and 1876, when the federal Indian Act became the overarching legal framework controlling Indigenous peoples' lives. I submitted my report in July 2024 to inform the development of permanent installations and related programming.[4] Given the lack of publicly available information about this history, The Village at Black Creek and the research committee of First Nations representatives permitted me to adapt my research report into this book.

As it happens, The Village at Black Creek proved to be a useful anchor for thinking about Indigenous history—and Indigenous-settler interactions—in the Toronto region. Serendipitously, the Village—including the original farm that forms its nucleus—is situated on a tributary of the Humber River. The banks of the Humber served for millennia as a key transportation route and site for Indigenous habitation, including successive Wendat, Haudenosaunee, and Anishinaabe villages. The Humber watershed thus offers a convenient snapshot of Indigenous histories that are the context for understanding developments in the Toronto region in the nineteenth century as well as contemporary land claims and ongoing Indigenous connections to historical territories in the greater Toronto area.

The first homesteaders on the site, Elizabeth Fisher and Daniel Stong, were "ordinary" people, not members of the elite, the people most often blamed for colonial actions. They were Palatine Germans from Pennsylvania, not British. Yet, by settling on this plot of land and building a farm, their actions had repercussions for the land and Indigenous peoples. The extent to which they had contact with Indigenous peoples is unknown, but close relatives of Elizabeth Fisher held Methodist camp meetings on Yonge Street that were attended by large numbers of Indigenous people.

Although segregation and social distancing increased over time, my research revealed significant interactions between Indigenous and settler peoples, both positive and negative, in the early nineteenth century. These interactions came about through missions, trade, mutual aid, technology transfers, intermarriage, and participation in the War of 1812. I was able to identify individuals, interrelated families, and other social networks that played key roles in establishing relations of power or forms of resistance in the region. These are illustrative examples; I have not identified all such relations.

With its church, school, mill, European-style homes for individual families, and a farm that grew European crops and supported European farm animals, The Village at Black Creek also represents what Indigenous peoples were supposed to achieve through the "civilizational agenda." Beginning in the 1820s, churches and the colonial government encouraged Indigenous peoples to transform themselves into Christian farmers, establish their own "settled" communities, and abandon hunting. Over the next two decades, in the face of unprecedented loss and change, many Indigenous people adopted Christianity and tried out farming as a strategy for survival and renewal. They struggled to protect their families, lands, and lifeways while also engaging with new ideas and forms of community—out of necessity.

That Indigenous peoples as well as settlers founded new communities in the nineteenth century is rarely acknowledged. As settlers were establishing new farms and villages, Indigenous peoples were being pressured to give up their lands and relocate to new settlements—often repeatedly. However, when they tried to adopt the kind of agricultural and village life that The Village at Black Creek represents, they experienced radically different outcomes. The histories of the Coldwater-Narrows Reserve west of Orillia and the Credit Mission Village on the Credit River provide important points of comparison and reveal how Indigenous displacement and settler immigration were fundamentally linked.

Ben Cousineau, Chippewas of Rama, member of the research committee for the Changing the Narrative project | Photo by Robert Snache

Research committee member Marcie Sandy, representing the Lands and Resources Department of the Six Nations of the Grand River Elected Council | Photo courtesy of Marcie Sandy

A Collaborative Research Process

Where Histories Meet is perhaps the first historical account of the Toronto region created through a genuinely consultative process with the five First Nations currently living in the area. Research committee members reviewed, provided feedback on, and approved the original research directions, questions, and methodology of the Changing the Narrative project and hence of my archival and secondary-source research. They reviewed two drafts of the report, including maps and images, and offered valuable feedback and numerous suggestions for improvement. Beausoleil First Nation also reviewed the manuscript while the Huron-Wendat Nation did not take up our invitation to do so. As a white scholar, I am enormously grateful for the guidance I received. Research committee members advised me to pay attention not only to colonialism's impact on First Nations but also to their strategies for creative adaptation, resilience, and resistance and made many contributions that ensured this perspective was well supported.

Because archival evidence and secondary sources such as books and articles reflect the biases of collectors and authors and the fragmentary nature of surviving evidence, Alan Corbiere and I interviewed twenty Knowledge Keepers and Elders who were suggested by the participating First Nations. Notably, several were descendants of historical figures discussed in this book. We asked them about the history of their communities and what should be conveyed at The Village at Black Creek or to Canadians generally. Alan reviewed the interviews, provided analysis, and suggested excerpts that might be particularly useful; I make considerable use of his analyses in the following paragraphs. Because the interview process was delayed by pandemic lockdowns, the interviews were not integrated into the original research report but appear in this book as commentary. Given that colonialism is not "over," they provide crucial perspectives on colonialism's consequences and meaning in the present and for the future.

I think they need to know the truth that Black Creek Pioneer Village was manufactured. That it was a manufactured landscape. That's important. And then, I guess, on the flip side of that coin, they need to know that our people were here, even though we don't have necessarily stories of my great-great-great-great-grandfather going there and harvesting wood, or something. It doesn't mean that our people weren't here. It wasn't terra nullius. It wasn't empty.

—Kelly LaRocca, Mississaugas of Scugog Island[5]

This book, then, is a place where the archival record, oral tradition, and Indigenous perspectives on written history, family memory, and genealogy meet. In some communities, such as Six Nations, there is some unbroken oral tradition, such as the Haudenosaunee Great Law of Peace. In others, the chain of transmission has been interrupted. Darin Wybenga, historical interpreter and research committee representative for the Mississaugas of the Credit, commented, "And one thing I will say is that we don't have a long memory about our own history. We really don't... Because there is really no oral tradition around here about these things. We really, really suffer from that."[6] Wybenga noted the loss of place-based stories: "I long to hear some of those old stories from way back... wonderful stories about the little people by the Credit River and the big monster that used to live in the whirlpool out by Burlington Bay. I would love to know those stories."

Both community members and outsiders are affected by this loss of knowledge. As Elder Garry Sault of Mississaugas of the Credit noted, "There wasn't much anybody knew about who we were and what we were. It's like we faded away from history."[7] Most interviewees attributed this loss to the influence of the Christian churches and government repression. Margaret Sault of Mississaugas of the Credit commented: "Well, a lot of things were forbidden to them, like Powwows and different things, and the government tried to keep them apart [from other Indigenous communities] and not to participate in those things."[8]

Elder Rhonda Coppaway of Mississaugas of Scugog Island highlighted the loss of Indigenous language speakers as another threat to knowledge of oral tradition. "Our oldest member passed away a couple of years ago and she was our only language speaker. So we've come almost full circle that way, where the whole community spoke the language and now there's... We're trying to revive that. It's a little bit difficult, but there seems to be energy in the community to want to push forward... So with that Elder passing, our stories, right, are important to hold on to and it's [difficult]... We just probably don't have the information that we should."[9]

Yet all the interviewees knew their community's and family's history as felt experience, including intergenerational trauma, which is often passed down wordlessly. In addition, as Alan pointed out, many values, practices, and knowledges were learned from parents or grandparents without being identified or labelled as Traditional Knowledge. As Elder and former Chief Carolyn

King of Mississaugas of the Credit said, "I'm going to say that just the same way that we just used things, because that's what my mom did or my grandma did, that I don't relate it to something that was a long time ago. It was just something that we did."[10]

In many cases, the interviewees' understanding of their community's history came from their examination of archival records and secondary sources, usually written by non-Indigenous people, supplemented with what they learned from Elders, often in response to the immediate need to defend Aboriginal and treaty rights—and their territories—from encroachment. Elder Margaret Sault, who spearheaded land claims research for the Mississaugas of the Credit for decades, explained, "I'm just kind of learning the traditional history and how they merge, or how they complement, one another. The written word and the historical, traditional side. I'm just kind of learning and piecing those together."[11] Kory Snache of Chippewas of Rama described a similar process: "I do a lot of independent research in archives all over the place. Googling things and trying to decipher what is legitimate and what isn't. And I think that's half the battle. And kind of correlating it with other information."[12] Some took up this research so they could pass knowledge of their history on to the next generation. King commented, "I started to delve into the history, deeply into the Mississauga history, after I had my kids. You want to tell your kids, right?"[13] Others wanted to reinterpret history from Indigenous perspectives: Vicki Snache of Chippewas of Rama noted that what "is really important is to allow for us to be part of creating the narrative . . . If we were to have a part in creating the story, then it needs to be from our voice so that it can be told in a respectful and nonbiased way."[14]

Darin Wybenga spoke about how new oral traditions were being created through this process of research and reinterpretation. As Alan Corbiere noted in his report on the oral history interviews of members of the Mississaugas of the Credit, "This statement actually accords with Bruce Granville Miller's call to recognize Indigenous oral historians not as static 'jukeboxes' that kick out the same 'tune' (story) on demand, but as historians who constantly reinterpret their history as new information comes to light from multiple sources, assisting in the creation of a more fulsome and dynamic retelling of history."[15]

This book includes numerous excerpts from these oral interviews, providing crucial perspectives on the history it explores, especially in the concluding chapter. Nevertheless, the history presented in the main text has been gleaned primarily through archival and secondary sources because interviewees generally spoke of the more recent past rather than the period before 1876. Even so, the interviewees' perspectives deepened my understanding of the consequences of European colonialism and the persistence of Anishinaabe and Haudenosaunee culture, lifeways, knowledge, and values. Their words and the photographs they so generously shared with me make the living presence, persistence, and creativity of First Nations palpable. To my mind, their words carry the soul or spirit of this book, and I, as a non-Indigenous historian, acknowledge my responsibility to respect and uphold them. Ultimately, though, I selected the historical evidence, interviewees' quotes, and images. Any errors or biases are my own.

To allow for a nuanced history that does not homogenize the experiences of Indigenous peoples—or Indigenous Nations—I've drawn on the rich individual histories of the Mississaugas of the Credit, Mississaugas of Scugog Island, Chippewas of Rama, Chippewas of Georgina Island, and Six Nations of the Grand River. The northern and western hinterlands of Toronto in the nineteenth century most centrally involved the ancestors of the Chippewas of Rama, Chippewas of Georgina Island, and Mississaugas of the Credit. Although the Mississaugas of Scugog Island are located closest to Toronto today, they used a different river and portage route via Oshawa for transportation and trade, interacting primarily with other Mississaugas in the Peterborough area. However, they had significant connections with the Anishinaabek of Lakes Huron and Simcoe and were visited by Mississauga Christians from the Credit Mission. Some Scugog people moved briefly to the Coldwater reserve in the 1830s.

The Haudenosaunee of the Grand River lived at some remove from the region north of Toronto but were influential in Indigenous-settler relations throughout south-central Ontario, particularly during the early settlement period. Mohawk War Chief Joseph Brant served as the main interlocutor between the Haudenosaunee, other Indigenous Nations, and the British. He was guided by and reported to the Haudenosaunee Confederacy Chiefs. In subsequent decades, there were frequent interconnections between the Mississaugas of the Credit and the Haudenosaunee, and they became neighbours when the Mississaugas moved to New Credit in 1847. Haudenosaunee contact with Anishinaabek north of Toronto appears to have been less frequent, although they met occasionally at Grand Councils.

To this day, local First Nations have overlapping claims to territory and different versions of key historical events, including inter-Indigenous conflicts and treaties such as the Dish with One Spoon Wampum agreement (c. 1700). These differences are rarely discussed in print, although they have profoundly shaped relations between First Nations and with governments and settler populations. This book is attentive to this plurality of viewpoints. At the same time, all Nations were affected by the same colonizing dynamics and their current differences were often created or exacerbated through these dynamics. Indigenous people of various Nations also helped one other, shared information, visited one another, intermarried, and relocated from one community to another.

Conflicting historical interpretations among First Nations have legal ramifications. For example, the Six Nations assert rights of consultation in the Toronto area based on the Nanfan Deed of 1701 (which they maintain is a treaty) and their seventeenth-century presence in the area. Some of their claims are disputed by other First Nations. Because several issues discussed in this book are currently under litigation (and may be for some time), we worked together to find ways to acknowledge and express these differences neutrally. Where necessary, I include both versions of disputed historical events in the main text or footnotes. In quoted excerpts from the interviews, however, interviewees express their own perspectives that others may not share.

Including rival historical interpretations isn't ideal from the perspective of any individual First Nation, though it's helpful for understanding the overall lay of the land. At the request of the First Nations, I include the following disclaimer: "The involvement of the several First Nations in the research for this book in no way limits their ability to make factual and legal arguments in a court of law that may be contrary to any findings contained in this publication." The Six Nations of the Grand River crafted a separate and more specific disclaimer.[16]

The title *Where Histories Meet,* then, refers to various forms of contact and contention among different historical accounts, including my own struggle to work respectfully with conflicting Anishinaabe and Haudenosaunee historical narratives. As a white historian, I do not feel it's my role to adjudicate between these narratives given, on the one hand, the history of colonial "divide and rule" policies and, on the other, the colonizer's need to assert a unitary and dominating narrative to control others. I have come to recognize that these divergent accounts are emblematic of the unruly nature of narrative itself. They are, in part, new origin stories arising from colonial circumstances. There's creative energy in letting them be and respecting both even as the Canadian legal system insists on winners and losers.

This book is a partial history of Indigenous-settler relations viewed from a particular perspective and shaped in part by the parameters of the original research project. It is suggestive and illustrative. There are many other histories to be told, particularly of Indigenous peoples to the east and northeast.

It is also partial because of the colonial and gender biases of the archives. Most of the Indigenous individuals in the archival record are male Christianized leaders who cooperated with colonial authorities and supported (at least for a time) the adoption of the civilizational agenda. Indigenous women rarely appear outside of brief mentions of Indigenous or white men's wives or the occasional photograph—yet interesting questions can still be asked about their lives. Archival information about non-Christians is also sparse and the circumstances of their lives opaque. As research committee member Ben Cousineau of Chippewas of Rama commented, "It's difficult because the people who probably had the most effect on our community's history, we've forgotten. Because the knowledge that we have is mostly coming from government and colonial sources and records."[17] Another caveat is that genealogical information, especially on Indigenous individuals, is often difficult to confirm. While participating First Nations have had the opportunity to review relationship charts, I welcome new information and corrections.

A Few Words about Terminology

Spellings of personal names, ethnonyms, and place names differ substantially from document to document in the archival record and among different groups in the present. In general, original spellings are retained in quotations. When a modernized name or word is substituted or added, this is indicated by square brackets. Because there are several systems of orthography for rendering Indigenous names and languages in roman script, I decided to use, in consultation with Indigenous members of the team and research committee, the most common ethnonyms and spellings.

The term "Indigenous" is used in preference to other more general or outdated labels. Here, it refers to First Nations people rather than Inuit or historical Métis. The term "Indian" is retained in quoted historical texts and when it's used in a legal sense to refer to those with "Indian status" or to government agencies with "Indian" in their name, such as "the Indian Department." In a few cases, highly pejorative terms have been replaced by modern neutral terms in square brackets.

Numerous, confusing, and overlapping ethnonyms exist for various groups, with many variant spellings. "Anishinaabek / Anishinaabeg" (adjectival and singular form "Anishinaabe") is an umbrella term for culturally and linguistically related peoples, including Ojibwe / Ojibway / Chippewa (To Roast until Puckered Up, possibly referring to the puckered seams of Ojibwe moccasins); Michi Saagiig / Mississaugas (River with Many Mouths); Odaawaa / Ottawa (People Who Trade); Bodewadmi / Potawatomi (Keepers of the Fire); Algonquins; and Nipissings. In this text, I most frequently refer to Chippewas and Mississaugas, as these are the names most commonly used at present.

The Six Nations (Five Nations up to the 1720s) or Haudenosaunee Confederacy are also known by the French name "Iroquois" and include the following Nations: Onödowa'ga (People of the Great Hill) / Seneca; Gayogoho:no (People of the Great Swamp) / Cayuga; Onoñda'gega (People of the Hills) / Onondaga; Onyota'a:ka (People of the Standing Stone) / Oneida; and Kanien'kehá:ka (People of the Land of the Flint) / Mohawk.[18] The Haudenosaunee became known as the Six Nations when they were joined by the Skarù:rę (People of the Hemp Shirt) / Tuscarora in 1722. Here, I will refer to the Mohawk, Oneida, Onondaga, Cayuga, Seneca, and Tuscarora.

Many individuals had both Indigenous and "Christian" names in the period under study. At first mention, the Indigenous name (if known) is given first, then its English translation (if known), followed by a Christian or English name, if any. As some individuals preferred to be known or became widely known by one name or the other, subsequent usage may differ among individuals.

PART ONE:
The Toronto Carrying Place

1

Toronto's Indigenous Name

On August 24, 1793, a party of Anishinaabek from the Lake Simcoe area attended the naming ceremony for a military outpost that would later become the City of Toronto. John Graves Simcoe, the first lieutenant-governor of Upper Canada ("Canada West" from 1841–67; present-day "southern Ontario"), ordered a royal salute fired in honour of the Duke of York's victory over the French in Flanders and named the post York. Elizabeth Posthuma Simcoe, the wife of the lieutenant-governor, wrote that the Anishinaabek appeared to be "much pleased" with the firing of the cannons; one of them took Simcoe's young son Francis in his arms "and was much pleased to find the child not afraid, but delighted with the sound."[1]

The exciting but peaceful detonation of the cannon and the sense of celebration and friendliness between two peoples are poignant. There's also an evident cultural difference in an Anishinaabe Ogimaa (Head Chief) holding and paying sympathetic attention to the child of another man, the child of a foreign leader at that, something an upper-class British man, let alone a high-ranking official such as Simcoe, would likely never do. At the moment of Toronto's conception, then, the histories and cultures of Indigenous and settler peoples were already in dialogue, and new relationships were being created in all their complexity. What the Anishinaabek didn't know was that Simcoe considered the place's existing name, "Toronto," "outlandish."[2] In renaming it York, Simcoe was incorporating and subsuming this Indigenous place into imperial Britain.

The name "Toronto" reflects the ancient connection between the Lake Ontario waterfront and Lake Simcoe. The word appears to have referred to the five-thousand-year-old fish weirs and gathering place at the Narrows between Lake Simcoe and Lake Couchiching (now Atherley Narrows). The most widely accepted theory of the original meaning of "Toronto" is that it comes from the Mohawk word "Tkaranto" (Where there are trees in the water), a reference to hundreds of wooden stakes placed by Indigenous peoples at the Narrows and later called Mnjikaning (Fish fence) by the Anishinaabek.[3]

So the Fish Fence has been around for five thousand years. Pieces of it. You read their research, the various archaeologists that dove and saw. They would wonder why something was only two

The five-thousand-year-old Mnjikaning fish weir at Atherley Narrows. In 1615, Samuel de Champlain noted that the Wendat caught large numbers of fish there | Parks Canada, Nick Van Vliet, Underwater Archaeology Team, 41M144T, 1992.

thousand years old beside something that was four thousand years old. Because they only replaced what was missing. You didn't tear down the whole thing and put a nice new one in.

—Elder Mark Douglas, Chippewas of Rama[4]

The Toronto Carrying-Place Trail along the Humber River was a major Indigenous portage route from western Lake Ontario to this ancient fishing ground, gathering place, and site of regional councils. The French labelled Lake Simcoe "Lac Taronto" and the Humber River Portage route "Le Passage de Toronto." Subsequently, the name came to be applied to the bay at the river's outlet in Lake Ontario and then to the coastline near it. The Lake Simcoe Anishinaabek who attended Simcoe's ceremony almost certainly travelled along the Carrying-Place Trail to reach the lakeshore.

Anywhere where you wanted to go in what's now Ontario, you had to go through those lakes. You had to go through that slot at the Narrows. If you want to go east, west, south, whatever, you had to go through the Narrows. You had to go through Mnjikaning, where the barriers are. So it was a strategic choke point.

—Kory Snache, Chippewas of Rama[5]

14 WHERE HISTORIES MEET

The Toronto Carrying-Place portage routes along the Humber and Rouge Rivers to Lac Toronto (Lake Simcoe) as documented by Jean Baptiste Louis Franquelin, *Carte de l'Amerique Septentrionnale*, in 1688. Note the Seneca villages of Teiaiagon and Ganetsekwyagon at the mouths of the Humber and Rouge, respectively | Courtesy US Library of Congress

The Humber Trail was one of two main local portages to Lake Simcoe (the other was along the Rouge River) and a key connector to a web of Indigenous canoe routes that spanned the continent. The river was too shallow to be navigable along much of its course, but the 45-kilometre portage along its banks provided a useful shortcut to the upper Great Lakes. The portage bypassed the far lengthier water route through Lake Erie and the St. Clair River to Lake Huron and linked diverse peoples through long-distance travel for trade, regional councils, and warfare.

They used to travel back and forth on all those rivers . . . If they went visiting anybody, they'd take the rivers.

—Andrew Big Canoe, Chippewas of Georgina Island[6]

For example, Anishinaabek travelled roughly 800 kilometres from the Sault Ste. Marie area via the Toronto Carrying-Place Trail along the Humber to attend the 1764 Council at Niagara, hosted

1 | Toronto's Indigenous Name   15

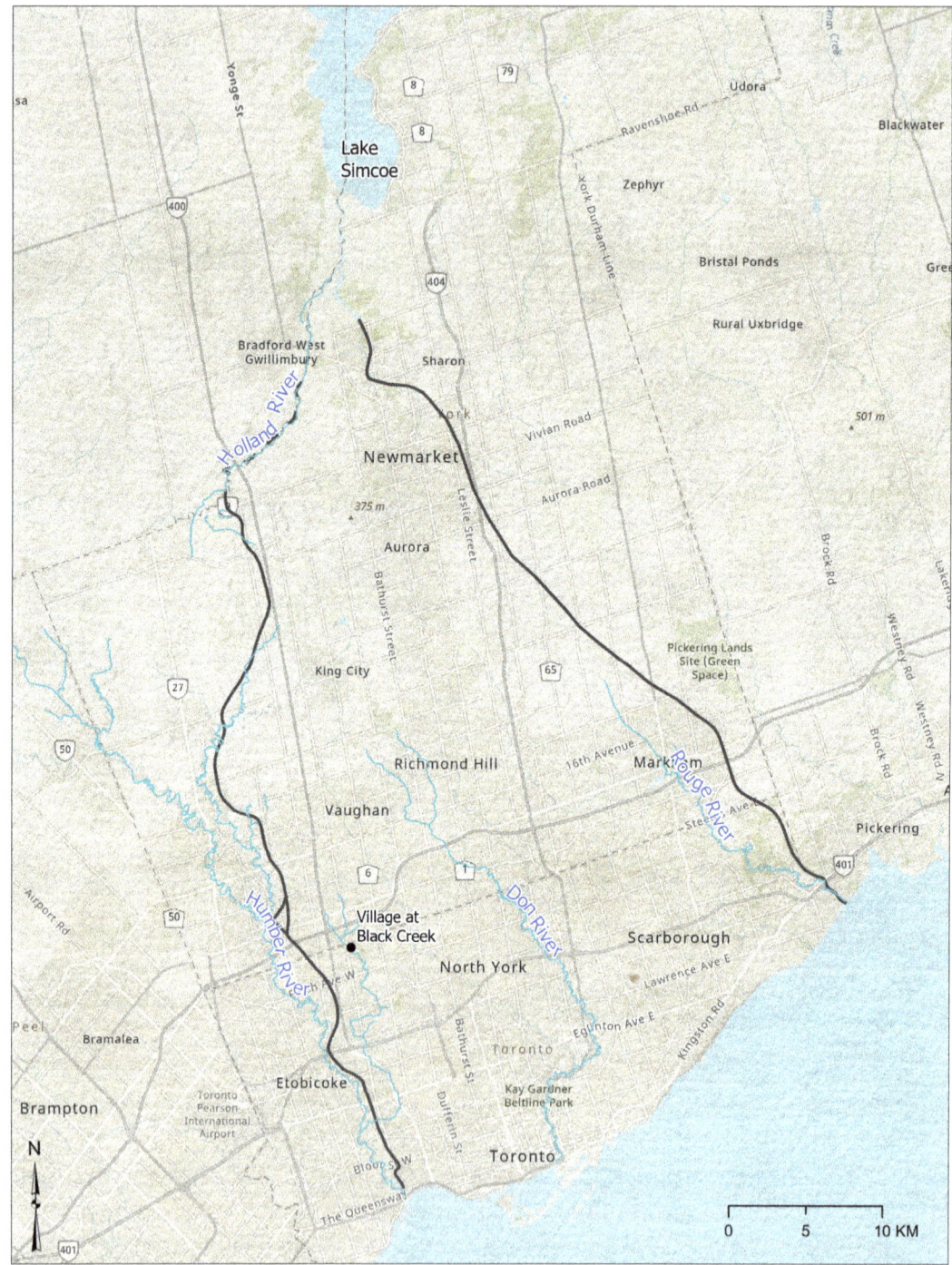

The approximate routes of the Toronto Carrying-Place Trail (east and west) superimposed on a present-day map of the region

by the British. The Anishinaabek's prisoner, fur trader Alexander Henry, described the journey:

> The next day was calm, and we arrived at the entrance of the navigation [Matchedash Bay] which leads to Lake aux Claies [the weirs at the Narrows of Lake Simcoe]. We presently passed two short carrying-places at each of which were several lodges of Indians, containing only women and children, the men being gone to the council at Niagara . . . On the 18th of June, we crossed Lake aux Claies, which appeared to be upwards of twenty miles in length. At its farther end we came to the carrying-place of Toronto. Here the Indians obliged me to carry a burden of more than a hundred pounds weight. The day was very hot, and the woods and marshes abounded with mosquitoes; but, the Indians walked at a quick pace, and I could by no means see myself left behind. The whole country was a thick forest, through which our only road was a footpath . . . Next morning at ten o'clock, we reached the shore of Lake Ontario. Here we were employed two days in making canoes, out of the bark of the elm-tree, in which we were to transport ourselves to Niagara. For this purpose the Indians first cut down a tree; then stripped off the bark, in one entire sheet, of about eighteen feet in length, the incision being length-wise. The canoe was now complete, as to its top, bottom and sides. Its ends were next closed, by sewing the bark together; and a few ribs and bars being introduced, the architecture was finished. In this manner, we made two canoes; of which one carried eight men, the other, nine. On the 21st, we embarked at Toronto, and encamped, in the evening, four miles short of Fort Niagara, which the Indians would not approach til morning.[7]

The site-specific installation *From Water to Water: A Way through the Trees*, Bonnie Devine, McMichael Canadian Art Collection, 2022 | Courtesy of McMichael Gallery and the artist

Note that the Anishinabek and Henry crossed Lake Simcoe on June 18 and arrived at Lake Ontario the next morning at ten o'clock. They had carried heavy packs along the rugged portage route for approximately 29 miles or 47 kilometres.[8] This portage was so useful that over the

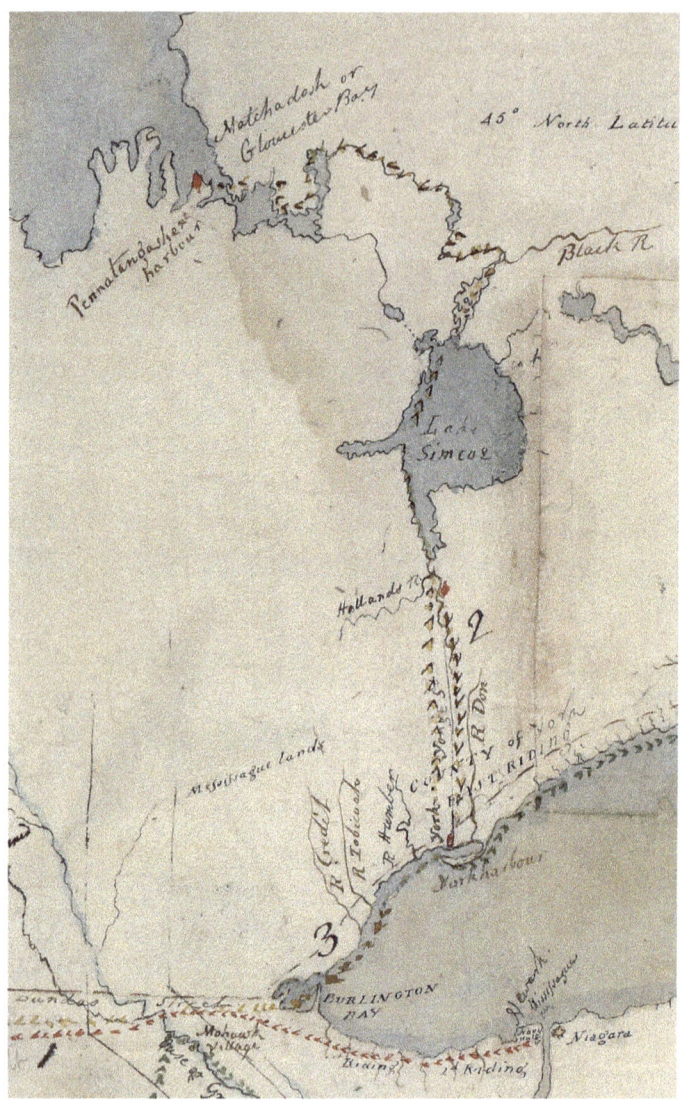

John Graves Simcoe's 1793 journey to Matchedash Bay. The dotted line is the portage route, and the solid line to the east indicates his proposed road (Yonge Street) | From Simcoe, "Sketch Map of Upper Canada"

centuries Wendat, Haudenosaunee, and Mississauga / Anishinaabek peoples had, at various times, built villages along the Humber and its tributaries. The Mississaugas referred to the portage as Cobekhenonk / Cobechenong / Gabekanaang, which has been translated as "Leave the canoes and go back."[9]

> *They had that Carrying-Place, and it was important to them. All the waterways were important to them. But that one was more because it went to Lake Simcoe... The Carrying-Places were highways to them.*
>
> —Margaret Sault, Mississaugas of the Credit[10]

After the French arrived in the late seventeenth century, control of the Toronto Carrying Place ensured access to the rich furs of the Muskoka area and fed into a range of political dynamics, including competition between New France and New England for colonial dominance. That struggle ended with New France's defeat in 1760. Facing a new possibility of American invasion in 1793, John Simcoe hoped to use the Toronto Carrying Place to keep Upper Canada securely within British North America.

For this reason, several weeks after the founding of York, Simcoe, accompanied by several British officers and Indigenous guides, followed the Toronto Carrying-Place Trail north to the west branch of the Holland River. From there, they canoed to Lake Simcoe and then headed west via the Severn River and several portages to

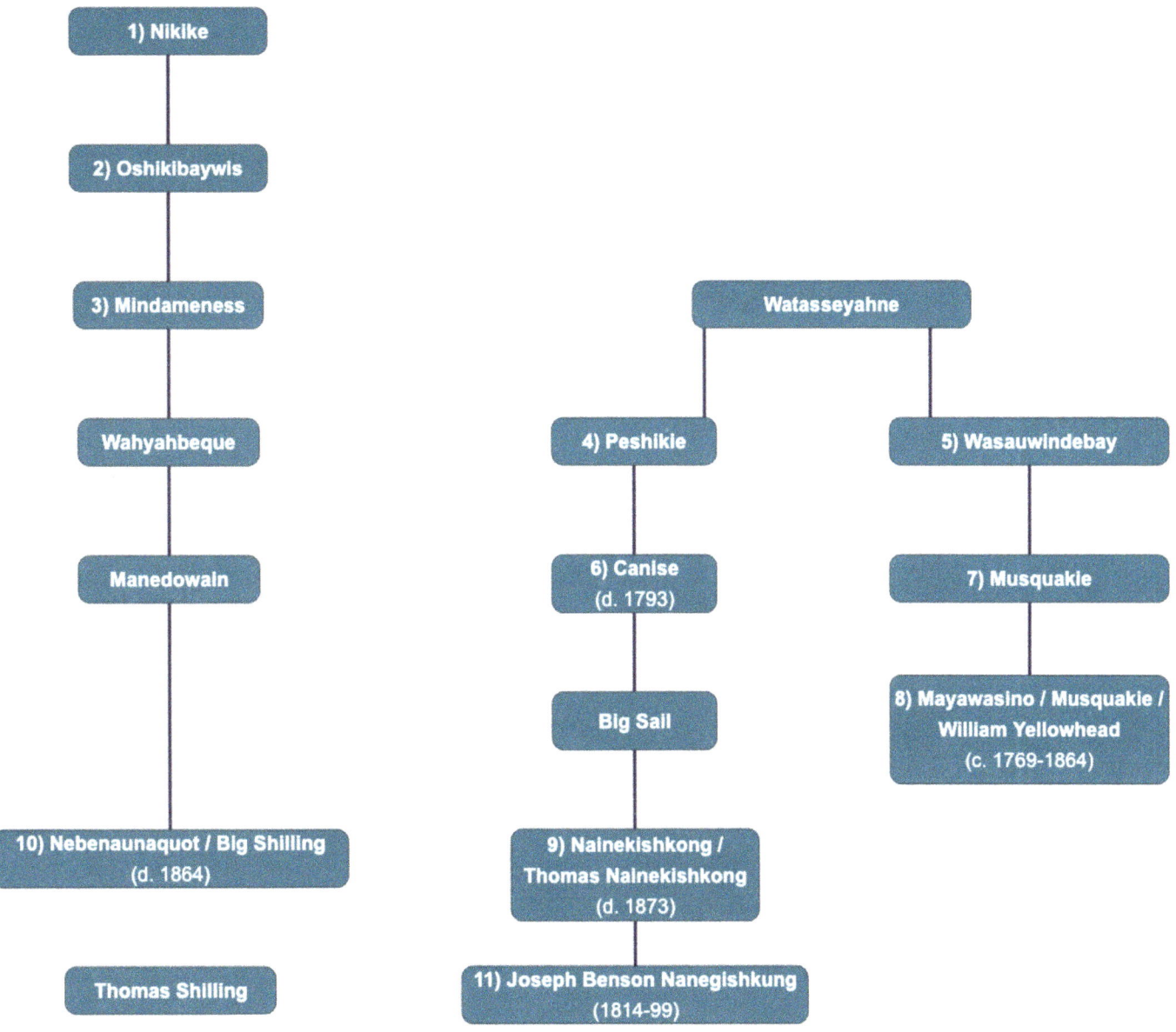

Chiefs of Lakes Huron and Simcoe in the seventeenth, eighteenth, and mid-nineteenth centuries | Courtesy of Beausoleil First Nation and reformatted by Ludia (Eon Seon) Bae. The numbers indicate the order of succession.

Matchedash Bay and Penetanguishene on Georgian Bay. Simcoe's aim was to assess this inland route for defence purposes. Given that tensions still simmered between the British and recently independent Americans to the south, he hoped that Penetanguishene's harbour would be suitable for a naval base.

Alexander Macdonell described numerous interactions with Indigenous peoples along the way: "Soon after making our fires, the Great Sail and his family (Messessagues [Mississaugas]), who were encamped further up the river, came to visit their Great Father, the Governor, to whom they presented a pair of ducks, some beaver's meat, and a beaver's tail. His Excellency gave them some rum and tobacco."[11]

However, as later recorded by Elizabeth Simcoe, her husband arrived at the camp of the Chief who had held Francis in his arms (here, named Canise) only to discover that the Chief and his eldest son "were lately dead, and their widows and children were lamenting them."[12] They likely died in the smallpox epidemic that devastated Anishinaabe communities around Lake Simcoe that year—one of the first consequences of European contact.

Simcoe found the Carrying-Place Portage route extremely arduous, especially the large wetlands that had to be traversed at Holland Marsh. On his return journey, he hoped to find an easier route: "The Governor went to see a very respectable Indian named 'Old Sail,' who lives on a branch of Holland's River. He advised him to return by the eastern branch of it to avoid the swamp."[13] Back at York, Simcoe concluded that the portage route was unsuitable for British military transport and ordered the construction of a road from York to Holland Landing. The opening of this road, later known as Yonge Street, was a major turning point in the development of the area, marking the end of the Toronto Carrying Place as the principal thoroughfare connecting western Lake Ontario to the Upper Great Lakes.

Historically, these two major transportation routes—the Toronto Carrying-Place Trail and Yonge Street—were the main physical links among Indigenous Nations and between Indigenous Nations and newcomers. Although Yonge Street facilitated widespread on-the-ground British colonization and hegemony, the traffic went both ways. Anishinaabek from Holland Landing, Lake Simcoe, Lake Huron, and the Muskoka area visited Yonge Street or York to speak with colonial officials, negotiate treaties, deliver petitions, trade furs, pick up supplies, trade goods, attend Christian religious meetings, and receive treaty "presents." (Although called presents, these gifts were not unilateral expressions of beneficence on the part of Europeans but an expected part of a system of reciprocal exchange necessary for treaty making.) They met with Indigenous visitors from Haudenosaunee and Anishinaabe communities to the east and west along the lakeshore and beyond. In fact, Yonge Street facilitated the spread of new ideas and social movements among Indigenous peoples.

The significance of these routes to both newcomers and Indigenous peoples suggests that we can better understand Indigenous history and the history of Indigenous-settler relations in the

Elizabeth Simcoe, *Canise or Great Sail, Chippewa Chief*, 1790s | Courtesy of Toronto Public Library, Canadian Documentary Art Collection, X18-27B.

The late Emerson Benson Nanigishkung of Chippewas of Rama, descendant of Canise / Kenis and an interviewee | Photo by Victoria Freeman

Toronto area through this larger regional lens rather than in the isolated silos of stand-alone accounts of individual First Nations, individual town histories, or the settler history of York or Toronto.

Emerson Benson Nanigishkung, a member of Chippewas of Rama First Nation, was a direct descendant of Canise, the Chief who held Francis Simcoe in his arms at the founding of York and who died in the epidemic of 1793—a powerful reminder of the continuity and persistence of

Carl Ray, *Muskrat and Vine,* 1974 | Photo by Bryant Ross, Coghlan Art

the turtle had given up his back for that. And everyone tried, but the only one who came back with any earth in his tiny paw was Wazhushk, muskrat, and today we call him Wazhushk, Muskrat Earth or the Black Earth. We all have a different name for Earth. Our Earth is Aki, being in the Earth, on the Earth, at the Earth.

— Emerson Benson Nanigishkung, Chippewas of Rama[14]

His words are a reminder that Indigenous lands are richly storied and that the worldviews of Indigenous peoples and the cultural contexts for their historical actions and decisions are only minimally evident in the archival record. These stories are both old and new—some elements are ancient, but each generation interprets the stories and their teachings anew to assist them in meeting new challenges.

Indigenous peoples in the region, despite more than two hundred years of colonial settlement. He shared his version of the Anishinaabe Great Flood re-creation story, with a local spin.

> *The land around Holland Landing, it's all black earth, what we call wazhushk, wazhushk being muskrat. That black soil . . . when you look at it east and west, you'll see that black soil. What [that] brings to my mind is the Great Flood, where all the animals were on a log with Nanaboozhoo. And all the animals tried to dive down and get some earth because*

2

Deep Time in the Humber River Watershed

Let's dip back into the deep "before" time of Emerson Benson Nanigishkung's story. Indigenous peoples have lived in North America since time immemorial. They were the first humans to inhabit the two American continents, and their cultures were developed here. There's currently no consensus on the earliest date for the Indigenous presence in the Americas. Archaeological research confirms that Indigenous peoples have been living in at least some areas of Turtle Island (North America) for more than 20,000 years, but new evidence continues to push back the date.[1] By comparison, the oldest continuous European settlements in what is now Canada are a little over 400 years old.

The time scale for an Indigenous presence in North America is so vast it's hard to comprehend: Indigenous peoples were here during the Pleistocene era before agriculture or metallurgy had been invented anywhere in the world and before livestock animals were domesticated. The world of ancient Indigenous peoples was vastly different from our world and from their world at the time of the arrival of Europeans. The global climate was considerably colder, and most of the animal species present 14,500 years ago or longer are now extinct.[2]

Indigenous peoples have lived in the Toronto region since at least 11,000 BCE, possibly earlier.[3] There's archaeological evidence that they hunted mastodon in the Red Hill Valley in Hamilton 13,000 years ago, after the approximately 2-kilometre-thick glaciers that covered the region for thousands of years melted.[4] Footprints discovered by workmen digging a tunnel under Toronto Bay in 1908 (but unfortunately destroyed at the time) are thought to have been 10,000 years old.

Over millennia the ancestors of today's Indigenous peoples adapted to numerous ecological changes, including the melting of glaciers; the rise and fall of water levels in local lakes, rivers, and drainage systems; periods of warming or cooling; and changing vegetation and animal life. The earliest known peoples in the Toronto area were nomadic hunters who followed herds of large mammals over tundra. When climate and landscape features changed to mixed deciduous forest around 7000 BCE (about the time of the ancient Sumerians in what is now Iraq), Indigenous peoples were drawn to bountiful flora and wildlife—including deer, fish, ducks, and wild rice—along local rivers.

Agriculture was invented independently in several regions of the world. Indigenous peoples in southern Mexico domesticated corn (also known as maize) about ten thousand years ago, and seed

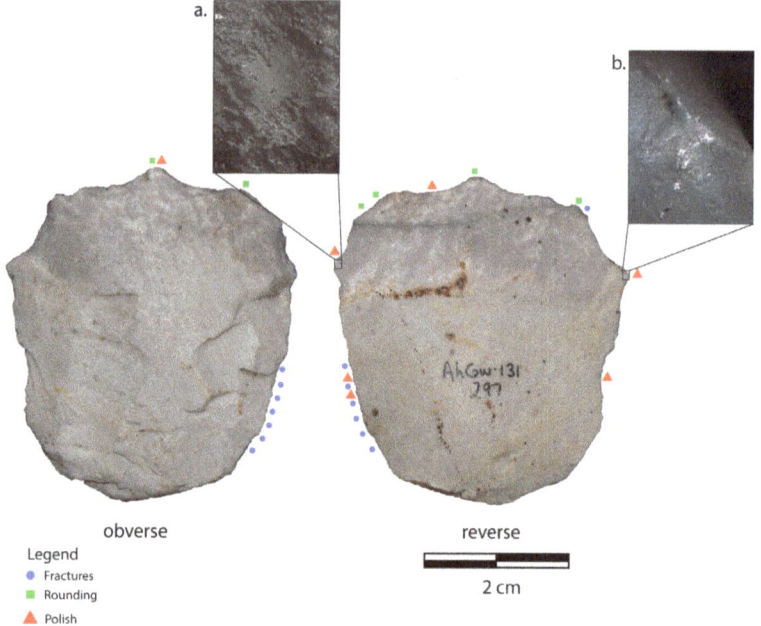

A 13,000-year-old tool recovered from the Red Hill Valley showing traces of mastodon blood | Courtesy of Archeological Services Inc.

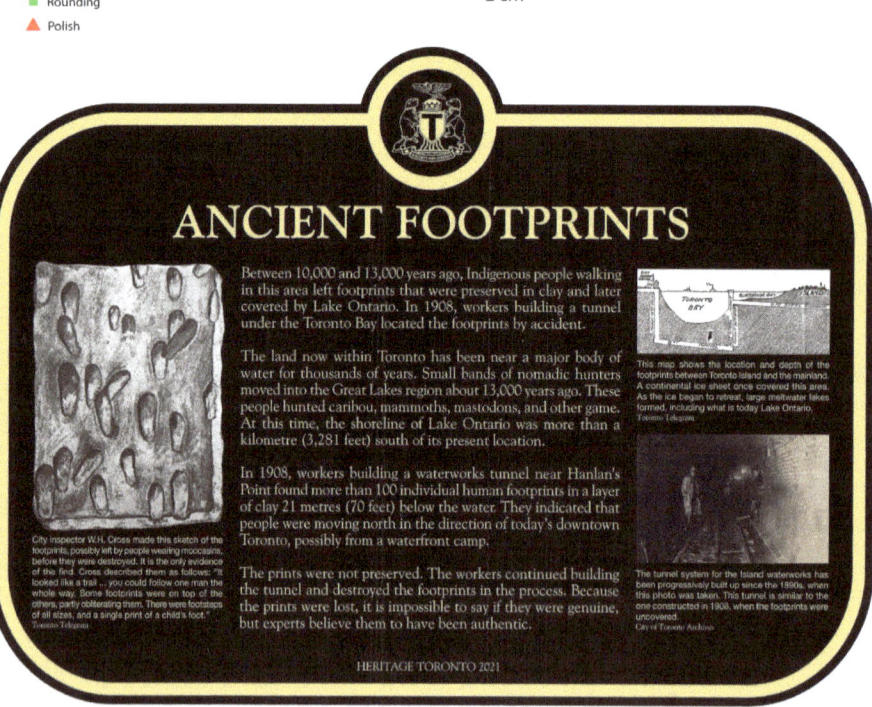

Heritage Toronto commemorative plaque about the 1908 discovery of ancient footprints of adults and a child beneath Toronto Bay | Courtesy of Heritage Toronto

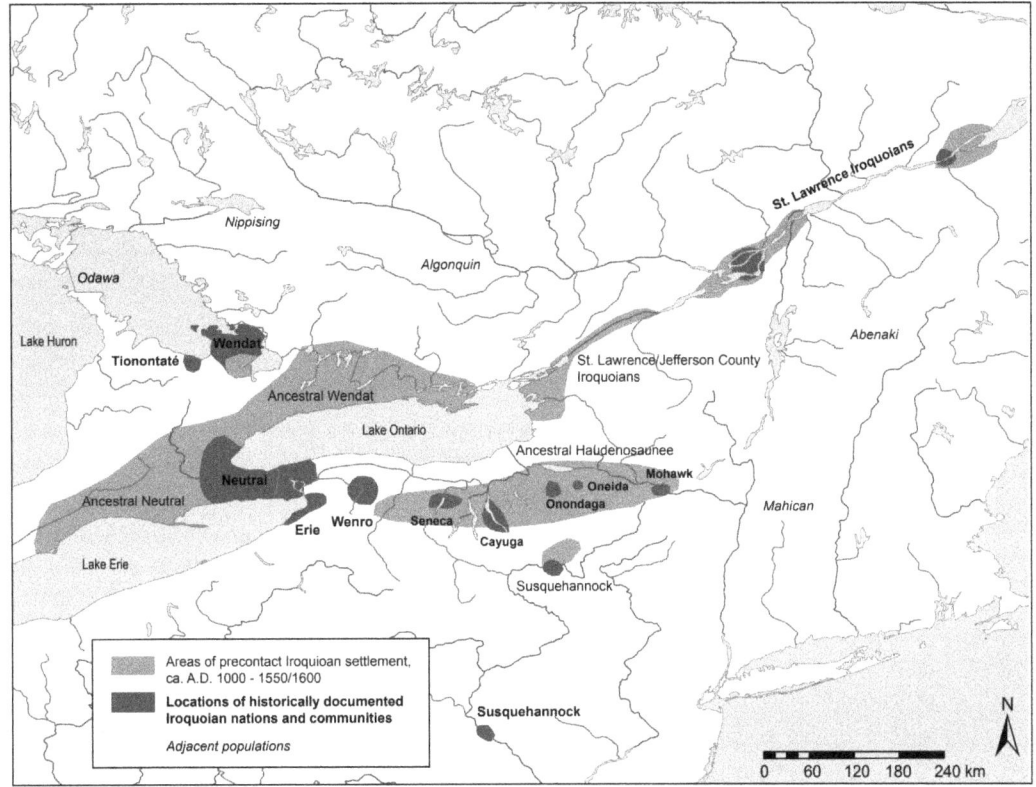

Wendat and other adjacent Iroquoian societies. The Odawa / Odaawaa, Nipissing, and Algonquin are historical Anishinaabe neighbours | Birch and Williamson, "Navigating Ancestral Landscapes in the Northern Iroquoian World"

corn and corn-growing technology were gradually shared with peoples to the north. By 800 CE (possibly earlier), some Indigenous peoples on the north shore of Lake Ontario were planting corn.[5] As horticulture spread and new crops were introduced, some groups established semi-permanent villages along the region's rivers, while others continued to move seasonally to hunt, fish, and harvest and then gather in larger groups in spring and fall.

Over time, two distinct cultural patterns emerged: the Wendat, Attawandaron (Neutral), and Haudenosaunee, who were semi-sedentary horticulturalists; and the Anishinaabek and related peoples, who followed the older hunter-gatherer way of life. Scholars would later categorize the horticulturalists as "Iroquoian," which caused confusion as the category included other sizable and related groups, such as the Wendat and Attawandaron—"Northern Iroquoians"—who were culturally similar but politically distinct from those known as "Iroquois" or Haudenosaunee.

Indigenous peoples developed ways of living and flourishing that supported living lightly on the land. They created cultural practices that ensured sustainable interconnections between land, water, and all beings. They passed on their knowledge, lifeways, values, and cultural identity through stories rooted in the land.

> *We had governance systems. We had protocols, etiquettes, and relationships with other Nations. We were stewards of the land and the waters.*
>
> —Vicki Snache, Chippewas of Rama[6]

> *Everything they had would have been things they made. What we call crafts today ... And, of course, they made quill boxes and ash baskets. Water vessels and sap vessels. Those were made from porcupine quills, from sweetgrass, from birchbark, from sinew. And all those things were gathered.*
>
> —Ben Cousineau, Chippewas of Rama[7]

Three Indigenous Nations

Today, three Nations—Wendat, Onödowa'ga or Seneca, and Mississauga / Anishinaabek—claim the Toronto area as their historical territory. All had villages in the Humber watershed and used the Toronto Carrying-Place Trail. They maintain connections and relationships to the area and have ancestral connections to earlier peoples of the Great Lakes region whose names aren't known to us.

Wendat Villages on the Humber River and Black Creek

From roughly 1200 to 1600 CE, Wendat peoples (later called Huron by the French) lived in large, palisaded Longhouse villages surrounded by extensive corn fields, including along the Humber River and its tributaries. Skandatut (near present-day Kleinberg) was the largest of these villages, housing an estimated two thousand people. A fifteenth-century village overlooking Black Creek was located just south of today's York University, a short walk from what is now The Village at Black Creek. Archaeologists named it the Parsons site after the farm family who owned the site when it was first excavated in the early 1950s. The palisaded village housed up to fifteen hundred people in forty to fifty Longhouses; beyond the village, the inhabitants grew the Three Sisters (corn, squash, and beans) in fields that extended in an estimated 1-kilometre radius, including much of what is now York University.[8]

The Wendat were allies and trading partners of the Anishinaabe peoples who lived along the Canadian Shield to the north and the Bruce Peninsula to the west. The Attawandaron / Neutrals, who were Iroquoian speakers like the Wendat and Haudenosaunee, lived just to the west of the Wendat. Some appear to have had a presence in the Wendat villages along the Humber.

Beginning in the 1300s, Wendat communities gradually moved their villages north to the region known as Huronia or Wendake, to the west of Lake Simcoe and especially on the Penetanguishene Peninsula. There, they joined the Wendat Confederacy of four (possibly five)

Wendat bird effigy found along the Humber River | Courtesy of Toronto and Region Conservation Authority

Ekionkiestha' National Longhouse. A reconstruction of a Wendat longhouse, Musée Huron-Wendat, Wendake, Quebec | Photo by Stéphane Audet

Interior of Ekionkiestha' National Longhouse | Photo by Neufast, Creative Commons Licence Attribute-Share Alike 3.0 Unported Licence, Wikimedia Commons

2 | Deep Time in the Humber River Watershed

Nations. It is believed that the last Wendat communities left the Toronto area about 1610, although it remained Wendat hunting territory until 1649–50.

In the early 1600s, the Wendat became allies and trading partners of the French. Explorer Samuel de Champlain overwintered with them in Huronia in 1615. That same year, Etienne Brulé might have travelled the Humber route from Huronia to Lake Ontario with several Wendat companions on their way to the country of the Susquehannas.

Contact with the French exposed the Wendat to epidemic diseases, notably smallpox, that decimated the Wendat population, reduced their military strength, destabilized their culture, and led to many conversions to Christianity, fuelling internal divisions. In 1649–50, Seneca and Mohawk warriors of the Haudenosaunee Confederacy travelled north, likely along the Humber Portage route, and attacked the Wendats in the Lake Simcoe / Georgian Bay area. The Wendat Confederacy was defeated and broken up.[9]

Many Wendat fled to Quebec, the Detroit / Windsor area, and beyond, while roughly half were absorbed (as captives or adoptees) into the Haudenosaunee Confederacy. After 1650, some Wendat and members of the neighbouring Tionontaté / Petun Confederacy, which had also been defeated by the Haudenosaunee, regrouped in the Detroit area and became known as the Wyandot. The Neutrals were also defeated and absorbed by the Haudenosaunee; they no longer exist independently.

Today, the dispersed Wendats have regrouped as the Huron-Wendat Nation of Wendake, Quebec, the Wyandot of Anderdon Nation in Michigan, the Wyandot Nation of Kansas, and the Wyandotte Nation in Oklahoma, and have formally renewed the Wendat Confederacy. The Huron-Wendat of Quebec are the spokespeople for their heritage in Ontario, working to repatriate artifacts, rebury uncovered human remains, and ceremonially protect and honour their ancestors in the Toronto region. They have collaborated with other local First Nations on regional heritage projects such as the Shared Path, an installation of story circles and interpretative signage along the Humber River.

The Seneca Village of Teiaiagon

After the 1649–50 defeat of the Wendats, the Haudenosaunee Confederacy established villages along the north shore of Lake Ontario, and the Toronto area came under the control of the Onödowa'ga or Seneca. As the fur trade expanded, the area became strategically important because the Humber and Rouge Rivers gave access to the best furs, which came from the North. The Seneca transported them via Lake Ontario to the French at Montreal and the more distant Dutch and English, their military and trading allies, along the Hudson River in what is now New York State. In the 1670s, French fur traders and explorers began to visit the large village of Teiaiagon along the Humber and its sister village, Ganatsekwyagon, on the Rouge.[10]

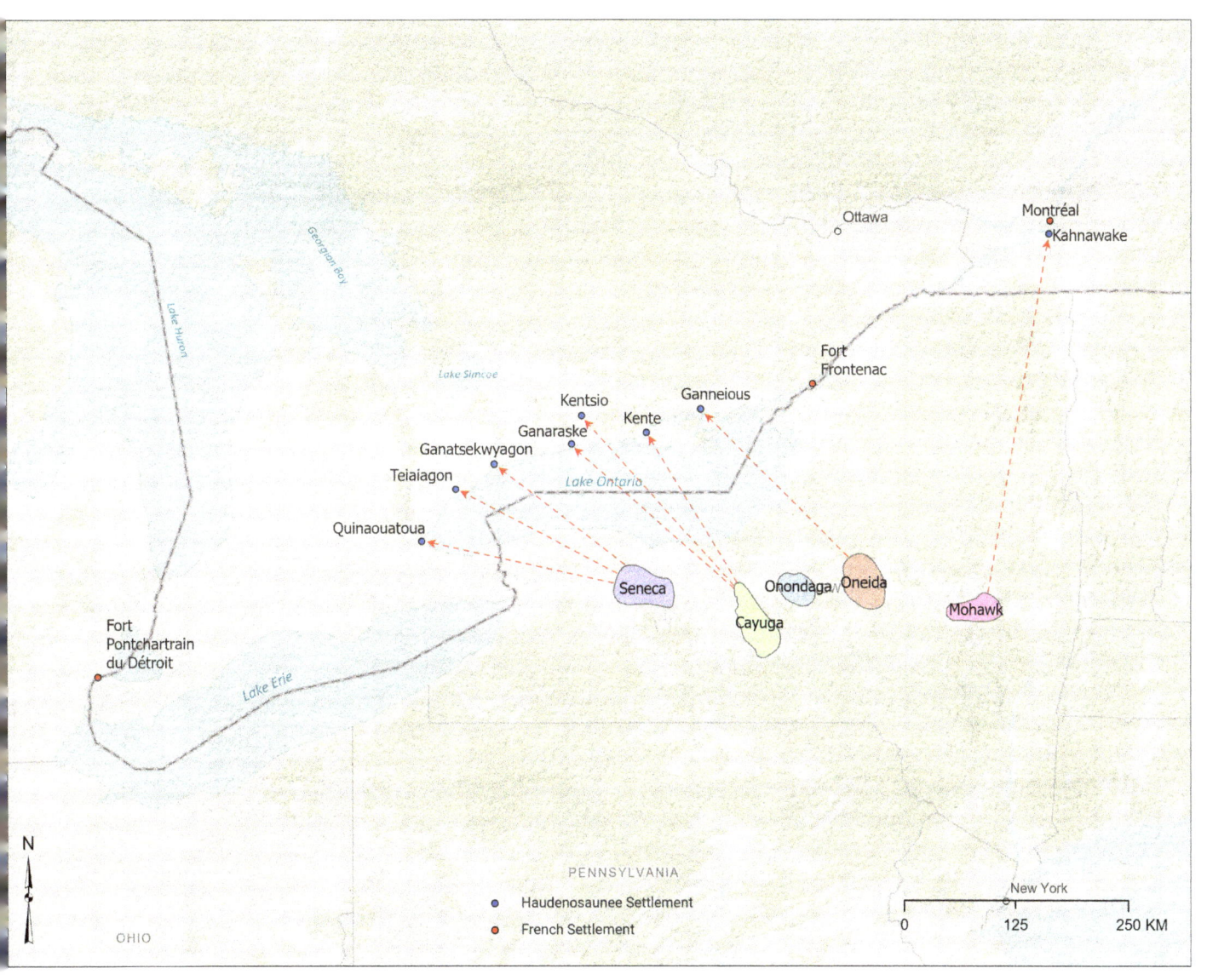

Haudenosaunee villages on the north shore of Lake Ontario in the late seventeenth century. The exact location of the small outpost of Quinaouatoua (Tinawatawa) at the head of the lake is still disputed.

Humber and Black Creek watersheds

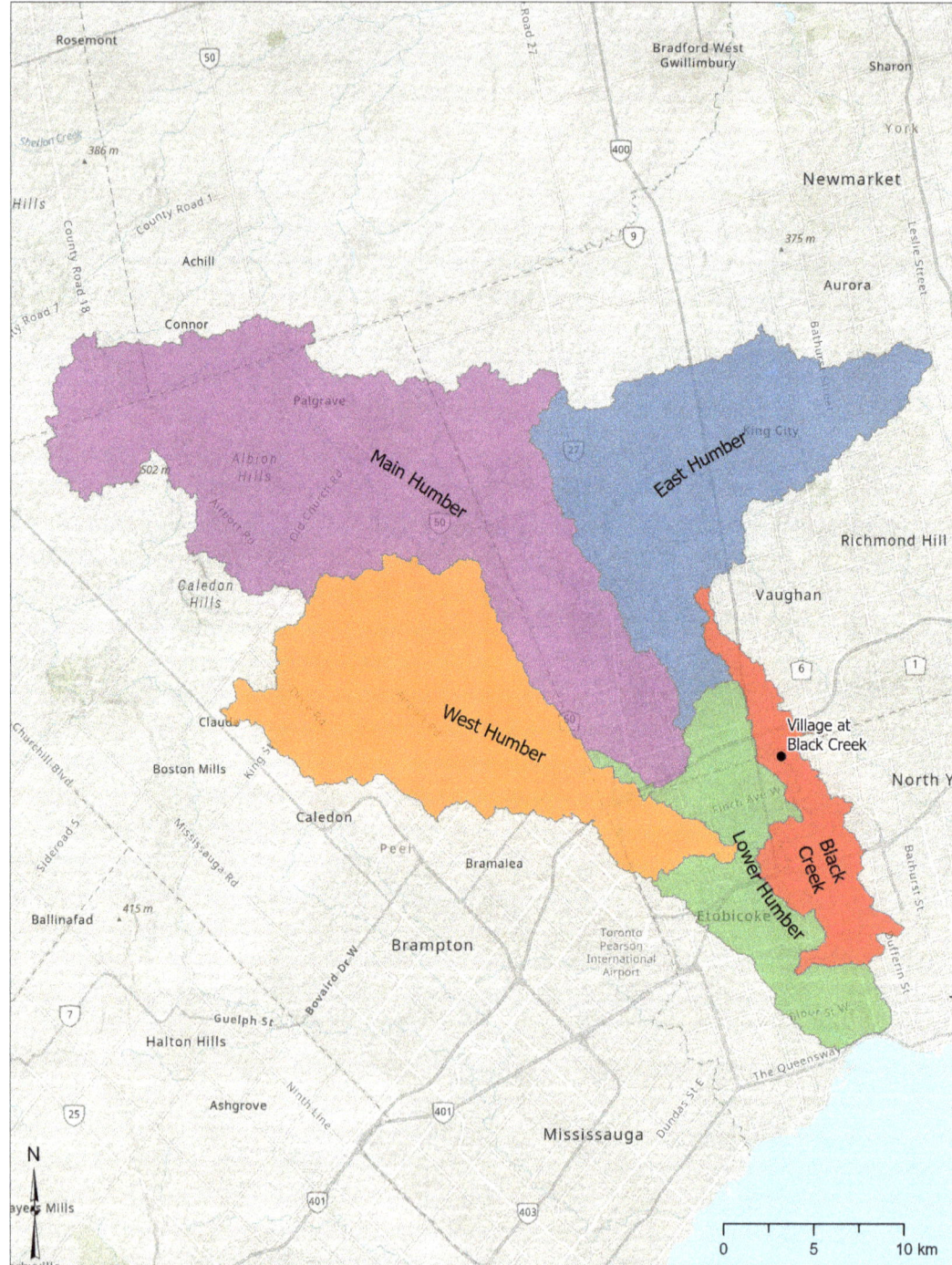

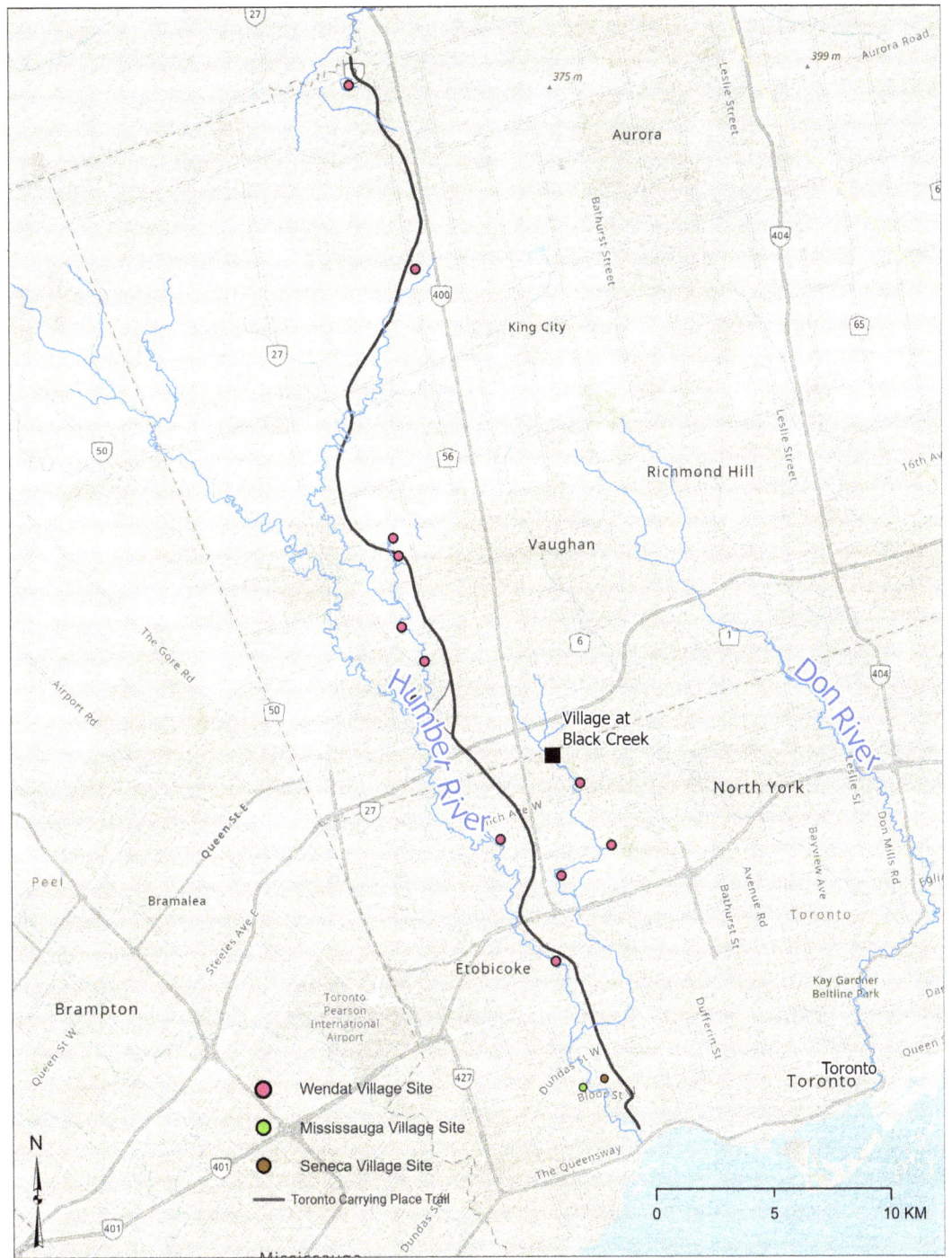

Historical Wendat, Seneca, and Mississauga villages on the Humber River

Reproduction of a moose antler comb from Teiaiagon, c. 1680s, Toronto | Photo by John Howarth, courtesy of Archeological Services Inc.

About 1700, following warfare with the French and Anishinaabek, the Seneca abandoned these villages and returned to their territories south of Lake Ontario. According to Anishinaabe oral tradition, the Haudenosaunee were defeated and forced to leave the north shore of the lake, and the Mississaugas took over the territory by right of conquest.

After prolonged attack, ourselves, our allies, come down, cross Georgian Bay. Attack. Had our first battle at Orillia. At least that's what we say. Orillia. Then split our forces off, our big force, into two forces. One group went eastward [to] Rice Lake, Alderville, those folks, and the Mississaugas of the Credit ancestors travelled down the Humber River [Toronto] Carrying Place and fought at this end of Lake Ontario and drove out the Haudenosaunee at this end.

—Darin Wybenga, Mississaugas of the Credit[11]

The Haudenosaunee dispute this narrative. According to their oral tradition, the Five Nations allowed Mississauga occupation through diplomatic agreement. They also negotiated with the British to retain and protect their rights to their hunting territories on the north shore of Lake Ontario through the Nanfan Deed of 1701. In the view of the Haudenosaunee, they did not relinquish their title to lands in present-day southern Ontario acquired by the right of conquest over the Wendats even after it was occupied by the Anishinaabek / Mississaugas. Today, the Six Nations of the Grand River (near Brantford, Ontario) assert treaty rights to the Toronto area that are contested by the Mississaugas of the Credit.[12]

The Mississauga / Anishinaabe Village on the Humber

Unrelated culturally to the Wendat or Haudenosaunee, the Anishinaabek were allies of the

Mississauga routes into southern Ontario

2 | Deep Time in the Humber River Watershed

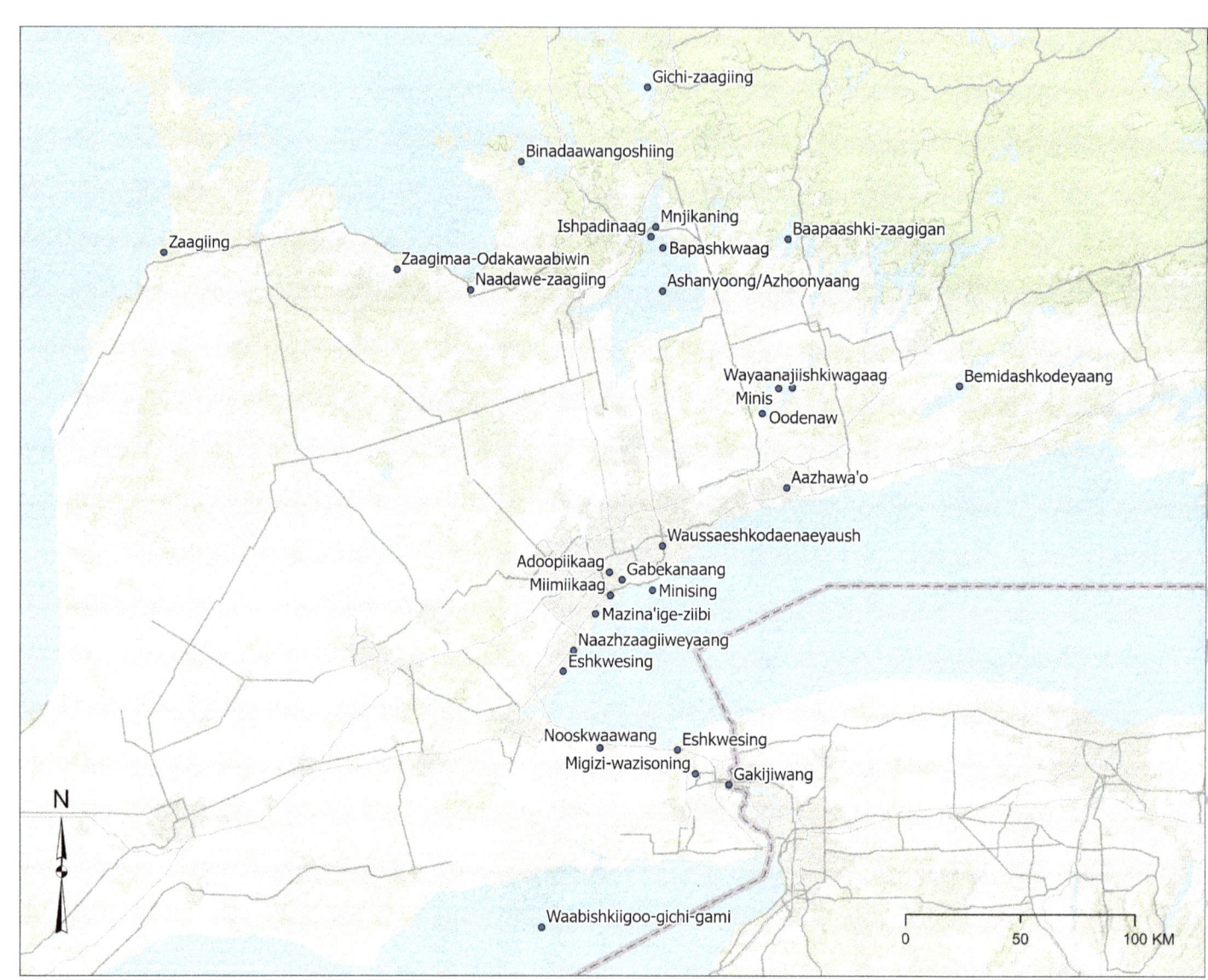

Anishinaabe place names

Wendat and French. In the early 1600s, they lived in territories around Lakes Huron and Superior. According to Anishinaabe oral tradition, around the 1660s they began pushing south. They attacked the Haudenosaunee and drove them from the Anishinaabe territories the Haudenosaunee had invaded after defeating the Wendats in 1650. In subsequent decades, the Anishinaabek moved into the former territories of their Wendat allies along the north shore of Lake Ontario.

Anishinaabek who moved south from near the Mississagi River on the north shore of Lake Huron to the north shore of Lake Ontario around 1695 came to be known to Europeans as the Mississaugas (possibly derived from Michi Saagiig, referring to a river with many mouths, or the Anishinaabe word for "eagle.")

The Mississaugas came from the North Shore. This is the more recent story, but the Creation story brings us in from the East Coast. We're still related all around the Great Lakes with all the different people.

—Carolyn King, Mississaugas of the Credit[13]

One group of Mississaugas travelled south via the Humber Portage route and established control and stewardship over territories from the Rouge River in the east to Long Point on Lake Erie in the west. They established a summer village on the west bank of the Humber across the river from the abandoned Seneca village of Teiaiagon and another on the Rouge at the former site of Ganetsekwyagon. The Mississaugas then established camps along all the major rivers and their Council Fire (seat of government) and main village at the mouth of the Credit. They became known as the Mississaugas of the Credit. The Humber Portage connected them to related Anishinaabek who established territories around Lake Simcoe, eastern Georgian Bay, Lake Scugog, and Peterborough.

The Anishinaabek moved seasonally to hunt and fish, plant gardens, process maple sugar, and gather berries, roots, and medicines. In the spring and fall, they gathered in large numbers at major fishing sites such as Mnjikaning (or the Narrows) and at the mouth of the Credit River, where they held Councils, socialized, found marriage partners, and conducted ceremonies. After living in villages over the summer, they dispersed in winter into smaller family hunting groups in the interior forests.

The Mississaugas traded furs with the French, who built their first trading post on the Humber in 1720. Yet even during the period of nominal French control, and especially after concluding a diplomatic agreement with the Six Nations in 1700–1701, which granted them safe passage through Haudenosaunee territory, the Mississaugas also traded with the English at Albany.

Regional Alliances and Agreements before 1787

Indigenous peoples have long traditions of diplomacy and treaty making, often activated and commemorated through Wampum. Wampum

Replica of Dish with One Spoon Wampum, handmade by Ken Maracle, a Faith Keeper of the Lower Cayuga Longhouse and a member of the Cayuga Nation, Haudenosaunee Confederacy, Deer Clan. The replica was purchased for use by University of Windsor faculty and staff in their teaching | Photo provided by Leddy Library, University of Windsor

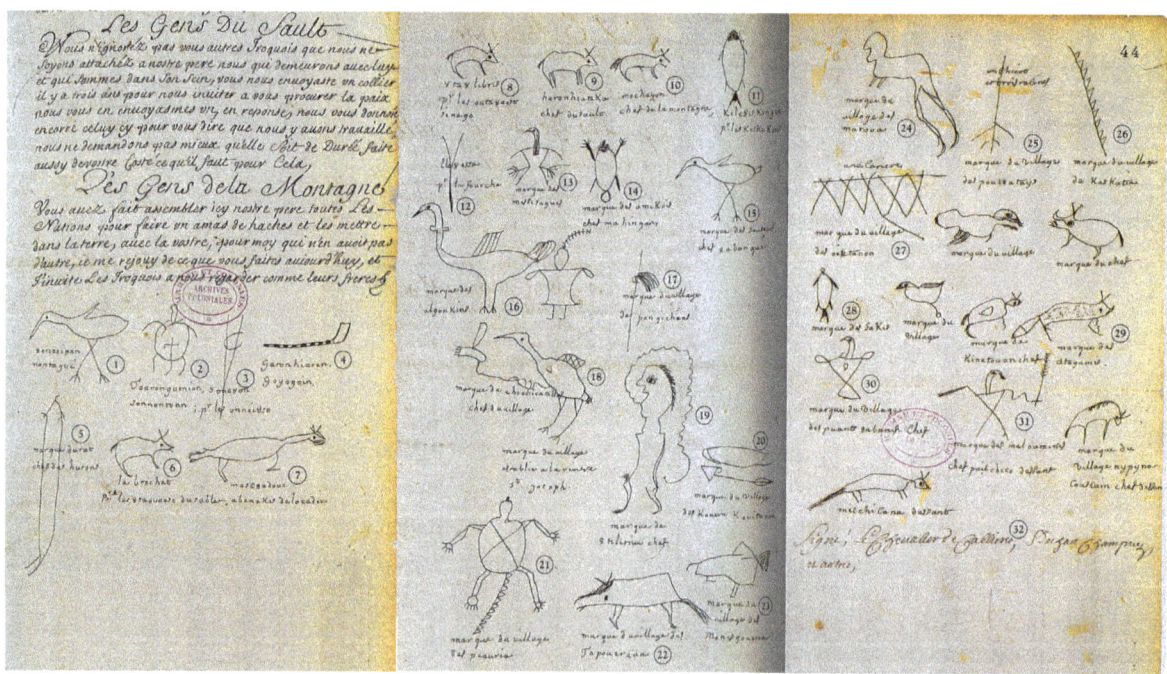

Indigenous leaders used their Doodem marks rather than personal signatures to sign agreements with Europeans. These are from the Great Peace of Montreal in 1701 | Wikimedia Commons

is a string or belt made from beads fashioned from purple and white marine shells. According to Haudenosaunee oral tradition, Wampum was first used ceremonially by the Peacemaker and Aienwatha / Hiawatha, the founders of the Haudenosaunee Confederacy.

Considered a living presence with the power to manifest stories, Wampum was exchanged during meetings between Nations of the Great Lakes region to demonstrate respect and serious intent. Wampum's symbolic designs embodied the words and pledges made in its presence and their permanence. Successive generations of Wampum Keepers were responsible for maintaining the oral memory of treaties and reciting the meaning of a Wampum Belt in Councils where they were renewed. Unfortunately, colonial disruption hindered the intergenerational transmission of the meanings of some Wampum symbols, complicating the interpretation of some historical agreements in the present. Cultural and archival research is being undertaken to try to recover these meanings.

In 1700, after a long period of warfare exacerbated by the fur trade and competing alliances with the French and English, the Anishinaabek (including the Mississaugas) and the Haudenosaunee concluded a peace agreement commemorated in the Dish with One Spoon Wampum. In eastern North America, a shared dish or kettle is an ancient metaphor in Indigenous diplomacy. It figures in many treaty relationships and alliances, including the Great Law of Peace that unites the Nations of the Haudenosaunee Confederacy and appears to have been used in agreements

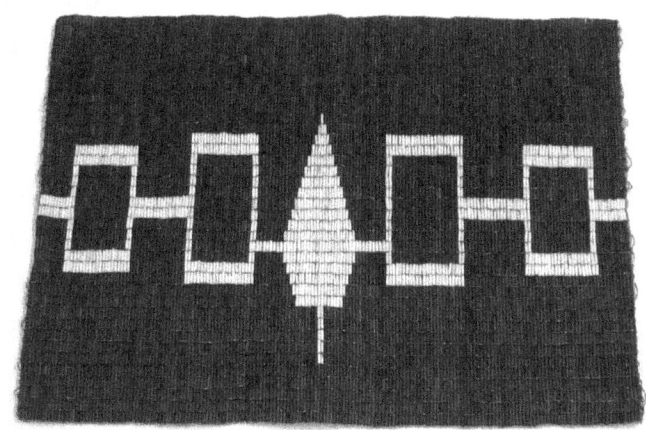

Replica of the Five Nations or Aienwatha / Hiawatha Wampum Belt of the Haudenosaunee Confederacy | Photo courtesy of Jake Thomas Learning Centre

between the Haudenosaunee and Anishinaabek before the version agreed to in 1700–1701. The metaphor was key to the 1701 regional peace negotiated at a gathering of thirteen hundred delegates from thirty-nine Indigenous Nations from across eastern North America convened at Montreal by the French. The Great Peace of Montreal ended a near century of conflict, often referred to as the Beaver Wars, between the French and their Indigenous allies and the Haudenosaunee.

Present-day Toronto land acknowledgements often refer to the Dish with One Spoon as an agreement to share the resources of the Great Lakes region. But the terms are remembered

Regional Anishinaabe Council Fires (seats of governance) as represented in the Eternal Council Fires Wampum Belt and interpreted by Chief Musquakie / William Yellowhead in 1840. The actual Wampum Belt has not survived. Clan symbols are reproduced from Chiefs' Doodem signatures on treaty documents and indicate the Doodem responsible for maintaining each Council Fire or seat of governance. In his reading, Musquakie mentioned Sault Ste. Marie as the site of the first Council Fire but did not specify the Doodem. However, the Crane is the predominant Doodem at that location.

differently by the two parties. The Haudenosaunee maintain that the agreement is to share the resources on the north shore of Lake Ontario (they also claim a right to north shore resources through the Nanfan Deed, negotiated with the British in 1701).

So, in the 1700s, the Great Peace at Montreal, where we all came together, forty Nations came together and put an end to the Indian Wars. It was called the Dish with One Spoon Treaty, where we all agreed to share these lands in a respectful manner for the environment, conservation. We all were to keep that dish clean and leave enough for our other brothers to share from. It was not an ownership issue to those lands, because title and ownership was foreign to us.

—Phil Monture, Six Nations of the Grand River[14]

The Anishinaabek dispute that the agreement was to share the land and resources unconditionally. Instead, they insist that the peace agreed to in 1701 recognized territorial sovereignty and that a second Wampum Belt, the Yellowhead or Eternal Council Fires Wampum Belt (also part of the peacemaking process between the Anishinaabek and Haudenosaunee), provides persuasive evidence that the sharing of resources was intended to be conditional upon intertribal diplomacy and permission.[15] Now lost but described in detail at a joint Council in 1840, it signified Haudenosaunee recognition of regional Anishinaabe Council Fires, including at the Narrows (Mnjikaning) and Credit River, the Clans responsible for them, their duties, and where and when resources were to be shared with the Haudenosaunee.[16]

I know, politically, our people were bound with a number of different communities through, not just our Nation, but communities through Wampum. Chief Yellowhead [Musquakie] was a Wampum carrier and speaker . . . He carried that one Wampum. He was the speaker of that one Wampum that encapsulated all the different communities; mentioned all the different communities that were surrounding our territory of Rama.

—Kory Snache, Chippewas of Rama[17]

Wampum was also exchanged with Europeans. Military and trading alliances were negotiated following Indigenous protocols and included extensive gift giving. The French and English gave their allies annual presents to maintain their loyalty and signify their ongoing good intentions. These alliances recognized Indigenous sovereignty and were key to the commercial competition between the English and French in the fur trade.

Going right back to the 1613. Our Two Row [Wampum] and the relationship we're supposed to have with the Dutch.

Our peace, friendship, and respect . . . and how we were to respect each other's governments, never trying to impose their laws upon us and likewise, us upon them. To the 1664, when Great Britain wanted a similar treaty with the Five Nations, which we honoured.

—Phil Monture, Six Nations of the Grand River[18]

3

Trade and Colonial Rivalries

The fur trade was one of the earliest forms of sustained contact between Indigenous peoples and European newcomers. The Toronto Carrying-Place Trail linked fur traders with regions to the north, especially the fur-bearing region of Muskoka. French fur traders and those of mixed Indigenous and French heritage (and, later, British traders) sought beaver fur because felt hats had become fashionable in Europe and beaver fur could be turned into waterproof felt. In exchange, Indigenous peoples gained access to metal knives, copper pots, needles, mirrors, blankets, woven cloth, ribbons, and guns and ammunition.

French Trade on the Humber, 1660s–1759

The main route of the fur trade was from Georgian Bay to the French River through Lake Nipissing to the Mattawa River and then down the Ottawa River to Montreal. But the two portage routes along the Humber and Rouge Rivers allowed Indigenous traders to send furs to the French in Montreal (via Lake Ontario) or to the English at Albany (on the Hudson River) and, later, Fort Oswego (on Lake Ontario) depending on who offered the best prices and highest-quality trade goods—usually the English. Because beaver was extirpated in their territories south of Lake Ontario, the Seneca established themselves on the Humber and Rouge Rivers to access the Canadian Shield's best fur-bearing regions.

The French began trading with the Seneca at Teiaiagon in the 1660s. The introduction of sailing vessels on Lake Ontario in 1678 promoted the use of the portage route along the Humber River since it had good anchorages near its mouth for larger vessels.[1] The principal trade good on offer was alcohol.

In 1720, after the Mississaugas gained control of the area, the French established their first trading post, the Magasin Royal, at the site of Teiaiagon, but it was short-lived. Competition from the English on the lake's south shore led the French, in 1750, to build a larger trading post, known as Fort Toronto, at the mouth of the Humber. It was soon relocated to the east (at the site of today's Exhibition Grounds) and described, in 1757, as "Toronto, or Saint-Victor, a small fort made of stakes on Lake Ontario, to

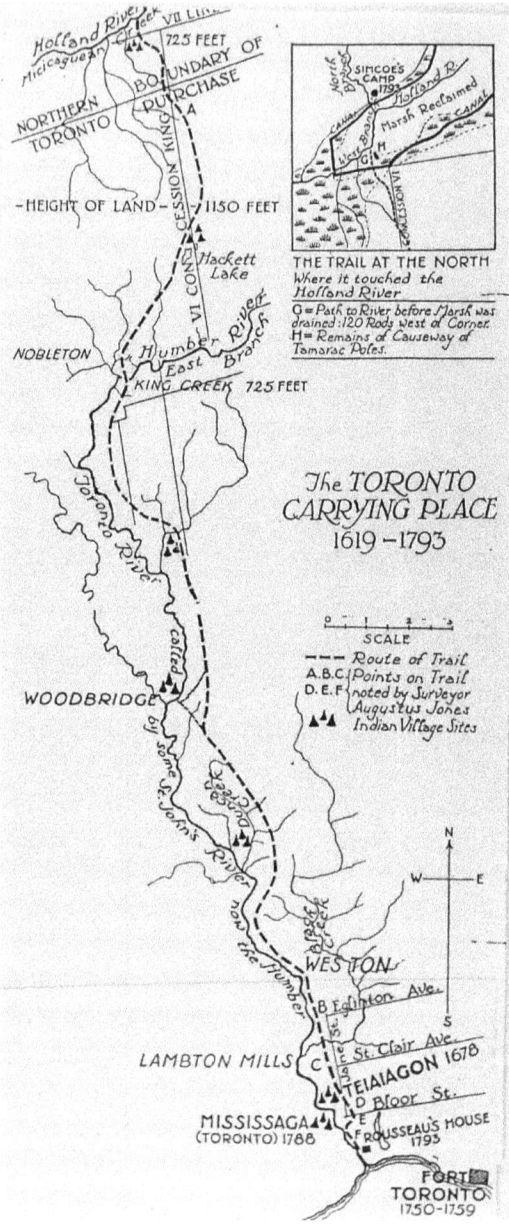

The Humber route of the Toronto Carrying-Place Trail | C.W. Jefferys, from Robinson, *Toronto during the French Régime*

sell l'eau de vie [brandy] to the [Mississaugas] in order to counterbalance the trade that happens at [Oswego]."[2]

Competition between France and Britain resulted in a series of intercolonial wars in the eighteenth century that extended through much of eastern North America. In addition to regular troops and militia, both colonial powers relied on the military service of their Indigenous allies. The Anishinaabek (including the Mississaugas), the "Canadian Iroquois" of the St. Lawrence Valley,[3] and others fought on the side of the French, and the Six Nations and others fought on the side of the British—though these Indigenous warriors were often reluctant to fight each other. Towards the end of the Seven Years War, in 1759, the French abandoned and destroyed Fort Toronto (also known as Fort Rouillé). Although the British and Haudenosaunee defeated the French in 1760, France's Indigenous allies were not conquered.

After 1760, the Mississaugas traded exclusively with the English, who claimed the region as their own.

> *And things were going more or less fine until the French were expelled by the British . . . Because the French never wanted our lands. They wanted a trading post here or a chapel there or some small thing, and they more or less were friendly to us. They intermarried with us. Learned the language. And they weren't greedy for anything except beaver pelts.*
>
> —Darin Wybenga, Mississaugas of the Credit[4]

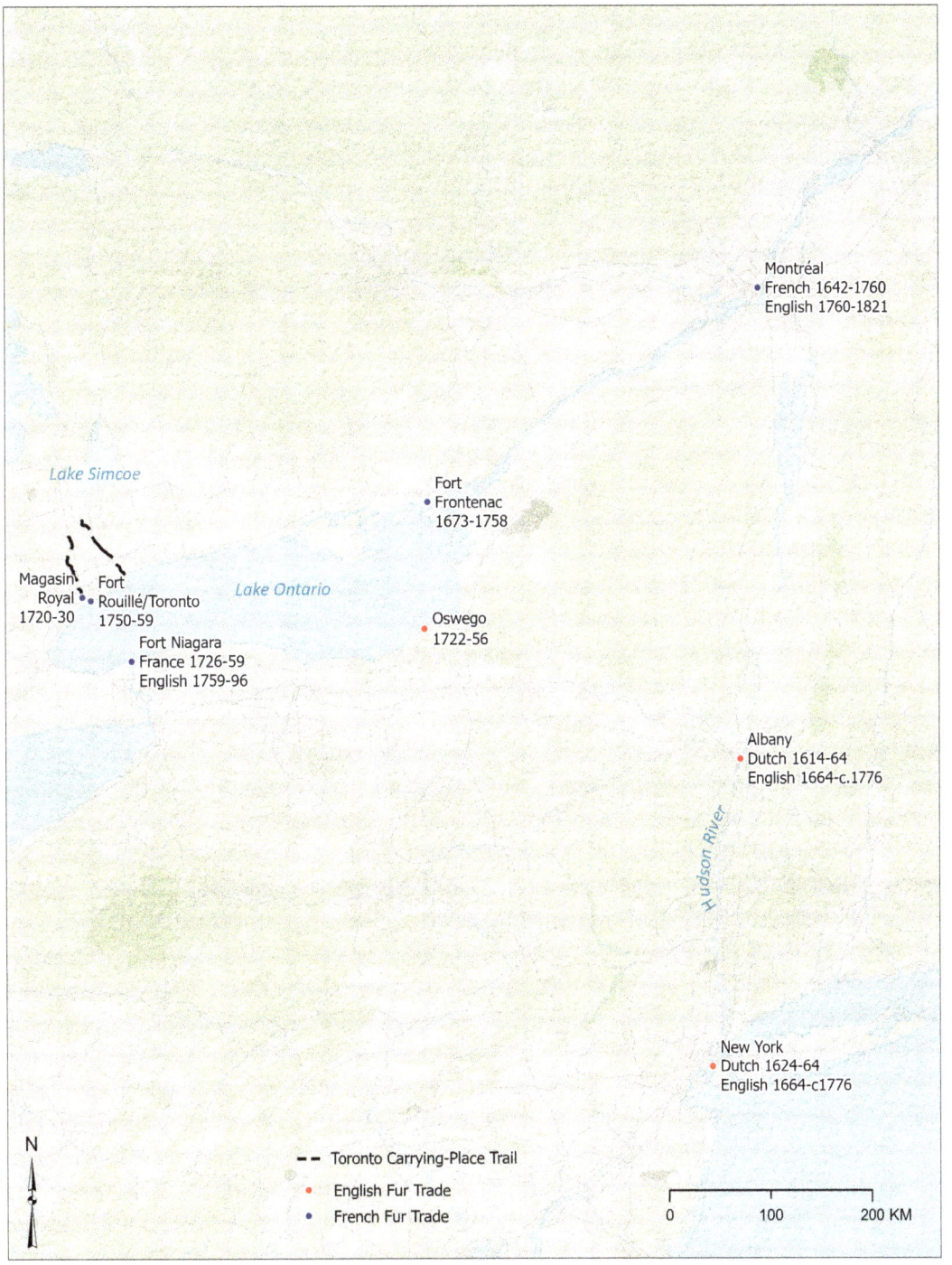

Fur trade from the Humber River to French and English trading posts and centres in the eighteenth century

43

Illustration of the Twenty-Four Nations Wampum presented by Sir William Johnson to the Anishinaabek and other Nations at the 1764 Treaty of Niagara | Adapted by Kaia'tanoron Dumoulin Bush from her illustration for *A Treaty Guide for Torontonians*

Illustration of the Covenant Chain Wampum presented by Sir William Johnson to Britain's Indigenous allies at the 1764 Treaty of Niagara | Adapted by Kaia'tanoron Dumoulin Bush from her illustration for *A Treaty Guide for Torontonians*

After Britain's defeat of New France in 1760, Toronto Mississauga Chief Wabbicommicot and most local Mississaugas chose not to fight with Pontiac in the Indigenous resistance to the British that broke out in 1763; in fact, Wabbicommicot helped bring about a peaceful resolution. Wabbicommicot then attended the massive 1764 Council at Niagara, which extended the existing Covenant Chain alliance between the Haudenosaunee and English to France's former allies, including the Anishinaabek. The Treaty of Niagara laid the foundation for peaceful relations in what became Canada. The British promised that Indigenous peoples would never live in poverty and could call on the British in times of need—promises still recalled today.[5]

The British Trade after 1760

The Council at Niagara also set British exchange rates for trade goods and furs and restored trade that had been disrupted by Pontiac's War. As the British extended control over the Toronto area, fur traders, licensed and unlicensed, returned to the Humber. They mostly traded alcohol, but they also sold more useful trade goods.[6] Jacques Duperon Baby (of the Detroit fur-trading Baby family) received a licence to trade in 1762, but the extent of his trade is unknown. (Sometime after 1816, his son James Baby—a politician, judge, wealthy landowner, slave owner, speculator, and member of the Family Compact—would buy fifteen hundred acres on the east bank of the

Humber and build a large home at the site of Teiaiagon, now Baby Point, north of Bloor Street.[7] In 1830, he was appointed one of the trustees for the Six Nations of the Grand River trust funds. He was later removed from that office.)[8]

The first legal fur traders of note under the British were French traders Jean-Bonaventure Rousseau and his son Jean-Baptiste Rousseau. In 1770, Jean-Bonaventure Rousseau received a licence to trade at the Humber River. The merchandise in his first trading expedition included 80 imperial gallons (360 litres) of rum, 15 imperial gallons (73 litres) of wine, four fusils (light flintlock muskets), 300 pounds of gunpowder, and 16 hundredweight (approximately 1,792 pounds or 813 kilograms) of shot and balls.[9] In 1774, Rousseau Sr. delegated the trade on the Humber to his son Jean-Baptiste, known as St. John Rousseau to the English. The river became known as St. John's River.

Another trader who may have been trading on or near the Humber as early as 1775 was Joseph Shepard, a Loyalist who came from the United States in 1774 and became a "roving Indian trader in the vicinity of York."[10] He married (Maria) Catherine Fisher, sister of Elizabeth Fisher Cummer and an aunt of Elizabeth Fisher Stong, who lived at the farm that forms the nucleus of The Village at Black Creek.[11] Shepard settled on Lot 16, northwest of Yonge and Sheppard (the street was named after him).

Impact of the Fur Trade

The fur trade began as an exchange for mutual benefit. It depended on Indigenous labour and alliances with Indigenous people and provided Indigenous people with access to highly valued, labour-saving European trade goods. It built on networks of exchange and reciprocity already established between Indigenous Nations over great distances. It mimicked Indigenous practices of reciprocal gift giving central to their cultures, governance, and spiritual practices, and bonds of trust and amity, including marriage and other forms of kinship, formed between Indigenous and European peoples. For example, in 1771, Nanebeaujou, one of the Head Chiefs of southern Georgian Bay, came to trade on the Humber and adopted English fur trader Ferral Wade as his son. The trading relationship was enhanced through fictive kinship, ensuring that both Wade and his followers acted responsibly—as relatives. Wade described his adoption in a letter to his employer, Sir William Johnson:

> He told me to sit by him that he wanted to speak to me. he then pulled Out ten strings of Wampum & spoke as follows, It gives me and my people great pleasure that you Intend to Continue among Us. now that we know where to [obtain] supplies to our Liking. keep up your Spirits and be Assured My people will Look on this house as their Own then taking me by the hand he now took me as his Child, and All the Indians should Look on me as such. then holding up the Strings

those is Like your Writing they don't tell Lyes. you may depend on having a Great Many Indians this fall & Winter treat them kindly when they Come.[12]

Over time, the fur trade's negative impacts became clearer. Contact with Europeans exposed Indigenous peoples to lethal European diseases to which they had no acquired immunity. Trade also incorporated Indigenous peoples into wider European economic relations, ensnaring them in relations of credit and debt, in a market system in which prices could fluctuate considerably according to distant and capricious economic forces beyond their control—but usually to the advantage of Europeans. As a result, they also became increasingly subject to European law.

The fur trade imported an exploitative form of resource extraction that contradicted the Indigenous practices of conservation and maintaining balance in ecological relationships. It undermined the spiritual relationship between Indigenous peoples and fur-bearing animals. The drastic reduction in beaver populations changed water levels, which altered the relationships between other plant and animal species. The trade also altered the balance of power between Indigenous Nations, between those who had easy access to pelts and those who didn't, and between those who had early access to guns and those who didn't. Within communities, the intensification of the fur trade along with intermarriages between European fur traders and Indigenous women altered relations between Indigenous men and women.

Although historians have labelled it the "fur" trade and highlighted the useful goods exchanged for furs, a key trade item was alcohol, an intoxicant previously unknown to Indigenous peoples. Its use—for a variety of reasons—appears to have led to addiction for some and widespread social disruption, which many Indigenous leaders tried to stop. From a fur trader's point of view, alcohol was an ideal trade good because it could be consumed quickly and could be addictive, fuelling demand. In the 1670s, French fur traders from Fort Cataraqui (present-day Kingston) got the entire village of Teiaiagon (including children) drunk for three days.[13]

The Mississaugas complained frequently that the fur traders only sold alcohol. In the 1820s, they complained that fur traders were forcing alcohol on them and threatening them with violence if they became sober. Alcohol was absolutely central to the trade—and intimately connected to colonial processes.[14]

According to historian Peter Schmalz, the highest officials in the British Indian Department made their fortunes through the alcohol trade, even though they were witness to the destruction it wrought. Both Europeans and Indigenous people commented on the havoc created in Indigenous communities by the alcohol traders at York, and the appeals of abstinence-focused Christian movements such as Methodism can only be understood in relation to this devastation. Alcohol also became a source of friction between the Mississaugas close to York and other Anishinaabek from Lakes Huron and Simcoe, who were initially less affected by its ravages.[15]

As Europeans despoiled Indigenous fishing and hunting grounds, and as diseases killed huge numbers of Indigenous peoples, alcohol misuse became a marker and symptom of Indigenous trauma. Yet its continuing presence in the fur trade was complex. Indigenous peoples demanded that fur traders make it available to them and favoured traders who did.

The provision of alcohol enmeshed local peoples in global systems of human exploitation, notably the slave trade. The alcohol that traders offered to Indigenous peoples was increasingly produced by enslaved African peoples on Caribbean sugar plantations, generating immense wealth for British slaveholders and investors. Later, alcohol would be a factor in the development of a local sex trade.

Paradoxically, local fur traders often had good relations with Indigenous people or were part Indigenous themselves. Many learned Indigenous languages and had at least a rudimentary understanding of Indigenous culture and protocol. They learned to use Indigenous technologies such as canoes and snowshoes to meet Indigenous trappers in their own world. They certainly had far more contact with Indigenous peoples than most settlers.

PART TWO:
Founding York

4

Early British Treaties

After the defeat of Britain in the American War of Independence (1775–83) and the formation of the United States of America, Britain tried to increase the population of its remaining North American colonies. It needed to defend its territories against further hostilities from the United States and provide land for "Loyalists"—people who lived in the Thirteen Colonies (America) and supported the British. To facilitate these goals, the British negotiated a series of poorly documented agreements with the Mississaugas.

> *It wasn't until the British become the only game in town that we start to get problems. And that's when the treaty-making process begins. And that's, of course, where the problems really begin for us.*
>
> —Darin Wybenga, Mississaugas of the Credit[1]

The war divided the Haudenosaunee Confederacy over how best to protect their territories in the colony of New York: some Nations fought for the British, others for the Americans. Those Haudenosaunee (principally Mohawks) who supported Britain lost their homelands and followed War Chief Thayendenegea / Joseph Brant to Canada. Their lands were ceded to the United States through the Treaty of Paris, a move bitterly opposed by the Haudenosaunee.

> *We challenged the King by what right he had to do that. We only gave him permission to walk upon our lands and share them. He had no authority to cede it away."*
>
> —Phil Monture, Six Nations of the Grand River[2]

In 1784, the Mississaugas agreed to provide land to the west of Lake Ontario for settlers and Six Nations Loyalists, in what became known as the Between the Lakes Treaty. As Mississauga Chief Pokquan explained to colonial officials, "We are Indians, and consider ourselves and the Six Nations to be one and the same people, and agreeable to a former, and mutual agreement [the Dish with One Spoon], we

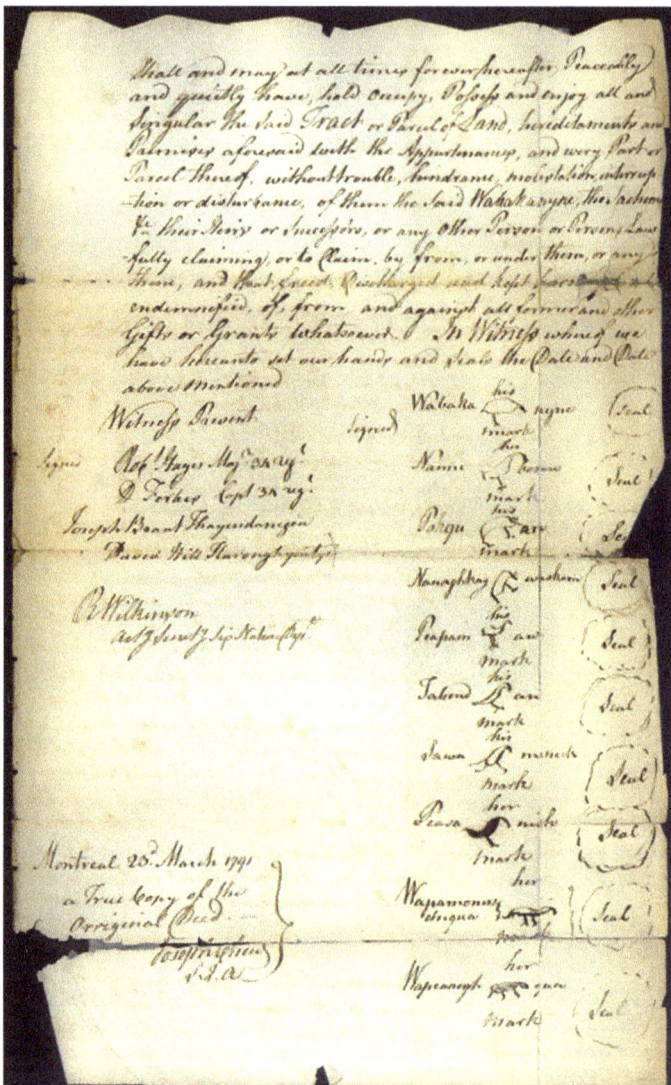

Indenture for lands at Grand River, 1784. This is a true copy of the original deed. The top signatory is Wabakinine, and the last three are principal women | Copy of deed from the Mississaugas, May 22, 1784, correspondence and memoranda received by the Surveyor General's Office, Archives of Ontario, RG 1-1, vol. 2, p. 145

are bound to help each other."[3] The 1784 Between the Lakes Treaty is recognized by Canada but not by the Haudenosaunee.[4]

In the Haldimand Proclamation of 1784 (regarded as a treaty by the Six Nations), the British granted 6 miles (10 kilometres) on either side of the Grand River from its mouth to its source to the Six Nations in perpetuity, in recognition of their loyalty.[5] A 1785 census recorded that more than 1,400 Haudenosaunee, including almost 450 Mohawks, had arrived from south of the new border and were re-establishing their communities and Nations along the Grand River. They were joined by 400 people from other allied Indigenous Nations.

The new arrivals greatly outnumbered the Mississaugas of south-central Ontario, who counted just over 500 people at the time. Their presence substantially altered the political landscape, especially since the Haudenosaunee had been British allies for far longer than the Mississaugas—for more than a hundred years.[6] Joseph Brant soon became an important intermediary between the Haudenosaunee, the British, and other Indigenous Nations.

The Johnson-Butler Agreements and the First So-Called Toronto Purchase

Because Britain feared the Americans coveted its remaining North American territories, it sought further land cessions from the Anishinaabek to ensure military control of the entire north shore of Lake Ontario and the route from York to Matchedash Bay on Georgian Bay.

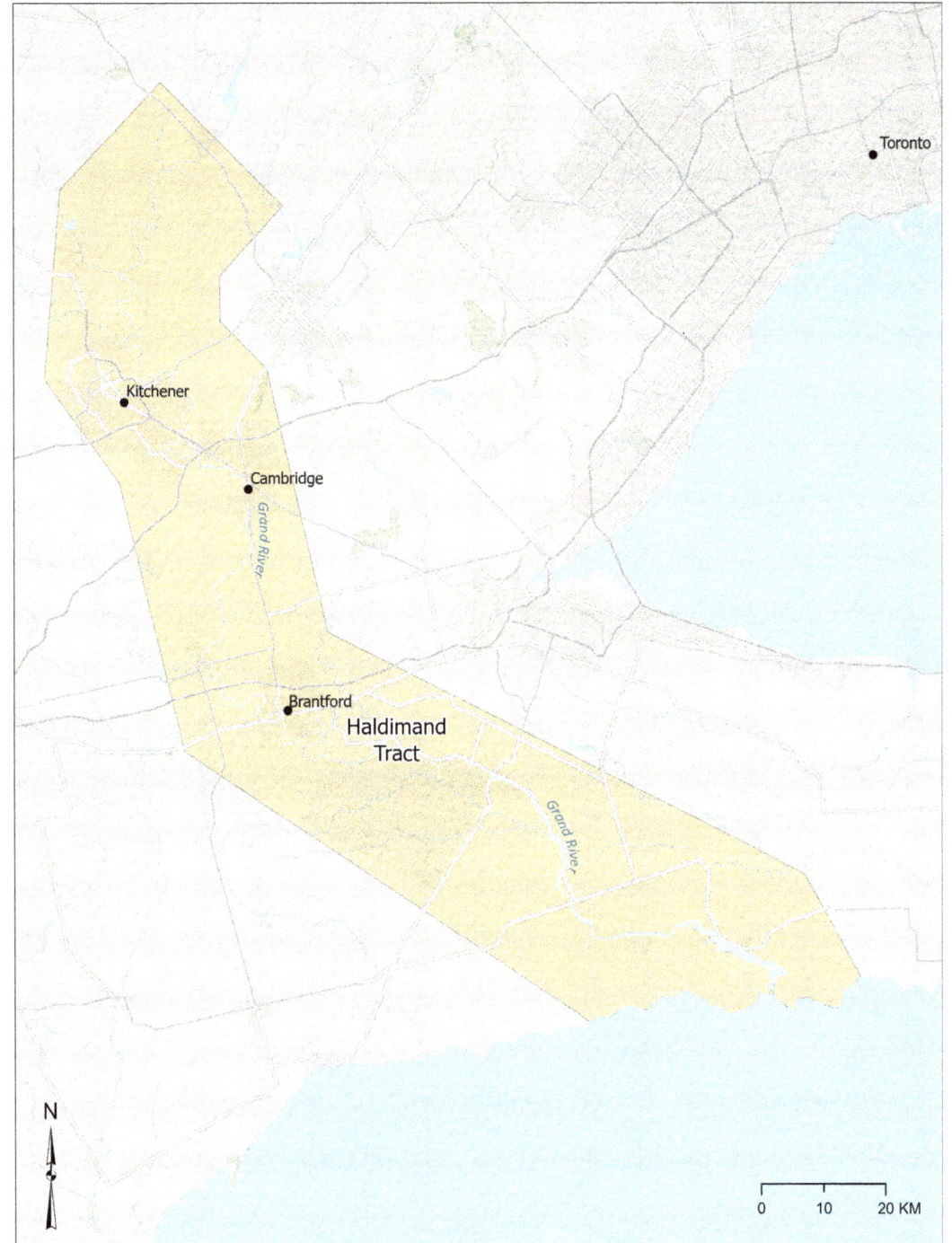

Lands granted to the Six Nations through the Haldimand Proclamation of 1784, as surveyed by Augustus Jones, 1791. The size and exact boundaries of the original lands granted to the Six Nations through the 1784 Haldimand Proclamation vary in existing maps and are currently under litigation.

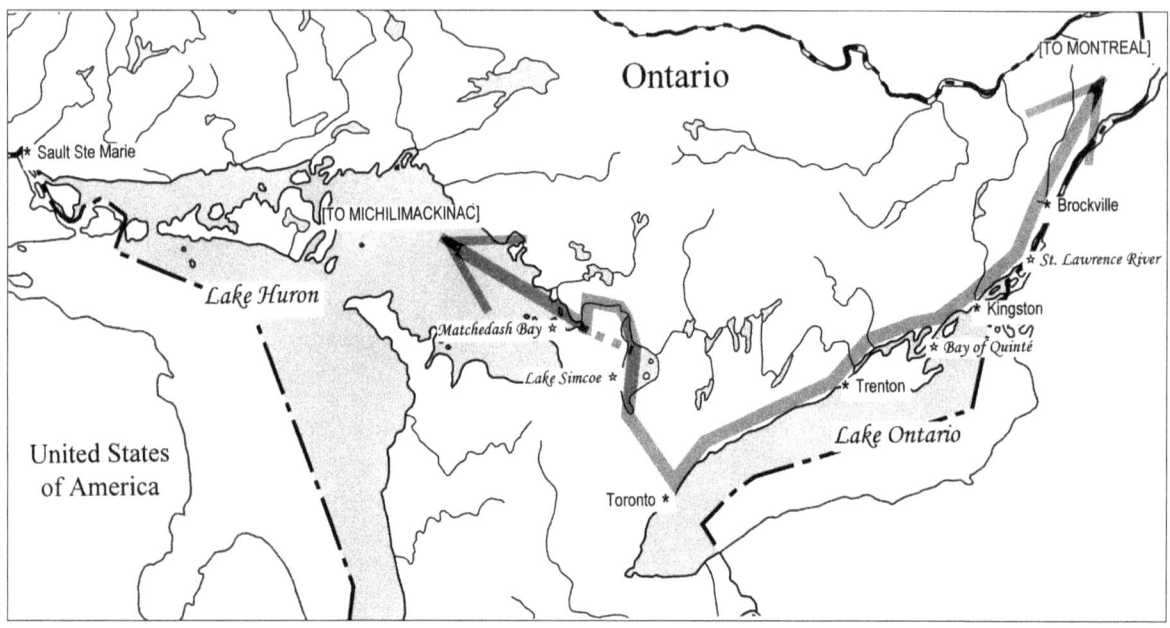

British land purchase strategy, 1783–88 | Reimer, "British-Canada's Land Purchases, 1783–1788"

The so-called Collins Purchase, a poorly documented agreement in 1785 between Simcoe and the Chippewas of Lakes Huron and Simcoe, was probably not a land cession but granted the British right of passage over the portage route west of Lake Simcoe to Matchedash Bay.[7] Discussions in 1787 and 1788 with the Mississaugas, the Chippewas of Lakes Huron and Simcoe (including Chief Canise), and others led to other poorly documented land cessions. In 1787, an agreement was made between Sir John Johnson, head of the colonial Indian Department (and son of Sir William Johnson, who negotiated the 1764 Treaty of Niagara), and the Mississaugas concerning the lands at Toronto, including the waterfront and the Toronto Carrying-Place Trail.

From the beginning, the Mississaugas and the British had different understandings of what they were agreeing to. The British intended a land cession, and the negotiations bore a superficial and ultimately deceptive resemblance to Indigenous treaty making in terms of the protocol followed. But the basic assumptions differed substantially. Anishinaabek used land differently than the British: Anishinaabek did not live in permanent villages or farm large areas (though they maintained small gardens). They held their land in common rather than individually, although some areas

Unknown artist, portrait of Sir John Johnson, n.d | Courtesy of McCord Museum, M17590

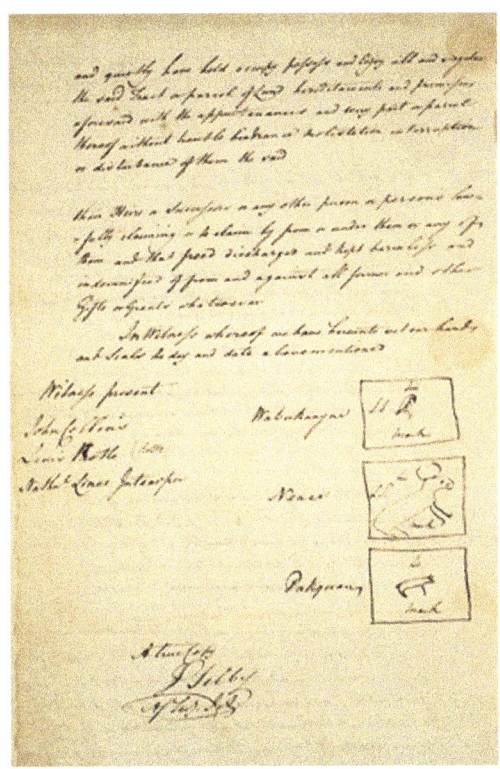

Clerk's manuscript copy of incomplete 1787 Toronto Purchase indicating Doodems of three Mississauga Chiefs, including Wabakinine | Library and Archives Canada, RG 10, D-10a, series A, vol. 1841, reel T-9938, GAD REF IT040

were assigned to different family groups for different uses. The Mississaugas likely understood their agreements with the British as allowing the British to use certain lands in exchange for ongoing annual presents, rather like a lease or rental agreement, not a permanent transfer of ownership, the British intention. Although the Mississaugas welcomed the trade goods offered, they were induced to make agreements because the British promised great assistance to the Mississaugas—teaching them to farm, for example, and free passage across surrendered land to hunt and fish as before. The Mississaugas could not have envisaged being swamped by a flood of settlers, who would outnumber them ten to one, transform the landscape, erect fences, impose their

4 | Early British Treaties   55

own laws, and ignore British promises that the Mississaugas could hunt and fish on ceded lands.

> *You know the Mississaugas of the Credit were part of the Mississauga Nation, along with Scugog, Alderville, Hiawatha, Curve Lake . . . and those are the ones that, as the Mississauga Nation, signed treaties. And then the Mississaugas of the Credit, when Indian Affairs or the federal government at the time wanted them to settle, they kind of broke apart, and they became the First Nations they are today.*
>
> —Margaret Sault, Mississaugas of the Credit[8]

Problems with the agreement soon became apparent. In 1788, the first survey of the lands was not completed because of a dispute with Head Chief Wabakinine over the eastern and western boundaries. Surveyor Alexander Aitken reported that Wabakinine had been successfully "prevailed upon" by Colonel John Butler to extend the boundaries eastward from the Don River to the eastern end of Ashbridges Bay and westward from the Humber River to Etobicoke Creek.[9] Not wishing to anger the Chief further after Butler and other officials left, Aitken did not complete a survey of the northern boundary. Gifts were given to the Mississaugas in 1788, which the British recorded as payment for the land, but it's not clear how the Mississaugas understood them since gifts were customary as an expression and renewal of alliance.

This is the list of gifts given to the Mississaugas of the Credit in 1788 as payment for the Toronto Purchase of 1787, according to Nathaniel Lines, interpreter.[10]

6 Bales Strouds [coarse woollen cloth]
4 Bales Moltons [linen cloth]
4 Kegs Hoes
8 Half Barrels Powder
5 Boxes Guns
3 Cases Shott
24 Brass Kettles
10 Kegs of Ball
200 lbs Tobacco
1 Cask containing 3 Gro Knifes
10 Doz. Looking Glasses
4 Trunks Linen
1 Hogshead containing 18 pieces Gartering
24 Laced Hats
30 Pieces Ribbon
3 Gro. Fish Hooks
2,000 Gun Flints
1 Box 60 Hats
1 Bale flowered Flannel
5 Bales Blankets
1 Bale Broad Cloth
5 pieces embossed Serge
1 Case Barley Corn Beads
96 Gallons of Rum

At the same meeting in 1788, an agreement was said to have been made for lands along Lake Ontario's north shore to present-day Belleville, but no deed, treaty document, or record of payment for this "Gunshot Treaty" (purportedly ceding lands as far inland as a gunshot could be heard) has ever been discovered. In addition, it appears that the northern route to Matchedash Bay, discussed in the 1785 Collins Treaty, was confirmed at this time.[11]

> *Those early treaties, I always say we went in with a certain amount of . . . I don't want to use the term "naiveté." We didn't go in with a clear understanding, a clear mind of what we were truly entering into. I think we had the mistaken assumption that we would be still sharing these lands. The British would do their thing on the lands, and we would do our thing. We knew they would build villages, and we knew they would put roads through. We knew that. We weren't stupid. We knew what went on south of the border. We knew that. But we still expected to carry on our lifestyle. I don't think we were ready for the onslaught of people that came. All of a sudden, when you find fences springing up and plowed fields and stripped forests and a salmon fishery that doesn't work so well anymore.*
>
> —Darin Wybenga, Mississaugas of the Credit[12]

> *I think they just thought they were being, like, "Yeah, we can share the land." But the idea of consultation would continue— which didn't.*
>
> —Kory Snache, Chippewas of Rama[13]

The Establishment of York

In 1793, Lieutenant-Governor John Graves Simcoe established York at the best harbour on Lake Ontario's north shore. Originally conceived as a military post, York was made the official capital of Upper Canada in 1796. To make it their own, the British sought to transform the area's mental and physical landscape. Simcoe renamed Cobhekhenonk / Gabekanaang the Humber River after a river in England; Lake Simcoe, which had been called Ashanyoong / Azhoonyaang (Place of the Calling) by the Mississaugas, was named after Simcoe's father. Simcoe replaced so many Indigenous place names with English ones that Mohawk War Chief Joseph Brant sarcastically observed: "Gen. S[imcoe] has done a great deal for this province, he has changed the name of every place in it."[14]

Blank Deed

A year later, in 1794, the British became aware that the precise boundaries of the land cession at Toronto were unaccountably missing from the only treaty document that could be located. Governor Lord Dorchester informed Simcoe:

> A plan . . . has been found in the Survey'r General's Office, to which is attached a blank deed, with the names or devices of three chiefs of the Mississauga Nation, on separate pieces of paper annexed thereto, and witnessed by Mr. Collins, Mr. Kotte, a surveyor, since dead, and Mr. Lines, Indian Interpreter, but not being filled

Mary Ann Burges, portrait of Elizabeth Simcoe, 1790 | Courtesy Toronto Public Library Digital Archive, JRR3264

Jean Laurent Mosnier, portrait of John Graves Simcoe, 1791 | Courtesy of Toronto Public Library Digital Collection, OHQ2-PICTURES-S-R-1

up, is of no validity, or may be applied to a land they possess; no fraud has been committed or seems to have been intended. It was, however an omission which will set aside the whole transaction, and throw us entirely on the good faith of the Indians for just so much land as they are willing to allow, and what may be further necessary must be purchased anew, but it will be best not to press that matter or show any anxiety about it.[15]

Subsequent inquiries of Sir John Johnson (who had negotiated the agreement), the interpreter Nathaniel Lines, and other witnesses all produced different accounts of the boundaries agreed to.

Elizabeth Simcoe, *York Harbour, Looking West from the Mouth of the Don River*, c. 1793 | Courtesy Toronto Public Library Digital Archive, PICTURES-R-3235

The vagueness of the surrender document and these inconsistencies led the British to conclude the deed was indeed invalid and the exact lands it covered in doubt. Although they knew they did not have a valid deed to the lands at Toronto, they did not reveal this to the Mississaugas and settlement proceeded apace. Colonial officials would not find a solution to this problem until 1805.

5

Turning Indigenous Territory into Private Property

From 1781 to 1850, a series of agreements (interpreted as land cessions by the British and treaties by the Anishinaabek) opened virtually all Indigenous lands in southern Ontario to settlement. In the British legal system, following the acquisition of title, the first step was surveying the land and dividing it into rectangular lots to sell or grant to settlers. Surveying was a concept alien to First Nations, who recognized intercommunity or territorial boundaries between Nations with physical features such as heights of land between watersheds. The surveyor thus played a key role in the conversion of Indigenous territories into colonial private property. Often, he needed relationships with Indigenous people to carry out his work.

The story of surveyor Augustus Jones highlights the role of intermarriage in developing alliances between Indigenous and European people. The son of a Welsh immigrant to the colony of New York, Jones accompanied his extended family north in the 1780s. Over the next two decades, he became a key figure in early Indigenous-settler relations. Through marriage, he developed strategic partnerships with key leaders among the Mohawks at Grand River and the Mississaugas of the Credit. Jones learned to speak both Anishinaabemowin and Mohawk. His survey records include a valuable list of Mississauga place names for the rivers and other features of the Toronto area. His extended family relationships established early networks of cooperation between some Indigenous leaders and settlers and between some Mississaugas and Haudenosaunee. Not all Indigenous peoples approved of the results: an uneasy mix of personal interest, networks of power and privilege, and loyalties to multiple communities divided Indigenous communities over how much to trust and work with such intermediaries.

According to historical geographer R. Gentilcore, "No other surveyor in Upper Canada surveyed and subdivided so much important land."[1] Named deputy surveyor of the Nassau District in 1791 (renamed the Home District in 1792), Jones was a man of prodigious energy. He surveyed most of the townships from Fort Erie to the Head of the Lake (now Hamilton); the Haldimand Tract (lands along the Grand River); the waterfront along the north shore of Lake Ontario from Toronto to the Trent River; town plots for York and Newark (Niagara); York township, Etobicoke Township, and Scarboro (later Scarborough); the western boundary of the Toronto Purchase; and the Lake Simcoe area. He also surveyed two key roads that opened vast lands for settlement: Dundas Street, which linked Lake Ontario and the Detroit frontier, and Yonge Street, which connected Lakes Ontario and Simcoe.

> *[For place names] we have to rely on Augustus Jones, the deputy provincial surveyor. What does he do? He writes down all the names of the rivers and creeks all around the western end of Lake Ontario. And, for the most part, they were pretty accurate.*
>
> —Darin Wybenga, Mississaugas of the Credit[2]

In 1795, Jones was directed to survey and open a cart road (what would become Yonge Street) from York to Lake Simcoe. He was given thirty soldiers of the Queen's Rangers (a Loyalist military unit) for road construction. Surveying began in January 1796, and on February 16 Jones reached Holland Landing (on the Holland River), a distance of almost 55 kilometres.

The northern part of Yonge Street (extending from today's Aurora to Holland Landing) traversed land that lay beyond the northern limit of the nebulous Toronto Purchase, which was already known to be invalid. (Confusion about the status of the lands along the northern stretch of Yonge Street had led to the search for the 1787 deed.) The land lay within the territory of the Anishinaabek of the southern Lake Simcoe area (known today as the Chippewas of Georgina Island). It is not clear if the land had been properly ceded.

In 1798, Head Chief Musquakie (known to the English as Yellowhead) of the Chippewas of Lakes Huron and Simcoe apparently confirmed that the lands south of Lake Simcoe had been surrendered in 1788.[3] The Johnson-Butler agreement had purportedly also ceded waterfront lands east of the Toronto Purchase from Scarborough to the Belleville area. But in 1923, when commissioners investigated Indigenous grievances prior to the signing of the Williams Treaties, the Mississauga Nation claimed that they had never ceded seven townships lying immediately south of Lake Simcoe.[4] In fact, the Williams Treaties commissioners found no records confirming that the land had been ceded through any treaty. For this reason, the commission included a description in Clause 2 of the 1923 treaty—more than a century after the land had been granted to settlers.

Augustus Jones and His Mississauga Family

During the winter of 1793–94, Augustus Jones hired Wahbanosay / Wabenose (Walks in the Dawn), the Mississauga Eagle Doodem (Clan) Chief, as a guide for the Yonge Street survey. Wahbanosay was the Ogimaa of the Mississaugas at Burlington Bay and would later sign land cessions for Treaties 8 (Burlington Heights), 13 (the 1805 Toronto Purchase), and 14 (Mississauga / Burlington).

Doodem signature of Wabenose / Wabahnosay on Toronto Purchase of 1805 (Treaty 13) | Library and Archives Canada, RG 10, vol. 1841, IT 038, Indian Affairs' consecutive number 13; August 1, 1805, Toronto Purchase, LAC, RG 10, D-10a, series A, vol. 1841, reel T-9938, GAD REF IT 038 (GKS ID: 1596)

That Jones depended on Wahbanosay's deep knowledge of the land is revealed through this story, told by Kahkewaquonaby (Sacred Feathers) / Peter Jones, son of Augustus Jones and grandson of Wahbanosay: "I heard my departed father say, that when he started to run Yonge Street, he planted his compass by the shore of York Bay, and got my grand-father to set the point of the compass for Holland Landing on Lake Simcoe. My father then followed the course set by the Indian, and came within twenty rods of striking the point aimed at, after running more than 30 miles through a vast wilderness."[5]

A few years later, Augustus Jones entered into a country marriage (i.e., according to Indigenous custom rather than a Christian marriage) with Wahbanosay's daughter Tuhbenahneequay, later known as Sarah Henry, whose mother was Naishenum.[6] Augustus Jones and Tuhbenahneequay would have two children, Thayendenaged / John Jones, born in 1798, and Kahkewahquonaby / Peter Jones, born in 1802. Both would become important figures in the history of the area. After her relationship with Jones ended, Tuhbenahneequay married Chief Mesquacosy, with whom she had eight children. Today, a grove of 150 ancient oak trees along the Toronto Carrying-Place Trail is named in her honour.

Wahbanosay and another wife, Puhgashkis, were the parents and Tuhbenahneequay the half-sister of influential Mississauga Chief Nawahjegezhegwabe (Sloping Sky) / Joseph Sawyer, who would serve as Head Chief of the Mississaugas of the Credit from 1829 to 1863, alongside Wahbanosay's grandsons, Peter and John Jones, who also became Chiefs.

Augustus Jones and His Mohawk Family

Augustus Jones also married Sarah Tekarihogen of Six Nations of the Grand River in 1798 in an Anglican ceremony, meaning that for a few years he was partnered with both Sarah and Tuhbenahneequay. Sarah was the daughter of [Henry] Tekarihogen of the Turtle Clan, the "acknowledged first chief and sachem of the Mohawks" and his wife, Catherine.[7] Henry had been named Tekarihogen (a very prestigious hereditary title and position, named after one of the founders of the Haudenosaunee Confederacy) by his mother or grandmother Sarah, the Turtle Clan Matron and Head Clan Matron of the Mohawks. In Haudenosaunee governance, the Head Clan Matron was responsible for naming the Head Chief, and each Clan Matron named the Male Sachem or Chief of their Clan. Clan mothers could also "dehorn" or depose leaders who did not fulfill their leadership responsibilities.

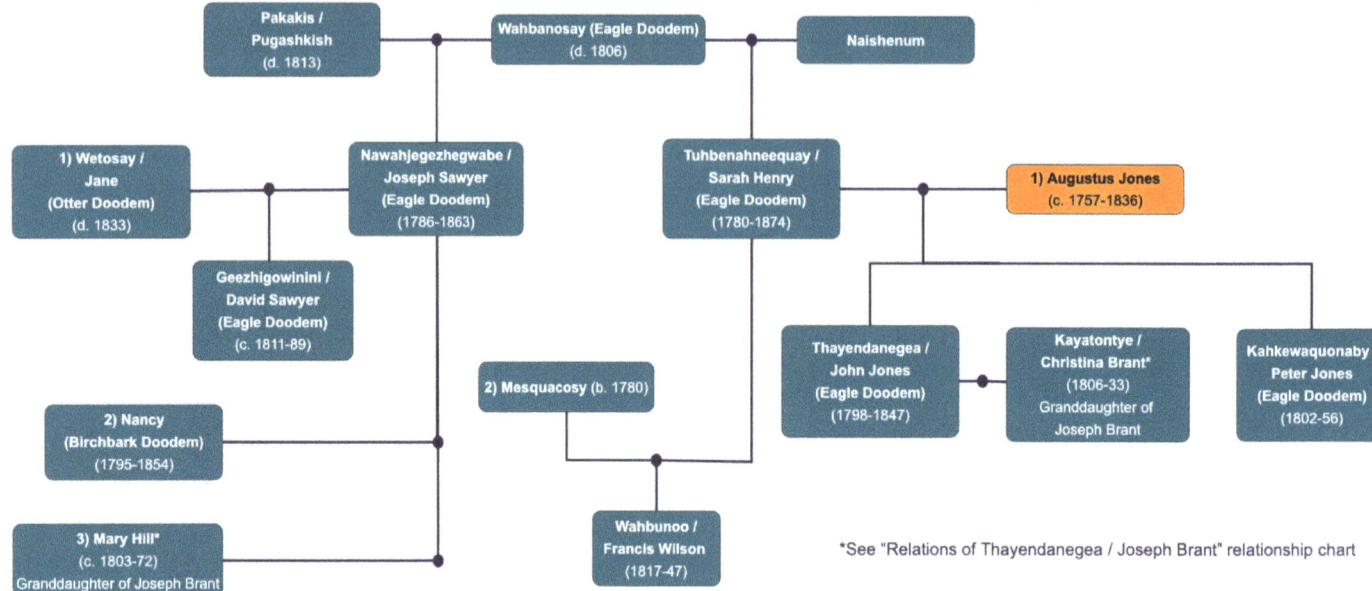

Mississauga relations of Augustus Jones (c. 1757–1836) | Victoria Freeman and Ludia (Eun Seon) Bae. Numbers indicate the order of marriages

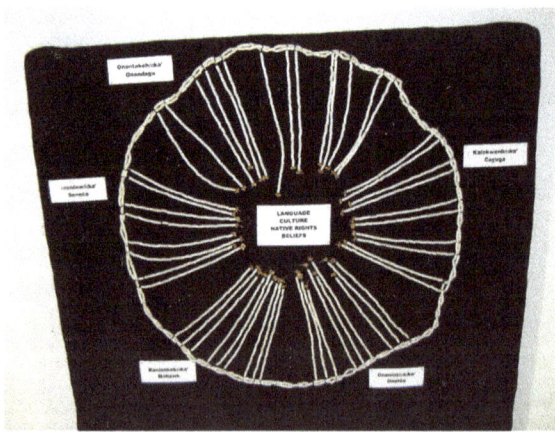

Replica of the Circle Wampum of the Haudenosaunee Confederacy. Equal strands of Wampum represent the Fifty Chiefs of the Confederacy, while the longest strand represents the people. Tekarihogen is the name / title of one of these Chiefs | Photo courtesy of Jake Thomas Learning Centre

Having two wives proved to be untenable for Jones. Indigenous men could have more than one wife if they could support them (and some European fur traders had multiple country marriages in different regions to secure access to Indigenous kin trading networks and their own safety). But Augustus Jones was a settler who wanted the respect of his Christian settler neighbours. He felt increasing pressure to end his relationship with Tuhbenahneequay (who refused to convert to Christianity), especially after he and Sarah joined the Episcopal Methodists in 1801. He ended his relationship with Tuhbenahneequay the following year and lived permanently with Sarah, though he maintained a lifelong connection to his Mississauga sons and at one point brought them to live with his Mohawk family. Sarah and

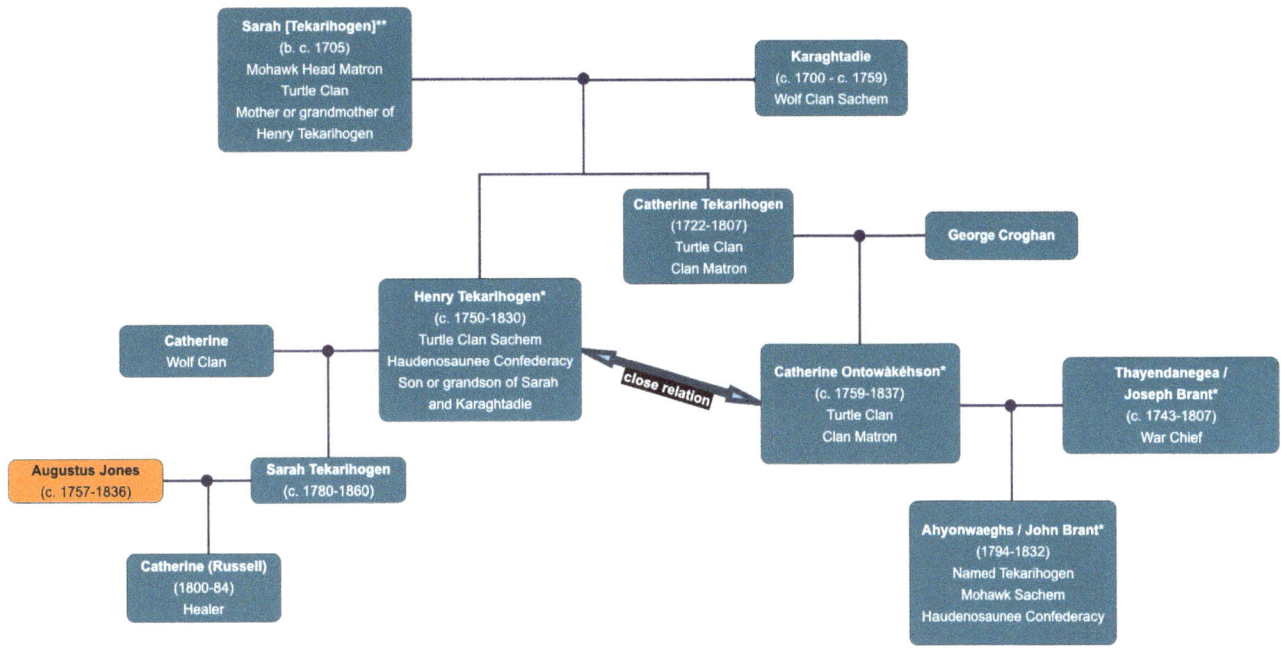

Haudenosaunee relations of Augustus Jones (c. 1757–1836) | Victoria Freeman and Ludia (Eun Seon) Bae

Wedding announcement of Augustus Jones and Sarah Tekarihogen, *Upper Canada Gazette, or American Oracle*, May 12, 1798

> MARRIED] At the Grand-River about three weeks since, A. JONES, esq. deputy surveyor, to a young lady of that place, daughter to the noted Mohawk warrior TERRIHOGAH.
>
> "At each kind glance may their souls unite,
> While love's soft sympathy imparts
> The tender transport of delight,
> Which beats in undivided hearts."

George Romney, *Thayendanegea / Joseph Brant*, 1776 | National Gallery of Canada, acc. no. 8005

Augustus would have eight children of their own at Grand River.

Perhaps Augustus Jones met Sarah Tekarihogen through Joseph Brant, for whom Jones conducted numerous surveys along the Grand River (Brantford, once Brant's Ford, across the Grand River is named after him). Brant and Augustus Jones built their houses at opposite ends of Burlington Beach and became close friends. Jones named his first son by Tuhbenahneequay "Thayandenaged" after Brant, and in 1823 Thayandenaged married Christina Brant, Joseph's granddaughter.

Educated in colonial schools and well-dressed, with "civilized" manners, Brant was an active participant in the elite social life of the colony and the most influential Mohawk leader in the eyes of British colonial administrators. Elizabeth Simcoe, wife of the lieutenant-governor, entertained him at dinner: "He had a countenance expressive of art or cunning. He wore an English coat with handsome crimson blanket, lined with black, and trimmed with gold fringe, and wore a fur cap; round his neck he had a ring of plaited sweet hay [sweetgrass]. It is a kind of grass which never loses its pleasant scent. The Indians are very fond of it."[8] In fact, sweetgrass is a cleansing spiritual medicine.

In marrying Sarah Tekarihogen, Augustus Jones became Joseph Brant's relative in addition to his close friend. In 1779, Joseph Brant had married Catherine Ohtowa'késon, the daughter of Catherine Tekarihogen (a close relative of Henry Tekarihogen) and the powerful Pennsylvania fur trader and Indian agent George Crogham. These relationships, and others created through intermarriage between Indigenous women and members of the Indian Department or fur traders, created an intercultural network of power brokers that advanced certain interests. Many of these relationships facilitated land dealings.

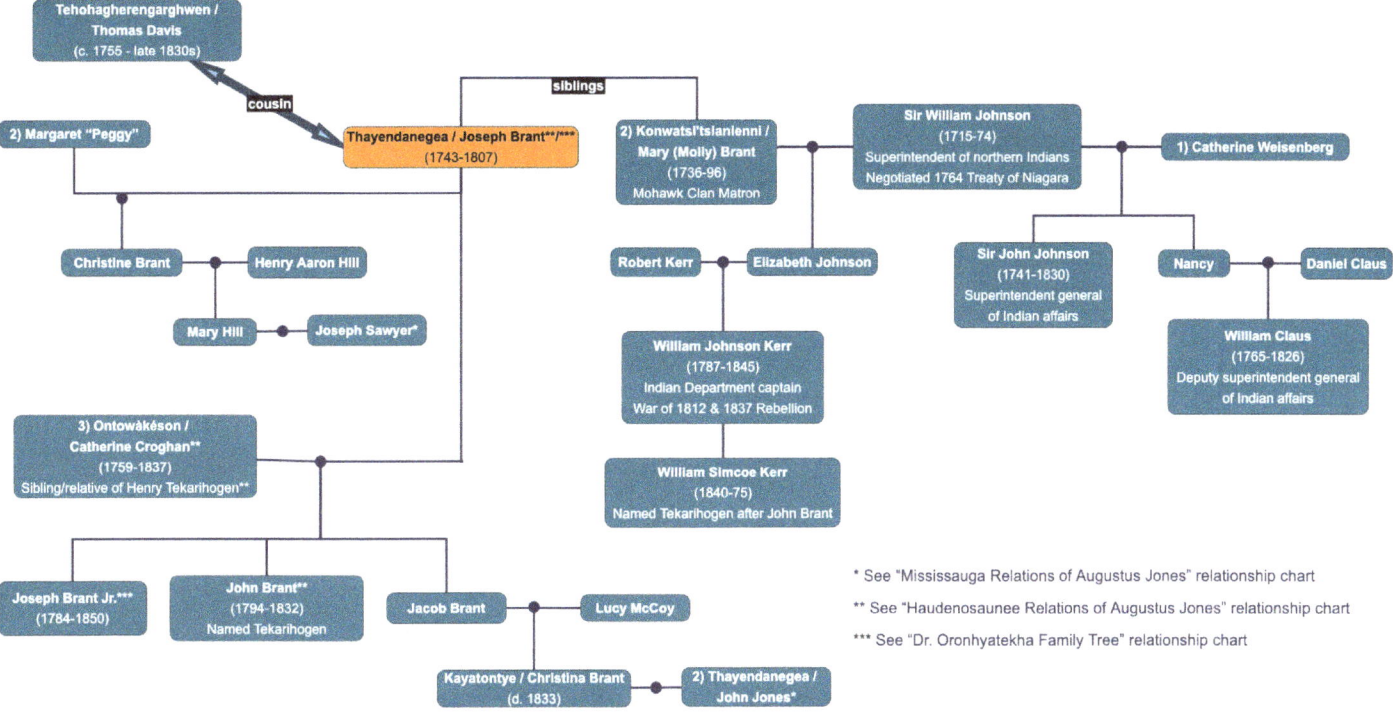

Relations of Thayendanegea / Joseph Brant (1743–1807) | Victoria Freeman and Ludia (Eun Seon) Bae. Numbers indicate the order of marriages

Augustus Jones, Henry Tekarihogen, Joseph Brant, and the Haldimand Tract

The Haldimand Tract would prove to be an early laboratory of Indigenous-settler relations. Augustus Jones allied with the Haudenosaunee faction who, like Brant and Henry Tekarihogen, opposed traditionalist Haudenosaunee and followers of the new Longhouse religion of Seneca prophet Ganiodaio / Handsome Lake, which combined some elements of traditional and Christian teachings. Jones' faction promoted Christianity, British education, and accommodation with settlers. Controversially, Brant argued that Haudenosaunee should grant settlers long-term leases for significant portions of the Haldimand Tract. The resulting trust fund would guarantee Haudenosaunee economic self-sufficiency, a necessity in his view if they wanted to remain self-governing allies and not subjects of the British Crown.

Colonial officials rejected Brant's proposal, in part because they opposed the idea of white men being tenants of Indigenous landowners. Also, according to the Royal Proclamation of 1763, which unilaterally established the relation of Indigenous peoples to the Crown in British law, Indigenous peoples could only sell their land to the Crown, not to individuals. Hence, according to the British, Indigenous peoples did not own their land in fee simple, as Brant asserted. It could not be disposed of as they pleased.

Nevertheless, Brant and Tekarihogen leased or sold large portions of the Haldimand Tract to Loyalist friends who had lived near them in New York and who they believed would assist the Haudenosaunee in learning Western-style farming.[9] These Loyalists included Palatine Germans who had come with the Haudenosaunee from New York and Pennsylvania after the American Revolution. (Some of these Palatine Germans were related to those who, like the Stong and Fisher families, later came to the Toronto area.) Through Brant, Jones was granted two huge tracts of land on the Haldimand Tract.[10] Brant also sometimes made Jones his agent in land purchases and named him one of his executors.

Some Haudenosaunee opposed Brant's policy of leasing out their lands to settlers, and they challenged the validity of Brant's leases to Jones, among others. For example, in 1809, the Six Nations Council included the following resolution, among many problematic land sales: "Brothers, We had forgot to mention 4800 acres marked out for Mr [Augustus] Jones near the Delaware Village—as we have never agreed to this we forbid his getting it."[11]

Traditionalists at Six Nations attempted to dehorn Henry Tekarihogen in 1811 because of his involvement in these land issues, but these efforts failed. He continued as Tekarihogen into the 1820s. In a pattern that would become familiar to Indigenous peoples, those leaders who favoured accommodation with settlers became increasingly powerful in their communities, regardless of their position within traditional governance structures, in part because of their links with colonial officials. In the process, traditionalists (particularly non-Christians) and traditional governance by Hereditary Chiefs were undermined, even though Indigenous peoples were still self-governing.

Problems with Jones' original survey of the Haldimand Tract persist to this day. Also, although Brant wrestled some concessions from the government and sold or leased a majority of the Haldimand Tract to settlers, the resulting ambiguity over title created a legal morass.[12] Colonial officials appropriated Six Nations trust funds for unrelated purposes and kept poor records. Two centuries later, the Six Nations are still trying to regain control of the development of their lands on the Haldimand Tract and reassert their sovereignty and traditional governance.

Augustus Jones' support for Brant's position on land sales may have been the reason he abruptly ceased working as a surveyor in 1800. By then, government officials were actively working to undermine Joseph Brant's influence and approach to selling or leasing Six Nations land.[13] Jones retired to his Stoney Creek farm near present-day Hamilton but later moved to the Haldimand Tract. Although his influence declined, in the coming decades, his Mississauga sons, who became known as John and Peter Jones, would have a profound influence on Indigenous peoples and their relations with newcomers.

6

Indigenous-Settler Encounters

The goodwill in evidence at York's 1793 naming ceremony did not last. In 1796, Wabakinine, Head Chief / Ogimaa of the Mississaugas at the western end of Lake Ontario and a signatory of the original Toronto Purchase of 1787, was killed while defending his sister from sexual assault by an off-duty Queen's Ranger on the Toronto waterfront. Wabakinine's wife also died a few days later of her injuries. The murder of their leader and the acquittal of his assailant at trial outraged the Mississaugas and sparked a major crisis in the colony.[1] Tensions between settlers and Indigenous peoples were already high since another Mississauga Chief had been murdered at Kingston just a few years previously and other killings by settlers had gone unpunished.

Chief Wabanip, the brother of Wabakinine's wife, found Augustus Jones at work along the Thames River and asked him to accompany the Mississaugas to Niagara to demand justice from colonial officials. Large numbers of Anishinaabek from across the Great Lakes flocked to Niagara "in great concern for the loss of a favourite and experienced Chief." Jones conveyed the Mississaugas' deep distress to Peter Russell, the administrator of Upper Canada who had replaced Simcoe, on leave. To defuse the crisis, Russell promised justice and offered additional gifts and provisions. But the situation remained tense for many months. Russell wrote:

> I cannot, however, shake off my apprehensions that some unfortunate family may yet, notwithstanding fall a sacrifice to their resentment, for Wabikanyn had many relations among the Chippewas and Lake Indians, and was greatly beloved by them, especially as they are not insensible of our present incapacity to punish them to any effect—for they mentioned this to Mr. Jones and proposed to him to join them should they prevail upon the Lake Indians to join them in revenging the many injuries they had received from us in this and other instances they enumerated.[2]

Jones later reported to his superiors that Nimquasim, a prominent Chief from Lake Huron, had met with other Anishinaabek at a York tavern "to open a war against the English to get Satisfaction, for what had been done; saying that he had at the Place of his residence, a great number of young warriors,

George Theodore Berthon, portrait of Upper Canada administrator Peter Russell, c. 1890 | Courtesy of Toronto Public Library Digital Archive, JRR407

that he could bring out at his command."[3] York and its neighbouring townships had a population of only 675 settlers and 135 soldiers, so it was extremely vulnerable to a coordinated Indigenous attack.[4] Although the local Mississaugas were few in number, they were allied with the powerful Western Alliance of Anishinaabek, Wyandot, Shawnee, Miami, and other Indigenous Nations, who were rumoured to have the backing of Britain's enemies, France and Spain. Russell ordered the inhabitants of York to assemble and provide themselves with "arms and ammunition for their Mutual Defence." He requested that four thousand small arms be sent to Upper Canada. Later, he requested that two blockhouses be built and that the number of troops in the colony be increased.

Given deepening tensions with Joseph Brant over Haudenosaunee land sales, the British feared the Mississaugas would form a military alliance with Brant and the Six Nations. But Brant convinced the Mississaugas that an armed uprising would fail given Britain's overall military superiority (beyond its evident weakness at York). To avoid an open confrontation with Brant, Russell accepted Brant's Haldimand Tract land sales, even though they contravened the Royal Proclamation.

The attack on York never materialized, but Wabakinine's death marked a turning point in the Mississaugas' relationship with settlers and the Crown. Their trust had been broken, and they were increasingly wary of British intentions and promises.

Spooked by the unrest, the British appointed James Givins (also spelled "Givens") the first Indian agent at York. His instructions were to distribute the annual alliance presents to the Mississaugas separately from the Haudenosaunee and to otherwise keep them apart. In a 1797 letter marked "Secret and Confidential," the Duke of Portland outlined the primary duty of the new appointee: "Fomenting the jealousy which subsists between the Mississaugas and the Six Nations, and of preventing, as far as possible, any junction or good understanding taking place between those two tribes. It appears to me that the best and safest line of policy to be pursued in the Indian Department is to keep the Indians separate and unconnected with one another, as by this means they will be in proportion more dependent on the King's Government."[5] The policy of sowing division and preventing "connections or confederations" was generalized across the colony. Portland elaborated:

> They [Indian Department officials] shall distribute His Majesty's presents in such manner, and with such suitable solemnities . . . as to produce the most powerful effect on the Indians, and to leave the strongest impressions on their minds, of their dependence on His Majesty's bounty, for the benefits they receive . . . Such measures . . . added to the growing settlement of the Province, which must furnish the means of civilizing the Natives, and of interposing large tracts of settled country between them, cannot fail, e'er long, to put them in a very advantageous position, as well with regard to themselves, as to the Province, without the possibility of their ever becoming an object of alarm, or even of inconvenience.[6]

Despite these efforts, and although the Mississaugas and Haudenosaunee had shelved plans for a military attack, these two Nations were renewing and strengthening their alliance for other purposes.

The Mississauga-Haudenosaunee Alliance of the 1790s

By the mid-1790s, the Mississaugas understood that giving up or sharing land to strengthen their alliance with the British had not served them well. A huge amount of their territory had been alienated under British law for a pittance. They were becoming impoverished as settlers transformed the landscape around them, making their traditional way of life increasingly difficult. They were becoming dependent on annual presents and revenue from land sales to sustain themselves.

When the British approached the Mississaugas to sell their remaining lands on Lake Ontario to the west of the Toronto Purchase (the southern portion of the city of Mississauga), the Mississaugas sought out Joseph Brant's assistance. Brant had influence with colonial administrators and had succeeded in selling land at market prices. Before his death, Chief Wabakinine had also asked Brant to be a guardian of their lands and to act as their spokesman and negotiator.

In 1798, Mississauga Chief Wabanip reported to the commander of the Queen's Rangers:

> Father, Our Brother Capt. Brant sent us these strings of Wampum this spring to invite us to his village to Council—On our arrival he told us the reason he sent for us was to join our hands and hearts to those of the five Nations and to tye them

so fast as never to be separated again; that we may become one people, and in future the five Nations expect to see us every spring at their Council fire to consult with each other, & if any injury happened to one or the other, they were not to do anything without first consulting each other in Council. Father, He gave us this Belt which now tyes us and the five Nations, and I now tell you that we were very much pleased at what our Brother Capt. Brant told us.[7]

The British were shocked when their first attempt to buy the waterfront tract west of Toronto was met with this response by Joseph Brant to Peter Russell: "I do not think it reasonable that the land should be taken from the poor Mississaugas for a shilling an acre, only to give away to individuals to make money of."[8] Colonial officials then tried to undermine Brant's role with the Mississaugas. They tried to pressure the Mississaugas to break their alliance with the Six Nations and made the delivery of the Mississaugas' presents conditional on "good behaviour," rather than a right based on their past military service and alliance.[9] Hostile officials such as William Claus (head of the Indian Department in 1799) sidelined Brant, especially when they received word that the French and Spanish would not support an uprising among the western Nations allied with the Mississaugas and Six Nations. Brant also came under increasing criticism from the Haudenosaunee for giving up huge swathes of the Haldimand Tract to white settlers.[10] By 1805, when colonial officials met with the Mississaugas of the Credit to replace the invalid deed for the Toronto Purchase of 1787 and acquire more land to the west, Brant was no longer the Mississaugas' negotiator. They were on their own.

The Mississaugas actually were, for a short time, known as the Seventh Nation of the Six Nations. But divide and conquer always was Indian Affairs' or the federal government's thing to keep them apart.

—Margaret Sault, Mississaugas of the Credit[11]

Invalid Title to Toronto Area Lands

Until 1805, the British did not actually have a valid title to the lands they were disbursing, but they believed they did until 1794. When the purported "deed" of the 1787 cession resurfaced that year with no description of the boundaries of the lands ceded, the British tried to rectify the problem without telling settlers or the Mississaugas.[12] Peter Russell explained the situation in 1798:

> We were exceedingly alarmed on reading the paragraph which related to the Purchase made at Toronto in 1787, which if more generally known, would probably shake the tranquillity of many respectable persons, who have risked nearly their whole property within its limits. For should the whole of that transaction be invalid, as your Excy and Lord Dorchester have judged it to be, the King's right to

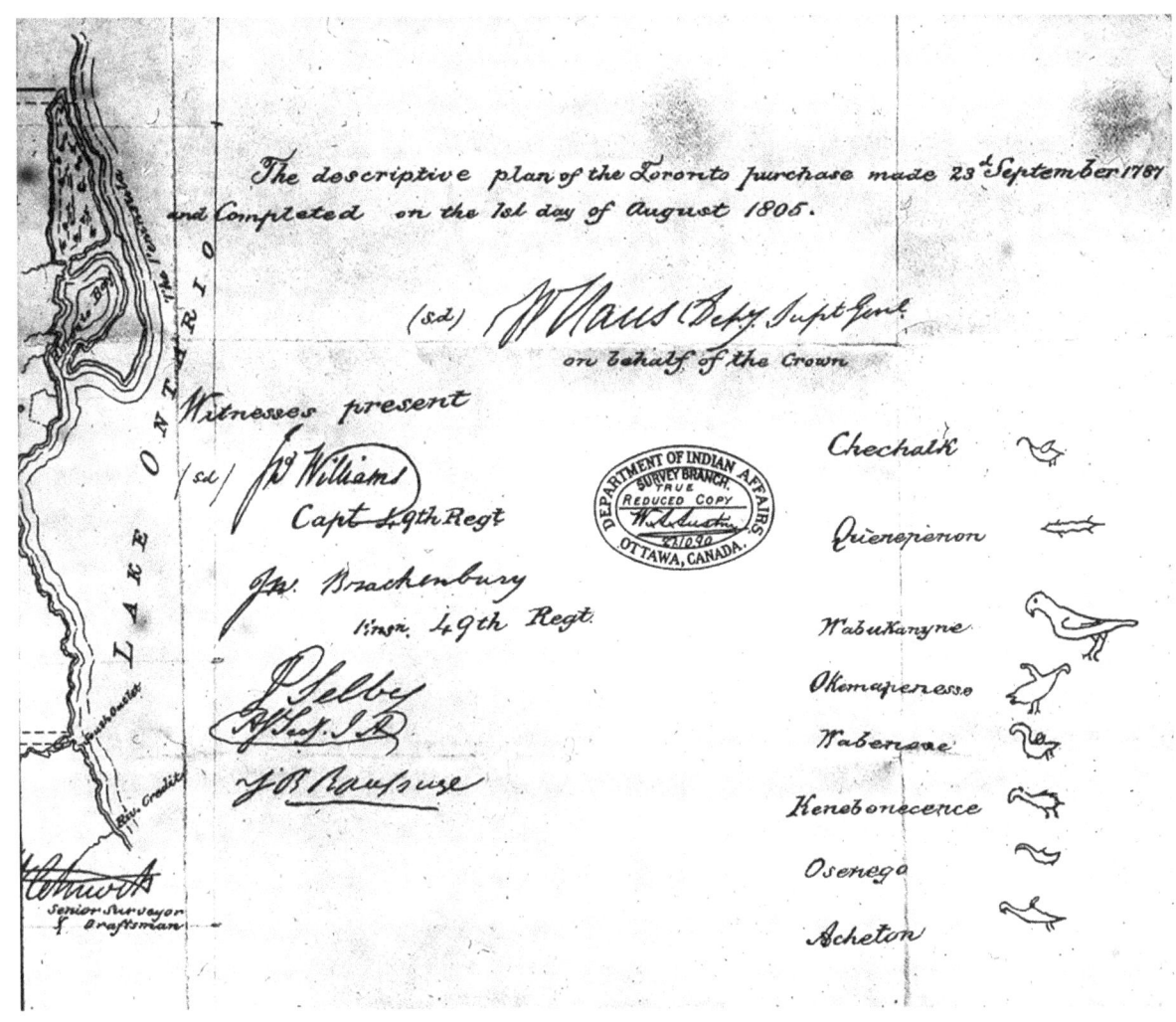

Doodem marks of the Mississauga signatories to the 1805 Toronto Purchase | Courtesy of City of Toronto Archives, fonds 1231, item 175

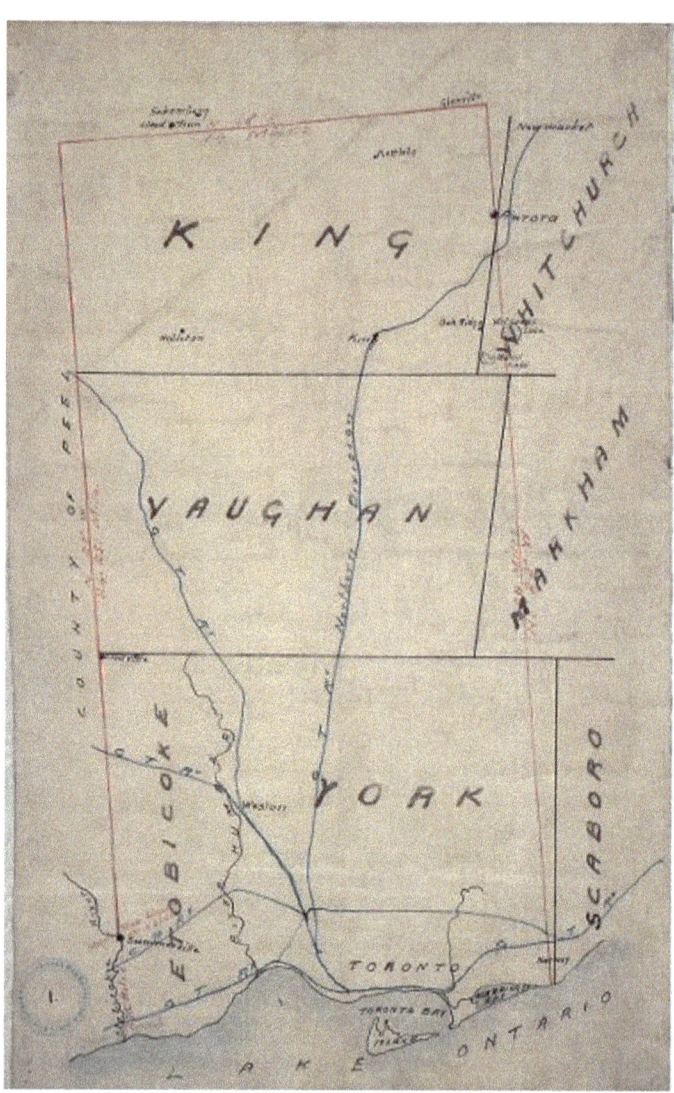

The boundaries (in red) of land deemed to have been ceded in Treaty 13 (1805), according to a 1911 map | Courtesy of Toronto Public Library Digital Archive, MsX.1918.1.6

any of the land between the Rivers Etobicoak & Don, may become very doubtful; and our tenure of the intermediate space (involving a great many cultivated farms, as well as the seat of government) might consequently be at the mercy of the Messisagues, who, if they were apprised of the circumstance, might be induced to give trouble with a view of making their own advantages from it.[13]

The issue of legal title wasn't resolved until 1805.

The Toronto Purchase of 1805 and the Head of the Lake Purchase of 1805–1806

The breakdown of trust between Indigenous Nations and settlers accelerated Indigenous dispossession. In 1805, British negotiators met with the Mississaugas to acquire all the land along the lakefront and major communication routes, determined to remove Indigenous peoples from areas of potential settlement or conflict. To do this, they also needed to revisit the Toronto Purchase and legally establish its boundaries.

By this time, the Mississaugas were suffering considerable hardship, and they no longer knew with certainty the boundaries agreed to by their Chiefs in the Johnson-Butler treaties of 1787–88. The British increased the size of the land cession without their knowledge or compensation.[14] They apparently resorted to subterfuge to do so.[15] The Mississaugas of the Credit signed Treaty 13, known today as the Toronto Purchase of 1805.

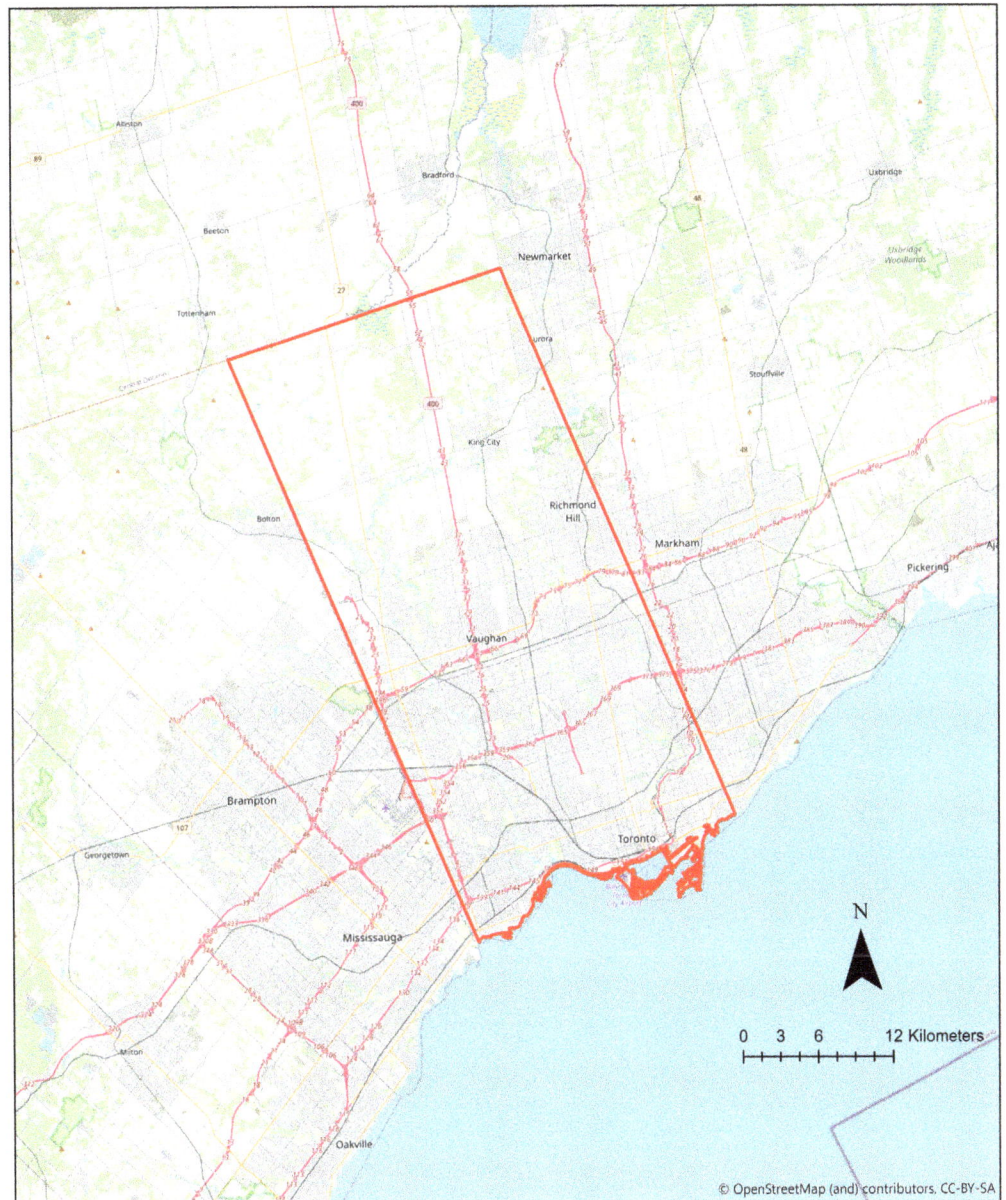

Treaty 13 boundaries superimposed on a modern road map

The Toronto Purchase Treaty, No. 13 (1805)

The British colonial government acquired legal title to 250,808 acres of land north from the Toronto waterfront to roughly Aurora and east from Etobicoke Creek to Ashbridges Bay.

The final cession differed considerably from Sir John Johnson's recollection ten years after the 1787 agreement he'd negotiated: a ten-mile square along the Lake Ontario waterfront, two to four miles on either side of the Humber River, and another ten-mile square at the northern end of the Toronto Carrying Place. (The Mississaugas eventually received some redress through the Toronto Purchase Land Claim settlement agreement in 2010.)[16]

After the Mississaugas signed the 1805 "confirmation" of the Toronto Purchase of 1787, Crown negotiator William Claus pressured them to give up their waterfront lands west of Etobicoke Creek to Burlington. Chief Quinepenon / Kinepinew (Golden Eagle) responded: "I hope you will open your ears and attend to what we have to say . . . when Sir John Johnson came up to purchase the Toronto Lands, we gave them without hesitation, and were told we should always be taken care of, and we made no bargain for the Land, but left it to himself." Chief Quinepenon acknowledged the pressure that the Mississaugas were under: "I speak for all the Chiefs & they wish to be under your protection as formerly. But it is hard for us to give away more Land: The Young Men & Women have found fault with so much having been sold before: it is true we are poor, & the Women say we will be worse, if we part with any more land."[17]

Nevertheless, with little remaining bargaining power, the Mississaugas ended up ceding the waterfront lands to the west of the Toronto Purchase in what became known as the Head of the Lake Purchase or Treaty 14. The price was roughly 2.5 per cent of its market value at the time.[18] However dubious its legal origins, once title to the land was confirmed and the land divided and granted or sold to settlers, the land system was self-perpetuating.

By then, the die was cast. We were already largely dependent on European trade goods. And sickly . . . and disease-ridden at the time, so we couldn't . . . we just didn't have the numbers to stand up to the Crown in any way, shape, or form.

—Darin Wybenga, Mississaugas of the Credit.[19]

7

Settlers on Indigenous Lands

My father used to say we had a very lax immigration policy back then.

—Sherry Lawson, Chippewas of Rama[1]

Upper Canada's founders were hostile to American democratic ideals and wanted to create a new territory in the image of Britain and its institutions, including a landed aristocracy. In 1791, when Upper Canada was separated from Lower Canada (Quebec), John Graves Simcoe became the first lieutenant-governor. He and other colonial officials awarded large land grants to British settlers and military officers, some of whom became government officials, magistrates, and so on. But this attempt to create a British landed gentry in North America was unsuccessful.

For one thing, Britain was far away. Loyalists, on the other hand, were just across the border and in need of land. On February 7, 1792, Simcoe issued a proclamation inviting those in the newly declared United States of America who remained loyal to the British Crown to come to Upper Canada. American immigrants were welcomed because they already had experience in clearing and farming North American lands and could quickly move their families at their own expense rather than requiring a government subsidy for ship's passage from Britain. They were offered two hundred acres of virtually free land per family and lower taxes than in the United States. To obtain a land grant, a male settler swore an oath of allegiance to "the King in his Parliament" and paid minor fees. Within two years, he had to build a home, clear 10 metres of land across the front of the property for a road, and clear and fence 10 acres.[2]

From the beginning, the British government, loath to spend money on the colony's development, tried to make the colony self-financing. In the 1790s, trade remained minimal, and agriculture was mainly for subsistence rather than surplus. Officials resold lands acquired at below-market prices from the Mississaugas to build infrastructure.[3]

Settler Attitudes towards Indigenous Peoples

Early settlers from the Thirteen Colonies had various ideas about Indigenous peoples. They brought with them attitudes forged over almost two hundred years of uneasy coexistence and sometimes extremely violent conflicts over land—including King Philip's War (1675–77)—which hardened anti-Indigenous prejudice. Immigrants from America and Europe arrived with preconceptions shaped by stories told by explorers and travellers about the supposed customs and nature of "Indians." They presumed they were culturally and religiously superior in a "natural" hierarchy of societies and peoples. A common misbelief was that Indigenous peoples did not properly use their land so they had minimal rights to it. These attitudes led to friction. In 1797, Peter Russell issued a proclamation promising the "utmost severity" against anyone doing injury to the "fisheries and burial places" of the Mississaugas, a widespread problem.[4]

> *I kind of get the feeling that unless we were needed for something, we weren't really liked. Unless we were needed for our trading or our goods or our knowledge, then we were just kind of another class of people who were off to the side and in the background and looked upon as lesser.*
>
> —Ben Cousineau, Chippewas of Rama First Nation[5]

Some negative attitudes changed through contact. Elizabeth Simcoe, disparaging of the first Mississaugas she met in Kingston in 1792, came to view them more positively.[6] People who worked in the Indian Department (located at Niagara and then York) had greater familiarity with Indigenous cultures and languages than the newcomer population at large, even though it served Britain's interests. At one point, before 1800, six of eighteen of the highest-ranking officials were married to Indigenous women, and another five were of partial Indigenous descent.[7]

In the nineteenth century, settler concepts of racial difference hardened into cruel stereotypes. These attitudes were not just mistaken beliefs based on observable differences, but useful concepts that encouraged and justified the takeover and exploitation of another people's land for imperial and individual ends. Yet on the ground, and especially in the first years of European settlement, actual contact between Indigenous and settler peoples had a variety of outcomes. Indigenous peoples often extended hospitality to the newcomers and worked with them for mutual benefit. Some settlers—a minority—returned this hospitality.

> *I've been at some of their homes when their grandparents talk about people that I've heard of in our community from way back. "Yeah, my grandmother was friends with this person from Rama" or "My friend was friends with this person." So there are always good exchanges. Because*

they'll just tell you, like, "Oh, yeah, we've always thought the Indians are good people." They say things like that and you're, like, cool.

—Kory Snache, Chippewas of Rama[8]

Who Were the Settlers?

Extensive settlement of the Humber River / Black Creek watershed and area north and northwest of York did not occur until after the founding of York in 1793. The largest group of settlers were so-called late Loyalists who arrived from Pennsylvania, New York, and New Jersey before the War of 1812. Unlike the United Empire Loyalists who arrived during or just after the American Revolution, late Loyalists were motivated more by the possibility of acquiring land or escaping persecution for their pacifism than loyalty to the British Crown. Most were poor farm families with little education. Others were labourers or tradespeople. Many were recent immigrants to the United States.[9]

A minority of the Loyalists were from a more prosperous social class and had served as British officers. Some had fought alongside warriors such as Joseph Brant in the American Revolution, for example, in Butler's Rangers (led by John Butler, who later helped to negotiate the Johnson-Butler agreements of 1787–88). Many of these veterans would go on to serve in the Indian Department, which was staffed by military officials until 1830.

The colonial administration encouraged settlement along Yonge Street so farmers could help clear, maintain, and defend the vital transportation and military link. The Chippewas from Lakes Huron and Simcoe also used Yonge Street to travel to York to sell their wares or confer with colonial officials. They often camped on the lands of sympathetic settlers, such as the farm of Jacob Munshawa (Jr.) at the rise just south of Thornhill.[10]

Areas adjacent to Yonge Street and in the Don River watershed developed rapidly and supported several larger villages and other infrastructure (such as stagecoaches), while the area north of York between Yonge Street and the Humber remained largely agricultural. Smaller hamlets and villages served local needs. Yet only a part of Yonge Street had been provisionally surrendered through the 1787–88 agreement, and the northern boundary of ceded territory had yet to be established. Even after 1805, the status of lands north of what would become Newmarket to Lake Simcoe was still uncertain.

The settlers who took up farms in the area north of York were ethnically diverse, principally Palatine Germans but also other Americans, Quakers, French Royalists, British settlers, and Black immigrants from the American colonies. Several groups immigrated en masse and formed close-knit groups that could preserve their distinct identities more readily than they would have in the nascent United States.

Detail from "A Map of the Province of Upper Canada Describing All the New Settlements, Townships," Sir David William Smyth, 1800. Note the "Old Indian Fields" south of Lake Simcoe, the unceded Mississauga territories to the west, the salmon fisheries at the mouths of the rivers, the lands granted to the French Royalists, and Six Nations lands along the Grand River | Courtesy of University of Toronto Libraries

The Palatine or Pennsylvania Germans

Palatine Germans (popularly referred to as Pennsylvania Germans or incorrectly as Pennsylvania Dutch) were the most numerous Loyalist group to settle north of York. The majority arrived between 1798 and 1805. Originally from the Rhine River region of Germany known as the Palatinate, they fled famine, war, and religious persecution beginning in 1709. Many went to England but were offered homes in Pennsylvania or along the Mohawk Valley in New York by Queen Anne, who reportedly sought permission for their settlement from the Mohawks Sachems visiting her in England.[11] Thousands of other Germans followed. Some of the Germans who came to Upper Canada, especially those who had lived in the colony of New York before the Revolutionary War, had lived close to the Haudenosaunee (especially the Mohawks and Oneidas) with permission from Haudenosaunee Clan Mothers. They "communicated, drank, worked, worshipped and traded together, negotiated over land use and borders, and conducted their diplomacy separate from the colonial governments."[12]

The Palatine Germans in New York were attacked in November 1757 by a raiding party of about 200 Mississauga and Canadian Haudenosaunee warriors from Kahnawà:ke and 65 French troops and Canadian militiamen. The attackers burned the town of German Flatts, killed about 40 inhabitants, and took 150 captives, mainly women and children, back to New France. During the American Revolution, Joseph Brant led 150 Haudenosaunee warriors loyal to the British

William Berczy, self-portrait, 1783 | Courtesy of Royal Ontario Museum ©ROM, 989.282.1

Crown, and Captain William Caldwell commanded 300 Loyalists in an attack that destroyed the same town, then held by the American forces, although, in this instance, few Germans were killed. Despite these attacks, after the American Revolution, many of the Palatine Germans of the Mohawk Valley accompanied Brant and Loyalist Mohawks to Niagara. At the invitation of Brant, they settled mainly in the counties of Dundas and Grenville on the Haldimand Tract in Upper Canada, but another related group came to the area north of York.

William Berczy, *Thayendanega (Joseph Brant)*, c. 1807 | National Gallery of Canada, acc. no. 5777

Nehkik, portrait of Samuel Peters Jarvis attributed to William Berczy, 1794 | Courtesy of Royal Ontario Museum, ©ROM, ROM2016_15391_11

In 1794, the Executive Council granted land developer and artist William Berczy and his partners a large land grant in Markham Township with a contract to finish building Yonge Street north from York to Lake Simcoe within one year. Sixty-four families of German settlers from New York and Pennsylvania established German Mills on a branch of the Don River two miles east of what would become Thornhill and is now part of Markham.[13]

Berczy's settlers cleared part of the townsite of York and 24 kilometres of Yonge Street (Eglinton to Elgin Mills), but they weren't able to complete the road within the stipulated year. By the winter of 1795–96, about one-third of the Markham settlers had returned to Niagara, and Berczy's grant was revoked, although some settlers remained."[14] William Berczy painted one of the most famous paintings of the Mohawk leader, likely in 1807, the year of Brant's death. As art historian Gloria Lesser comments: "It was in his capacity as a land developer that Berczy met Joseph Brant in 1794, and the union between them and John Graves Simcoe, the first Lieutenant-Governor of Upper Canada, consolidated their mutual political and financial prospects."[15] Berczy is also credited with painting the portrait of two-year-old Samuel Peters Jarvis, son of the first provincial secretary and registrar, William Jarvis, who later became chief superintendent of the Indian Department. The child was given the name "Nehkik" (Otter) by the Mississaugas.

The Palatine Germans from Pennsylvania had originally been invited to Pennsylvania by William Penn, the famous Quaker and founder of the colony, an iconic "friend to the Indian" because of his conciliatory relationship with the Lenni Lenape, with whom he had concluded a peace treaty in 1682. But later Pennsylvanians abandoned Penn's progressive policies. In Pennsylvania and most other colonies, "unrelenting settlement expansion and violence became the norm" and so-called Indian wars erupted as the frontier moved westward.[16]

After 1800, a large number of Mennonite or Lutheran Germans from New York and Pennsylvania settled north of York. Many were related to or knew one another. In the first generation, they tended to marry within their own community. By 1805, approximately four thousand Pennsylvania Germans had arrived in Markham, Vaughan, York, Pickering, Scarborough, and Whitchurch townships in York County and townships in Waterloo County that had been created from Block Two of the Haldimand Tract.[17]

The Fisher, Stong, and Kaiser Families

The Fisher, Stong and Kaiser families who established farms on lands that would become The Village at Black Creek were of German origin from Pennsylvania. Elizabeth (Fisher) Stong inherited a 200-acre lot when her brother Jacob Fisher died of camp fever during the War of 1812. Daniel Stong and Elizabeth (Fisher) Stong married in 1816 and began clearing land and building their first home. To the south, the Kaiser family settlement, called Kaiserville, eventually included a blacksmith shop, carpenter shop, wagonmaker's shop, a store, a sawmill built by John Dalziel, and an ashery.[18]

Jacob Fisher Jr., Elizabeth's uncle, acquired significant land holdings in York and founded the village of Fisherville."[19] The nearby village of Newtonbrook, along Yonge Street between Finch and Steeles, was framed by the Fisher family mills on the west branch of the Don to the west and the Cummer Mills on the East Don River to the east. Both mills were owned by families related to Daniel and Elizabeth (Fisher) Stong. Jacob Cummer; his wife, Elizabeth (Fisher) Cummer; and their three children had travelled from

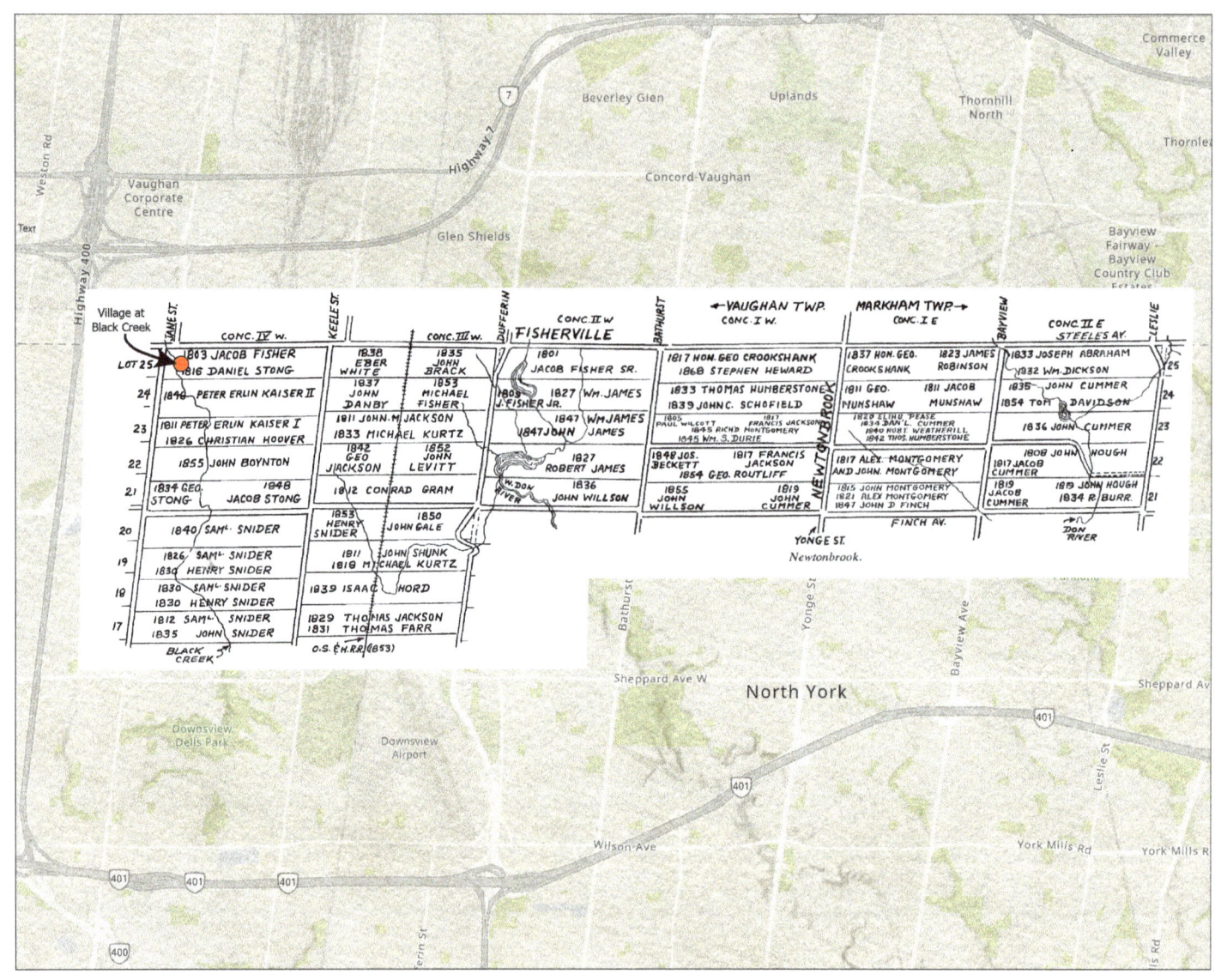

Early settlers near The Village at Black Creek

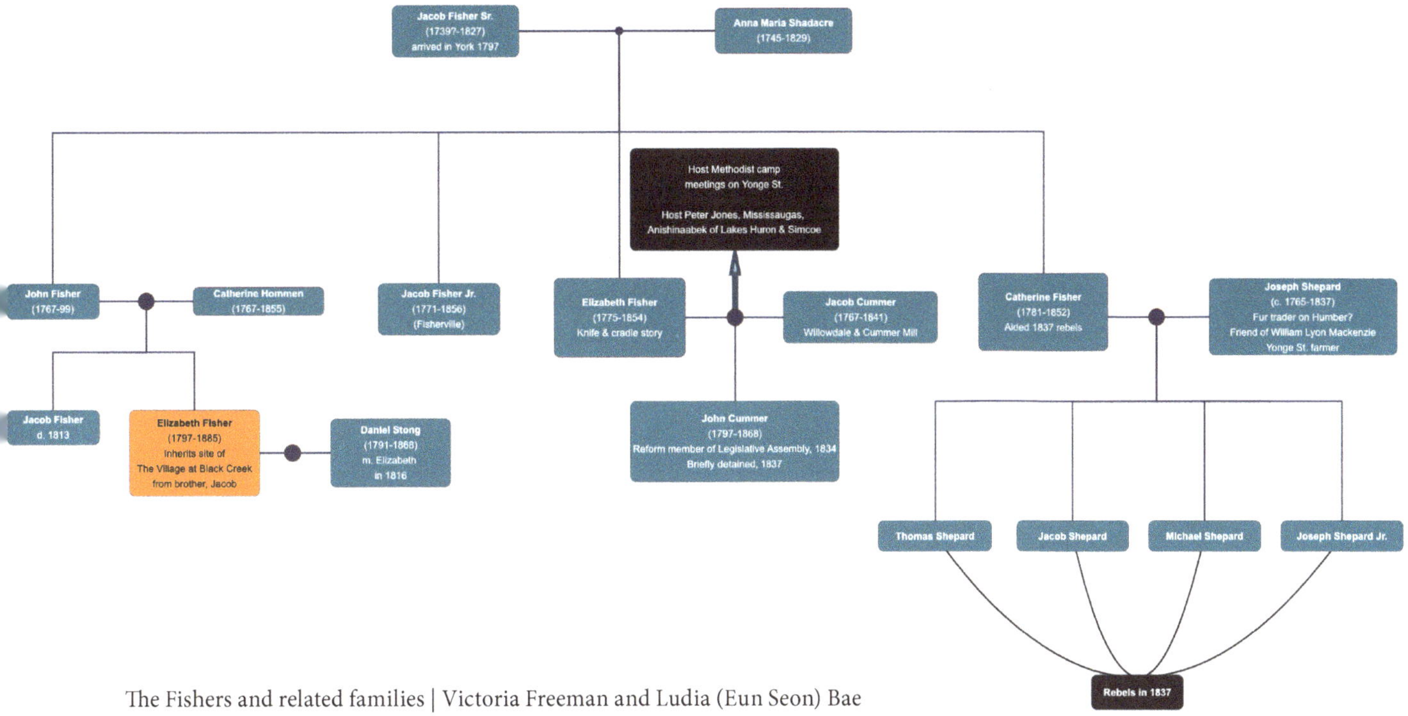

The Fishers and related families | Victoria Freeman and Ludia (Eun Seon) Bae

Daniel and Elizabeth Stong's first house, 1816. The Stong house is the oldest building at The Village at Black Creek | Courtesy Toronto and Region Conservation Authority

7 | Settlers on Indigenous Lands

Cradle said to have been gifted to Elizabeth Cummer by an Anishinaabe man from Lake Simcoe. Some Cummer descendants question this provenance, given the cradle's Pennsylvania German design. Would an Anishinaabe man have made a cradle of this type? Did he receive it in trade from German immigrants? Or did the story become attached to it at a later date? | Photo courtesy of Sarah J. McCabe

Pennsylvania to York County with Elizabeth's father, Jacob Fisher Sr., and her brother John Fisher (Elizabeth's father) in 1797.

Although Elizabeth and Daniel Stong's personal experience with Indigenous peoples is unknown, Elizabeth's aunt, Elizabeth Cummer, related a story about her encounter with an Anishinaabe man from the Lake Simcoe area:

> During these early days, it is said that Elizabeth Cummer was at work in the kitchen in the pioneer dwelling, when an Indian came to the door and manifested his admiration for an ordinary kitchen knife which was on the table. Fearing him and anxious to have him leave, Mrs. Cummer gave him the knife and thought nothing more of him. Later, this Indian came back, making a journey from Lake Simcoe, and bringing as a gift for her a cradle which the Indian had fashioned in honor of her infant son John, for he heard that he was the first white child born in the wilderness north of Toronto.[20]

In *Pioneering in North York*, Patricia Hart comments on this incident as reflecting an Indigenous ethic of reciprocity: "It was an Indian custom to return gift for gift."[21] As Catherine Sims notes, "Ojibwa oral tradition as well as documentary sources confirm that to the Ojibwa people, giving gifts was the most important means through which humans could communicate with the spirits and with each other." Thus, the gift of the cradle was more than a gesture of hospitality: "In Ojibwa culture, presents conferred responsibilities on the receiver."[22] Reciprocal gift giving created and affirmed an ongoing relationship for mutual benefit. Gifts communicated peaceful intent and one's regard and respect for the other; they acknowledged interconnection and accepted responsibility to maintain the relationship.

Remarkably, the cradle said to have been gifted to Elizabeth still exists and remains in the Cummer family—it was exhibited in 2015 at the North York Historical Society. The cradle is of typical Pennsylvania German design, so the Indigenous man either traded for the cradle or made it himself.

The Society of Friends / Quakers and Children of Peace

In 1800, Timothy Rogers obtained an 8,000-acre land grant for a Quaker settlement in York County (King and Whitchurch Townships), and he led the first group of Quaker families from Vermont and Pennsylvania the following year. More Quakers followed.[23] In 1801, Quaker Joseph Hill built a mill at the site of the town of Newmarket; he dammed the East Holland River to create a millpond (now Fairy Lake). The first Quaker meeting house, the oldest religious building erected north of Toronto, was built in Newmarket in 1807; the second, dating from 1810–12, still stands. A splinter group led by David Willson, the Children of Peace, built the Sharon Temple. Soon, according to local historian Ethel Wilson Trewhella, "all along Yonge Street, from Aurora to Holland Landing, also the northwestern part of Whitchurch Township and the southwestern part of East Gwillimbury Township were almost entirely settled by pioneer Quakers."[24] The Quakers helped clear and build much of the northern part of Yonge Street.

The Quakers of Pennsylvania had a long (and somewhat mythologized) history of amicable relations with Indigenous peoples, going back to Pennsylvania's founder, William Penn. According to historian Alan Taylor, one of the reasons the Quakers were attracted to Upper Canada rather than the Ohio Valley, another destination for settlement, was "because the British kept the peace by treating the Indians more generously than did the Americans."[25] The British, for their part, welcomed the Quakers as exemplary and peaceable farmers. To encourage their move to Upper Canada, Simcoe made it known that they would be welcome and enacted militia laws that exempted pacifist groups such as the Quakers, Mennonites, and Tunkers (later Brethren in Christ) from militia service upon the payment of a small fee. A further reason the Quakers, Mennonites, and Tunkers preferred Upper Canada to the United States was because of British policies that safeguarded their distinct identities.[26]

The Quakers on north Yonge Street had considerable contact with Indigenous peoples because of their proximity to the Holland River, a key transportation route.

> *That community of what is now Georgina Island resided all around Holland Landing. The mouth of Cook's Bay. Because that area was a huge staging ground for wild rice, waterfowl, and the rivers were used for harvesting.*
>
> —Kory Snache, Chippewas of Rama[27]

French Royalists

In 1798, Augustus Jones laid out lots along Yonge Street for forty French Royalists who had gone into exile after the French Revolution. These émigrés, who with their families made up a group of about 170 settlers led by Count Joseph de Puisaye, settled in Uxbridge, Gwillimbury, and Whitchurch Townships in York County. Fearing an Indigenous attack from the north, Peter Russell suggested that de Puisaye's men be provided

aristocrats made poor farmers. By 1800, most had left. Those who remained did not receive patents to their lands until 1806, and by 1807–1808, most of the remainder had sold and moved away.

One of de Puisaye's settlers, Laurent Quetton St. George, arrived at the Windham Settlement in early 1799 and for the next few years engaged in the fur trade before moving to Niagara and York. Known as Wau-be-wayquon (White Hat) to the Anishinaabek, he set up a store in York and trading posts near the Narrows and at Amherstburg across from Detroit. He learned at least rudimentary Anishinaabemowin, and his Anishinaabemowin vocabulary list is preserved at the Toronto Reference Library. St. George Subway Station is named after him.

The Queen's Rangers

Many original lot owners in the area north of Toronto were former soldiers of the Queen's Rangers, who like the French Royalists, were given land in the 1790s to defend York from potential Indigenous or American attacks from the north. They were also given a substantial block of land in Etobicoke to defend York's western flank.

Most members were veterans of the American War of Independence from New York and Pennsylvania. They accompanied Simcoe on his first visit to York in 1792. The following year, about one hundred sailed to York, cleared ground on the waterfront, and constructed the blockhouse, storehouses, barracks, and palisade of Fort York, where they were stationed. They also began constructing Yonge Street, originally

Unknown artist, *Laurent Quetton St. George*, 1815 | Courtesy of Toronto Public Library, Canadian Documentary Art Collection, V 3-46c

weapons to form a local defence force: "Their numbers may moreover contribute to fill up an uninhabited space, thro' which an Indian Enemy may at present advance to the Destruction of this Town before we can possibly receive sufficient warning of their approach."[28] Although twenty-two 200-acre lots were granted for what became known as the Windham settlement, the French

intended for defensive purposes. By early 1796, the road extended to Holland Landing. Most of the Rangers sold their lands to the Pennsylvania Germans.

Early British Settlers

Some British settlers came directly from Britain. Others immigrated to the American colonies before the Revolution and made their way north as United Empire Loyalists. They were still perceived as British, as opposed to American-born Loyalists, whose families had lived in the American colonies for longer periods. They received more extensive land grants, according to their rank, and joined a relatively small number of British families to form a new colonial elite in York. Some of these families acquired multiple land holdings, including north of Toronto.

Early administrative positions were often filled by British officials. Some returned to Britain after a few years while others remained in the colony, including British military officers, most of whom had fought in the War of Independence. The number of British settlers would increase significantly after the War of 1812.

Early Black Settlers

During the American Revolution, British officers encouraged freed slaves to join Loyalist forces. An unknown number of Black soldiers, including Richard Pierpoint, fought for Butler's Rangers alongside Mohawks and other members of the Haudenosaunee Confederacy.[29]

> TO BE SOLD,
> A BLACK WOMAN, named PEGGY, aged about forty years; and a Black boy her son, named JUPITER, aged about fifteen years, both of them the property of the Subscriber.
> The Woman is a tolerable Cook and washer woman and perfectly understands making Soap and Candles.
> The Boy is tall and strong of his age, and has been employed in Country business, but brought up principally as a House Servant—They are each of them Servants for life. The Price for the Woman is one hundred and fifty Dollars—for the Boy two hundred Dollars, payable in three years with Interest from the day of Sale and to be properly secured by Bond &c.— But one fourth less will be taken in ready Money.
> PETER RUSSELL.
> York, Feb. 10th 1806.

1806 advertisement for the sale of Peggy Pompadour, an enslaved woman owned by Upper Canada administrator Peter Russell, *Upper Canada Gazette*, February 22, 1806 | Archives of Ontario

After the war, some Black Loyalist veterans, including Pierpoint, sought refuge in Canada and were offered land grants on the Niagara Peninsula. However, other free Black people and some who had escaped from enslavement to fight for the British came to York. At the same time, many well-to-do white Loyalists brought their enslaved African "servants" with them to Canada. For example, Sir John Johnson, superintendent-general and inspector general of Indian Affairs from 1782 until 1830 and negotiator of the 1787 Toronto Purchase, brought fourteen enslaved people to Lower Canada.[30] While a 1790 act passed by the British government assured British immigrants to Canada that their slaves would remain their property, in 1793, Lieutenant-Governor Simcoe passed a law banning the importation of enslaved people and decreed that all enslaved children born in Upper Canada after 1793 would be free at the age of twenty-five.

In 1799, out of a total non-Indigenous population of two hundred, about fifteen people of African heritage lived in York and another ten east of the Don River. Six of the fifteen were "owned" by William Jarvis and five by Peter Russell.[31] Thus, many of those who interacted with Indigenous peoples were also shaped by the general cultural acceptance of hierarchies of rights, privileges, and freedoms.

So early interactions with settlers, I would say, from what I've heard, is half good, half bad. I've heard of our people going and stealing from settler cabins and stuff when they just hacked them out of the woods and threw up, like, a cedar cabin. I've heard of stories of our people going at night and robbing . . . but then having to return items because they would get caught, and their Chief says, "Take that back. We want to keep peace between our people." Don't infringe upon them. Let them do what they're doing and they'll let us do what we're doing, kind of thing. Keep relations peaceful. I've heard of that happening.

—Kory Snache, Chippewas of Rama[32]

PART THREE:
Changing Relationships

8

The War of 1812 and Its Aftermath

Indigenous peoples and settlers faced the threat of American invasion during the War of 1812 and fought—sometimes side by side, other times separately—in several key battles, including the Siege of Detroit, the Battle of Queenston Heights, and the Defence of York.

The York Militia was a volunteer militia unit drawn from settlers. It consisted of three infantry regiments from York and the York region, including Etobicoke, Scarborough, and Durham (Pickering and Whitby). The 1st Regiment of the York Militia fought at the Siege of Fort Mackinac, Detroit, Queenston Heights, and York; the 2nd at Detroit, Queenston Heights, and Lundy's Lane; and the 3rd at Detroit, Queenston Heights, and York.[1] Several settlers from The Village at Black Creek area—such as E. Kaiser, Jacob E. Kaiser, Jacob Snider, and Abraham and William Burkholder—participated in these conflicts, as did Joseph Shepard and possibly Daniel Stong.[2]

Jean-Baptiste Rousseau, lieutenant-colonel in the 2nd York Militia and captain in the Indian Department, was "on Service with the Indians during the late War until the month of November, 1812, and on the 16th of the said month was taken ill when on duty, having been actively employed the whole of that season on a deputation to the Indians at Lake Huron, &c."[3] He served at the Battle of Queenston Heights.

Peter Robinson, who later became a prominent fur trader, organized a rifle company attached to the 1st York Militia: "This company, made up of experienced woodsmen, travelled overland to join in Major General Isaac Brock's successful attack on Detroit on August 16, 1812."[4] Andrew Borland, who also became a local fur trader, volunteered at age seventeen to serve in Captain Robinson's company. At the end of July 1812, this rifle company marched to the Grand River Tract where General Isaac Brock was recruiting Haudenosaunee warriors.[5] George Martin, a Sachem of the Haudenosaunee Confederacy and the grandfather of Oronhyatekha (Dr. Peter Martin), played a major role in persuading Haudenosaunee warriors to support Brock and fight at Amherstburg / Detroit in 1812. He also acted as interpreter at the Battles of Beaver Dams and Fort Niagara.[6]

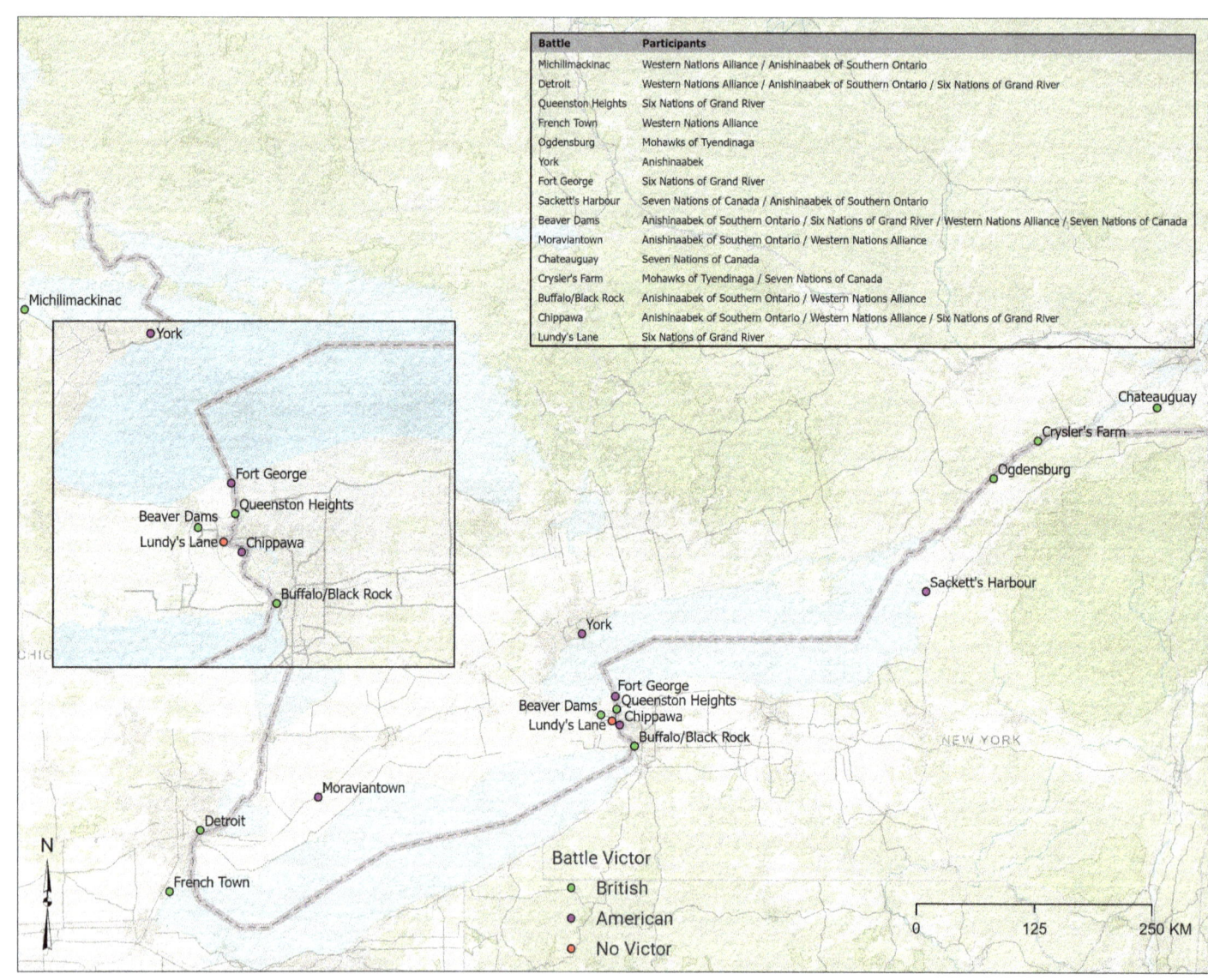

Indigenous engagement in selected battles of the War of 1812

Sir Isaac Brock had to make promises to the Five Nations that they would protect our lands because many of the Five Nations said, "We've got to stay home and stop the squatting that's happening upon our lands."

—Phil Monture, Six Nations of the Grand River[7]

Brock played on American fears of Indigenous warfare by sending General Hull, the Detroit commander, a summons to surrender. He warned Hull that once the battle commenced, the large Indigenous force would be "beyond my control." Hull, for his part, warned, "No white man found fighting by the side of an Indian will be taken prisoner."[8] On the night of August 15, 1812, some 530 First Nations warriors, including Anishinaabek from Lakes Huron and Simcoe, followed Tecumseh and other leaders across the Detroit River in canoes and landed below the fort. The next morning, the British followed with 300 regulars, 30 Royal Artillery, 400 militia, and 70 Haudenosaunee from Grand River led by John Norton. General Hull, fearing a massacre, surrendered without firing a shot.

Indigenous warriors, including Six Nations and Anishinaabe fighters, outnumbered Britain's regular troops in several battles and played a key role in important victories. Like the settlers, they fought to protect their homelands and families, but they fought as allies of the British rather than as British subjects. They were not naive about Britain's intentions towards them or their remaining land. They considered the British the lesser of two evils since the American government and settlers were more aggressively taking over Indigenous territories to the south.

When you read about the War of 1812 . . . lo and behold, I find out that Lawrence Herkimer [Wybenga's ancestor] is in the war, and he's a messenger between Fort York and Niagara-on-the-Lake. That was pretty exciting! He didn't have the shiny red coat. Or maybe he did. I don't know.

—Darin Wybenga, Mississaugas of the Credit[9]

Keeping abreast of what my ancestors did, my grandfathers did, at the time, as Chiefs, one Nanigishking, Thomas Nanigishking, a warrior of 1812.

—Emerson Benson Nanigishkung, Chippewas of Rama[10]

By this point, the Mississaugas needed to demonstrate their loyalty to the Crown to receive the presents they depended on. Further, the British had promised an Indigenous-controlled territory and buffer zone between the British and Americans in the much-contested Ohio Valley—a promise they abandoned in peace negotiations with the Americans and the Treaty of Ghent in 1814.

The Mississaugas, led by Chief Wahbanosay, and the Chippewas from Lakes Huron and Simcoe, led by Musquakie (or Yellowhead) and Assance (Little Shell), engaged the Americans, who arrived by ship to attack Fort York on April 27, 1813. Indigenous fighting forces were often accompanied by officials from the Indian Department who spoke their languages, and in this case, Indian agent James Givins served with the Mississaugas of the Credit.

Elder Garry Sault related that the Mississaugas camped at the Humber River. When the American Navy got blown off course, they saw the fires of the Mississaugas and so loaded their longboats and rowed ashore to attack the greatly outnumbered warriors, who bravely returned fire. After a brief skirmish, heavy fire from the Americans forced them to retreat through the woods.

> *We lose five of our Chiefs there in this little battle. They retreat up the Humber, and when they get to around where High Park is, they set up on top of the bluffs, and they showed the Americans that they were sharpshooters too.*
>
> —Garry Sault, Mississaugas of the Credit First Nation[11]

The Americans, realizing they had landed in the wrong place, retreated and moved east to re-engage with the British at Fort York. The wounded Mississaugas were tended by Given's wife at his home. Mississauga leader Peter Jones remembered:

I was too young to take up the tomahawk against the enemy, and therefore was not engaged in the war. Well, however, do I recollect being told that the "Yankees" were coming into Canada to kill all the Indians, and wondering what kind of beings the Yankees could be, I fancied they were some invincible munedoos [Spirits]. My old grandmother, Puhgashkish [wife of Wahbanosay], was supposed to have been killed at the time York, now Toronto, was taken by the Americans, for being [disabled] she had to be left behind when the Indians fled into the backwoods, and nothing was ever afterwards heard of her.[12]

The invading force of about two thousand Americans had already captured the fort by the time the Six Nations arrived on the scene. The Americans invaded and looted the town of York and occupied it for nearly two weeks.

Chief Musquakie suffered a severe facial injury when a ball shattered his jaw at the Battle of York. Because of his injury, he passed on the chieftainship to his son, William Yellowhead, also known as Musquakie.[13]

In 1815, William Claus, the deputy superintendent-general of Indian Affairs, presented the "Pledge of the Crown [Wampum] Belt" to the Haudenosaunee, Mississaugas, and other allies to represent the interwoven "love and friendship" between them and promised that they could keep their customs.[14] In recognition of their service, Chiefs Assance and Musquakie received medals from the Crown.[15] Although the Anishinaabek

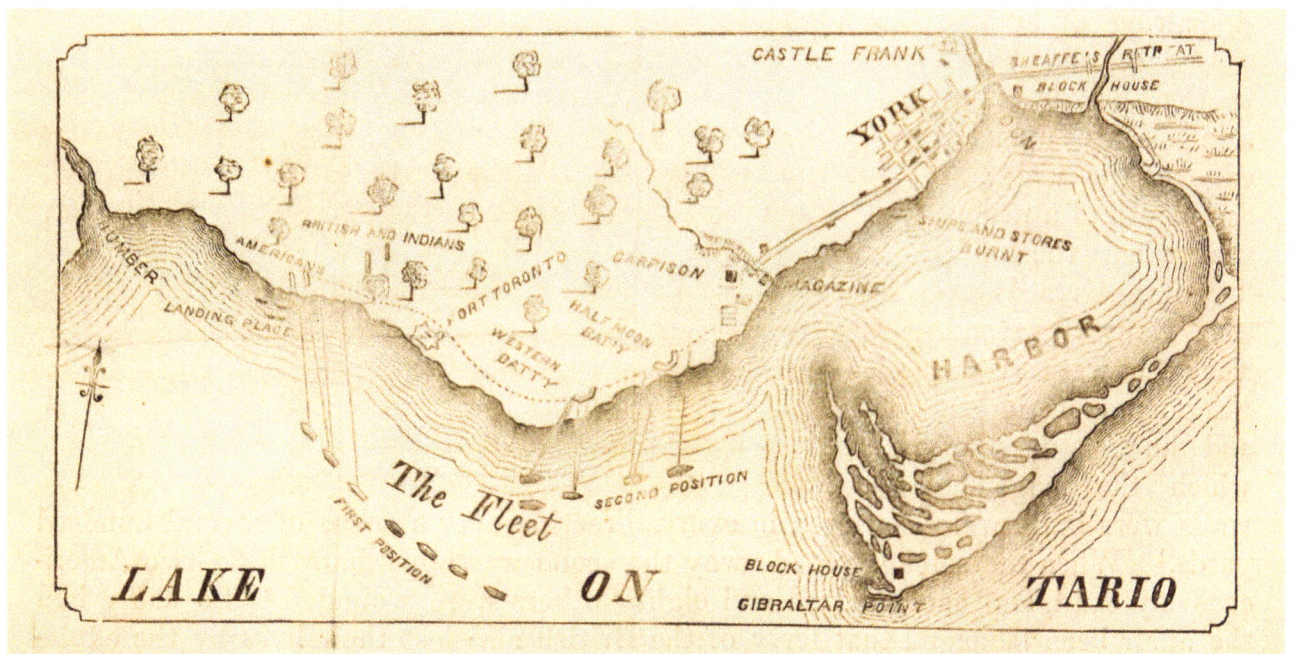

"The Mississaugas and Chippewa at the Battle of York, April 27, 1813," in Benson J. Lossing, *The Pictorial Field-Book of the War of 1812* (New York: Harper and Brothers, 1868)

Six Nations veterans of the War of 1812, 1882. John Smoke Johnson is at left | Library and Archives Canada, C-085125, MIKAN ID 3530023

8 | The War of 1812 and Its Aftermath

and Haudenosaunee had been told they would receive pensions for their war service, no muster roll of Indigenous warriors was kept (as it was for the British army and the militia). General Drummond called for a Council to be assembled on March 3, 1815, at Burlington Heights. There, he told the assembled Nations, including the Anishinaabek, "Chiefs and Warriors: I have given directions that the money promised to the widows of the Chiefs and warriors killed in action shall be paid in the course of 15 or 20 days, also the pensions promised to those worthy men who have been disabled by wounds received in action."[16] It appears they never received them.

Later in the nineteenth century, a new Canadian patriotism invented a more heroic version of the militia's exertions in the War of 1812 and downplayed or completely ignored the contributions of Indigenous warriors other than Tecumseh.[17] Jones reflected: "The Ojebways, as well as other Indian tribes, rendered the British great assistance in fighting the Americans. In that war many of our fathers fell, sealing their attachment to the British Government with their blood. It is generally believed, that had it not been for their efficient and timely aid, Canada would have been wrested from the Crown of Great Britain."[18]

Indigenous Dispossession after 1815

It is often said that neither the British nor the Americans won the War of 1812. It is clear, however, that Indigenous peoples lost. Despite fighting in disproportionately higher numbers and contributing significantly to the defence of Canada, their military and political influence declined once peace was established and the British no longer needed Indigenous allies. Settlers and colonial officials viewed them not as treaty partners in an ongoing mutually beneficial relationship but as impediments to economic development. The British saw presents, long given to renew treaty relations and maintain loyalty, as an expensive and unnecessary burden on a treasury depleted by war.

We are no longer allies. We are now just an annoyance, basically. So instead of being the wartime partner, that trading partner and so on, we are just in the way of development.

—Ben Cousineau, Chippewas of Rama[19]

Giving, reducing, withholding, and delaying presents had been a British tactic to ensure compliance since the 1790s, when the Duke of Portland advocated this strategy to ensure the Mississaugas would sell their lands west of York at a price dictated by the British:

They must be brought to consider themselves in no way entitled to those presents; that they are indebted for them to his Majesty's spontaneous bounty, and owe them solely to his paternal regard for their welfare and comfort—That it is therefore incumbent on them to shew their gratitude to His Majesty for the benefits they receive from him by promoting to the utmost of their power, the interests of His Government in Canada.[20]

Given the huge cost of the War of 1812, the British sought ways to reduce Indian Department expenditures. Although they continued to give annual presents, hold Councils, and pay lip service to the alliance, presents were reduced, adding to the hardship experienced by Indigenous groups whose game and fish had been depleted and whose hunters had often been prevented from hunting on ceded lands.

Between 1815 and 1824, the settler population of Upper Canada doubled from 75,000 to 150,000, while the Indigenous population remained at about 8,000. By 1840, the settler population had grown to nearly half a million.[21] Ten years later, it reached nearly 1 million. To serve this huge influx of immigrants, Indigenous Nations were pressured to cede more land to provide acreage for new farms. Yet much of the land already ceded was inaccessible to settlers because it had been designated as Crown or Clergy Reserves. One-seventh of every surveyed township was reserved for the colonial government and one seventh for the Church of England, the colony's official church.

Greatly outnumbered, Indigenous peoples were induced to sign land cessions for almost all their remaining territory. If they didn't, the government threatened, squatters would simply take over their lands or steal timber or other resources. According to historian Gerald M. Craig, "To a very large extent, Upper Canada was settled by squatters, and it was never practicable to evict very many of them; the speculators and the government simply had to make terms with them."[22] It does not appear that the government tried very hard to protect Indigenous lands against such depredations.

In 1818, the Mississaugas ceded 648,000 acres north of the previous Head of the Lake Purchase up to the territories ceded that same year by the Chippewas of Lakes Huron and Simcoe (Ajetance Treaty 19 and Lake Simcoe–Nottawasaga Treaty 18, respectively). Mississauga Chief Joseph Sawyer and John Jones (Mississauga son of Augustus Jones and brother of Peter Jones) recalled that William Claus, deputy superintendent-general of the Indian Department, persuaded them to put their remaining lands "in trust" with the Crown in 1820 by telling them: "The white people are getting thick around you and we are afraid they, or the Yankees will cheat you out of your land, you had better put it into the hands of your very great Father the king to keep for you till you want to settle, and he will appropriate it for your good and he will take good care of it, and will take you under his wing, and keep you under his arm, & give you schools, and build houses for you when you want to settle."[23]

Following this advice, the Mississaugas of the Credit signed over virtually all their Toronto-area lands, including on the Credit River, believing they would be held in trust and protected. They later learned the agreement had been recorded as two land cessions (Treaties 22 and 23) and the land subdivided and sold off.

The Mississaugas never intended to cede their lands on the Credit. In 1828, they discovered to their horror that they retained legal title to a mere

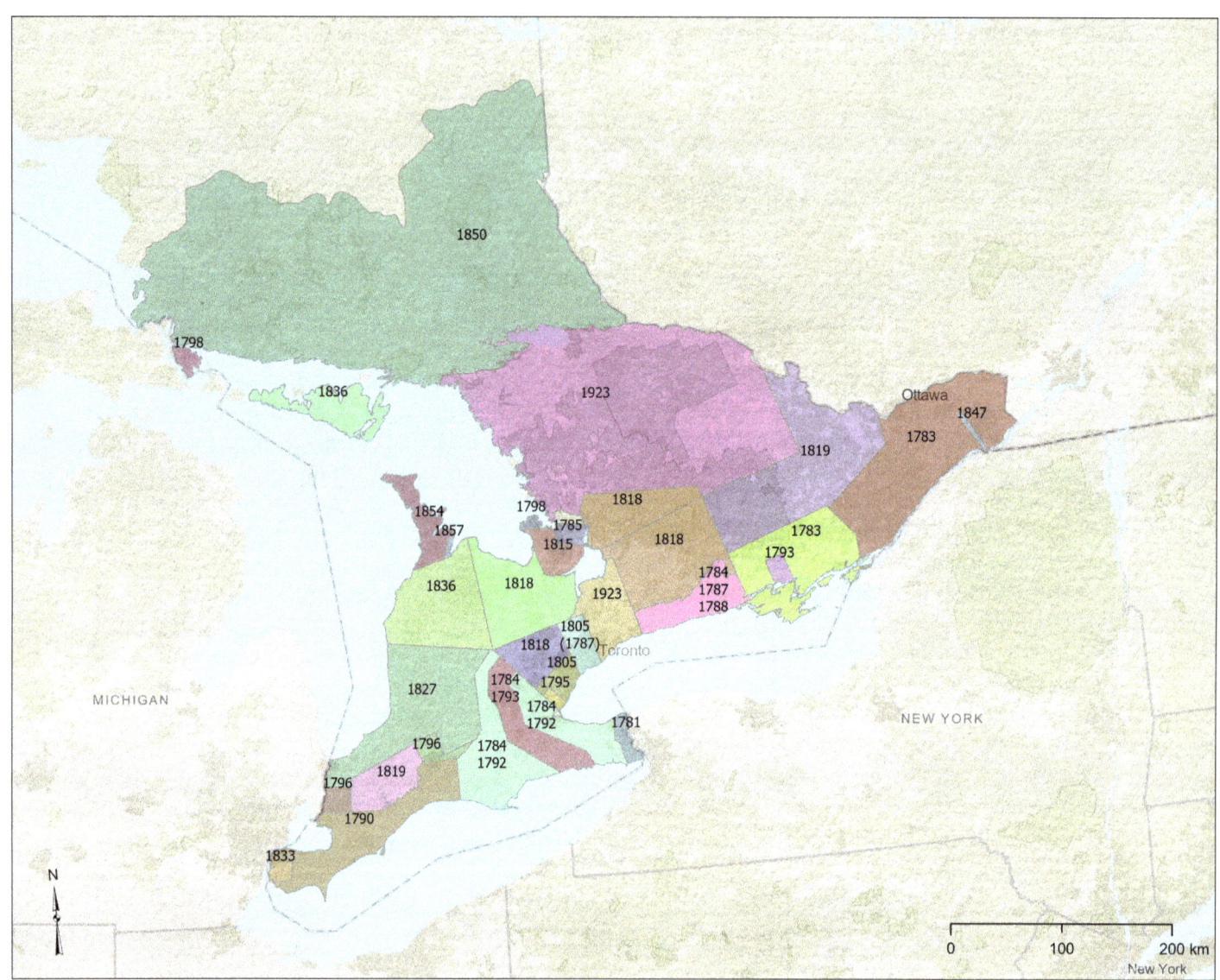

Anishinaabe land treaties in Ontario, by date. Some treaties had to be renegotiated, revised, or confirmed, which is why there is more than one date indicated

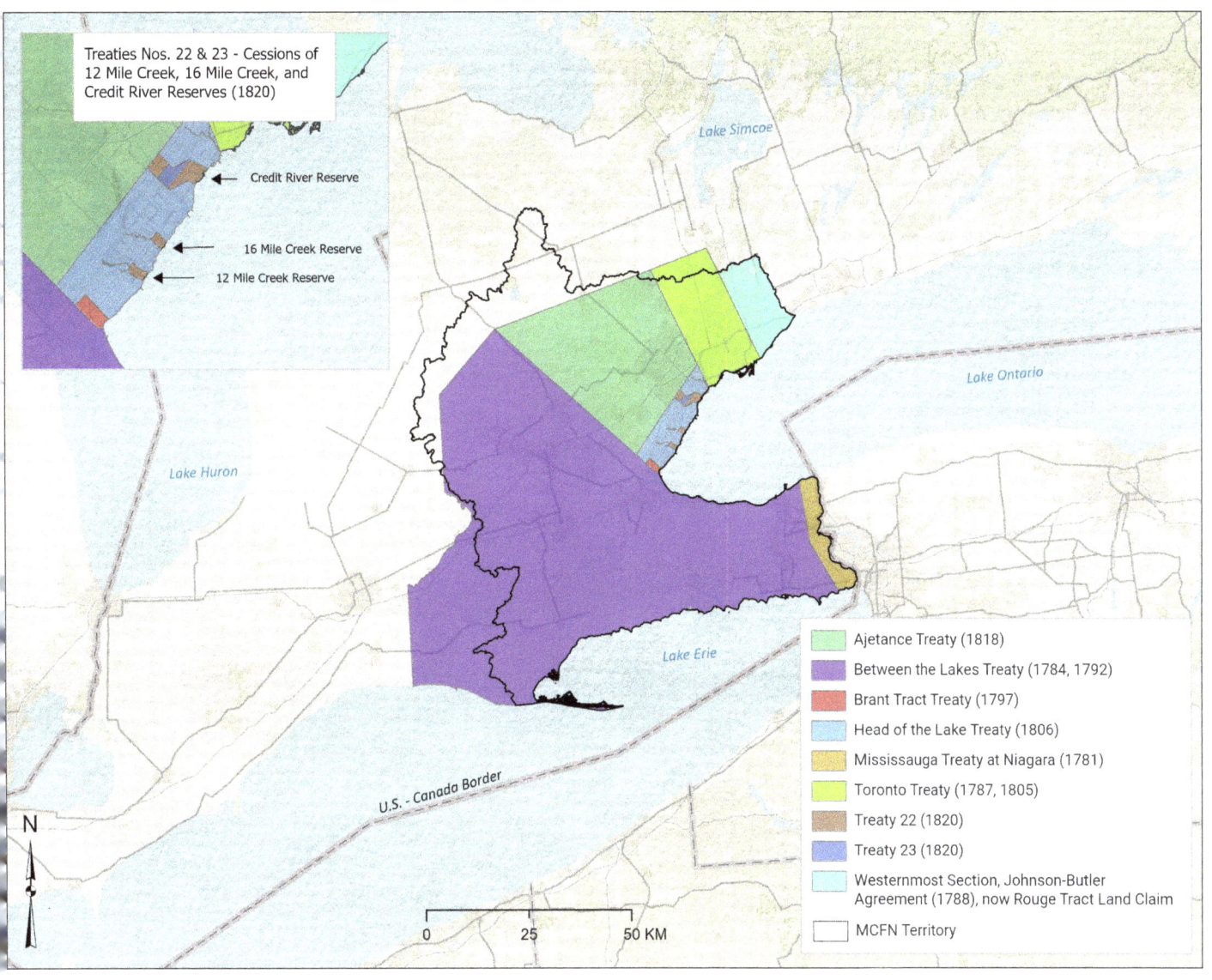

Mississaugas of the Credit land treaties, 1781–1820

8 | The War of 1812 and Its Aftermath

200 acres on the east side of the Credit River, on the other side of the river from their village. They could be forced from their village at any time. Chiefs Sawyer and Jones stated: "Several years ago we owned land on the twelve mile creek, the Sixteen and the Credit. On these we had good hunting and fishing and we did not mean to sell the land but keep it for our children for ever."[24]

In this and other instances, Indigenous intentions and the law of the land—Indigenous law—had no standing in the eyes of colonial officials. Only British understandings of these supposedly mutual agreements were deemed valid. British law prevailed.

> *So we went from 4 million acres of land in 1781 to 200 acres of land on the east bank of the Credit River [in 1820].*
>
> —Darin Wybenga, Mississaugas of the Credit[25]

After the War of 1812, the Chippewas of Lakes Huron and Simcoe were likewise dispossessed of vast territories. The first land cession was the 1815 Lake Simcoe Purchase (Treaty 16).[26] The ceded territory was 250,000 acres of rich farmland in the area west of Lake Simcoe and south of the Matchedash Tract, from Kempenfelt Bay to Penetanguishene Bay, for a one-time payment of 4,000 pounds. The government wanted to secure the route to Georgian Bay for North West Company traders so they could use the Toronto Carrying-Place Trail and avoid American interference.[27] This cession included the Penetanguishene Road (now Highway 93), built

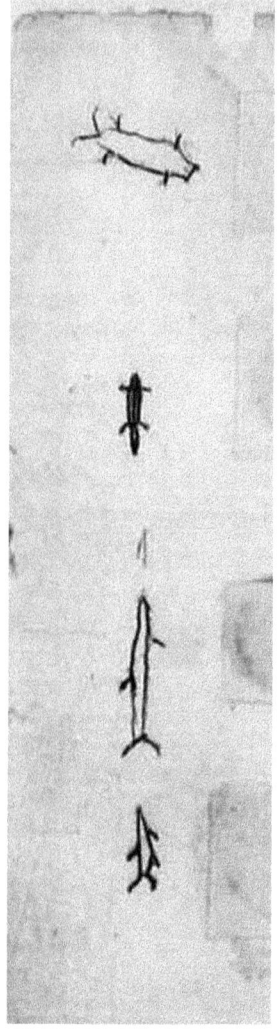

Doodem signatures on Lake Simcoe–Nottawasaga Treaty 18, signed October 17, 1818, at Holland Landing. The top Doodem mark is Musquakie's reindeer mark | Library and Archives Canada, RG 10, Chippewa Indians, 1592000 Acres Huron Tract, vol. 1842/ITO58, reel T-9938z

for military purposes during the War of 1812. It was signed by Chiefs Snake, Musquakie, and Assance. The provincial commissioner, Elisha Beman, and James Givins were among those who signed for the Crown.

The Lake Simcoe–Nottawasaga Purchase (Treaty 18), the Rice Lake Purchase (Treaty 20), and the Ajetance Treaty (Treaty 19) were all signed in 1818, opening up most of central Ontario to settlement. Through Treaty 18, the Chippewas of Lakes Huron and Simcoe ceded more than 1.5 million acres for an annual payment of 1,200 pounds to be shared between the three bands. The area was surveyed into townships between 1820 and 1836 but with the understanding that the Chippewas had not given up their rights to hunt and fish.[28]

Our history is like many other First Nations in Canada. We once called a massive territory ours. And then it shrunk down to a couple of thousand acres through a series of treaties and surrenders or alleged surrenders and so on.

—Ben Cousineau, Chippewas of Rama[29]

But speaking of land, 1818 . . . to me that was devastating. How can that be? How can that happen?

—Emerson Benson Nanigishkung, Chippewas of Rama[30]

Some Anishinaabek were dispossessed without any treaty or compensation. Some of the lands of the Mississaugas of Lake Scugog were ceded through the Rice Lake Purchase of 1818, but land on the west side of the lake was not formally ceded until 1923. The Mississaugas were simply pushed aside as lands were granted to settlers.

British Immigration after 1815

After the War of 1812, the imperial government rejected Simcoe's policy of promoting American settlement. Lieutenant-Governor Sir Francis Gore forbade magistrates to administer oaths of allegiance to Americans, which made it nearly impossible for Americans to secure title to land. Even American-born settlers already established in Upper Canada were not automatically granted the same citizenship rights as British settlers. To offset the risk of disloyalty and republican political sympathies infecting the colony with democratic ideas, the British encouraged and subsidized immigrants from Scotland and Ireland. A huge influx arrived after the Napoleonic Wars, when crossing the Atlantic was safer. Many immigrants were poor Irish or Scots, but a smaller number were from educated, well-to-do English families. They became incorporated into the ruling elite and entrenched British culture on Yonge Street.[31]

Lord Selkirk also brought British colonists to Red River (near what is now Winnipeg), but they left that colony in 1815–16 because of conflict with the Métis. Seventeen men and their families travelled via Penetanguishene and arrived at Holland Landing. Their extreme poverty led many to hire themselves out along Yonge Street. A number moved to West Gwillimbury in 1819.

British immigration peaked in the 1840s, bolstered by large numbers of Irish fleeing the potato famine. But the Irish had been the most

A version of the 1834 City of Toronto coat of arms from James Cane, *Topographical Map of the City and Liberties of Toronto*, 1842 | Courtesy of Toronto Public Library, T- 1842-LARGE

numerous British immigrants since the 1820s. A large number settled in York / Toronto but others sought land in the farming districts. In most of the counties north of Toronto, the Irish constituted at least 20 per cent of the population with large concentrations in neighbouring Peel and north in South Simcoe. By the 1850s, there was an Irish enclave in Newmarket and Irish towns in the Humber Valley. By 1871, 43 per cent of Toronto's population was of Irish origin.[32]

Many British settlers and colonial officials in Upper Canada and Great Britain saw themselves as part of an expanding British Empire, particularly after the Napoleonic Wars, which ended in 1815. For many, the superiority of British culture and government went unquestioned. It was their right to rule over other peoples, although some British officials in the Colonial Office in England, motivated by a genuine if paternalistic humanitarianism, acted as a partial check on settlers and their governments in their dealings with Indigenous peoples.[33]

For many, imparting British culture—"civilization"—to Indigenous peoples was seen as a "gift." Others were skeptical that Indigenous peoples could be civilized at all.

Black-Indigenous Relations after the War of 1812

As they had done during the American Revolution, Black soldiers fought in the War of 1812, notably alongside Indigenous allies in the Battle of Queenston Heights. After the war, they pressed the British government for the military land grants promised to soldiers. In 1819, fifteen Ontario "men of colour" were granted 100-acre lots in Oro Township (southwest of Lake Simcoe), but not all took up their grants. A second wave of refugees from the United States arrived between 1828 and 1831. Eventually, about sixty Black settlers and their families acquired land in the area. The government hoped they would help provide provisions to the fort at Penetanguishene and, if war with the United States broke out, help defend the region.

This settlement was south of the Chippewa communities at the Narrows and the later Coldwater-Narrows Reserve on land ceded by the Anishinaabek in the 1815 Lake Simcoe Purchase (Treaty 16), but the nature of their interactions is unknown. Black settlers were among the first agricultural settlers in the area, but many did not stay long, as the land was of poorer agricultural quality than elsewhere. After 1831, when Oro Township was opened to white settlement, the value of the land increased. Many Black settlers sold their properties and relocated elsewhere. By 1900, their settlement had disappeared.[34]

After the War of 1812, secret routes along Indigenous pathways or military trails also brought enslaved freedom seekers from the American South to refuge in Upper Canada. By 1834, the year after slavery was abolished in the British Empire, the population of York was 9,000, including at least 400 Black residents. According to the 1842 census, Toronto had 470 and the Home District 803 "Coloureds" across various townships.[35] The Township of York held the second-highest population of Black residents outside of St. John's Ward in Toronto proper. Etobicoke Township, to the west of York Township, had the next largest Black community, and thirty Black residents were counted in Vaughan Township.[36]

Fragmentary evidence suggests the relationship between Indigenous peoples and Black people was complex, given the exploitative context of British and white supremacy. For example, Mississauga Methodist missionary Peter Jones viewed enslaved Africans with compassion, expressed support for abolition, and visited an abolitionist organization in England in 1838, but he also reproduced popular racist tropes that placed Africans at a lower level of civilization than Indigenous peoples. The Credit Mission Village passed legislation in 1844 to prevent a Black husband of a Mississauga woman from living in the village.[37] While some Haudenosaunee provided aid to those escaping slavery, Joseph Brant is believed to have owned more than thirty enslaved Africans.[38] At the same time, given the forced transportation of enslaved Africans to North America, and their need to seek refuge and freedom from slavery in Canada, their position as "settlers" in relation to Indigenous peoples and lands was different from that of colonizing white Loyalists or British settlers.[39]

9

The Postwar Fur Trade along Yonge Street

After 1814, there was renewed interest in transporting furs from Georgian Bay, Penetanguishene, and Muskoka to York via Yonge Street and from there to Montreal, the headquarters of the powerful North West Company of fur traders. When the portage route along the Humber was superseded by Yonge Street, Newmarket became the centre of trade because of its proximity to the Holland River, the gateway to Lake Simcoe and beyond. Holland Landing, the northern terminus of Yonge Street, became an important point of transfer from land to water transportation, briefly replacing York as the location for present distributions to the Anishinaabek.

> *There were trading posts everywhere. You had one down at Toronto, near the mouth of the Humber, later it would be on the Humber. You had one at Holland Marsh at Holland Landing. And then Newmarket. And then you had one at the Narrows in Atherley, right outside of Rama. And then you had one over at Balsam Lake. And then there was another one just east of that. Literally, at every portage route, there was a trading post.*
>
> —Kory Snache, Chippewas of Rama[1]

As fur traders moved through the territories of the Chippewas of Lakes Huron and Simcoe, they encountered three related groups led by Head Chiefs Musquakie, Snake, and Assance. Many of these Chippewa had family hunting territories to the north in Muskoka, while some hunted along the Holland River.

> *The Snache family [previously spelled Snake], our harvesting grounds were the east and west branch of what's now the Holland River. Our family [were] the harvesters that utilized that whole area, all the way towards Schomburg, and all the way towards—I guess . . . I don't know what's down the east branch—I guess towards Newmarket. That was my family's harvesting grounds.*

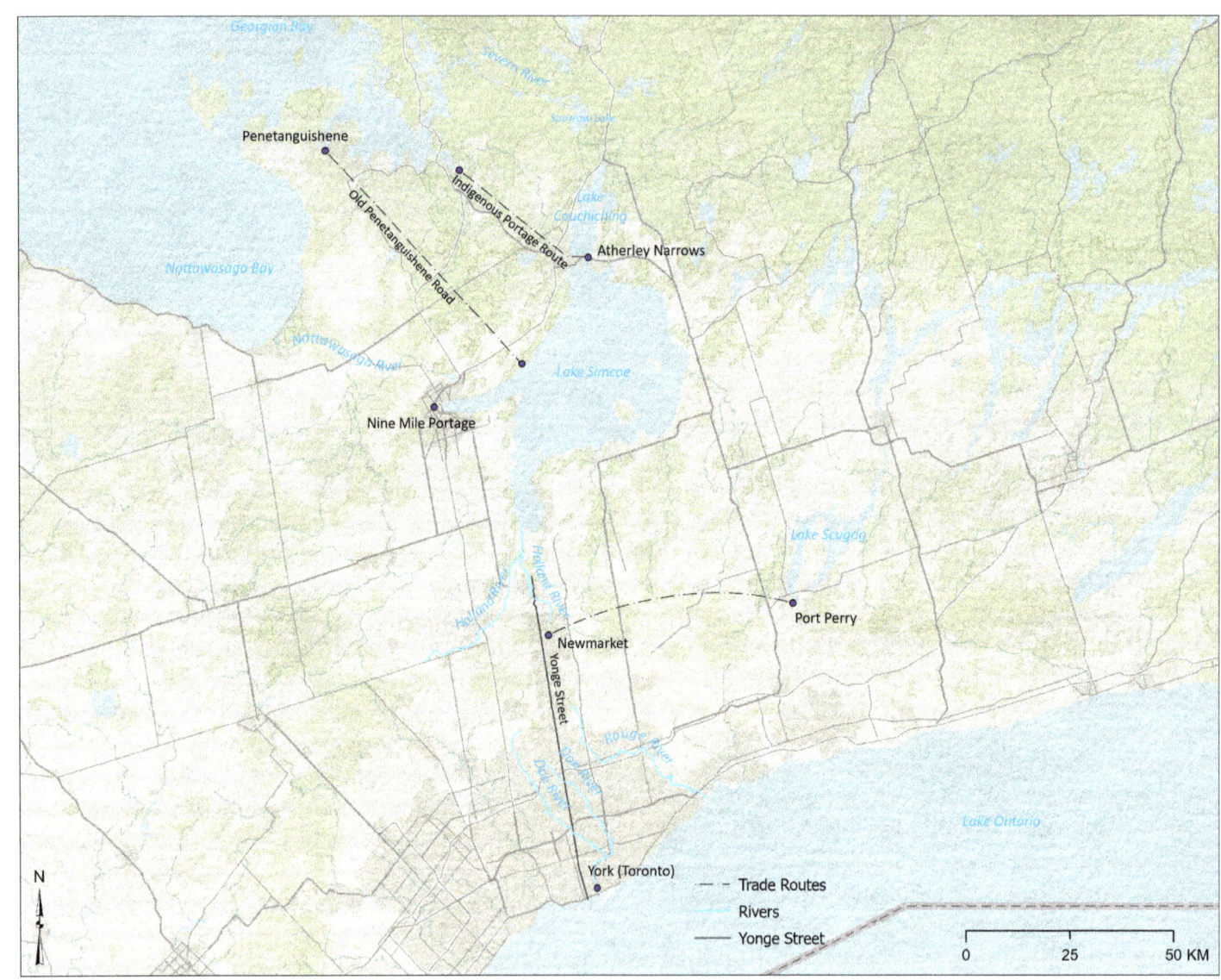

Regional fur trade via Newmarket and Holland Landing

Two groups of fur traders became especially prominent in the area north of York through their trade at Newmarket and Holland Landing. These groups branched out into other related businesses, such as milling, distilleries, retail stores, and transportation. Some of these traders or their families were of mixed Indigenous / European heritage. All had extensive interactions with local Indigenous peoples.

I know that our ancestors travelled south right into York for trading. Down at the Toronto Carrying Place through Holland Landing, all those areas, and traded at York and around York. So I think those would have been good experiences and good relations. I think they'd have to be to maintain the trading relationship. The negative ones I've read about and heard about seemed to be based around alcohol, at least in this area.

—Ben Cousineau, Chippewas of Rama[3]

Interviewee and cultural land-based educator Kory Snache of Chippewas of Rama First Nation | Courtesy of Kory Snache

And we used to call that river Gichiziibi, which means, basically, the "large river outlet" or "large river mouth."

—Kory Snache, Chippewas of Rama[2]

To the east of Lake Simcoe, traders encountered Mississaugas related to the Mississaugas of the Credit and those in the Peterborough area. Led by Chief Crane, they moved between Lake Scugog, Mud Lake (later Curve Lake), and Balsam Lake. This latter group traded mainly along the rivers and portage routes leading to Oshawa, but they also came to Newmarket.

Borland & Roe: Intermarriage in the Fur Trade

William Roe grew up in Sandwich (now Windsor) where he and his siblings received "good educations, intermingled freely with the surrounding Indian children and learned their language fluently."[4] He arrived in York in 1807 and moved to Newmarket after the War of 1812

John Kuna, *Dawn on the Holland River*, 2018. This mural depicting the Newmarket fur trade was painted on an exterior wall of the Buckley Insurance Brokers building, Newmarket, across the street from the site of the 1814 Borland and Roe trading post | With permission of the artist

with his father-in-law, William Laughton, also a partner in the fur trade and, later, in a steamship business.

Andrew Borland is believed to have been born in Pennsylvania of unknown and possibly mixed parentage. He arrived in Canada either in 1808 or 1810. One source indicates he drove cattle north along the Hudson River to Montreal then travelled along the north shore of Lake Ontario to York, accompanied by Jacob Gill, a carpenter from the state of New York. Borland worked briefly as a clerk in Darcy Boulton's store at York before setting up a Newmarket trading post with Roe to intercept traders heading for York, and another at Coldwater. They also established trading posts at the Narrows between Lakes Simcoe and Couchiching and farther north. He purchased 5 acres of land in Newmarket in 1815.[5]

Settler histories record that "Mr. Borland had a thorough knowledge of the Indian character, as well as of the language of the neighbouring tribes, and had acquired considerable influence over them."[6] While such descriptions of "friends to the Indian" are often settler hyperbole, Borland did

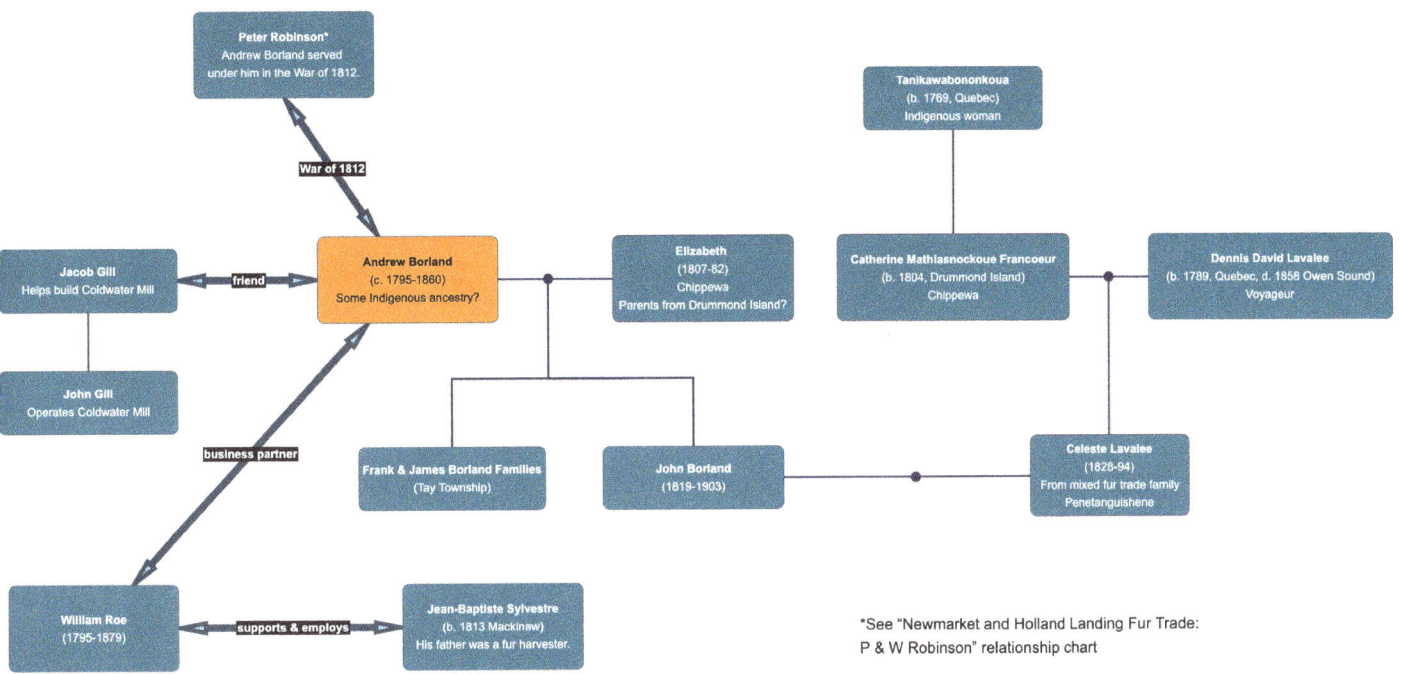

Borland & Roe, Newmarket fur traders, and their connections | Victoria Freeman and Ludia (Eun Seon) Bae

speak Anishinaabemowin and had close relatives who were Indigenous. He married Elizabeth, an Anishinaabekwe.[7] They were married in a country marriage (i.e., according to Indigenous protocol, not in a Christian church) around 1819. One source indicates she was born in 1797, making her twenty-two when she married, but census information suggests she could have been as young as twelve.[8] (If the latter is correct, this is very young, even by the standards of the day, though a significant number of settler women had their first child by the age of sixteen, and Anishinaabe girls often married at age fourteen or fifteen.)[9]

According to historian Gwen Reimer, "It was common practice for fur traders on and inland from the eastern shore of Georgian Bay to take up Indian wives in that period [the early to mid-nineteenth century]."[10] A country marriage ensured the safety of the fur trader and his access to furs through his wife's kin. It also gave his wife and her family access to valued trade goods. The women made essential items such as snowshoes, winter clothing, and footwear and often acted as interpreters, negotiators, and guides. According to Reimer, these traders were the only Europeans in the area at the time practising intermarriage. While some fur trade marriages were purely

BAPTISTE SYLVESTRE.

Born at Mackinac, on All Saints' Day, 1813; removed to Penetanguishene and Newmarket in 1816.

Jean Baptiste Sylvestre, photographer and date unknown | Osborne, *The Migration of Voyageurs from Drummond Island to Penetanguishene in 1828*

transactional and temporary, Elizabeth and Andrew's marriage lasted until he died in 1860. She is remembered by descendants as "the real head of the family."[11] She was active in the community and acted as a witness to several marriages in her later years, when she lived in Coldwater, one of the two villages originally established as part of the Coldwater Reserve.

Andrew and Elizabeth's son John Borland appears on a list of seventy-five voyageurs and their families, largely people of mixed Indigenous / French Canadian heritage, evacuated from Drummond Island to Penetanguishene in 1828 after Drummond Island was deemed to be US territory. Many had served as soldiers for the British or worked in the fur trade for the North West Company and had married Indigenous women or their mixed-heritage daughters. Their children had likewise become soldiers or traders. While most received land in the vicinity of Penetanguishene, several collected furs in Muskoka and some traded at Newmarket. Some of the women married local fur traders.[12]

John Borland, only about eight years old, likely travelled with his mother (the list does not include the names of married women). They travelled to Newmarket where the Borland family expanded and lived until the 1830s before moving to Coldwater. John married a woman of mixed Indigenous / French heritage, Celeste Lavallee. As an infant, she had travelled on the same boat from Drummond Island to Penetanguishene with her mother, Catherine Mathiasnockoue Francouer, and her father, voyageur Denis David Lavallee, originally from Sorel, Quebec. Celeste's maternal Indigenous lineage is known back to her grandmother, Tanikawabononkoua.

One other mixed-heritage fur-trading family from Drummond Island is known to have worked for or brought furs to Borland and Roe. Jean-Baptiste Sylvestre recalled that from 1816 "my father came to Newmarket with his furs": "There were only a storehouse and two small log huts at the [Holland] landing. My father made arrangements with Mr. Roe, merchant at Newmarket, who sent me to school, and then I engaged to drive team for him and make collections all over the country. I met a party of young people in Georgina [on the south shore of Lake Simcoe] and played the fiddle all night for them while they danced."[13]

These relationships with Indigenous peoples paid off handsomely for Borland and Roe: "The Indians at that time came to Newmarket in large numbers to exchange their peltries for supplies. These parties sometimes numbered as many as three or four hundred, and the value and extent of the trade may be realized from the fact that sometimes Mssrs. Roe and Borland obtained furs at one time amounting to fifty thousand dollars."[14]

There was a darker side to this trade. Local fur traders were not above threatening Indigenous peoples who tried to break free from the destructive trade in alcohol. Mississauga missionary Peter Jones related the traders' hostility to Indigenous Methodism (which required abstinence from alcohol): "Friday 22nd [June 1827].—Cautioned my brethren this morning against believing the traders when they threatened to hinder them from embracing Christianity, as W. Snake, the Chief, informed me that Mr. Bolen [Borland] and P[hilemon] Squires had threatened to flog him if he did not leave off attending the meetings, and said many other things to intimidate him in becoming a Christian. Indeed, from all accounts the traders are exasperated at the Indians becoming a praying and sober people."[15]

Perhaps because of injuries sustained in the War of 1812 or a gradual decline in the fur trade, Andrew Borland moved into another line of work. In 1832, he was appointed captain of the wooden paddle steamer *Colborne*, the first to make daily trips from Holland Landing through the Narrows to the Chippewa village that later became Orillia, the starting point of the Coldwater Road. The steamer completed the modernization of the Toronto Carrying-Place transportation route.

By mid-century, as the fur trade became less important to the area's economy and as the settler population boomed, white settlers in urban areas such as York increasingly frowned upon intermarriages. Families such as the Borlands came under pressure to downplay their heritage and identify as white, especially if they lived in settler communities where colonial and racist attitudes were a given. Census records reveal changing racial identifications over time. Some branches of the Borland family retained their Indigenous identity, especially in less settled areas or in more marginal occupations. For example, the 1901 census for Tay Township (east of Penetanguishene) lists two Borland families as "Chippewa English Breed." Frank and James Borland both worked in the lumber trade. James' son George was a river driver.[16]

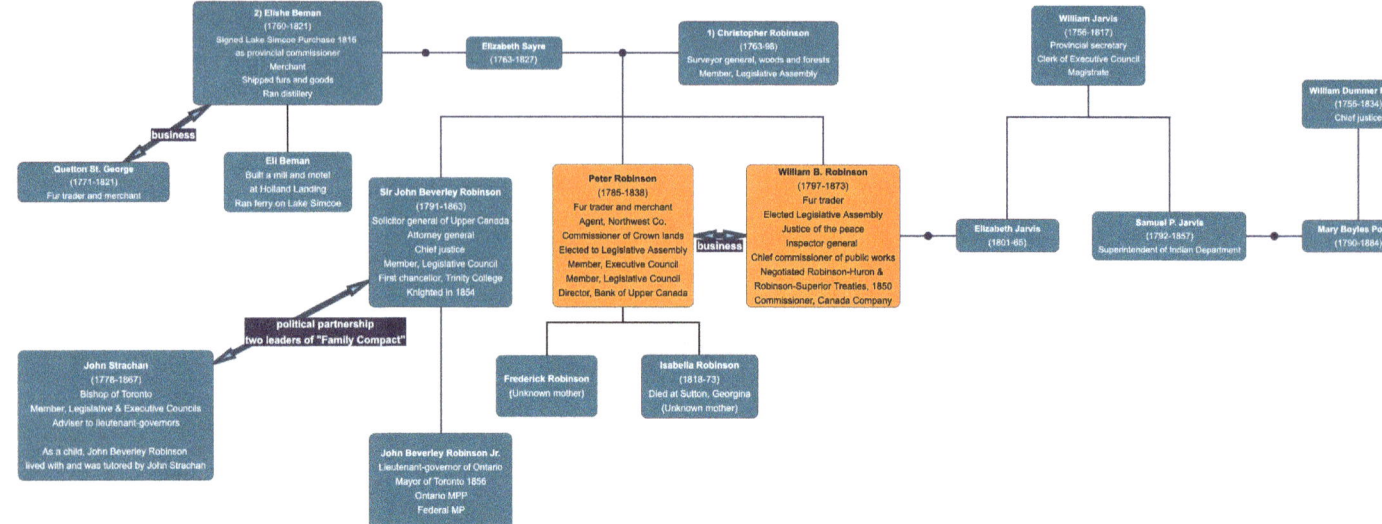

Peter and William Robinson, fur traders of Newmarket and Holland Landing, and some of their connections | Victoria Freeman and Ludia (Eun Seon) Bae. The numbers indicate the order of marriages

Another downside was the loss of Clan identity. And if their father was white, they kind of lost their Clan. Because the Clan follows from the father [for Anishinaabek]. And if you have a white father, it's gone.

—Albert Big Canoe, Chippewas of Georgina Island[17]

The Robinson Family and the Family Compact

A second set of family connections in the Newmarket fur trade was not facilitated through intermarriage but rather through family connections to the governing elite, illustrating how the fur trade contributed to local networks of entrenched power and privilege.

Elisha Beman came to York in 1795 from New York, where he had served as a Queen's Ranger under Lieutenant-Governor Simcoe during the American War of Independence. He soon opened a tavern and ran a business selling provisions and baked goods, becoming one of York's wealthiest residents. In 1802, he married Esther Sayre, the widow of Christopher Robinson. In 1803, he and Esther moved to a house built by Christopher's son Peter Robinson near the Holland River. The next year he began establishing various businesses at Newmarket, including mills, a store, and a distillery, while also maintaining his business interests in York. He shipped furs and potash for French Royalist fur trader Quetton St. George, distilled and milled grains in Newmarket for local markets, and sold goods obtained from wholesalers in York and Kingston. His son Eli built a mill and hotel at Holland Landing and opened a ferry and boat service on Lake Simcoe. The schooner was "chiefly manned and occupied by Indians."[18] Both worked closely with Peter Robinson, who was building a wholesale retail enterprise in Newmarket / Holland Landing.

Beman was also a land speculator and served as a constable and justice of the peace. As a provincial commissioner, he was a signatory to the Lake Simcoe–Lake Huron Purchase in 1815, which ceded a large tract of land between Lake Simcoe and Lake Huron. Elisha Beman's store and mills became the nucleus of Newmarket and were taken over by his stepson Peter after his death.

Peter Robinson was a wealthier, better-educated, and better-connected Loyalist than most of those who came to Upper Canada.[19] His father, Christopher, was a lawyer and United Empire Loyalist from a prominent Virginia slave owning family who had acquired a great deal of land in Upper Canada, served as an elected member of the House of Assembly, and was a founder and bencher of the Law Society of Upper Canada. Peter Robinson moved with his father and mother to York in 1798 (from Kingston) and established himself in Newmarket in 1812. He opened a mill and bought lots on Yonge Street for the site of what became the village of Holland Landing. He soon became an agent of the North West Company and the pre-eminent fur trader in Newmarket.

In 1815, George Head, the elder brother of later lieutenant-governor Sir Francis Bond Head and the author of *Forest Scenes and Incidents, in the Wilds of North America* (1829), visited Newmarket and noted in his journal that Robinson "kept a shop in the house where we now were, which was plentifully stocked with all manner of commodities, particularly such as were suited to the wants and tastes of the Indians: it was in fact, the great mart to which all those in this part of the community resorted to furnish themselves with the different articles of which they stood need,—flour, cheese, blue cloth, powder and shot, for the men, and all sorts of millinery and ornament for the [women], such as flaring gown patterns, beads, and rings for their noses."[20]

That Peter Robinson moved in different circles than Andrew Borland and his family is evident from his career. Robinson was elected to the House of Assembly for York East in 1816 and for York and Simcoe in 1820, along with William Warren Baldwin, father of reformer Robert Baldwin. He was named director of the newly established Bank of Upper Canada in 1823. Yet in 1823 and 1825 he also sponsored the immigration of 2,500 impoverished and dispossessed Irish Catholic tenant farmers and their families to Lanark County, Carleton County, and the Peterborough area. In 1827, he became commissioner of Crown lands, a post he held until 1836, during which time he approved sales, appraised land, collected money from the sale of Six Nations lands, and

Peter, William B., and John Beverley Robinson | Peter Robinson and William B. Robinson, Toronto Public Library, Canadian Documentary Art Collection, C-2-23b and C-2-23a; *Sketch of Sir John Beverley Robinson* by George Richmond, Toronto Public Library, Canadian Documentary Art Collection, JRR315

settled Black veterans and Loyalists in Oro Township. Tory in his politics, he represented York on both the Legislative and Executive Councils. He died in 1838.

Peter Robinson was listed as unmarried at his death, but his will made provision for two children of an unknown mother or mothers. Whitchurch historian Marjorie Richardson reportedly found evidence that his prominent family "tried to suppress the fact Peter married a North American First Nations woman."[21]

Peter's younger brother William Robinson also lived in Newmarket and joined his brother in the firm P. and W. Robinson. He married Elizabeth Jarvis, daughter of William Jarvis and the sister of Samuel Peters Jarvis, who was married to the daughter of Chief Justice William Dummer Powell. Robinson established two trading posts, on Lake Joseph and Georgian Bay. He became known as "one of the chief Indian traders throughout northern Ontario" and enjoyed a reputation for fair dealing among Indigenous peoples.[22] In 1833, he moved to Holland Landing. He was named a justice of the peace and was elected to the Legislative Assembly for Simcoe County numerous times between 1830 and 1854. He gave "lavish grants of land to Tories" to get elected in 1836. In 1844 he was named inspector general, and he was a member of the Legislative Council in 1844–45. Then, in 1846, he became chief commissioner of public works. He also acquired land in Seneca Township on the Haldimand Tract.

For the Anishinaabek and other Indigenous peoples, William Robinson's name is associated with the Robinson treaties. He negotiated the first Robinson Treaty in 1843 (for 700 acres in the District of Simcoe, to be held in trust for the Chippewas of Lake Simcoe and signed by Musquakie). He then negotiated the Robinson Huron and the Robinson Superior Treaties of 1850–51, which became models for the Numbered Treaties negotiated in western and northern Canada after Confederation. In a groundbreaking revenue-sharing clause, the treaties tied annuities to resource revenues, but these promises were not honoured by the Crown, which capped annuities at four dollars per person in 1870. In 2024, the twenty-one First Nations named in the Robinson Huron Treaty agreed to a $10 billion settlement for past annuities.[23]

Mississauga Methodist missionary Peter Jones related an incident that reveals another side of William Robinson—his Eurocentrism—and the injustice inherent in the imposition of British law. Jones interpreted for Chief John Assance when he appeared before Robinson, who was a justice of the peace, at Newmarket in 1828: "The Matachedash chief had complained about a white man who had severely beaten one of the members of his band, but Robinson refused to issue a warrant to arrest the man because the chief could not cite the day of the month when the beating occurred."[24] This incident is described in George Playter's *History of Methodism*:

> The chief gave a fine reprimand to the magistrate. Said he: "I have been abused again and again by your people, and no notices has been taken of them for their bad conduct; and I thought the reason you did not take notice of us was because we were so wretched, ignorant, and drunken; and consequently not worthy of regard. But now our eyes are opened to see our miserable condition, and in seeing we have endeavored to forsake our former evil ways. I cannot suffer any more from your young men, without having justice done to the offenders. Consider what I say."[25]

The third of the Robinson brothers, John Beverley Robinson, was named attorney general of Upper Canada in 1814 and served as chief justice from 1829. He was also a member of the powerful Legislative Council. Along with John Strachan, the first Anglican bishop of Toronto, he headed what became known as the Family Compact, a small tightly knit group of men from interrelated families and their associates who dominated the government of Upper Canada in the 1820s and 1830s.

About half the Family Compact's members were second-generation Loyalists who, like Robinson, were "brought up in the tradition of unswerving devotion to the King and Mother Country." The rest were born in Great Britain or sons of British immigrants. The Executive Council, senior officials, and members of the judiciary were conservative, Anglican, anti-American, and determined that Upper Canada should remain part of the British Empire, "the grandest, the freest, and the noblest political organization that man has ever developed."[26] Advocating a "balanced" government of King, appointed executive, and elected Legislative Assembly, as well as an official church (the Church of England), they were openly contemptuous of democratic ideas such as universal male suffrage and oblivious or hostile to Indigenous forms of governance (as were virtually all settlers). They ensured that like-minded men received positions throughout the colony as sheriffs, magistrates, militia officers, and so on. They were interested in trade, banks, canals, settlement schemes from which they could profit. They also supported a huge increase in British immigration in the 1820s and 1830s to offset the influence of the majority of settlers, who were American-born.

The Rise of an Agricultural and Industrial Economy

The fur trade at Newmarket peaked in 1825. The Yonge Street route was increasingly bypassed after the North West Company merged with the Hudson's Bay Company in 1821, and most furs were transported through York Factory on Hudson Bay directly to England rather than through Montreal, where most local traders had previously sent their furs. Upper Canada's economy, once based mainly on the fur trade, became increasingly focused on agriculture and industry.

10

Deforestation, Farming, and Milling

Upper Canada's settler colony developed within an ethic that didn't question the rampant exploitation of resources or the need to "tame the land."[1] Both the land and Indigenous peoples were considered wild and in need of civilizing.

In fewer than one hundred years, dense forests of pine, beech, hard and soft maple, white and red oak, black and white birch, basswood, ironwood, hickory, cedar, elm, ash, cherry, tamarack, and other trees were transformed into farmland by "an army of axe-wielding settlers and woodsmen."[2] The environmental impacts of farming and logging had enormous consequences for Indigenous peoples.

Alexander Macdonell's 1793 journal of Simcoe's expedition to Penetanguishene provides a glimpse of the pre-colonial landscape along the Humber:

> In the early part of the day, went over a pine ridge; but from ten till six in the evening, when we encamped, went through excellent land for grain or grass, the trees uncommonly large and tall, especially the pine. Crossed two small creeks which emptied themselves into the Humber, on one of which (Drunken Creek) we dined, and encamped on the second. The land through which we passed is chiefly wooded with maple, bass, beech, pine and cedar.[3]

Peter Jones, in *History of the Ojebway Indians* (1861), commented that Mississaugas rarely cut down living trees:

> In addition to this belief in the immortality of their own souls, they suppose that all animals, fowls, fish, trees, stones, &c., are endowed with immortal spirits, and that they possess supernatural power to punish any who may dare to despise or make any unnecessary waste of them ... In their heathen state they very seldom cut down green or living trees, from the idea that it puts them to pain; and some of the pow-wows [Traditional Healers / Shamans] have pretended to hear the wailing of the forest trees when suffering under the operation of the hatchet or axe.[4]

To establish farms, new settlers had to cut down and remove the roots of trees, clear brush and burn debris, drain wetlands, drive off or kill wildlife, and build houses, barns, and fences from timber. Once farmhouses were built, they needed to be heated with wood, and as more immigrants arrived, the demand for wood increased exponentially. As William Cronon calculated for New England (which has a similar climate): "A typical . . . household probably consumed as much as thirty or forty cords of firewood per year . . . [which] meant cutting more than an acre of forest each year. In 1800, the region burned perhaps eighteen times more wood for fuel than it cut for lumber."[5]

As accessible forests disappeared, tree poaching became a problem, including on Indigenous lands, where settlers used a variety of subterfuges to gain access. For example, in 1837, John Jones, Peter Jones' brother and one of the Credit Mississauga Chiefs, was imprisoned for debts. He had been cutting timber on the Credit Reserve, as was his right, unaware that a white man had gained an irregular lease to some of it through a Mississauga youth not empowered to sign away land rights. The supposed tenant charged Jones with trespass, and the court ruled in the white man's favour and imposed a fine, which Jones could not pay.[6] (The judgment was eventually overturned.)

> *They came over here and they were cutting all the trees down. They never got permission to come over and do it. And Joseph Snache sent a whole bunch of warriors over and kicked them off.*
>
> —Andrew Big Canoe, Chippewas of Georgina Island[7]

By the early twentieth century, many areas, including the Oak Ridges Moraine, had lost over 90 per cent of the original tree cover. According to historical geographer David Wood, "On the moraine north and west of Toronto," woodland in Albion Township "went from 40.2 to 7.8 per cent, Caledon Township from 36.8 to 8.1 per cent, and King Township from 33.6 to 6.5 per cent . . . [between] 1860 and 1910."[8] Cleared land dried more quickly and washed into streams in greater amounts.

As the forests were chopped down, "birds and insects, the panoply of ground-dwelling animals, the species in the ground, and aquatic life—all were affected."[9] Farmers imported seeds from Europe for fields and gardens, some of these imported plants were invasive and altered ecological relationships between local flora and fauna.

Farming also greatly affected groundwater. As Wood notes: "Quite apart from the desirability of good water for humans and their animals, all the wildlife depended on water. Whole natural communities were built around available water, whether on the surface or in the ground, but the aim of agriculture was to drain off 'excess' water so that the land could be used for growing crops."[10] By the twentieth century, the counties of southern Ontario had drained between 20 per cent and 80 per cent of their wetlands.

> *So entire ecosystems wiped out, basically. These places that we've been going to for thousands of years look very different now, not just to us, but also animals, who don't*

go there anymore because it's different. It's so quick. It happens so quickly.

—Ben Cousineau, Chippewas of Rama[11]

Wildlife Reduction and Restrictions on Indigenous Hunting

The importation of farm animals such as sheep, pigs, and cattle; planting forage crops; and selective grazing that favoured some native plants over others also altered ecological relationships.

According to Wood, settlers typically viewed wildlife as either useless or dangerous pests, as sources of fur or food, or as legitimate targets for recreational shooting. Bears, wolves, and foxes were killed because they preyed on domestic animals and passenger pigeons and deer because they ate crops. Beaver, fox, mink, marten, otter, and muskrat were hunted for fur. Deer, ducks, wild turkeys, and passenger pigeons could be hunted for food or sport. Even squirrels or raccoons were shot for sport.

Virtually all forms of wildlife were greatly reduced, and some species, such as the passenger pigeon, once so numerous as to darken the sky, were rendered extinct in less than a century. Wild turkeys also became extinct locally. In 1822, wild animals were reported to be scarce in regions near York. In the early 1840s, a writer could say that "the living, breathing denizens of the forest are various; but their numbers are fast diminishing before the destructive progress of civilization."[12]

As Wood comments, "The custom of hunting for food or pleasure seemed to be considered a right in nineteenth-century Ontario. In 1837 the Reverend Featherstone Osier complained about hunters in the Newmarket area: 'The people . . . are very careless about all connected with religion. On the Sabbath . . . more guns [are] heard firing than on any other day of the week.'"[13]

Hunting went on (as in most parts of the New World) as if there were no limits to the resources. Indigenous hunters were forced to compete with settlers for increasingly scarce game that they relied on for food. Although treaties with the Mississaugas and Chippewas specified that they could hunt and fish on ceded lands, settlers fenced their farms and warned Indigenous hunters and gatherers they'd be shot if they ventured on farmers' lands. In 1805, at a Council at the Credit, Chief Quinepenon told colonial authorities of this betrayal: "The inhabitants drive us away instead of helping us, and we want to know why we are served in that manner—Colonel Butler told us the farmers would help us, but instead of doing so when we camp on the shore, they drive us off & shoot our Dogs & never give us any assistance as was promised to our old Chiefs . . . The Farmers call us Dogs & threaten to shoot us in the same manner when we go on their Land."[14] This devastation is still remembered by First Nations.

All along there, Fox Island, Snake Island, all along there, their fishing grounds and their hunting grounds and Holland

10 | Deforestation, Farming, and Milling

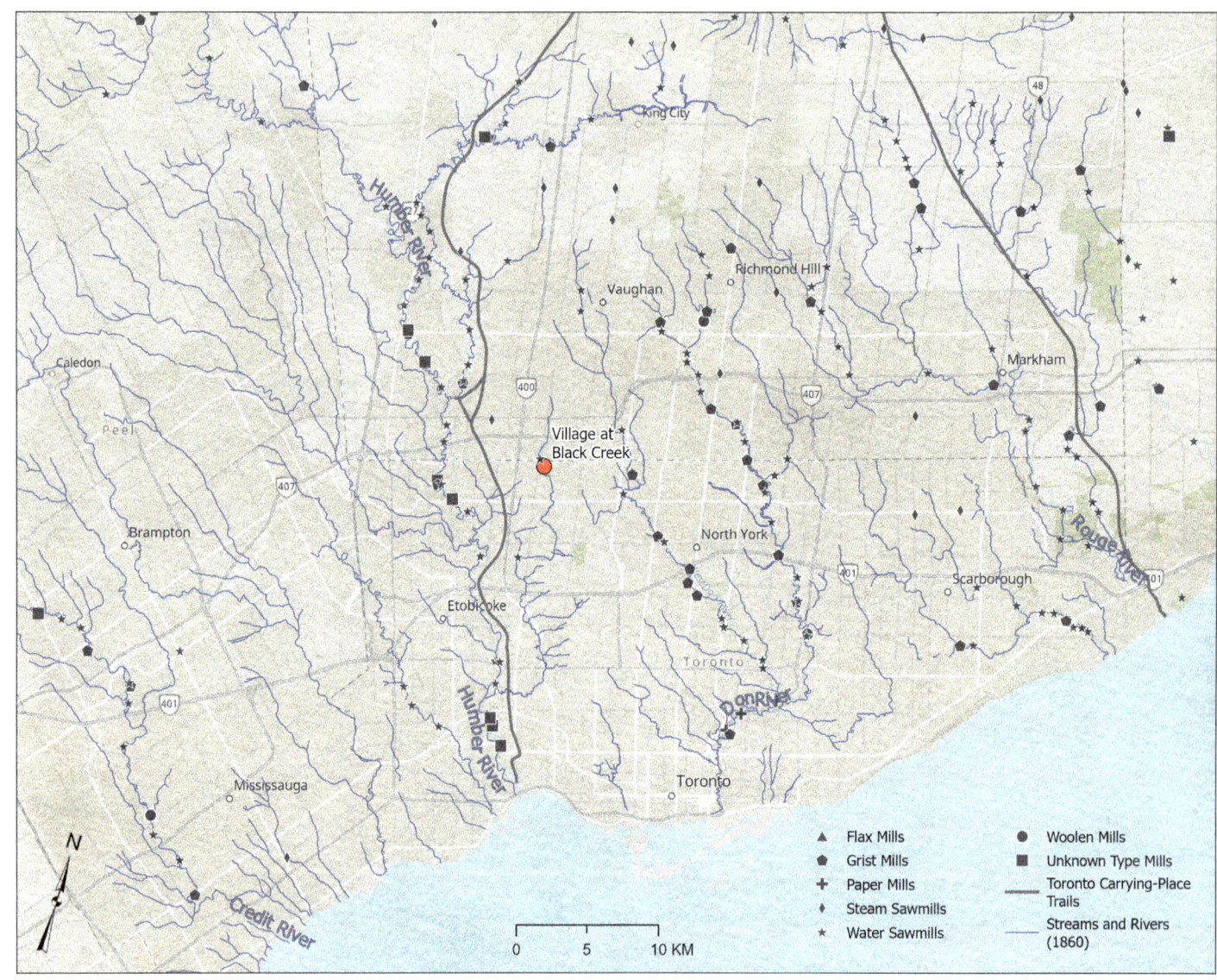

Mills in the Greater Toronto Area, 1859–60

Roblin's Mill at The Village at Black Creek was originally located in Ameliasburg, Prince Edward County | Courtesy of Toronto and Region Conservation Authority

Landing and the swamp. There was lots of fish. Lots of game. Deer . . . Our people would pick what they need and that would be it . . . There used to be lots of deer, here, across the lake from us on the south shore of Lake Simcoe. There's no deer there now. The farmers and the people that call themselves sportsmen shot them all.

—Andrew Big Canoe, Chippewas of Georgina Island[15]

Milling and Its Impact

In 1791, Lieutenant-Governor John Graves Simcoe proposed that the government provide materials for watermill construction, which he considered "universally necessary" and "a great inducement to the settlement of lands."[16]

Mills were key to the expansion of settler agriculture and settlement. Sawmills cut lumber into boards and beams for houses and barns while gristmills ground wheat into flour for bread. There were 201 sawmills in the Home District in 1840 and 275 in 1848. By 1860, there were upwards of twenty mills in Vaughan Township alone.[17] Prospective farmers and artisans sought locations near mill sites, and distilleries were often built near gristmills so that poorer-quality grains or grains such as rye could be distilled into alcohol, which was used (and abused) by settlers and loggers. Later, carding and textile mills were introduced to prepare and weave wool into clothing and other items.

Mills were essential to settlers but also a precarious venture. Dependent on local water conditions, mill owners could be ruined by low flows in summer or damaging floods in spring and fall. Many local mills succumbed to indebtedness or changing environmental conditions in their first years of operation.[18] Government support was often critical to their establishment.

As watermills proliferated, sawmills transformed large swathes of forests into lumber for local infrastructure, imperial warships, and export to Britain. Other mills began to process grains, textiles, paper, and minerals, for local consumption and global circulation. Tree cover disappeared, settler agriculture expanded, and once abundant fish populations dwindled, threatening the sustenance of Indigenous peoples, particularly the Mississaugas, who relied on fish for food.

The King's Mill on the Humber River, 1793, and changes to the river's course over time

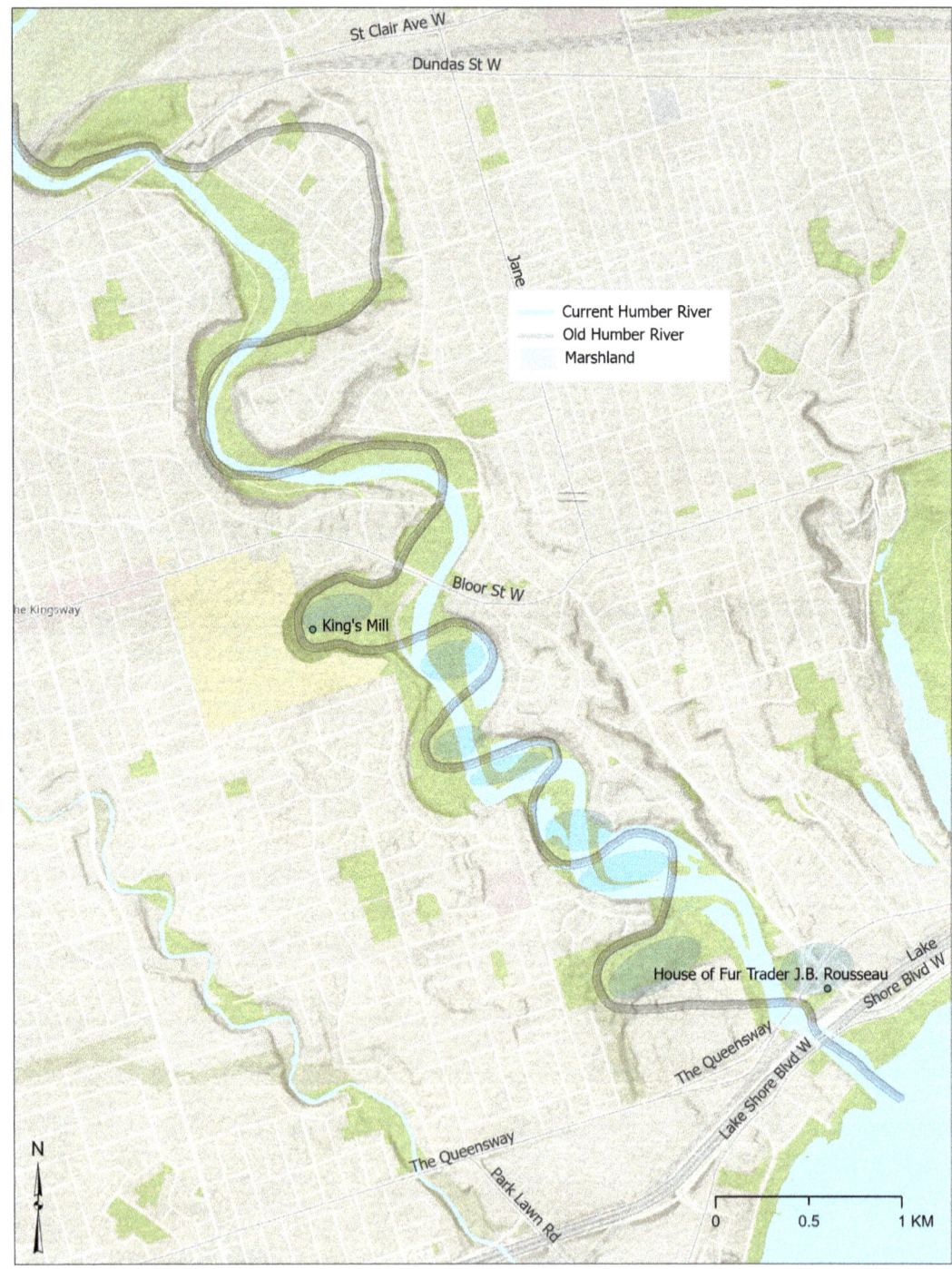

And wherever they put a mill, the Indians lost the fish. Because as soon as they put the mill in, it changed the water level, and it took away the fisheries, so there wasn't food to eat. Because the Mississaugas are fishers. Even our Doodems are fish. There are Doodems that are fish.

—Carolyn King, Mississaugas of the Credit[19]

Deforestation and Milling on the Humber

In 1793, Simcoe decided to move the government shipyard from its exposed position in Newark (now Niagara-on-the-Lake) to the banks of the Humber River. Completed in October 1793 near the present-day Old Mill Inn, the King's Mill processed lumber for Royal Navy gunboats constructed at the Humber shipyard. Many more mills would follow along with mill-based communities such as Weston and Lambton Mills. The Black Creek tributary provided water and power for the settlers near today's Village at Black Creek.[20]

Early mills needed to be situated near river systems because they needed waterpower or steam power to operate. Dams also made it easier to catch fish. Before European contact, the rivers on the north shore of Lake Ontario were notable for their abundant fisheries, particularly salmon. Anishinaabek and Haudenosaunee harvested salmon intensively yet sustainably. The Humber was a noted spawning ground in the eighteenth century, and fish could be killed at night by torchlight and spear alone. A canoe of two people could amass eight to ten barrels of fish in a single night.[21]

A few years following the construction of the King's Mill in July 1796, Augustus Jones noted there had been "a great quantity of salmon as well as other fish destroyed by the wheels of [a] sawmill."[22] He suggested that racks could be used to protect fish and keep them away from the fast-moving wheels.

Sawmills typically dropped sawdust and wood debris through slatted floors directly into the water, clogging and slowing streams and covering gravel where salmon laid eggs. As sawdust accumulated, it created anaerobic conditions that smothered fish fry and other aquatic life. The removal of forest cover next to waterways raised water temperatures, increased erosion and run-off, lowered water volume through evaporation, and reduced the insect life that juvenile salmon depended on for food.[23]

Many toxic materials were dumped in the water. Especially during early settlement, farmers burned wood to produce potash and pearlash. Wood ashes were used to manufacture gunpowder, glass, medicine, soap, and textiles, and the area around Lake Ontario supplied British industry. Lime refuse, a by-product of ash production, was often dumped into the water while tanneries, soap factories, and other industries also released toxic chemicals.[24]

In 1806, Mississauga Chief Quinepenon protested to the government about the pollution of north shore rivers: "Our Waters on this River are so filthy & disturbed by washing with Sope & other dirt that the fish refuse coming into the River as usual for which our families are in great distress for want of food."[25]

Deforestation affected water flow on the Humber and its tributaries. The depth of the Humber dropped so much that by 1860 timber could no longer be floated down the river. By 1885, some stream flows had been so reduced that fish no longer returned to spawn.[26] This food source for the Anishinaabek (and settlers) eventually disappeared altogether.[27] Meanwhile, floods became increasingly severe, wiping out many of the mills that had contributed to this environmental destruction.

Milling on Yonge Street

Milling was also key to the settlements on Yonge Street. In the 1790s, before a mill was established close by, at least one settler on Yonge Street, Nicholas Miller, adopted the Indigenous method of pounding corn. "[He] set up the first gristmill in the area. It was a contraption that the settlers had devised from the Indian method of pounding corn in a hollowed-out tree stump. A heavy weight, such as a block of wood, was hung on a long pole set at right angles across the top of a notched post. The corn, which was placed in the hollow stump, was pounded by the weight either falling at the end of a rope or being swung down on the end of the pole, which acted as a lever or sweep."[28]

Research committee member Lauri Hoeg of Chippewas of Georgina Island and her daughter Hayley Williamson singing an honour song for the water at a land-based education session | Courtesy of Lauri Hoeg

Early mills were built by settlers on the west branch of the Don River at what became known as York Mills. John Cummer, son of Jacob Cummer and Elizabeth (Fisher) Cummer, owned a farm at Finch and Yonge. A side road ran to the Don River, where he ran a mill for his father from 1819. By 1851, he and his son (also named Jacob) had added a gristmill and woollen factory.

In 1794, William Berczy hired men to build a large house and mill, the beginnings of German Mills, a few miles east of today's Thornhill. The first mill in Vaughan was built in 1801. Settlers were drawn to Thornhill, named after Benjamin Thorne, who by 1830 was operating a gristmill, sawmill, and tannery. By 1848, it was the largest community on Yonge Street north of Toronto with a population of around 700 people.[29]

Elisha Beman and Peter Robinson would both operate mills at Newmarket, and Robinson also owned the Red Mill at Holland Landing.

The Mississaugas and Milling on the Credit

In May 1806, land surveyor Samuel Wilmot arrived at the Credit River to mark off the boundaries of the Mississaugas' reserve, which extended one mile on either side of the Credit, as agreed to in the Head of the Lake Treaty (Treaty 14). While surveying with a crew of Indigenous workers, he was instructed to "note Timber ... Pine & Oak for the Royal Navy south of [Dundas] Street."[30] The navy sought white pine timber for naval masts. When the British lost access to Baltic timber after the Napoleonic Wars, construction of sawmills and timber extraction accelerated. By mid-century, sixty or more mills had been constructed on the Credit River, and woodland cover fell to 67 per cent. It would fall to 9.5 per cent by 1911.[31]

Milling had numerous negative environmental impacts on Indigenous peoples, but some developed mills of their own, and Indigenous men were employed on logging crews. When the Mississaugas established the Credit Mission Village in 1826, they needed lumber to build European-style homes and facilities. Peter Jones went "with a party to Mr. Racey's mills [at Erindale on the Credit] to raft down boards for our school and meeting house."[32] In 1829, he recorded that the Mississaugas had agreed in Council to erect their own sawmill, which was operational the next year.

The Mississaugas of the Credit ended up operating two sawmills. Lumber was shipped by a schooner co-owned by the Mississaugas and Captain James McLean to lumber yards around Lake Ontario, including Niagara and on the Humber. (McLean was a Scottish immigrant married to a Mississauga woman.) As Wood notes, "In 1844, Port Credit was exporting a considerable amount of forest products—indeed, almost as much lumber as Toronto." Toronto exported over 1.5 million board feet of lumber at the time.[33]

As elsewhere, the impact of milling on salmon was catastrophic. Along the Credit, salmon populations were dwindling by 1846 and nearly disappeared in the next decade.[34] The last indigenous Lake Ontario salmon was recorded in 1898.[35]

PART FOUR:
The Civilizational Agenda

11

Indigenous Christianity

The end of the War of 1812 and peace with the United States transformed the relationship between settlers, the colonial government, and Indigenous people. The non-Indigenous population surged, but new settlers were not prepared or educated for an ongoing relationship with Indigenous peoples. Most had no understanding of treaty relations: they believed treaties were one-time land deals that had freed up Indigenous land without any ongoing obligation or relationship with Indigenous peoples required on their part. There was little concept of ensuring a mutually beneficial coexistence into the future. Indigenous peoples were expected to "die out" or defined as a problem to be ignored, pushed to the margins, relocated elsewhere, or eliminated through cultural transformation. Indigenous people living traditional lifestyles had no place in Upper Canada's developing economy.

The situation was particularly perilous for the Mississaugas of the Credit because of their proximity to York's environmental degradation and whisky traders. As a child, Peter Jones experienced firsthand the near disintegration of his mother's people as poverty, European diseases, trauma, and alcoholism took their toll. The Mississaugas suffered a high number of deaths, including the deaths of their Chiefs Wabakinine, Wahbanosay, and Quinepenon. Their numbers also dwindled as members relocated to Grand River or farther away from European settlers.[1]

At this low point, the Mississaugas feared they would not survive as a people. Given their low numbers and proximity to York, their survival strategy was to work with colonial partners to protect their interests as best they could.

In this context, colonial officials and some Indigenous people started to advocate the policy of "civilization"—though not necessarily for the same reasons. Colonial officials promoted civilization as a process of cultural remodelling that would save Indigenous peoples from the supposed dead end of their own cultures and societies. Civilization would also save money by turning hunters into self-sufficient farmers who would not need presents or government support. (This discourse ignored the fact that that the Haudenosaunee had been farmers before Europeans arrived.) Conveniently, changing Indigenous land use would also free up "excess" Indigenous land, since, as farmers, they would use only the small plots they could clear.

By "benevolently" encouraging Indigenous people to abandon cultural and economic practices deemed harmful to British agricultural, industrial, and economic development, the British hoped to incorporate them into the colony and the larger British Empire, furthering the "progress" of both. Indigenous peoples, who were aware of the wars and violent land dispossession taking place in the United States, likely considered the British approach the lesser of two evils. As traditional food sources disappeared, there was also the simple question, What would they eat?

After 1815, many Indigenous peoples and settlers shared the belief that Indigenous peoples had to adapt to white society to survive. The goals of governments, some religious leaders, and some Indigenous people were temporarily aligned. In Indigenous communities, what form that adaptation should take would be a matter of considerable debate and soul-searching.

Converting Indigenous Peoples

A key concept of British imperialism globally and North American colonialism specifically was the conviction that Christianity was superior to all other religious and spiritual beliefs and that conversion was essential for the civilization and, hence, the survival of Indigenous peoples. The colonizers' stance was also defensive—Christianized Indigenous peoples would share a belief system with settlers, rendering them more knowable and trustworthy. Settlers hoped Christian ethics would lead Indigenous peoples to abandon their supposedly warlike ways and live peaceably in a single nation rather than as threatening independent Nations.

Most missionaries knew little about Indigenous spiritual beliefs and ethical systems, particularly those that prevailed before the havoc wrought by European colonialism. They ignored or devalued millennia of accumulated wisdom and spiritual practice that focused on ethical relationships with other beings and the land. Missionaries characterized Indigenous peoples as ignorantly living in darkness and sin.

> *I think some of the first buildings on every reserve were churches. And it happened at Rama too . . . The purpose of it was to get our people in there and get them Christianized and colonized . . . The sales pitch was, "This is the way, the only way, and your way isn't the right way." So our people went to the church.*
>
> —Ben Cousineau, Chippewas of Rama[2]

Some Indigenous converts agreed because Indigenous people were, indeed, going through a dark time. They had endured multiple traumas. A high death rate from unfamiliar diseases, loss of land and self-sufficiency, and other colonial dynamics had shaken the confidence of many in traditional worldviews and practices and suggested the need for radical change. Christianity, and especially Methodism, became a point of connection and interaction between many Indigenous peoples and settlers, though it also created serious divisions within Indigenous communities.

In 1819, the York Bible Society produced a report titled "Thoughts on the Civilization of the Chippewa and Mississaga Tribes of Indians Spread over the Province of Upper Canada." The report was co-authored by fur trader Peter Robinson, York Indian agent James Givins, and Duncan Cameron, former commander of the York Volunteers at the Battle of Queenston Heights and provincial secretary of Upper Canada. The report asked, "What may be the best practicable mode of civilizing the Indian tribes throughout this Province and communicating to them the Pious knowledge and the blessings of the Christian Faith?" Refuting "the General opinion entertained by those least acquainted with the manner of those Indians, which seems to be that all attempts at civilization will prove abortive," the report called for missionary activity to ease the inevitable transition to an agricultural life. "He may be a hunter for half a century or more; but European civilization and agriculture surrounding this spot will lessen the game and . . . certainly in the end make him a tiller of the land."[3]

The report's recommendations likely influenced Sir Peregrine Maitland, lieutenant-governor of Upper Canada. A year later, he developed a plan to establish Indigenous settlements with schools to teach basic literacy and useful skills for agriculture and frontier industry. This training would be provided in a religious and moral context provided by Anglican missionaries. The plan was not implemented immediately, however, because the Church of England was sparsely represented in frontier areas—and the Methodists beat them to it. In fact, although some Indigenous peoples had been exposed to Catholicism through French missionaries in the 1600s and early 1700s, and although many Mohawks were nominal Anglicans, the 1820s and early 1830s witnessed a remarkable surge of conversions to this more egalitarian form of Protestant Christianity.

Methodism had emerged in eighteenth-century Britain as a more experiential form of Christianity, one that stressed personal reformation and a direct relationship with God. Less hierarchical than Anglicanism, Methodism gained many adherents among the poor and disadvantaged and those who sought more equitable social relations in England and North America.

In 1802, Nathan Bangs, an American Methodist saddlebag preacher, preached to Indigenous peoples in Upper Canada. Their positive response made him a strong advocate for Methodist missions in the colony. The Episcopal Methodists, originally based in the United States, became particularly enthusiastic about Indigenous conversion beginning in 1816, following an unprecedented wave of conversions among the Wyandot in Ohio by a Black Methodist lay preacher named John Stewart.[4] In Upper Canada, this wave of conversions began at Grand River.

The Mission at Grand River

The British and Foreign Bible Society, a non-denominational Christian Bible society, was

The British had a far longer positive association with the Haudenosaunee through the Covenant Chain alliance established in the 1660s than with the Anishinaabek, who had been allies of the French until 1760.[6] Even before the Mohawks relocated to the Haldimand Tract from their homelands in New York, many Mohawks had converted to the Church of England, adopted European-style clothing and housing, and adopted some European farming practices. In fact, the Mohawk Chapel in the Mohawk Village (now Brantford) was the first Anglican church in Upper Canada, though for years it lacked a regular Anglican preacher. Services were usually led by catechist Henry Aaron Hill (brother-in-law of Joseph Brant). Elderly Mohawk Chief Henry Tekarihogen sometimes read prayers in Mohawk.[7]

Mohawk Chapel, Brantford, built in 1785 | Photo by Norman Einstein, Wikimedia Commons

The Methodists viewed the Mohawks' conversion to the Church of England as superficial. In fact, they considered the non-Christian Cayuga and Onondaga "the most moral and orderly of all the Indians": "The Cayugas and Onondagas were very unfriendly to the Gospel on the ground that the Mohawks were no better for it," an observation many Indigenous people also made about white Christian settlers.[8] Many Senecas, Cayugas, and Onondagas had found an alternative to Christianity in the teachings of Seneca prophet Handsome Lake. His visions reinforced cultural continuity yet also adapted traditional spiritual practices, social structures, and relations to the land to ensure Haudenosaunee survival in the face of dwindling game and a reduced land base. Handsome Lake incorporated some elements of

founded in Britain in 1804. Its first translation project for Canada was the Gospel of John into Mohawk in 1804.[5] Many colonial officials considered the Mohawks the most civilized of Indigenous peoples, mainly because they lived in settled villages and were horticulturalists (as well as hunters). But to the consternation of would-be civilizers, women, not men, exercised jurisdiction over and cultivated their extensive fields.

Jacques Gérard Milbert, engraved by M. Dubourg, *Camp Meeting of the Methodists in N. America*, c. 1819 | Courtesy of Library of Congress, Washington, LC-USZC4-772

Christian belief and European lifeways into his teachings—such as men tilling the land for crops, domesticating animals, and building European-style houses. He also warned against alcohol abuse, selling land, and becoming involved in white men's wars. His prophetic vision of environmental destruction and the end of the world warned Haudenosaunee to be respectful in their relations with the earth and all beings.[9] Although many Haudenosaunee eventually converted to Methodism or other Christian religions, it was partly through Handsome Lake's teachings that the Haudenosaunee were able to preserve many elements of their original culture, languages, and ceremonies for future generations.

The Methodists, who insisted upon sobriety, noted with approval the way Haudenosaunee traditionalists handled cases of excessive alcohol use: "In the case of a drunken member of the tribe, the chief men would summon him to a council meeting, at which united efforts would be made to produce humility and reformation, partly by exhortations and entreaties, and partly by exacting, publicly, certain humiliating ceremonies. In obstinate cases, councils had been held for a fortnight, before signs of contrition appeared."[10]

Methodism gained a toehold at Grand River in 1822, when Thomas Davis, a Mohawk Chief "well disposed towards the Gospel," invited a lay preacher to his home.[11] American Methodist

Seth Crawford and missionary Alvin Torry came to Grand River in 1823 and began preaching at Davis' house. Dramatic conversions ensued. Several Mohawks responded strongly to the Methodist emphasis on a direct relationship with the Creator. The highly emotional services led some non-Methodist Mohawks to comment that the preachers used wolves' brains as medicine to make the people cry and shout.[12]

By 1823, the Methodists counted thirty members at the mission at Grand River, which became known as Davisville (after Chief Davis). Following the conversions of Polly Jones (daughter of Sarah Tekarihogen and Augustus Jones) and her Mississauga half-brother Peter Jones at a camp meeting at Ancaster that year, Indigenous Methodism spread rapidly. Camp meetings were "evangelistic, religious, revival gatherings held in frontier forest clearings where enthusiastic preaching, inspired singing, impassioned praying, deep personal reflection and come-to-Jesus conversions were commonplace."[13] Camp meetings often offered Indigenous peoples and settlers their first positive contact with each other—in some cases, deep and lifelong friendships resulted.

Peter Jones, the Mississaugas, and the Methodists

Kahkewaquonaby / Peter Jones had lived with his father's Mohawk family at Grand River since 1820. He was given the Mohawk name Desagondensta (He Stands People on Their Feet) and, at the urging of his father, was baptized into the

Matilda Jones, *Portrait of Kahkewaquonaby, Reverend Peter Jones*, 1832. Matilda Jones, an English portrait artist (no relation), painted this portrait during Jones' first visit to England | Victoria University Library (Toronto)

Anglican Church. But Jones remained skeptical of the truth of Christianity: Christian settlers were "drunk, quarreling, fighting and cheating the poor Indians, and acting as if there was no God."[14]

Rev. James Spencer, M.A, *Chief [Joseph] Sawyer of the Credit*, c. 1846 | Toronto Public Library, John Ross Robertson Collection, JRR 4 [Framed]

After his heartfelt conversion to Methodism at Ancaster, Jones became an extraordinarily effective exhorter and lay preacher. In 1827, he was the first Indigenous person to be granted a licence as an itinerant Methodist preacher. He became a fully ordained Methodist minister six years later. Over a decade as preacher and minister, he converted hundreds of Indigenous people, especially Anishinaabek. Jones spoke to the Mississaugas and other Anishinaabek in their language and translated and interpreted Christian concepts, hymns, and sections of the Bible so they were comprehensible within Indigenous worldviews. His sincerity was palpable, and he spoke with personal knowledge of the deep pain and trauma people were experiencing on multiple fronts.

> *He really goes for Christianity in a big way. And it's a very moving conversion experience you read in his diary. The man never loses his devoutness. Even when I read his diary and stuff, I'm thinking, okay, give it a rest sometimes. You don't have to be that religious. But nevertheless, he is, and I kind of admire him for that. Right to the very dying end.*
>
> —Darin Wybenga, Mississaugas of the Credit[15]

A key element of Methodism's appeal was its insistence on abstinence from alcohol. Jones detested drunkenness for the "evil it had done to my poor countrymen, many thousands of whom have had their days shortened by it, and been hurried to destruction."[16]

Peter Jones' mother, Tuhbenahneequay, became one of the first Credit Mississauga converts. When Jones returned to the Credit River to tell his Mississaugas relatives of his conversion, his mother accompanied him back to Davisville and was baptized "Sarah Henry." She then brought her nephew David Sawyer to be converted. David walked back fifty miles to tell his father, Joseph Sawyer (later Head Chief), and his mother. Both converted.[17] Peter's brother John and his wife,

Christiana Brant (granddaughter of Joseph Brant), also joined the Methodist church. As word spread, more and more Indigenous people came to Davisville to see for themselves "whether the truth had been told."[18]

In 1824, the first Indigenous Methodist church was formally established at Davisville mostly by Indigenous converts. Peter Jones and Seth Crawford preached, and Thomas Davis offered his house for a school. Among its trustees were Augustus Jones and Peter's brother John Jones.

These activities changed the relationship between the Mississaugas and the Haudenosaunee—at least among those who converted to Methodism. Methodist commentator George Playter later commented that mutual mistrust and suspicion between the two Indigenous Nations persisted long after the war between them ended around 1700: "From that time, the two great bodies never entered into confederacies, never mingled in general councils, nor pitched their tents, nor held their festivals together. But since their Christian profession this animosity has ceased. The Mohawks, who possess the fertile flats of the Grand River, have invited their Missisaugah Brethren to occupy their lands, and reside among them. They now both plant in the same fields, send their children to the same school, and worship in the same assembly."[19]

Many of the Mississaugas of the Credit moved to Grand River. In 1825, they began planting corn and potatoes on land lent to them by Thomas Davis. In their annual report for that year, the Episcopal Methodists painted a glowing picture of these changes: "Their fields of corn have been pretty well cultivated, and promise a good harvest. Having signified to the Government their wishes to settle on their lands for civilization, they have received assurances of encouragement and aid, beyond their highest expectations, and they hope to be enabled to commence an establishment on the Credit in the course of another season."[20]

Mississauga Conversions on the Humber and Credit

In July 1825, the Mississaugas returned to their lands on the Credit in advance of receiving their annual presents and payments for surrendering their lands. While there, Peter Jones preached to a large crowd, and his words made a deep impression:

> The people flocked from all directions to hear me preach on the flats by the river side; we assembled here on the green grass that all might have an opportunity of hearing. I should judge there were about 300 people, Indians and whites. I spoke to my people first in Indian, and then exhorted in English; the power of the Lord came upon some of the Indians so that they fell to the earth, some rejoicing, and others crying for mercy. The congregation behaved very well, and a number of the gentry present expressed their surprise at what they saw and heard. Before sunset I held a class meeting with

the Indians; they spoke very feelingly of the dealings of God to their souls, and it was a time long to be remembered by us all. There were two of my nation present who joined with us to serve the Lord today—Bluejay and Benjamin Crane.[21]

Jones was especially gratified to convert Bluejay, "the most inveterate drunkard of the tribe."[22]

Although expressed through Christian imagery, Anishinaabe Methodism echoed older Indigenous revitalization movements. Prophets such as Neolin, who had inspired Pontiac, and Tenskwatawa, brother of Tecumseh, had reinvigorated Indigenous societies at critical moments. These movements likewise called for a ban on alcohol and a return to sober living. Like them, Methodism acknowledged the harm done to Indigenous peoples and did not stigmatize them as degenerates or "savages" fully responsible for their own misery, as many settlers did. Faced with colonial dynamics that reduced their agency as Nations, converts saw Methodism as a viable route to social equality because it stressed the personal reformation of both Indigenous and white sinners.

Methodism, as interpreted through Jones and other converted Mississaugas, explained current afflictions and losses. Its focus on confessing sins and praying for personal and communal redemption and salvation restored a sense of agency and hope. At a time when so many loved ones were dying, it promised an afterlife in a better place. Jones was exceptionally effective because he drew out the similarities between Indigenous spirituality and Christianity, affirming that both worshipped the same Supreme Being.[23] For a time, and in a bid to survive and reconstruct their devastated societies, many Mississaugas and other Anishinaabek embraced Methodism as a necessary, if revolutionary, social experiment. In doing so, some gained the strength to survive the cumulative effects of colonialism over the previous decades.

Yet conversion meant repudiating deeply held beliefs and practices, such as the beliefs that elements of the natural world were imbued with spirit and that one could be offered guidance by Guardian Spirits. Although Methodism acknowledged some aspects of the Mississaugas' historical and cultural experience, it denied others. Missionaries shamed and denigrated those who did not convert, depicting them as ignorant, sinful, inferior, and less civilized than the British or Indigenous converts. They warned of eternal hellfire—actions that today would be regarded as a form of spiritual abuse. They created division within Indigenous communities by giving converts resources, privileges, and protection and denying them to non-Christians. Pressure to convert made it less of a free choice and more of a necessity for survival.

The Mississaugas took up the . . . I'll say the white man's way . . . very early at the whole promotion or advocacy of Peter Jones because he says, right in the book, he's quoted as preaching to his people, saying that "if we don't act like them, they're going to kill us." So it was a concerted effort to convert them to be like them. He says that he never wanted to lose the language, but they did.

—Carolyn King, Mississaugas of the Credit[24]

Through conversion, the Mississaugas of the Credit, who numbered less than two hundred people, gained important political allies. White Methodists were involved in the humanitarian movement gaining ground in England and the United States. Many Methodists believed history and culture, not genetics, were responsible for the differences between nations. In their view, members of "primitive" and "savage" societies at the bottom of the hierarchy of nations could be redeemed through education, sobriety, conversion to Christianity, and the adoption of agriculture and private property in a civilizing process they believed was universal. The colonial secretary, Lord Glenelg, told Peter Jones, "Our forefathers the ancient Britons were once as barbarous as the North American Indians are; and as Christianity has made the nation what it is, surely it will do the same for the Indian tribes."[25] Over the next decade, humanitarians agitated against slavery and called for the protection of Indigenous peoples from the worst effects of colonialism, including the loss of their land rights and exploitation by alcohol traders—a benevolence that also, paradoxically, legitimized British colonial rule.[26]

Methodism thus offered the Mississaugas a new way to view their own culture and history while at the same time allowing Euro-Canadians to see the missionary brand of colonialism as a gift.

Presents, Prayers, and a Promise at the Humber

Peter Jones' 1825 letter to Indian Agent James Givins marked the first time a literate Mississauga wrote to an official in Upper Canada:

> By the request of Capt. John [Cameron] and others of the Mississagues in those parts, I take the liberty to write a few lines to you wishing you to send an information respecting their presents to what times you will be ready to issue them, or to what time would wish them to come down, there are about fifty of the Nation who have planted corn and potatoes, and who have embraced Christianity, and are attending to the means of education; they not wish to come down till they get a sure word from you, for they are at present busy hoeing their corn.[27]

After Jones preached to the settlers and Mississaugas gathered at the Credit, Givins requested that the Mississaugas come to the Council Fire at the Humber River, 19 kilometres east of the Credit, to receive their annual payments and presents. Arriving the night before, the Mississaugas set up their wigwams and assembled for prayers at sunset. Jones preached. Some Mississaugas listened, and others mocked the Christians. Among the mockers was a wife, now the widow, of Peter Jones' late grandfather Chief Wahbanosay. She later converted and became a devout Christian.[28]

The next day, Colonel Givins, some military officers, the Reverend Dr. John Strachan, his wife, and several "gentlemen" from York came to visit the Christian Mississaugas and view their progress while the presents were being distributed. Jones described the proceedings:

> While they were cutting and dividing the goods, I got the children together, and selected two hymns for them to sing. The Doctor, Colonel [Givins], and Lady Strachan were highly pleased. When the issue was over I assembled all the Christian Indians together; two of them read in the Testament and some in easy reading. The Doctor then spoke to us, expressing his happiness in seeing the work of the Lord among us. He then gave us some advice, thinking it would be best for us to settle on the Credit and erect a village, saying he thought the Government would assist us, and wished us to consult about the matter. After this he concluded with prayer. When the Doctor and Colonel left us we talked the subject over, and it was unanimously agreed that it would be best for us to take the Doctor's advice and settle ourselves at the Credit the next Spring.[29]

The Indian agent usually gave alcohol to those gathered for presents, but that day, "the Christian men had all agreed not to take the fire water . . . and begged the agent not to offer them to any of the Indians . . . For the first time, perhaps, the kegs were carried away from an Indian camp untasted and unopened . . . and the Christian Indians were never offered ardent spirit by the government agents afterwards."[30]

After these meetings, a large number of Indigenous people accompanied the Christian Mississaugas back to Grand River "to see and hear the great things spoken of." Settler Methodists took note: the Newmarket Branch Missionary Society sent 10 pounds to support "sending the Gospel to new and remote Settlements, and to the Indian Nations."[31]

In fall 1825, the lieutenant-governor, Sir Peregrine Maitland, promised to build twenty houses and a schoolhouse at the Credit River before spring. After wintering at Grand River, the Mississaugas returned to the Credit, but the houses were not yet built.

12

Yonge Street Camp Meetings

The Methodists were the first Christians to reach many new settlements in Upper Canada. Itinerant missionaries travelled circuits of small communities and preached to anyone who would listen. Services were conducted in people's homes, though larger outdoor camp meetings were also held. As their numbers increased, settler Methodists organized: the first meeting of Methodists in York was held in 1818. By 1820, York had 43 members, the Yonge Street Circuit, which stretched from York to Lake Simcoe, had 211.[1]

Anglicans were a small but powerful minority because they belonged to the official church and received funds and lands from the Clergy Reserves, a widely resented privilege. North of York, in the absence of assigned preachers, a few Anglicans held services in private homes led by lay readers, missionaries, or members of the military.

John Cummer—son of Jacob Cummer and Elizabeth (Fisher) Cummer and cousin of Elizabeth (Fisher) Stong—began to hold large Methodist camp meetings at the Cummer Mill east of Yonge Street and did so for many years. The area became known as Scripture Town and later Angel Valley. Peter Jones described a camp meeting in June 1826: "Started with a number of Indians to attend a camp meeting on Yonge Street, where we arrived the next day about noon. During the meeting (which lasted three days), a number of both whites and Indians professed to experience a change of heart, at the close, several Indians received the solemn ordinance of baptism."[2]

In July, Jones returned to Yonge Street with John Sunday and Moses, two Christian converts from the Bay of Quinte. They met with the Anishinaabek of Lake Simcoe and Lake Huron and attended a missionary meeting near Newmarket featuring the Reverend Egerton Ryerson. Ryerson preached to a large crowd of people in the open air. About thirty Indigenous people were present. After Ryerson's speech, Jones explained the key Christian doctrines and spoke a few words to white settlers "who were listening with profound attention." John Sunday also spoke.

The next day Jones and Sunday visited Anishinaabek camps in the vicinity.

Chief Snake rose up and said—"Brothers: We feel very thankful to you for your visit to us, to shew us how wretched and miserable we are in our present condition and to tell us what the Great Spirit would have us do to make us wise, good, and happy; for my part I am ready and willing to become a Christian. I hope that all my young men will become good and wise, and serve the Great Spirit." He then enquired when they should have a school. Another old man rose and spoke to the same purpose.[3]

A letter written by Egerton Ryerson relayed the content of Jones' sermons:

P. Jones introduced himself by saying, compassion for his brethren had induced him to visit them; and proceeded to discourse to them of the knowledge of God, the fallen state of man, and the plan of redemption through Jesus Christ . . .

He then enlarged on the wickedness and destructive consequences of intemperance; and asked them, "where are our fathers and grandfathers? where are all those nations of which our fathers told us, and who once filled all these woods? and why are we now wasted to a few? I will tell you, brothers: It is because of the Schootawaubooh (firewater) that made them drunk, and leads to other great wickedness. On this account the Great Spirit is angry with us. Intemperance brings sickness and death, and thus we waste away. "Now, brothers, unless we put away the *firewater*, and other wickedness, we shall soon die off, and there will be none of us left." He then stated what the good book required of them, in the several duties in life; and also what the Great Spirit had done for their brethren at the river Credit, and other places . . . The Governor is pleased at this change, and is now building us houses to live in. Our brethren at the Credit are now sending their children to school "that they may become wise, and know how to read the good book, which the Great Spirit has given us."[4]

For Jones and other Methodists, the main solution to the problem of alcohol was Indigenous peoples becoming Christians. Other solutions were secondary.

Following these and other Methodist meetings, the Mississaugas of the Credit were summoned to a Council at York. Indian agent James Givins delivered a message: the lieutenant-governor, Sir Peregrine Maitland, and Bishop Strachan were strongly opposed to the Mississaugas attending Methodist camp meetings. The Methodists were of American origin and perceived to be of dubious loyalty to the Crown. They were suspected of advocating democracy and republicanism. According to Jones, Givins stated

that if we persisted in going to any more of them, he [the governor] would cast us off, and have nothing more to do with us—that we could now take our choice, either to desist from attending Camp meetings, and retain the good will and aid of the Governor, or persist in going and lose his friendship and assistance. This was, indeed, a great trial to us, and I was for a few moments quite confounded and astonished, having been taught to believe that man was a free agent, and had a right to worship God according to the dictates of his conscience; and also that the King's laws granted all his subjects liberty to worship God as they felt it their duty... After a long consultation between ourselves, the Chiefs thought it advisable for the sake of what the Governor had done and was doing for us, not to oppose his will in this matter, particularly as we were just commencing a settlement, and endeavouring to improve in civilization.[5]

This was a moment of considerable disillusionment for the Mississaugas. It was clear to them that "Christians were against Christians, that worshippers of the Great Spirit were opposed to other worshippers, and that white men with the Great Book hated others who followed the Great Book."[6]

The Mississaugas acceded to the Governor's demand, and the government built twenty log cabins at the Credit, each with half an acre of land, which "fenced would be sufficient garden for a family." The men contributed 100 pounds (some earned by selling salmon), the women made baskets and brooms, and the children brought shillings to fund the school and meeting house. Soon, forty children were attending the school, taught by Peter Jones' brother John Jones.[7]

The government ban on attending camp meetings was soon ignored. George Playter related:

In June [1827], about 60 [Lake Simcoe Anishinaabek] collected together, from their northern roamings, 30 miles distant, to a camp meeting on Yonge Street, 12 miles distant from York [the Cummer site]. They even came a week before hand, and were kindly supplied with provisions by benevolent persons in the neighborhood, and with a suitable place at the campground. On the first day, in the afternoon, the horn was blown for the people to assemble for preaching... Their old bald-headed chief led the way, followed by the men, and then the women and children... Great interest was felt by preachers and congregation for these poor people of the forest. But other Indians were present; and though the head men of the Credit mission agreed to the demand of the Governor [to not attend camp meetings], yet every Indian man, woman and child was at this camp meeting. Whether the promise was retracted, or not exacted by the Governor, I cannot learn.[8]

Peter Jones described another large camp meeting held at the Cummer Mill the following year.

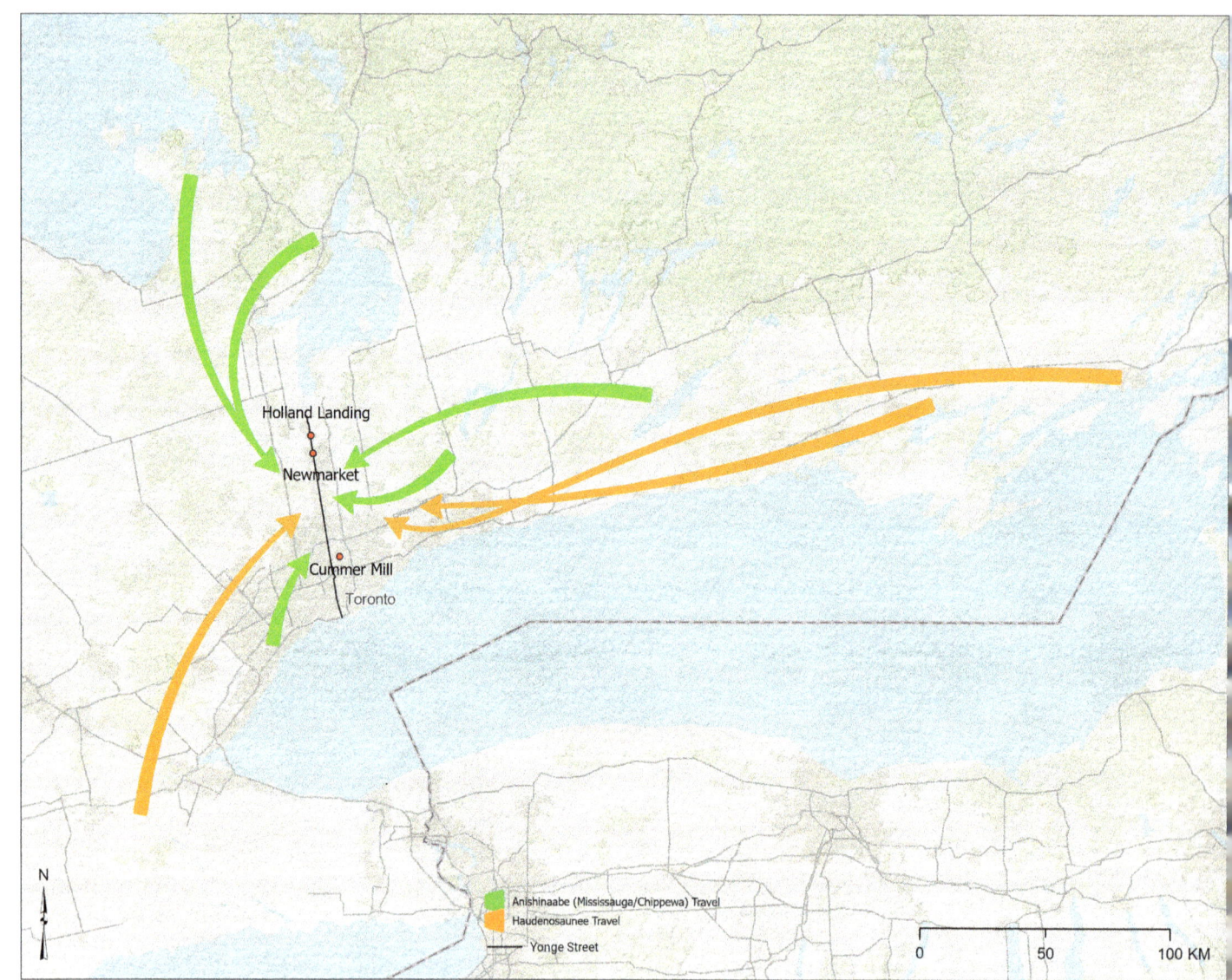

Indigenous attendance at Yonge St. Methodist gatherings

When we arrived we found between two and three hundred Indians collected from Lake Simcoe and Schoogog Lake. Most of those from Lake Simcoe have just come in from the back lakes to join with their converted brethren in the service of Almighty God . . . The Camp ground enclosed about two acres, which was surrounded with board tents . . . The Indians occupied one large tent, which was 240 feet long and 15 feet broad. It was covered over head with boards, and the sides were made tight with bushes, to make it secure from any encroachments . . . In this long house, the Indians arranged themselves in families, as is their custom in their wigwams.[9]

According to Playter, "The meeting began on Tuesday, and ended on Friday after; when about 30 whites and the same number of Indians, professed conversion. The heathen natives belonged mostly to John Asance's tribe, or the Matchadash Indians, from Penetanguishene. They lived on the river Severn, which connects lake Simcoe with the Georgian Bay . . . These were the most northerly Indians who had yet embraced the Gospel."[10]

Peter Jones visited the Cummers several times and stayed at their home. On August 8, 1828, he recorded: "Started for Lake Simcoe; called on Col. Givins, who informed me that he would give the payments and presents to the Lake Simcoe Indians on Wednesday, the 13th inst. Stopped for the night at Brother J. Cumer's, Yonge Street, where I met with Brother J. Beatty, who was much engaged in behalf of the Indians, by forming Missionary Societies."[11] On July 4, 1832, "Left Toronto for Lake Simcoe in the afternoon, and rode to Brother Davis' for the night. In the evening at prayer meeting in Cumer's Chapel."[12]

Presents and Preaching at Holland Landing

In August 1826, Peter Jones, accompanied by five other Mississauga converts from the Credit, preached to about half of the six hundred Indigenous people from Lakes Huron and Simcoe who had gathered at Holland Landing to receive their annual presents.[13] He did so again in 1827.

The 1828 present distribution was described by George Playter: "August 13th [1828] . . . The Christian Indians numbered 390, heathens 65, and those connected with the French people 60; total 515. Four or five days, the Indians had been together, Peter Jones conducting meetings, and assisting the schools."[14] According to Peter Jones,

It took the Commissary all day to divide the goods, which consist of blankets, cloths, calicoes, shirting, hats, guns, rifles, powder, shot, balls, tin and brass kettles, pots, axes, silk handkerchiefs, ribbons, thread, brooches, &c. The amount of their payments is £1,200 per annum, besides the King's presents, which perhaps are nearly as much more; these, with frugality and economy, might be enough to clothe them all the year. In the evening I assembled the Indians and discoursed to them on the depravity of our nature, and the atonement made by Jesus Christ. They were very attentive.

Thursday 14th.—Colonel Givins commenced giving out the goods this morning. The mode of distribution was as follows: The men were seated in rows on the ground by themselves, the women and children in the same order—the Commissary then commenced giving one sort of goods to each individual until the whole of the various articles were disposed of.[15]

The Decision to Convert

The decision of Anishinaabe leaders to convert was usually carefully considered, given their influence over and responsibility to their followers. When they did convert, they played a strong role in converting members of their Nation. "The principal chief was consulted on the subject of Christianity; as also the next senior chief. The former said the Indians could do as they thought best; as for himself, he had not made up his mind on the subject. He would think about it till next spring. The other said he would be glad to be instructed; he would come to the Credit soon, and perhaps leave some of h[is] boys at the school."[16]

In 1827, while visiting Holland Landing, Peter Jones recorded: "The exhorters [lay speakers] . . . said that the number now obedient to the faith was more than one hundred; and that above forty professed a change of heart; also that the opposition of the traders was subsiding, and that only a few wicked French [likely fur traders] were still threatening to beat the Indians. They also informed us that Yellowhead, the great Chief, was much engaged in the good work, and had lately encouraged his people to be firm and faithful in serving the Great Spirit." However, he noted the next day that "a number of French Canadians were present, who were quite uneasy and threatened to beat Yellowhead."[17]

On another occasion, he recorded the conversion process of a medicine man: "During this day some of the Christian Indians came to inform me that a certain pagan powwow had intimated his intention of consulting his *munedoos* or *spirits* that evening, in order to ascertain from them whether it was right for the Indians to forsake the religion of their fathers to take hold of the white man's."[18] The following day, Jones noted the presence of the "conjuror" among the three hundred who came to hear him preach: "all paid good attention."

Jones also recorded the consultative process of another Chief:

> During this day John Asance, the Chief, brought a message to me from the head man of the Pagan Indians, accompanied with a string of wampum, stating that the reason he did not accept of the Christian religion, was, in consequence of a number of his people not being present at that place he could not consult with them and give a decided answer, but that next spring he would be able to let us know what he would do, and thought that he should meet our wishes and become a christian.[19]

Converted Chiefs played a key role in further conversions. Musquakie hosted a Methodist meeting on Chief's Island in Lake Couchiching in 1828 attended by three hundred. At Holland Landing, class leader Thomas Shilling (son of Chief Negenaunaquot / Big Shilling) recited the Ten Commandments in Anishinaabemowin and the congregation repeated his words. Chief William Snake influenced his people to attend the Methodist school built for them at Holland Landing. The Methodists' insistence on monogamy was strengthened when Chief Assance gave up two of his three wives (though he continued to provide for them).[20]

I know Chief Snake used to go meet with Egerton Ryerson. He was a good friend of Chief Snake. They used to go and meet in Toronto . . . And he actually asked Egerton Ryerson to bring Methodism to our people. We'd lost everything and we needed help.

—Kory Snache, Chippewas of Rama[21]

Christian converts were given or took on "Christian" names, and some came to prefer them over their Indigenous names. They also acquired surnames, often their father's name, such as "Chechalk." If a missionary society paid for a young person's education, its members often reserved the right to name the young person. For example, the Young Ladies Society of a Methodist chapel in New York City chose the name "John Summerfield," after an Irish evangelist, for a Mississauga convert. Many converted Anishinaabek received the names of Methodist leaders, for example, Enimokosy became John Wesley. Chief Joseph Sawyer was named after the missionary who baptized him.[22] Because the Indigenous names and Clans of some Christian converts were not recorded and were no longer used, many were lost to later generations.

My aunt married into Rama. She married a Snake. Ryerson Snake. And guess where the name came from? . . . They named a college after him, and now they've taken the name away.

—Albert Big Canoe, Chippewas of Georgina Island[23]

As Jones noted, some fur traders opposed conversions because they feared Indigenous people would stop drinking, become farmers, and no longer collect furs, putting the traders out of business. The Methodists relished tales of Indigenous converts resisting traders. In May 1827, Peter Jones recorded that he was

cast down in spirit, but being informed of the steadfastness of the Indians about Schoogog Lake, was encouraged still to trust in God, and cast all my care on him . . . Two white men went out to traffic with them for furs, taking with them two barrels of whiskey, hoping when they got the Indians into the bush they would be induced to drink, when they would be able to get their furs from them; but in this they were sadly disappointed, for after making one or two of them drunk, the Christian Indians went to them in a body and demanded the liquor, telling them they would not trade with them any more unless they gave it up; so the white men, sooner than lose their trade, gave up the whiskey to the Indians, who immediately took the barrels to the middle of the lake, cut a hole through the ice, tied weights to them and sunk them to the bottom.[24]

Jones recounted how his mother, Tuhbenahneequay, had resisted alcohol traders who were forcing alcohol on a group of women near York:

> A similar circumstance occurred to my mother when returning from Toronto in a canoe, in company with other Indian women. She informed me they were overtaken by a boat-load of white men, who came alongside, and then pulled out a bottle of whisky, asking them to drink. The women told them that they did not drink; but the men were urgent, saying, "Surely a little will do you no harm." The former still refusing, and the latter persisting, my mother held out her hand, saying, "Hand me the bottle." This being done, the white men thought they had prevailed. But, instead of that, my mother poured out the liquid fire on the opposite side of the canoe into the lake, and then returned the bottle empty to their tempters. The white men laughed and applauded, saying they had done perfectly right.[25]

Methodist John Carroll reported that other fur traders welcomed the changes they saw:

> The work of God in the conversion of the Indian tribes of our wilderness meets with no interruptions, neither from the traders, of which we had fears, nor any other description of opposers. We have avoided, as far as possible, all collisions, and in no instance do we interfere in the fur trade. Such is the power of grace, and such the changes on the manners of the Indians, that all seem convinced of its excellency and importance, and not a few of those who it was thought would lose in the trade by the Indians discountenancing the use of spirits, have thought the business more profitable, and on that account and for motives more worthy, have been friendly to the work, and in not a few instances have rendered material service. This is especially so with the traders on Lake Simcoe.[26]

Education and Training

Because Methodists believed in direct engagement with scripture as a core principle, literacy and education were key concerns. At the first meeting of the Canada Auxiliary Missionary Society in 1825, Thomas Davis and Peter Jones addressed the meeting and stressed the importance of establishing Indigenous schools, the need for Indigenous ministers, and the Mississaugas' desire for education.[27] Jones was convinced of the

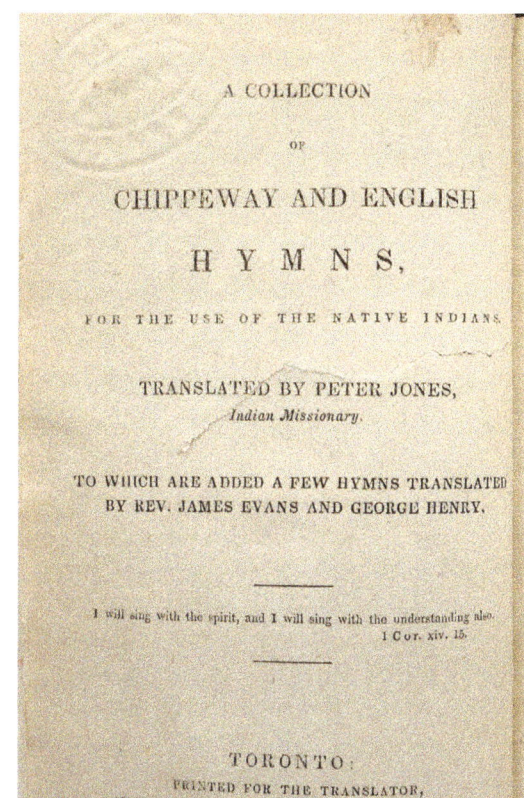

Title pages from *A collection of Chippeway and English hymns for the use of the native Indians*, translated by Peter Jones (Toronto, 1840)

value of Western-style education, which his father Augustus Jones had ensured he received.

Methodist schooling became a key site for advancing the civilizational agenda. The Mississaugas at the Credit River Mission Village were enthusiastic supporters of day school education: "Not surprising in a Christian village, one of the main objectives . . . was to create a literate population that could read and understand the Bible. A second objective . . . was the use of the day school as a first step in training teachers and missionaries to convert other First Nations people to Methodism."[28]

The curriculum was focused on reading, writing, Bible study, and hymn singing. Instruction was in both English and Anishinaabemowin and utilized teaching methods appropriate for Indigenous students.

Whereas in the settler schools, students were taught by the simple method of memorization and recitation, Mississauga students were taught using learning materials such as the abacus, picture cards, maps and globes that helped the students obtain direct experience of the information they were to learn. Also different from the settler schools was the number of subject areas covered during classes. While basic arithmetic and reading were taught in the settler schools, the Mississaugas were taught not only mathematics and literacy, but also geography, astronomy, geometry, English grammar, and science. Settler schools were rare in Upper Canada and, when they did exist, were often staffed with extremely unqualified teachers. The Mississaugas, on the other hand, had schools erected in their villages soon after their conversion to Christianity that were staffed by competent teachers—many of them of First Nations origins. The children of the Mississaugas of the Credit during the existence of the Mission village were far more literate tha[n] the settlers surrounding their village at the Credit.[29]

The Mississaugas' successful education was soon demonstrated to the colonial elite and offered as evidence that Indigenous peoples could, indeed, be "civilized." In 1828, for example, young Credit Mission school children were brought to York, where they sang and demonstrated their skills in reading and writing to the Methodists and at Government House.[30] Young Mississauga scholars "performed civilization" on many occasions, including in New York and elsewhere in the United States.

Since religious education was considered fundamental, Peter Jones, his brother John Jones, and other Methodists with knowledge of the Mississauga language were soon engaged in translating the Gospels, hymns, and other religious materials into Anishinaabemowin.

In 1827, the Episcopal Methodist Missionary Society reported that

> several benevolent persons set up a Sabbath school near New Market, to which the Indians, both children and adults, resorted in large numbers. Some members of the New Market Missionary Society having erected a temporary place for meetings and schools, the preachers of the circuit and the native exhorters from the Credit frequently discoursed to about 100 of the Simcoe Indians, who heard with great attention . . .
>
> By the middle of the present month (September) the Indians here will remove to their hunting grounds, when Mr. W. Law, who has been their teacher for 12 weeks past, will remove his school to an island in Lake Simcoe. Here, 20 miles from any white settlement, he will reside with the aged people and teach the children till the return of the hunters, which will be in the month of May next.[31]

By 1829, there were Methodist day schools at Six Nations, the Credit River, the Narrows and Matchedash in the Lake Simcoe area, and Grape Island and Rice Lake to the east.[32]

Building Relationships and Spreading the Message

Although the Credit Mission was a small community of about two hundred people, twenty-four members became missionaries, schoolteachers, or interpreters, spreading Methodism throughout Upper Canada and beyond. Peter Jones, Credit River converts, and the Mississaugas and Chippewas they converted created new patterns of mobility and communication between Indigenous communities.[33] Mohawk and Mississauga Methodists travelled together on missionary tours and attended meetings and services at Tyendinaga and other Mohawk communities on the north shore of Lake Ontario in addition to those at Grand River. Methodism and the new more sedentary, agricultural lifestyle spread to the Chippewas of Lakes Huron and Simcoe, east to the Mississaugas at Scugog and in the Peterborough area, and west beyond Grand River to the Oneidas, Munsees, Delawares, and Anishinaabek as far west as the St. Clair River.

Relationships also developed between Indigenous Methodists and settler Methodists who supported their aims, including Methodists in the United States and Britain. Converted Mississaugas travelled considerable distances on fundraising tours in the United States. Sometimes, they brought along young scholars to demonstrate their proficiency in hymn singing and Scripture reading. Jones and a few other high-profile Mississauga Methodists conducted missionary fundraising tours in Britain. On many of their journeys, Indigenous Methodists were hosted by settler Methodist families, forming ties of affection and respect. These warm ties often endured over long periods, at least until schisms and competition between the Episcopal and British Wesleyan Methodists in the 1830s and 1840s complicated relationships.

We had people coming to our mission village to go to temperance meetings, of all things. You have Peter Jones going out around in the neighbouring communities preaching. And he's welcome!

—Darin Wybenga, Mississaugas of the Credit[34]

The 1827 annual report of the Episcopal Methodists noted the extraordinary success of the Mississauga Methodists and advocated further education: "Like the first Christians, the converted Indians tell to their brethren the news of their salvation wherever they come, and feeling, as they do, the fulness of love which is in Christ Jesus for the heathen, they speak with a confidence and zeal which cannot fail to produce convictions."[35]

In 1828, the Missionary Society reported that there were ten Indian missions in Upper Canada with 800 members in the society and 1,200 baptisms in five years. Twelve schools were serving

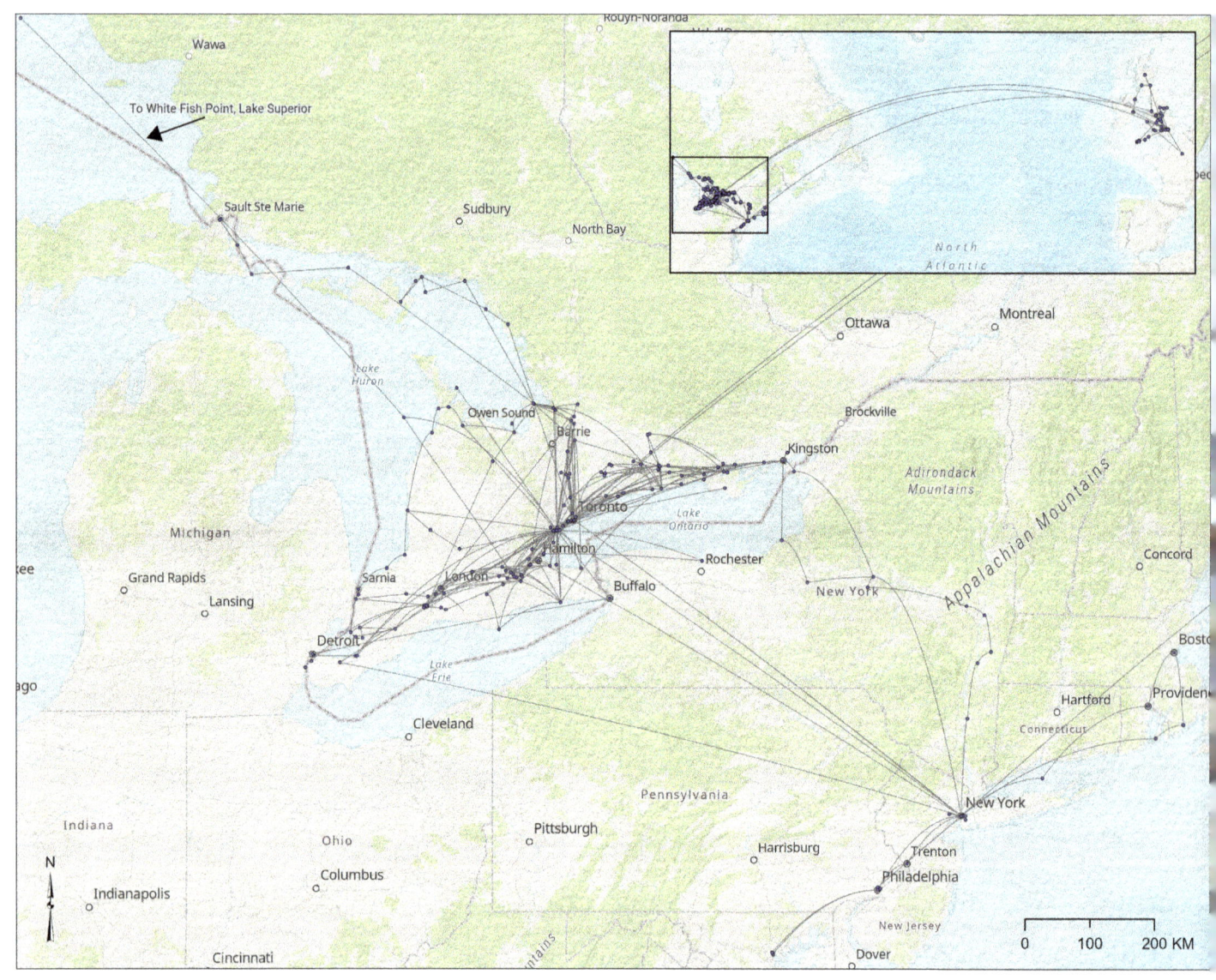

Missionary and fundraising travels of Rev. Peter Jones (Kahkewaquonaby), 1823–37

Elder Albert Big Canoe | Photo by Kim Big Canoe, courtesy of Chippewas of Georgina Island First Nation

"a new race of people."[37] They rejected the goal of "civilization" and did not wish to become like white settlers.

For Haudenosaunee and Anishinaabek, Christian conversions resulted in sometimes bitter divisions within their communities, particularly since colonial leaders preferred to deal with Christianized Indigenous leaders. They elevated those who favoured civilization and Christianity to positions of power, regardless of their legitimacy as leaders in traditional governance structures, and discounted and marginalized those deemed "pagan."

> *The last family that fought the conversion were the Nanigishkungs, the Benson family. They were the pagan Indians, they were called. They wouldn't ever transition over until really, really late.*
>
> —Kory Snache, Chippewas of Rama[38]

about 300 scholars. Peter Jones was formally appointed missionary to the Indian tribes. Indigenous converts made up a significant proportion of Methodists in the region near York. The Missionary Society recorded 576 members along Yonge Street and Whitby, 176 at York, and 400 on the Toronto circuit, as well as 345 Indigenous members at Newmarket and Lake Simcoe and 132 at the Credit Mission.[36]

By no means did all Mississaugas, Anishinaabek, or Haudenosaunee convert to Christianity. Some categorically rejected the lifestyle changes that Peter Jones and other Indigenous Christians advocated. Many rejected Jones' call to become

> *My great-grandfather was a Wesleyan Methodist. That's when the . . . there was no culture here, then. It was all religion. Culture had disappeared.*
>
> —Albert Big Canoe, Chippewas of Rama[39]

Given the much larger population of Haudenosaunee living at Grand River, there was strength in numbers; many saw no need to jettison traditional ways. Nonetheless, the minority

12 | Yonge Street Camp Meetings   155

who did convert became a powerful faction within the community. They were regarded by settlers (and themselves) as "progressives" and played leadership roles in negotiations with colonial officials.

Anishinaabek on Lake Ontario's north shore were far fewer in number than the Haudenosaunee. Swamped by the influx of settlers, they found it increasingly difficult to live a traditional hunting and gathering lifestyle close to York. Those who resisted conversion and civilization tended to move away from settlers and the largely Christian mission villages such as the Credit Mission.

Archival records offer only occasional glimpses of this resistance. At a General Council of the Anishinaabek and Haudenosaunee Confederacy held at the Credit River in 1840, "The council disapproved of the conduct of Kandoching and his people, in not attending this assembly after having been notified, and also of their saying that they supposed they were sent for in order to be talked to about the worthless Christianity."[40]

Inculcating British Gender Roles and Lifeways

Indigenous women who converted to Methodism were expected to learn and conform to European gender roles as wives, mothers, and keepers of Western-style households in single-family log houses with Western-style furniture such as beds, tables, chairs, and cupboards. For people used to a highly mobile lifestyle, this marked a major shift.

Non-Indigenous women played a key role training Indigenous women in Euro-Canadian domestic duties and general comportment. Settler women and women in Britain donated various items such as work bags containing pincushions, needle cases, needles, scissors, thread, bodkins, thimbles, and articles of clothing. Settler women taught Indigenous women in gender-segregated schools.

Mississauga women also drew on their traditional skills to raise funds for missionary work. Peter Jones' journal for 1830 records the efforts of the Dorcas Society at the Credit Mission, run by Miss Barnes, the female teacher: "The Dorcas Society has made about forty pairs of mocasins and a few pairs of gloves; and has sold twenty-one pairs of mocasins and two pairs of gloves for $40; the remainder of the mocasins sister Barnes took with her in order to sell for the Society."[41]

Indigenous girls and women adapted to these changes but also retained traditional skills and knowledge, such as paddling, medicine, and the manufacture of clothing or household items. In 1837, at a present distribution at Manitoulin Island, Peter Jones recorded that "there was a great canoe race of women of the different nations present."[42]

The resocialization of Indigenous women was also furthered through intermarriage. For example, Peter Jones' British wife, Eliza Field, played a major role in mentoring girls and women at the Credit Mission.

13

The Credit Mission

In 1826, the Mississaugas of the Credit moved back to the Credit River to live in the model village established for them by the government with the band's annuity funds—the fulfillment of an 1820 treaty promise. In 1827, the annual report of the Episcopal Methodist Church presented a glowing portrait of the "progress" of civilization at the Credit Mission:

> The whole community consists of 260 souls—the society of 120 [church members], is formed into six classes, with as many leaders. Three stewards have the management of their funds for religious purposes, and provide for the communion, and several exhorters frequently visit the neighbouring tribes, from 50 to 100 miles around them. Of those who belong to this body, two families only remain in a wandering state, several families having embraced religion during the past year. In the month of October they were put in possession of the houses erected by the government; but as 20 houses were insufficient to accommodate 40 families, the Indians are themselves fitting up several more. To these was added last fall, a house for meetings and schools . . . By the efforts of the Missionary (Mr. Ryerson), the building was erected, and the expense, £75 ($300) has been defrayed by the liberality of the inhabitants in the neighbouring towns. Mr. Jones's School during the year, has averaged 32; of these, 24 read in the testament, and English reader, and ten are writing. A number of these children possess minds of more than ordinary capacity for improvement, and being pious, the society may hope that, at no very distant period, the Saviour will employ them as messengers of mercy to other tribes of their pagan brethren. Indeed more than 20 of these children are now employed in the pleasing task of instructing their parents, for they are often heard reading in the testament the words of our Saviour.[1]

The report noted that "in the spring of this year, the Indians, out of their funds in the hands of the Government, purchased two yokes of oxen, one wagon, three ploughs, chains, harrow-teeth, hoes and other implements of husbandry, to commence the new business of agriculture. A few friends from York and Yonge street sent them a good Scotch plough, to break up the soil."[2]

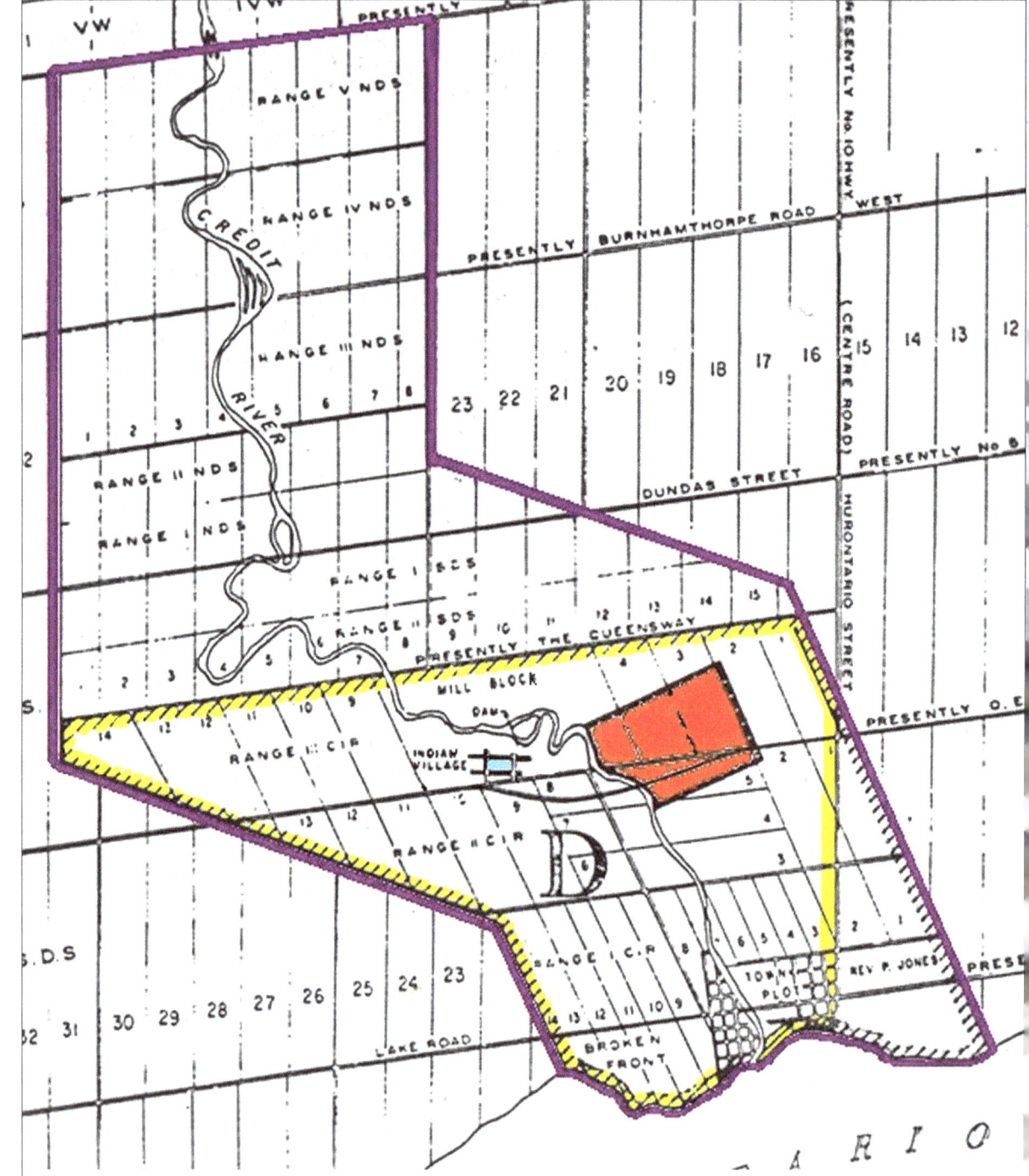

Credit Mission and land cessions on the Credit River. The area outlined in purple is the one-mile tract on either side of the Credit River reserved by the Mississaugas in Treaty 13A, signed in 1805. The area outlined in yellow is part of the area ceded in 1820 in Treaty 22. The red area is the two-hundred-acre reserve that was the only unceded land remaining after Treaty 23 was signed at the same time as Treaty 22. The blue area is the site of the Credit Mission Village (1826–47) | Courtesy of Heritage Mississauga

It was quite a source of contention when we first moved into the Credit River Mission Village. How do we hold land, for example? Do we hold this mission village in common, with no private ownership? So that was a big thing. Eventually, people decided, okay, we still hold land like the old ways. Everybody shares the land. The land belongs to everybody. We are attached to this land communally.

—Darin Wybenga, Mississaugas of the Credit.[3]

In 1828, the government ordered Indian agent James Givins to take a census of the Credit Mission settlement after the harvest. Note the high number of deaths, which still exceeded the number of births.

Men 64	Land cultivated 61 acres	Cows 27
Women 74	Wheat 65 bushels	Oxen 18
Children 88	Oats 23 bushels	Horses 11
Families 47	Indian corn 1,045 bushels	Hogs 122
Houses 30	Onions 9 bushels	Wagon 1
Births (year) 17	Beets and carrots 16 bushels	Ploughs 4
Marriages 2	Cabbages 670	Harrows 1
Deaths 19	Cartloads pumpkins 30	
Baptisms 40		
Members of church 132.[4]		

The Mississaugas received £470 annually from the government for lands surrendered, "and the King's presents were worth nearly as much more. Added to this, their hunting, fishing, manufacturing, the natives were in a comfortable

Sketch of John Jones' house at the Credit Village, from Egerton Ryerson's *The Story of My Life*

condition."[5] In fact, their living conditions compared favourably with many settlers.

In March 1828, the Methodist missionary James Magrath visited the Credit Mission. He reported that John Jones taught thirty-five boys while a female schoolteacher taught thirty-six girls. Both were taught reading, writing, arithmetic, and religion, but the Mississaugas wanted tradespeople at the village to instruct the boys. "The girls were also taught to sew and knit, and wanted to own spinning wheels. Miss Sillick said that the Governor ordered a supply of Bible and Testaments."[6]

Magrath inventoried 206 tilled acres and "a work-house for all Trades, a sawmill and a store for the merchants on the River." The villagers also manufactured baskets, moccasins, and gloves—"best gloves of deer skin, 7s. 6d. a pair."[7]

The village's economic success was so great that the band's missionary, Benjamin Slight, wrote in 1837: "A great proportion of the peasantry of even happy old England, might envy many in this village."[8] The village was comparable to the kind that The Village at Black Creek represents.

Stories of the Mississaugas' transformation into model Christian farmers appeared in the *Christian Guardian* (founded in York in 1829) and other Methodist newspapers and circulated throughout North America and Britain. They were regarded as the vanguard of Indigenous "civilization," countering the argument that Indigenous peoples were unredeemable "savages" doomed to extinction.[9]

Mission Governance

Elected Chief in 1829, Peter Jones created a legal code for the Credit Mississaugas. Approved by Council in 1830, it stipulated that "according to the old customs of our nation, the Chiefs shall be chosen by a majority of our people, and shall retain their office during life." The Head Chief was given "supreme authority" but had to govern according to Council-approved laws. A General Council, conducted according to our old customs and composed of at least two-thirds of households, would be held every year. New laws would be passed by majority vote. A vote of two-thirds would be required to choose a new Chief or Chiefs and to depose a Chief "for great offences, gross immorality, or notorious incapacity." Occasional Councils of "at least one chief and ten or more householders" could meet regarding "general improvement and welfare," including offences against timber use, residence, and lands, which were all held in common.[10]

By replacing consensus-based decision-making with majoritarian democracy, Jones' code diverged from the historical practice of Anishinaabe law and governance. But there were significant continuities. It is unclear whether Clan-based governance continued under the new code, but families remained central. Smaller Councils were used for day-to-day decision-making while General Councils (which required the presence of most families) made larger decisions about leadership and law. Land, timber, and the fishery continued to be held in common. The Council allocated land to families and approved its exchange or sale.[11] Most significantly, decision-making authority was derived from the community and its jurisdiction was respected by colonial governments. Between 1830 and 1847, the Mississaugas maintained self-government through their legal code.[12]

Because they served as intermediaries with white society, Methodist leaders were named Chiefs or assumed leadership roles in most communities. Peter Jones was made a Chief of the Credit band in 1829; his uncle Nawahjekezhegwabe (Joseph Sawyer) was elected Head Chief after the death of James Ajetance that same year.

Mississauga Literacy and Political Advocacy

The spread of literacy and the biculturalism of Peter Jones and a few others gave the Mississaugas powerful voices to call out government and settler mistreatment. Jones stated:

> Col. Givins issued our payments and presents. On reading the receipt of the land payments presented for the Chiefs to sign, I discovered a discrepancy between the amount of the original agreement and the amount of goods now received. The original agreement stated that the Credit Indians were to be paid for lands ceded to the Crown, the annual sum of £522 10s. currency, in perpetuity. Whereas the amount of goods now paid to the Indians, was £472 10s. Thus cutting of L£50. I directed the attention of the Inspecting Officer to the same, and asked him why this was done. He immediately called Col. Givins to explain to us why this reduction had been made. He replied that he was not at liberty to explain.[13]

In numerous letters and petitions, the Mississaugas affirmed their fishing rights and title to their land. For example, an 1829 petition to Sir John Colborne stated the Mississaugas had received the first Europeans as friends and granted them land to live on but were now being abused by their neighbours, who were destroying their fishery and obstructing their efforts to farm and be self-sufficient. The petition succinctly related their experience with treaties since the arrival of the British:

Father,

Your children who now petition you are a remnant of the great nations who owned and inhabited the country in which you now live and make laws; the ground on which you and your children stand covers the bones of our fathers for many generations . . . But the white man made us sick and drunken, and as they increased we grew less and less, till we are now very small. We sold a great deal of land to our great father, the King, for very little, and we became poorer and poorer. We reserved all the hunting and fishing ground, but the white men soon grew so many that they took all . . . We reserved one mile on each side of the Credit, where we now live. About four years ago, the Great Spirit sent to us good men with the Great Word, the Gospel of our Saviour, Jesus Christ, and we became a new people; we have thrown away our sins; we live in houses in a Village where we worship the Great Spirit, and learn his word and keep his Sabbaths; our children and young men learn to read, and many of our people from a distance have joined us. We now want the fish in our River, that we may keep our children at home to go to School, and not to go many miles back to hunt for provisions. We also catch Salmon, and sell them very cheap to industrious white men, who bring us flour, and other provisions, and cattle; and they say it is much better than to fish themselves. But now, Father, we will tell you how wicked white men have used us—These are almost all lazy drunken white men, who will not work. They come in the Fall and Spring, and encamp for many weeks close by our Village—they burn and destroy our fences and boards in the night—they watch the Salmon, and take them as fast as they can be come up—they swear and get drunk, and give a very bad example to our young people, and try to persuade them to be wicked like themselves . . . Others go to the mouth of the River and catch all the salmon—they put the offals of Salmon in the mouths of the River in the Lake; and often in the dark they set gillnets in the River, and stop all the fish. by these means we are much injured, and our children are deprived of bread.

Now, Father, once all the fish in those Rivers and those Lakes, all the deer in these woods, were ours; but your red Children only ask you to cause laws to be made to keep these bad men away from our fishery at the River Credit . . . and to punish those who attempt to fish here. We will not fish on Saturday night, Sunday night, and Sunday, but will let the fish pass up to our white brothers up the River.[14]

Legislation to protect the Mississauga fishery followed in 1829 but was only in effect until 1834.[15]

Oominewahjeween (Pleasant stream) / William Herkimer | By Arvilla Louise Thorpe, reproduced in Smith, *Sacred Feathers*

Resistance—Bluejay on the Humber and the Herkimer Faction

After enthusiastic conversions in the 1820s and early 1830s, some Anishinaabek became disillusioned with Methodism. They switched to other Christian faiths or went back to a more traditional lifestyle and worldview. Some traditionalists left the church but remained at the Credit Village. Blue Jay, an early convert in 1825, rejected

Research committee member Darin Wybenga, Traditional Knowledge and land use coordinator, Mississaugas of the Credit | Courtesy Mississaugas of the Credit First Nation

Christianity for reasons unknown and left the mission with a group of followers. Jones called them "the wicked Indians on the Humber" because they consumed alcohol.[16]

A more serious challenge to the changes initiated by Jones was a faction led by Lawrence and William Herkimer that included the Johnsons, Keshegoos, and Tobecos, all Christians and church members of mixed heritage.[17] In the 1830s, they challenged Jones' leadership and resisted his rejection of traditional Anishinaabe culture, particularly his insistence on European-style "family government" and physically disciplining children to "have them in complete subjection." Traditionally, no one had the right to command another, even a child. The Herkimers and their followers insisted that all Credit lands remain communal, while Peter and John Jones sought (and eventually received) individual landholdings.[18]

> *My family goes back to the very founding of the Credit Mission Village and maybe even a little bit before that. My fourth great-grandfather was Lawrence Herkimer, son of the fur trader Lawrence Herkimer, born at Rice Lake. And he moved to New Credit, well not New Credit, you know, the old Credit.*
>
> —Darin Wybenga, Mississaugas of the Credit[19]

The Jones faction tried to control behaviour to ensure conformity to Methodist discipline. For example, they passed a resolution "that James Tobeco be required to put away his fiddle."[20] But the Herkimer faction persisted in challenging Jones. From the available evidence, it appears that about one-third of the band remained traditionalists, about half supported the Jones brothers and their radical reforms, and roughly one-sixth were moderates such as the Herkimers who accepted some changes but resisted others.[21]

Views of Peter Jones and the civilizational agenda remain divided. As a recent Mississaugas of the Credit publication puts it:

> He is often vilified as a leader who "sold out" his people's culture and traditions in favour of a non-indigenous world and

life view. Others view Jones as a person striving to help his people cope, survive, and even prosper amidst the flood of incoming settlers to Upper Canada . . . It is somewhat ironic, that Peter Jones, the agent of transition, would help to preserve in the *History of the Ojebway* some of the cultural history that was lost.[22]

Maybe the government was successful in some things, but I think one thing they weren't as successful at was to get Peter Jones to assimilate, because it backfired . . . I can argue the good and the bad. But the thing was survival at that time. You had to do what you had to do to survive as a people and make those changes. You give and you take, and you try to gain back what . . . you can.

—Margaret Sault, Mississaugas of the Credit[23]

14

The Coldwater and the Narrows Settlement

The Coldwater Tract, that was the first reserve experiment where we were placed into a boundary.

—Vicki Snache, Chippewas of Rama[1]

Thirty-five years after he'd accompanied Governor Simcoe on his trip up the Toronto Carrying-Place Trail to Lake Simcoe and Matchedash Bay, Major General Henry C. Darling, military secretary to the colonial governor general and superintendent of Indian Affairs, authored the first formal inquiry into Indigenous welfare.[2] The 1828 Darling report reflected a liberal humanitarianism gaining influence in Britain and America. It recognized at least some of the harms caused by colonialism and the "white man's burden"—a moral if paternalistic responsibility to "improve" the condition of Indigenous peoples.

Impressed by the Credit River Mississaugas' transformation, Darling recommended a general policy of assimilation. As a first step towards social integration, all Indigenous peoples in Upper Canada should be congregated on temporary reserves (protected environments away from the worst influences of Western culture) to be educated, converted to Christianity, and taught to farm. This "civilization" policy would also benefit the British by reducing the need for presents or government support and freeing up more land.[3]

Darling recorded that 550 Anishinaabek occupied the region of Lake Simcoe, Holland River, and greater York.[4] Joseph Snake was identified as Chief of those whose territories covered Snake, Fox, and Georgina Islands in Lake Simcoe, the Holland River, and lands to the south (today known as Chippewas of Georgina Island).

Chippewa family traditional hunting territories, as described to the Williams Treaty commissioners, 1923, by United Indian Councils of Mississauga, Chippewa, and Potawatomi First Nations

Our family name, Snache, comes from ginebigowinini, which in Anishinaabe means "he is who is a snake" or "he can be a snake." Some people would say "snake man."

So the majority of the Snaches can trace their line back to their one person, within our community. So, from Georgina, we have Snake Island in Lake Simcoe, and that's named after Chief Joseph Snake. He was the Chief or the Ogimaa. He was the speaker and the representative of that people. So his Clan was a spokesperson for that community, for external business. So, in a Western way, that's their idea of a Chief. He has a big lengthy history.

—Kory Snache, Chippewas of Rama[5]

Musquakie / William Yellowhead led those whose territories bordered Lake Simcoe, including the Narrows/Mnjikaning (known today as Chippewas of Rama), and also served as Ogimaa or Head Chief of all the Chippewas of Lakes Huron and Simcoe. John Assance was Chief of the Chippewas to the west of Lake Simcoe along the Severn and Coldwater Rivers to Matchedash Bay (known today as the Chippewas of Beausoleil First Nation at Christian Island in Georgian Bay). The three Chippewa bands hunted over a wide territory and functioned independently but came together seasonally for Tribal Councils. According to Darling, Musquakie's people had expressed a desire to "adopt the habits of civilized life."

In 1830, the new lieutenant-governor, John Colborne, formally adopted the policy of civilization, which appeared to offer a more humane alternative to the American policy, articulated in the 1830 US Indian Removal Act, of forced "removal." (The act legalized the deportation of Indigenous peoples from their homelands in the eastern United States to the territories of other Indigenous Nations west of the Mississippi.) The Mississaugas of the Credit's rapid transformation into Christian farmers might have helped the Indigenous Nations of Upper Canada avoid a similar fate. Colborne had initially focused on slashing the Indian Department's budget but changed his mind after visiting the mission. That same year, Britain transferred the Indian Department from military to civilian control. The transfer signalled the end of Britain's need for military alliances and its intention to make Indigenous peoples fully subject to the colonial government.

The civilization policy marked the beginning of Canada's reserve system. Indian agents or superintendents would oversee the development of new settlements and provide livestock and agricultural implements, which would, in time, replace annual presents. British Wesleyan Methodists and Anglicans would serve as resident missionaries, replacing the Episcopal Methodists who had been responsible for the initial conversions. There would be two new model settlements: one at Sarnia and the other at Coldwater and the Narrows for the Chippewas, many of whom had already converted.

The Coldwater and the Narrows settlement would be administered by Superintendent Thomas Gummersall (T.G.) Anderson, a fur trader in the Upper Mississippi Valley who served as

William Sawyer, portrait of Elizabeth Ann (Betsy) Anderson, wife of Thomas Gummerall Anderson, 1854 | Courtesy of Margot Maddison-MacFadyen and the Huronia Museum

William Sawyer, *Thomas Gummersall Anderson*, 1854 | Courtesy of Margot Maddison-MacFadyen and the Huronia Museum

a clerk and interpreter at Drummond Island in Lake Huron before it was relinquished to the Americans. Like many Indian Department employees, he was married to a woman of mixed heritage. Elizabeth Anderson's grandmother was noted Anishinaabe fur trader Elizabeth Mitchell of Michilimackinac.[6]

Earlier Land Cessions

How and when the Coldwater and Narrows Reserves were acquired isn't clear. Britain claimed that it had purchased them in 1785 through the so-called Collin's Purchase. But Britain most likely acquired the Matchedash Tract through a cession in 1787–88. Discussions likely began at the Bay of Quinte, when presents were distributed and some kind of agreement for lands at Toronto was made or at least discussed.[7] "Kenease & his Band or Party" of Chippewas from Lake Simcoe, along with seven other Nations or parties, including the Mississaugas of the Credit, attended this Council.[8] A 1788 document describes the tract as "beginning at Toronto & running on each side of the Communication to Lake Huron."[9] But the only surviving record of the 1787 Council is a copy of the infamous "blank deed," which was never properly filled out or signed.

In 1798, the cession of Penetanguishene Harbour was finalized. During negotiations, the Anishinaabek apparently confirmed that the adjacent Matchedash Tract had been surrendered, although its boundaries and the terms were not clarified.[10] In 1836, James Givins, chief superintendent of Indian affairs, conducted an inquiry and concluded that only the cession's date was uncertain. However, in 1847–48, in a memorial to Governor General Elgin, the "Lake Huron and Simcoe Tribe of Indians residing at Snake Island, Rama and Beausoleil Island," claimed the Matchedash Tract "had never been ceded to the Crown."[11] Other claims to all or portions of the tract were made in 1859 and the early 1900s. The entire Matchedash Tract was included in the Williams Treaty of 1923.

Certainly, after the Penetanguishene Purchase of 1798 (Treaty 5), the British believed they had title to the Matchedash Tract and established a rough military road along the ancient Indigenous portage route running from Lake Simcoe to Matchedash Bay. This route, later known as the Coldwater Road (Highway 12), was used by the British to transport goods and troops to Georgian Bay between 1795 and 1812. By 1815, its military use had decreased. It became the main route for settlers granted lots along it or in the vicinity.[12]

Establishing the Reserve

In 1828, after virtually all their lands had been ceded through Treaty 16 in 1815 and Treaty 18 in 1818, the Chippewas were promised a reserve on the Matchedash Tract, where they would be free from settler interference. In 1830, Lieutenant-Governor Colborne approved the creation of the 9,800-acre (3,966-hectare) Coldwater-Narrows Reserve between Coldwater near Matchedash Bay in the west and Mnjikaning (the Narrows at Orillia) in the east. The villages at either end were linked by a 22.5-kilometre (14-mile) road that followed the portage route and a mile on each side of the road. Five to six hundred Chippewas and other Anishinaabek, including the Potagunasees / Bootaaganasiig who had recently arrived in Upper Canada from Drummond Island, were promised houses, farms, and religious instruction.[13] The long, narrow reserve was not large enough to provide significant opportunities for hunting.

> *They settled in Coldwater. Before that, though, they hunted everywhere. They travelled in family groups. They'd only come together, I think, in the winter, for an encampment. They hunted and fished. And they picked berries. They lived on a lot of berries back then.*
>
> —Albert Big Canoe, Chippewas of Georgina Island[14]

The Coldwater and the Narrows Reserve (1830–36) and present-day First Nations

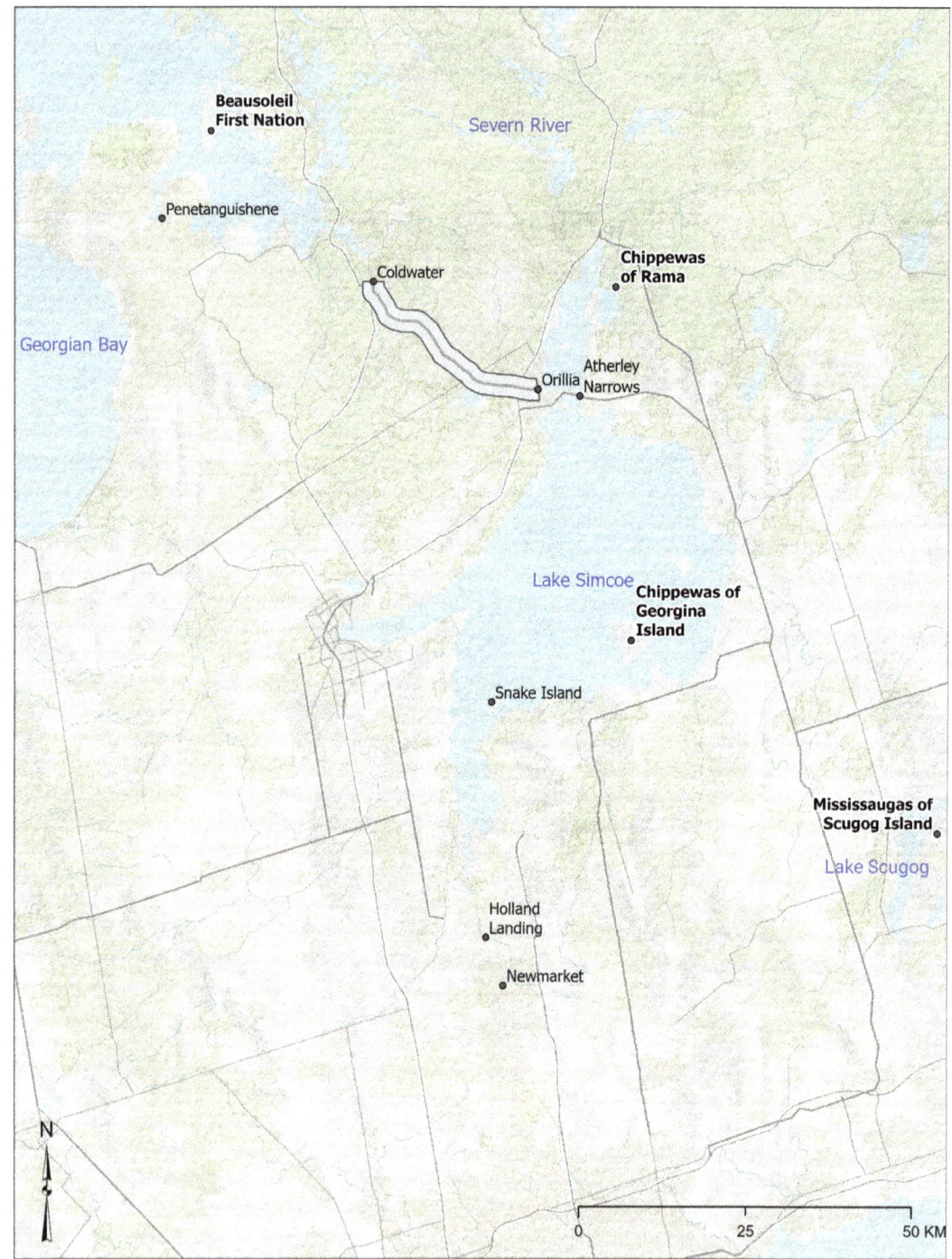

Sir Henry Byam Martin, *The Settlement of Coldwater,* 1832 | Library and Archives Canada, C-115022

Titus Hibbert Ware, *Shanty on the Coldwater Road, Orillia Township, Ontario*, 1844 | Toronto Public Library, PICTURES-R-1622

The initial plan was to survey the reserve into single-family farms strung out along the Coldwater Road, in the same manner as Yonge Street. But the road needed to be improved. In 1830, men from all three bands (plus the Potagunasees) received tools, oxen, and rations to clear and widen the road. Anderson directed that hay for oxen and horses be purchased from Mr. Roe of Newmarket. Eli Beman, son of Elisha Beman, provided axes, blacksmithing tools, and other necessities.[15]

From the beginning, the Chiefs had their own ideas about how the settlement should be organized. In July 1830, Chief Musquakie spoke out about the workers hired to build houses:

> I never heard our Father [the lieutenant-governor] say that the work men who were to make our Houses would be continually drunk. I heard from my father that we should never see that bad liquid, which rendered us so miserable in times past, that it would be kept out of our sight. I heard my father say, children, come and tell me if any person, no matter whom, takes any of that bad liquid into the Village that is about to be built for you and you may depend upon it that I will send them away. Ever since I was at the other side (meaning Penetanguishene) the workmen at this place have been drunk almost every day and particularly on Sundays. I wish to know by what authority this is done and who is the cause of it.
>
> I also ask my father to have our Village built like His Village at York vizt. the building in a line with streets as at York that we may see the people passing to and fro.[16]

Musquakie rejected the original plan to settle most of his people in houses stretched along the Coldwater Road. He asked that they be settled at the Narrows townsite with farmland located along the road. Seven of his young men and perhaps some from Snake's people could settle the portage road: "As for us old men, we intend to settle at the village you are building for us, & end our days there, & our children will be kept at school."[17] Given that fishing at the Narrows had long provided a reliable source of food, they wished to be near their fisheries rather than inland.

Anderson agreed that the village site was more conducive to children attending school, and he shared Musquakie's concerns about the dangers of white people and alcohol. He recommended that no more land should be granted to white settlers close to the reserve and that settler-owned land should be purchased by the government (the latter was not approved by his superiors).[18] Colborne directed that houses be built for the Chippewas on detached lots and reported that "they are now clearing ground sufficient to establish farms at each station for their immediate support, from which they will be supplied while they are bringing into cultivation their individual lots marked out for their residence."[19]

Of the two villages, Coldwater was intended for the Chippewas under Chief Assance, along with the Potagunasees / Bootaaganasiig. The village at the Narrows was for the followers of Musquakie and Snake. Oxen were purchased and crops planted, Anderson reported, and the department employed three labourers, a blacksmith, a surgeon, a farming instructor, and two schoolteachers.[20] But by early 1831, the Indian Department had spent 3,000 pounds on the settlement and was under pressure to cut costs. Anderson recommended reducing the number of government staff and no longer paying the Chippewas for making repairs to the road or for clearing land for their houses.[21]

Constructing houses was slow and more expensive than estimated. By 1832, the original contractor had received two-thirds of his pay but had only completed one-quarter of the work. He was fired. The next contractor, Eli Beman, did some work but refused to do the rest for the remaining amount and quit.[22] In early 1832, Anderson forwarded a list of buildings that still needed to be completed. The list included a building for teaching trades to the boys and girls, a blacksmith's forge for the same purpose, a large kitchen and dining room, a gristmill, a sawmill at Coldwater to replace another more distant one on the Severn, a house for the sick, a wash house, a large barn, and a sawmill and barn at the Narrows. By "employing a couple of Carpenters with the Boys who are to be taught the trade, many of them would be put up [at] a cheap rate."

Instruction in trades was a key part of the civilization plan. Anderson outlined the need to sow flax, provide spinning wheels, and employ a woman to teach the girls to spin. Buying raw wool would enable the girls to learn to make socks and cloth. Some of the boys should be supplied with leather and taught by a shoemaker to make shoes while others work in the blacksmith's forge. The making of pottery from local clay was also a possibility. An "active and practical farmer" was needed at the Narrows. Anderson concluded: "I may also observe that the affairs of the Establishment [appear] to have taken such a turn as in all human probability to ensure success."[23]

But the houses were not finished until 1833, and they were paid out of the First Nations' annuity funds because the government had refused to pay for their completion.[24] Over the next few years, the bands largely financed the reserve's development themselves.

Settler Intrusion and the Coldwater Road

They'd been promised a reserve where "no white man would be allowed to set foot."[25] But the Coldwater Road continued to be the main transportation route for settlers moving into the northwestern region of Upper Canada. Given that the reserve extended only one mile on either side of it, the road exerted an enormous influence on the Anishinaabek. Waystations for settlers were soon opened near the two villages, and fur traders, including Andrew Borland, operated nearby.[26] Band members went into debt to the traders while some settlers traded alcohol, trespassed on reserve land, and stole Chippewa crops.[27]

Alcohol "to a degree now unimaginable . . . saturated almost all arenas of work and leisure" among European settlers at this time. In the 1800s, overconsumption became an increasingly widespread problem.[28] For settlers, "Rum was cheap and often helped to relieve the anxiety of being isolated in a hostile environment."[29]

With so many settlers using the road, Colborne saw transporting settlers as another opportunity for the Anishinaabek to become self-sufficient.

> His Excellency thinks that all persons should be allowed to pass the new road with their own Horses, Carts, and Waggons, and baggage, but that the Indians should have a convenient establishment of Carts and Horses, formed at each end of the new Road, and under proper regulations, with a Batteaux stationed at Coldwater. And thus it is hoped the conveyance of Goods, will entirely fall into their hands, and His Excellency leaves it to your to fix a moderate price for the transport of baggage across the new road and to Pentanguishene.[30]

Anderson tried to interest the Chippewas and claimed they "expressed much satisfaction and promised to be very attentive to the business," but it didn't happen. Within two years, the Narrows' farming instructor, Gerald Alley, was operating a stagecoach.[31]

Despite promises that only band members would live on the reserve, Alley and Lewis, the first house builder, were given plots of land, intended to be temporary. Other white men acquired lots for speculative purposes.

> Mr. Alley informs that Mr. Mitchell has purchased from Borland & Roe 60 Acres of Land in the Vicinity of the Village, that several other Lots have been selected

about the Village, and that Mr. Lewis has purchased 200 Acres from the Land Company, near the little lake, three or four Miles from the Narrows. This kind of speculation, as far as the traders are concerned, can only be prevented I believe, by advancing to the Indians on account of their annuity a sum sufficient to keep a shop and thereby obtain their supplies at a cheaper rate than they can purchase them elsewhere."[32]

To solve the trader problem, officials proposed that the Chippewas should run their own store to become more self-sufficient and less in need of costly presents. Givins wrote to Anderson: "The Lieut. Governor approves of your plan for making the Indians storekeepers, and perhaps Yellow Head and the other Chief might be induced to consent to allow the stores required for their Shops to be purchased out of the land Payments." Colborne thought "a general Depot might be established at the Narrows for the reception of Furs." The Indian Department could purchase the furs at a higher price than the Chippewas could obtain from traders. If they could be sold in York or Montreal for more than the price paid, the balance could go to the Chippewas. "This plan would perhaps prevent Traders from settling among them. The Traders cannot be prevented from settling among the Indians by forcible means; But the property of Borland and [Roe] is in the hands of their Creditors."[33]

Anderson also suggested that the Chippewas start an inn for travellers. He was finding "the burthen of Gentleman travellers too heavy an expence for me to bear" since they stopped at his house along the way. He believed it would be "a convenience to the Traveller," one that would "push the Indians forward in every possible way to adopt the customs of whites . . . Of course no spirituous liquors would be allowed and merely eatables and bed kept by them, which they would find the means of providing without taxing their Land payments."[34]

Anderson instructed Givins to help them establish "a shop on their own account, and to make arrangements for the liquidation of their debts with the Trader."[35] If they had their own store and sold the goods at a low price, it would "render it unprofitable for traders to settle near their villages. At the same time a House of Entertainment [an inn] at said village should be Established by them, and some person appointed for a time to direct them in the management of it." Colborne approved of establishing a shop and inn at each village and proposed that the debts to the traders be paid in instalments (including Musquakie's debt to Philemon Squires, who along with Borland had threatened to beat Chief Snake if he became a Christian) once they secured John Assance's consent.[36]

Neither of these enterprises was established—perhaps because the Anishinaabek's annuity payments were already stretched, given their significant debts. Gerald Alley, responsible for advancing these ventures on the Chippewas' behalf, soon appropriated them. Alley was "a corrupt drunkard, little liked by his fellow government workers, who the Natives eventually said didn't know how to farm and had nothing

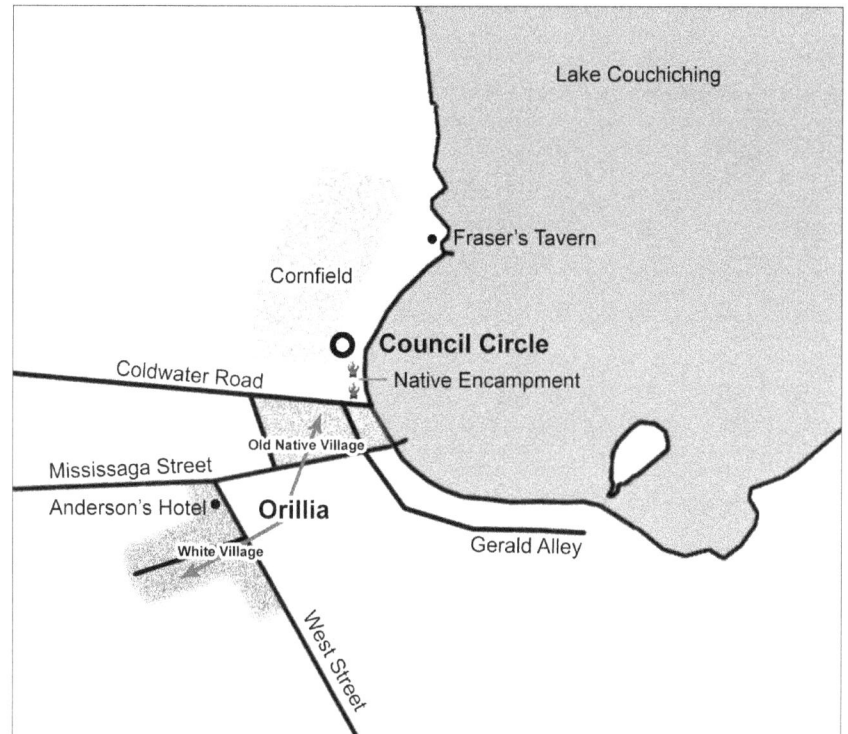

Chippewa and settler villages at Orillia, 1836

to teach them."[37] They complained that he "often smelled like a keg of whiskey."[38] As Anderson's man at the Narrows, Alley was tasked with running the supply depot, but he overcharged the Chippewas. He received permission to open a tavern on a dry reserve. Although the Chippewas complained about him and the Methodists forwarded a report to their mission conference outlining their complaints, Alley complained to the lieutenant-governor that the missionaries were encouraging disrespect to government authority.[39] He resigned from his position as farm instructor in 1832 but remained on-site.

In 1834, Anderson wrote Givins about the need for a "well-conducted" inn at the Narrows, now to be built and maintained by Alley: "There are two Inns at Newtown [the adjacent white village] & one other adjoining the South side of the reserve but they are disgraceful & unfit for genteel travellers to stop at."[40] Anderson thought a two-storey house could be built for 600 or 700 pounds and command a rent that would increase over time: "If the Indians themselves could afford to build it, it would be funding their money to advantage. If not, the site might probably be leased until the Indians could afford to pay for the Buildings, or . . . persons would be met with who would make the outlay provided they received, for a certain period, the usual interest for that outlay."[41]

The Chippewas never had enough money to take control of the enterprise. By 1834, Alley had also been given a land grant of 100 acres adjacent to the Coldwater Road despite the reserve supposedly extending a mile on either side. Alley then sold town lots to build a settler village 200 metres from the Chippewa village.[42]

Indigenous Milling

The proposed saw- and gristmills also drained the Chippewas' finances. Given the emphasis on land clearing and building houses, they needed a sawmill, but for the first years, they took timber to a mill on the Severn.

The government had planned to lend the Chippewas the money to build the mill. Once operational, the thinking went, the mills would pay for themselves by running twenty-four hours a day, milling for settlers and reserve residents. But in July 1832, Givins asserted that "the funds of the Department will not admit this season of any further advance" for the mill. The government would halt any further loans, despite proposing the initiative: "As the Mill is intended for the benefit of the Indians, and is an object of importance to them, if the Chiefs will appropriate £200 from their Land Payments, His Excellency will feel disposed to sanction its being applied to the Completion of the Mill."[43]

Chief Assance consented to the requisition of 200 pounds from his band's share of annuity payments. Beset by various difficulties, the mill finally opened in April 1833. By that time, the need for a gristmill was even more pressing. The reserve had produced between 300 and 500 bushels of wheat over the summer, and the Chippewas and settlers would have more to grind the coming year.[44] The Chippewas were pressed to use their annuity funds, and in 1833, the Chiefs consented to two more requisitions to cover the cost of construction. This was a significant drain since their total annuities amounted to only 1,200 pounds a year and they were also being pressed to pay off their debts to traders.

The government failed to discuss payment options transparently with the Chippewas. Anderson wrote: "On the subject I have not considered it necessary to consult the Indians at present, they being incapable of judging for themselves, they should and must submit to His Excellency's decision on the subject who is in fact their Guardian."[45] Thus, while the mill was said to be intended for the Chippewas' benefit, their annuities effectively subsidized government initiatives to encourage settlement.

The government rationalized its decision to end government support by arguing that it didn't want to stoke the jealousy of other Indigenous communities. The Royal Engineer, George Philpotts, wrote to Anderson: "[His Excellency] desires me to add that it is totally out of his power, with justice to the Indians in other parts of the Province, to advance more money for the Establishment at Coldwater, & therefore you will see that unless the Indians consent to complete the Mill in the manner proposed above, nothing more is likely to be done towards it."[46]

The Chippewas were demoralized by this drain on their finances. Assance stated at a Council: "Father if you give us what you have promised us our young Men will be very glad and will work hard. Father when you purchased our Lands you promised us a great many hundred Dollars a year, but we never see any money—there is a Mill now building and if we could but see the Money on the Table we should be satisfied . . . Father when shall we see the profits arising from the Mill, as yet we have not seen a copper."[47]

Although annuities were used to fund the mill, progress was slow. Andrew Borland's associate Jacob Gill carried out much of the building, under Anderson's supervision.[48] Finally, on May 6, 1834, Anderson reported: "About 600 Bushel of Grain has been ground at the mill the Toll of which has been divided amongst the proprietors [the Anishinaabek] and has supplied them with provisions to enable them to go on more cheerfully than usual with their spring farming."[49] The gristmill's costs totalled £1,591.13, paid from First Nations annuities. A farmer with sawmill experience was hired to provide instruction. As the sawmill and gristmill at Coldwater came into operation, plans were made to construct another sawmill at the Narrows—to be paid for in the same way.[50]

15

"Progress," Setbacks, and Strategies for Self-Sufficiency

So-called progress at Coldwater and the Narrows was decidedly uneven. Some families refused to live in log cabins and built wigwams instead. Half the residents gave up alcohol, but others, encouraged by alcohol traders, used alcohol excessively.[1] The school was attended sporadically as parents took their children out on the land for weeks at a time to learn traditional skills and engage in fishing, hunting and gathering, and syrup making. The Methodist Chippewas sometimes abandoned their farms to attend week-long camp meetings. At other times, T.G. Anderson had trouble finding workers for road construction or other manual labour.

> *We need to understand that we didn't live naturally as sedentary people. Our land base was much larger than a European land base would be. And our understanding, our relationship to the land different.*
>
> —Vicki Snache, Chippewas of Rama[2]

The behaviour and encroachment of settlers led the Chiefs to consider uprooting themselves to a more remote location. They made a formal request in 1832, but officials argued that the same would happen wherever they went.[3] Since they had already given up their land, they had few options.

Religious differences hampered collaboration, and intolerance stoked divisions. Although Musquakie advocated Methodism, sobriety, education, and farming, roughly half his people preferred their own belief system and did not convert. Meanwhile, bitter competition between the various Christian denominations increased strife and slowed the reserve's development. Although Peter Jones had converted many in the Lake Simcoe area in the late 1820s, colonial officials still mistrusted the Episcopal Methodists because of their involvement in opposition politics and their links to American Methodists. Officials approved the appointment of an Anglican missionary in 1830, and Anderson, himself a devout Anglican, "saw his own role as that of chief missionary."[4]

Titus Hibbert Ware, *Indians at Coldwater, Ontario*, 1844 | Toronto Public Library Digital Archive, PICTURES-R-205

The Potagunasees were Roman Catholics connected to the Ojibwe and mixed-heritage fur trade community near Penetanguishene and to Catholic Odaawaas / Ottawa led by Jean-Baptiste Assiginack, who had settled at Coldwater despite fierce opposition from the Anglican missionary. Chief Assance, who shocked many Methodist Anishinaabek when he converted to Catholicism from Methodism in 1832, complained that Anderson had refused to allow a priest access to the roughly one hundred Catholic Indians at Coldwater.[5]

Religious conflict led to conflict in education. Anglican missionaries were opposed to the Methodist school at the Narrows and set up a competing school, which failed because its teachers did not speak Anishinaabemowin.[6] At the annual present distributions at Penetanguishene, Anderson, Assiginack, Peter Jones, and Adam Elliot, agent for the Home District of the Society for

Converting and Civilizing the Indians, engaged in intense religious debate.[7]

How to respond to settler depredations became a matter of controversy. Musquakie intervened to stop the Chippewas' violent retribution against a travelling white surgeon who had desecrated an Indigenous grave and helped himself to a skull and other remains. Musquakie insisted that they trust the white man's law to render justice—but it didn't. This incident among others weakened the Chief's support among his people; he was perceived as too accommodating and conciliatory. Support shifted to some of his sub-Chiefs, notably Bigwin, Nanigishkung, and Negenaunaquot / Big Shilling, who took a stronger stand against the imposition of settler ways.[8]

At an 1833 Chippewa Council held at Coldwater, Musquakie spoke of the settlers' active interference: "My Father our Young Men take their Axes and go into the Wood, they do not however proceed far before they return to their homes . . . because the White Men are such close neighbors of theirs that they interfere with them."[9] This interference included intrusion on the reserve and outright occupation and possession of Chippewa houses. A white man named Laughton took possession of two houses built for the Chippewas and leased them to white men. Another house intended for the Chippewas, occupied by Gerald Alley, burned down in a fire.

Chief Assance complained that village residents were not receiving produce from the communal farms:

> Father you promised that you would have a small garden made for us, out of which we could get what would be necessary for ourselves and families. Father you promised us that the Children at school should have from the Farm what was wanted for them as likewise what was required for the Teachers and likewise our Superintendent . . . Father I cannot take any thing I want from the Farm, not a potatoe or Turnip or a grain of wheat . . . Father there was a great quantity of wheat here last year when I asked for any I sometimes got it and some times was refused—a great deal of it rotted and was lost and some of it remains at the North river now . . . Father it would have been better if those articles that were spoiled last year had been given to the old and helpless people . . . Father a great many of my Friends & Countrymen come here to see how I get on—when they arrive here they see that I am poor and have nothing, they go home and say that John Aissence had an empty hand.[10]

Taugaiwinnini, the speaker for the Potagunasees, identified other issues: "Father our Young Men are good Workmen and would make quantities of Hay—but they have no scythes. Father We wish to have a Milk Cow, we could Milk if we had any thing to Milk. We wish if His Excellency saw fit that he would be pleased to grant us another pair of oxen . . . Father we have always been anxious to raise Cattle and had we any thing to give them to eat we might succeed in so doing."[11]

Chief Assance pointed out that because their annuities were now being used to fund the mills, and because the government would not fund a blacksmith or a doctor: "We have no doctor here there is one at the Narrows but he seldom visits us."[12]

Anderson responded by blaming the Chippewas for failing to feed their cattle and not securing a constant supply of logs for the sawmill: "Had I not fed the Cattle, they would have starved and without my hauling logs the Mill would have remained idle."[13]

Clearly, the requirements of the civilization initiative were not well-communicated to the Chippewas and did not adequately factor in their deep attachment to their own modes of life. The mills required constant attention, whether for maintenance, labour, input materials, or outputs ready for market. Interruptions would render the whole arrangement unsuccessful and less than self-sufficient, particularly where debt was concerned. The following year, Anderson reported that in the Chippewas' absence, the mills continued to operate with hired settler labour: "The Saw Mill has undergone a good order and is Grinding more or less every day. The Indians being all gone, with most of their children to the Fishery, the school has not been attended."[14]

Early in 1835, four Chippewa Chiefs (but not Musquakie) petitioned the government to allow bands to manage all operations on the Coldwater-Narrows Reserve, including schools, gristmills, sawmills, and agricultural enterprises.[15] Anderson advised Givins:

> If the Indians would attend to their Farms and raise their own food, which they are certainly able to do with a little industry, instead of depending on the rent of the Saw Mill, and Grist Mill for food, they might be independant, and become valuable subjects. The Establishment is now in debt and it cannot pay Labourers to do all the work and at the same time supply Lumber free of Expence to the Indians without continuing a burden to the Government, whereas they would or ought to do every thing by their own labour.

Anderson favoured the government's continued control over the school, where he hoped the "civilizing" project would inculcate the discipline needed for the settler way of life: "I do not . . . consider it prudent that they should have the entire control of the School, but if His Excellency is pleased to exceed to their proposals in other respects they should of course support the School Establishment."[16] The Chippewas also wanted control over the mill back from its lessee, George Mitchell. When a spell of cold weather shut down the mill and made it impossible for the lessee to pay his rent, they regained control.[17]

In 1835, five years after the creation of the Coldwater-Narrows Reserve, Anderson reported favourably on its progress to his superiors. About 500 acres had been cleared, and each family had a farm under cultivation growing potatoes, corn, wheat, oats, and peas. Wigwams had been exchanged for log houses. Hunting "has in many cases been abandoned altogether" or no longer served as the only means of subsistence (though this might have been due to settler depredations and habitat loss). "Habitual intoxication is unknown," and instances of intoxication were

Titus Hibbert Ware, *Coldwater, Ontario*, 1844 | Toronto Public Library Digital Archive, PICTURES-R-203

Musquakie's substantial house at the Narrows Village was constructed by Jacob Gill for the Indian Department. It was made of wood sawn at a mill in Holland Landing and shipped to Orillia by boat | Hunter, *A History of Simcoe County*

seldom seen even though the "near approach of the White settlers" had rendered a ban on alcohol impossible. "The Sabbath is carefully observed—their religious duties strictly attended to, and reading and writing with a moderate knowledge of arithmetic is almost universal among the young people."

Anderson reported that Chiefs Assance and Musquakie now had frame homes, and schools existed at both Coldwater and the Narrows. A sawmill and gristmill were operating at Coldwater, and a sawmill was being built at the Narrows. On their own initiative, the Chippewas were building log barns and stables. Most Anishinaabek had adopted European dress and were manufacturing their own household furniture. They also understood the difference between barter and cash transactions, which would

Interviewee Mark Douglas, of Chippewas of Rama First Nation. Douglas is a founder and member of the Mnjikaning Fish Fence Circle, which protects the weir and sees that the site is honoured as a historical gathering place for Indigenous peoples | Photo by Robert Snache, courtesy of Chippewas of Rama First Nation

protect them from traders. The bands fished in the fall "as a source of profit, and not merely for their own food," and they had built "two Batteaux each capable of holding 40 or 50 barrels of Fish." Anderson continued, "Although obliged frequently to submit to irritating and extremely unjust treatment on the part of neighbouring White settlers, no Indian has during the whole period of my superintendence been complained of for any breach of the laws with one solitary exception, for the removal of part of a fence and that done in ignorance." He concluded that "this Experiment will appear incontestably to prove, that the Indian, under proper Treatment, is capable of being weaned from his savage Life, and of being made, under the Blessing of the Almighty, a good Member of the Church of Christ, and a dutiful and loyal Subject."[18]

All was not so rosy from an Indigenous perspective. Emblematic of the whole enterprise was the near destruction of the ancient fishing weir at the Narrows. In 1832, Andrew Borland was appointed captain of the wooden paddlewheel steamer *Sir John Colborne*, which made daily trips from Holland Landing to the village at the Narrows. In 1833, it was replaced by the *Simcoe*, which was bigger, faster, and flat-bottomed, making it less likely to get stuck in the Holland River's mud. This steamer, renamed *Peter Robinson*, was bought by Charles Thompson, who also ran a stagecoach from Toronto to Holland Landing.

Before then, shallow waters had kept ships out of Lake Couchiching and away from the Narrows village, rendering white settlement difficult. In 1833, the *Robinson* forced its way through the Narrows: its big sidewheels churned up the sandy bottom and destroyed much of the five-thousand-year-old weir.[19] The weir was damaged further when the channel was dredged to open it up for navigation. After 1833, the *Robinson* regularly brought settlers to the reserve wharf at the Narrows. From there, they travelled in large numbers to Coldwater along the Coldwater Road. At Penetanguishene, they boarded *Penetanguishene*, built by former fur trader Andrew Mitchell and partner Alfred Thompson and captained by Borland. The steamship ran from Penetanguishene to Sault Ste. Marie, transporting settlers and travellers into the northwestern regions of Upper Canada.[20]

PART FIVE:
Agency in Times of Struggle

16

The Quest for Secure Land Tenure

In 1831, Peter Jones wrote to the British secretary of state for the colonies on behalf of the Indians of Upper Canada:

> I wish to say something about our lands. My Indian brethren feel much in their hearts on this subject. We see that the country is getting full of white people, and that the hunting will soon be destroyed . . . It is our desire that whatever lands may be marked out for us, to keep the right and title ourselves, and not be permitted to sell them, not to let any white man live on them unless he is recommended by our council, and gets a licence from our father the governor. But we wish to feel that we stand on our own lands that our fathers left us.[1]

Jones had visited many Indigenous communities and understood that their hold on their lands was exceedingly precarious. In 1828, he learned the Credit Mississaugas had only 200 acres of unceded land and that their village was not part of that holding, even though the Mississaugas had tried to put their lands in trust for their children forever. In 1828, he visited the Mississaugas of Scugog and commented in his journal: "The Schoogog Indians in surrendering up their lands to the Government, made no reservation, as other tribes did; and therefore were dependent on the Government for the land on which they dwelt, and in which they laid the dead."[2] He was also aware of the Haldimand Tract land issues, as he had spent several years living with his father's Mohawk family at Grand River. He had been given explicit direction by the Anishinaabek of Lake Simcoe and Matchedash to speak on their behalf.

Jones' letter was forwarded to the lieutenant-governor. Sir John Colborne did not consider Indigenous peoples sufficiently advanced in colonial ways to be granted individual deeds for their lands: "I strongly recommend that in their present state His Majesty's Government should continue to act as their guardian." He stated that the lands set apart for them should be protected by the government "for the benefit of the Indians and their posterity." Large tracts of land had been reserved "by recorded agreement," and "they are all confident that their lands will never be taken from them."[3]

But Indigenous peoples were clearly not as confident in the security of their land tenure as Colborne believed. In 1832, T.G. Anderson sent an urgent message to Givins that a messenger from the

Mississaugas of the Credit had delivered the following message to the Chippewas of Coldwater and the Narrows: "I have been sent by our Chiefs to request the immediate attendance of your principle men at the Credit—a large assemblage of Indians will be there for the purpose of making some arrangements relative to their present situation. I am not at liberty to tell you what the subject is—that you will hear when you get there,—All I can say at present is, that we are poor and miserable, we have very little Land, in a few Years our children will not have wood to burn."[4]

Assance and the Potagunasees asked Anderson if the governor had ordered this Council or been informed of it. On being told that he had not, they said they wouldn't go or have any connection to it unless "their Father at York" wished them to attend. This decision likely reflected their dependent position, as they were still waiting for houses to be built. Givins replied to Anderson that the lieutenant-governor desired Anderson "to acquaint the Indians under your superintendence, that they have done perfectly right in not going to the Council at the Credit, that they well know that at the Credit, the Indians have more land secured to them than they can cultivate, and that the Tribes under your charge will also have as much land as they require, and that it will be duly set apart for their use and finally that all applications from their own Chiefs will be fully attended to without assembling at a distance from their homes."[5]

Yet, in September 1833, Chiefs Musquakie, Assance, and Taugaiwinini met with the lieutenant-governor's representative and called for deeds to their lands. Chief Musquakie stated: "Our Father [lieutenant-governor] likewise promised on your return from Coldwater to have two Deeds made out for our Lands one to made out on Parchment and the other on Common paper to be lodged in our hands before the Cold weather begins."[6] Chief Assance explicitly linked the fulfillment of government promises to his people's commitment to the reserve: "Father, you saw on the road our houses and our Lands I do not wish to abandon them I wish to improve them. Father if you give us what you have promised us our young Men will be very glad and will work hard."[7]

The precariousness of their tenure was driven home by the arrival at Coldwater of Mississaugas from the Lake Scugog area. The Mississaugas had been forced to relocate after settlers depleted game and a miller dammed the Scugog River, raising the water level by ten feet and flooding wild rice beds on Lake Scugog. In 1830, some Mississaugas followed Chief Jacob Crane to Mud Lake (present-day Curve Lake, near Peterborough) and, later, Balsam Lake, but others relocated to Lake Simcoe and the Coldwater Reserve.[8]

Considering the Creation of a Single Anishinaabe Territory

Because of ongoing encroachment on reserve lands and the diminishment of game and fish, many Anishinaabe Chiefs of central Upper Canada explored the possibility of one large settlement to protect their way of life. This was a new incarnation of the old dream of a protected homeland articulated in the Royal Proclamation of 1763. It had also been the goal of Britain's Indigenous allies during the American Revolution and later conflicts in the Ohio Valley. This vision had motivated Tecumseh to form his confederacy, ally with the British, and fight in the War of 1812.

In January 1836, Musquakie convened a Council at the Narrows to consider the possibility of a single settlement and "devise measures to prevent the ruin and degradation of our descendants."[9] The 1836 Council drew Chiefs from the Credit River, Rice Lake, Grape Island, Balsam Lake, Saugeen, French River, and the Coldwater-Narrows Reserve. If the government recommended removal to one settlement, the Council agreed that the only acceptable territory was at Saugeen, on the shores of Georgian Bay. It is not clear that they intended to give up their existing settlements as they also petitioned the lieutenant-governor for title to their lands that would "secure the property to ourselves and to our Children forever."[10]

The Chippewas demanded unilateral control of their mills and schoolhouse in August 1836 and the division of their land into 50-acre lots, each assigned to the head of a family.[11] The new lieutenant-governor, Francis Bond Head, agreed to hand over management of the mills and school but not the land division. Unbeknownst to the Chippewas, he was already planning to purchase the reserve.[12] In 2003, the Indian Claims Commission Chippewa Tri-Council Inquiry on the Surrender of the Coldwater-Narrows Reserve noted: "Little more than a year later, the reserve would be surrendered, making irrelevant all the progress that had been achieved there."[13]

Meanwhile, local settlers were complaining about the state of the Coldwater Road and petitioned Bond Head that the Chippewas should perform statute labour to maintain it, even though it was settlers who made heavy use of it and derived all the benefits. Anderson, to his credit, didn't think they should be forced.[14]

Sir Francis Bond Head and the Threat of Removal

Lieutenant-Governor Colborne's retirement in 1836 led to a radical change in policy. Bond Head did not believe Indigenous people could be civilized: "I firmly believe every person of sound mind . . . will agree, that an attempt to make farmers of the Red Men has been, generally speaking, a complete failure; that congregating them for the purpose of civilization has implanted many more vices than it has eradicated; and, consequently, that the greatest kindness we can perform towards these intelligent, simple-minded people, is to remove and fortify them as much as possible from all communication with the Whites."[15]

Instead, Bond Head aggressively pursued a policy of "Indian removal," akin to what was happening in the United States. Believing that Indigenous people would soon die out, Bond Head formulated a plan to relocate those living in central Upper Canada (including the Chippewas and Mississaugas but not the Six Nations) to rocky Manitoulin Island, where they could hunt and live in their traditional way during their final days.

Anna Jameson, *Sunset on Lake Huron from the Encampment of Chief Yellow Head*, 1837 | Library and Archives Canada, Peter Winkworth Collection of Canadiana, R9266-292

Bond Head ignored considerable evidence of successful transformation, perhaps because of his romantic sensibilities. He exalted the "noble savage" as being unalienated from nature and morally superior to civilized Europeans. He viewed industrial civilization as corrupt and artificial. He sought to preserve this natural man "like a museum specimen" until Indigenous peoples succumbed to extinction.[16]

The conviction that Indigenous people would soon disappear was common. British writer Anna Jameson spent a year in Toronto and travelled north to Manitoulin, Sault Ste. Marie, and Michilimackinac in 1837, where she encountered many Indigenous people and attended the annual distribution of presents. She believed that Indigenous peoples could not join modernity: "[They] do strike me as an *untamable* race," she wrote. "[T]here is a bar to the civilization of the Indians, and the increase or even preservation of their numbers, which no power can overleap . . . I can no more conceive a city filled with industrious Mohawks and Chippewas, than I can imagine a flock of panthers browsing in a penfold."[17]

"Kindness" was not Bond Head's only motive for wanting to relocate Indigenous peoples to Manitoulin. He wrote to Lord Glenelg, the colonial secretary:

> It was evident to me that we should reap a very great Benefit, if we could persuade those Indians, who are now impeding the

Artist unknown, portrait of Anna Brownell Jameson, 1844 | Hill & Adamson, Art Institute of Chicago, Wikimedia Commons

Manner I have detailed, will be better off than they were; that the Position they will occupy can bona fide be fortified against the Encroachments of the Whites; while, on the other hand, there can be no doubt that the Acquisition of their vast and fertile Territory will be hailed with Joy by the whole Province.[18]

Through Bond Head's efforts in the summer of 1836, the Anishinaabek ceded most of Manitoulin Island and the Saugeen Tract through questionable cessions that did not follow the treaty-making principles set out in the Royal Proclamation of 1763 or Lord Dorchester's further instructions. The cessions totalled about 3 million acres, including 1.5 million acres of Saugeen Ojibwe territory (Saugeen Tract Treaty 45 ½) and most of Manitoulin Island (Treaty 45).

On the way to Manitoulin Island that summer, Bond Head passed through the Coldwater-Narrows Reserve and met with Musquakie. There's no surviving record, but given that the bands had recently petitioned Bond Head for control over the reserve, Musquakie likely went into the meeting hoping to ensure the reserve's future.[19] But it appears the Chippewas were either asked or pressured to cede their lands. In October 1836, Givins wrote to Musquakie that the lieutenant-governor wanted to know "whether you are ready to give him an answer to the matter he spoke to you about when at the Narrows."[20]

Although Givins informed Anderson that the bands at the Coldwater-Narrows Reserve would be granted the right to manage their affairs effective March 31, 1837,[21] the surrender of the reserve

Progress of Civilization in Upper Canada, to resort to a place possessing the double Advantage of being admirably adapted to them (inasmuch as it affords Fishing, Hunting, Bird-Shooting, and Fruit), and yet in no Way adapted to the White population. I feel confident that the Indians, when settled by us in the

Saugeen "Indian Territories." Detail of Alexander Keith Johnston's *Canada*, 1844. The area labelled "Indian Territory" is the original Saugeen Tract, which was divided by surrender of the southern portion in 1836 (Treaty 45 ½). The Mississaugas of the Credit rejected moving to the northern Saugeen Tract because of its rockier, unfertile land | Courtesy of University of Toronto Libraries

was now the main issue. Chief Musquakie replied to Givins' letter: "As soon as I get an answer from the other Indians I have been consulting... I will immediately proceed to Toronto accompanied by three of my Indians and give an answer on the subject."²²

On November 26, 1836, Chiefs Musquakie and Assance, along with ten principal men from their bands and representatives from Snake's, signed the Coldwater Treaty in Toronto. Givins and William Robinson were among the witnesses, but Anderson—the official most involved and invested in the Coldwater-Narrows Reserve and directly responsible for it—does not appear to have been present. The financial arrangements were also unusual. The Chippewas of the Coldwater-Narrows Reserve agreed to give up the reserve for sale in exchange for the annual interest on one-third of the proceeds. One-third would be applied for the "general use of the Indian Tribes of the said Province," and the remainder would be applied "to any purpose (but not for the benefit of the said Indians) as the Lieutenant-Governor may think proper to direct."²³ First Nations would later assert that the Coldwater Treaty was one of several concluded in 1836 that had either been not agreed to or significantly misrepresented on paper.

A year later, Methodist leaders protested the injustice of these treaties and the attempted removal of the Indians to Manitoulin. In response, Bond Head explained his meeting at the Coldwater-Narrows Reserve the previous summer:

In the course of the inspectional Tour which I last Year made of the Province, I assembled, in the Months of August and September, the Indians, at each of these Places, and after explaining to them how much better, in my Opinion, it would be for them to receive Money for their Hunting Ground than to continue on it, surrounded as it was by the White Population, and consequently deprived as it was of its Game, I left them to reflect by themselves on what I had stated. The Chiefs of the Narrows and of Coldwater, after a long debate, became unanimously of the Opinion, that the Offer I had made to their Tribes was advantageous. They accordingly, on the 26th of November, came down in a Body to Toronto to beg me to carry it into effect.²⁴

In November 1840, Musquakie provided a different view in a letter to the next chief superintendent, Samuel Peters Jarvis: "Sir francis Bond Head came when we lived on Orillia drove us out of it to go and live on some of the island and so we did."²⁵ Musquakie's letter indicated that the Chippewas who travelled to Toronto deliberated for two days before coming to what was undoubtedly a difficult decision.

Six years after the Coldwater Treaty, a petition concerning the terms of the surrender was signed by the Chiefs of the Rama, Snake Island, and Coldwater Indians and forwarded to the governor general of Canada:

We wish to state to your Excellency that when Sir F. Bond Head insisted on our selling this Land and the bargain he had previously drawn out for us to sign, we were not made sensible of the full purport, so that we knew not the nature of the bargain. It may be proper for us to state to your Excellency . . . that up to the present period we have not received any money from the sale of the said Land . . . We are not fully satisfied that other people should participate in the money arrising from this sale—We conceive it to be our right to reap the benefit and not others. Also, the article of agreement is not satisfactory as it does not specify what the principal of the money comes to . . . In writing to your Excellency we wish to state particularly that the Grist Mill at Coldwater, and the Saw Mill near the Coldwater Road are not included in the Agreement and hence we shall continue to consider them as Indian property.[26]

That the Chippewa version of these events is closer to the truth is indicated by a letter Anderson wrote three weeks after the treaty was signed. Anderson reported that "the Indians are in a quandary quite undecided where to take up their future residence, they do not know what is best for themselves, and unless the Governor be pleased to direct them, the probability is they will again be scattered about the country, wretched objects of misery."[27]

Then they went down to Toronto under the leadership of Yellowhead, and the government told them they were going to sign a piece of paper and give them the rights to their land. Had the Natives sign a whole bunch of papers. They got home and had a lawyer read it, and what the government got them to sign was releasing all the land to the government. It wasn't a treaty.

—Andrew Big Canoe, Chippewas of Georgina Island[28]

Indigenous Resistance and Non-Indigenous Allies

Indigenous peoples protested when Bond Head offered them rocky Manitoulin Island rather than the fertile Saugeen Tract, and after he engineered the Saugeen's surrender by pressuring a few individuals of the band to sign.[29] For the first time, they received considerable support from non-Indigenous allies. In April 1837, Methodist missionaries protested the displacement of an unnamed group of Methodist converts who had cultivated and built homes and barns on their land, only to be moved after the surrender: "Justice and humanity unequivocally demand that the Indians be allowed to stay."[30]

A few months later, a petition by the "Resident and Ministers of the Wesleyan Methodist Church in Canada," reported "the strong feeling of dissatisfaction existing among the Indians in some of our Mission Stations." The petition stated that they had improved the lands in the belief that they'd belong to them and their children forever:

> [The] Saugeeng Indians have been induced to surrender certain lands to the Crown, which, in the opinion of the Indians generally, were not at the disposal of the persons who surrendered them,—not only from the fact that they were not the proprietors, but likewise, that a declaration of the Indians in Council had been forwarded to the late Lt. Governor, containing the deliberate, and unanimous decision of the Chiefs, assembled from different Tribes, that no person should have authority to cede or surrender the Saugeeng tract without the sanction of a general Council, and the concurrence of the hereditary and acknowledge Chief, and the late surrender having, in their opinion, been made without such sanction and concurrence, they consider it void, and maintain that the Chief of the said Territory is the rightful proprietor thereof.[31]

Eighty influential British humanitarians denounced Bond Head's policies in a petition to the governor general sponsored by the newly formed Aborigines Protection Society, a humanitarian organization based in England that declared "the Canadian Indians . . . the Society's first special care."[32] Protesting Bond Head's policy of obtaining extensive surrenders of fertile and developed reserves, the petition denounced the intention of exiling the Indians "to the 23,000 rocks of granite, dignified by the name of Manitoulin Island," which were "perfectly useless as Sir Francis admits, for every purpose of civilized life."[33] Many Methodists in Canada were active in the society, including Peter Jones, the society's Upper Canada representative.

While Bond Head was undertaking this program of removal, the British Parliamentary Select Committee on Aboriginal Peoples was also preparing a massive report, published in 1837, that was highly critical of the treatment of Indigenous peoples in Canada and other British colonies. It accused British settlers of treating Indigenous peoples immorally and contributing to their physical destruction and "moral degradation" through land theft, murder, the spread of sexually transmitted diseases, and the deliberate introduction of guns and alcohol.[34]

> The injuries we have inflicted, the oppression we have exercised, the cruelties we have committed, the vices we have fostered, the desolation and utter ruin we have caused, stand in strange and melancholy contrast with the enlarged and generous exertions we have made for the advancement of civil freedom, for the moral and intellectual improvement of mankind, and for the furtherance of the sacred truth, which alone can permanently elevate and civilize mankind . . . Through successive generations the work of spoliation and death has been carried on, until to the colonial possessions of the most religious nation in the world

the emphatic language of Scripture may with truth be applied—they are "the dark places of the earth, full of the habitations of cruelty."[35]

The report documented that Indigenous peoples had been and were losing their lives in large numbers across the Empire. Only by protecting, Christianizing, and civilizing Indigenous peoples could further deaths be prevented. Missionaries were thus seen as the only allies who could prevent corruption by alcohol traders and dispossession by rapacious settlers.[36]

The authors of the report assumed publicizing the historical wrongs of colonialism and the desperate situation of Indigenous peoples would outrage the British public and end the atrocities, as had been the case with the slave trade. Unfortunately, the report was opposed or ignored by most settlers and politicians in Upper Canada.[37] However, the *Christian Guardian*, the Methodist newspaper founded in 1829 in Toronto under the editorship of Egerton Ryerson, strongly criticized Bond Head's removal policy in several articles and challenged his narrative of irreversible Indigenous decline and incompatibility with Euro-Canadian society. The paper countered excerpts of Bond Head's correspondence with Lord Glenelg by describing the progress that had been made to establish viable farming communities and day schools.

> The principal difficulty with which the instructors of the Indians have had to contend in urging them to the cultivation of their lands had been, not their distaste for those employments, but the knowledge that they were in possession of no titles to their lands and were liable to be removed from them at pleasure, as some of them have been, after expended considerable labour. And since the design to banish them to Manitoulin has been known, these difficulties have been greatly increased. Their reasonable language has been—"Why should we learn to farm? If we improve our lands, others will be allowed to taken them from us; and if we go to Manitoulin, we cannot plough the big rocks." But the uniform opinion of the Missionaries is, that if settled on good land and their titles secured, they would become industrious, comfortable and contented.[38]

Largely in response to these well-organized campaigns, Bond Head's removal policy was abandoned after he was recalled to England in 1838.[39] This would not have happened without the involvement of Anishinaabe Methodists.

A key issue for the Chippewas of Coldwater and the Narrows was what would happen to their houses, mills, barns, and other improvements. On February 6, 1837, Chief Assance and twenty of his people seized the gristmill at Coldwater and the fall wheat held there. Assance stated that they wanted to ensure their children had food, but he also wanted to ensure that the mill and the wheat were included in the Coldwater property to be turned over to Indigenous control the following month. Settlers unsuccessfully petitioned

Bond Head against letting the Chippewas control the mill.

Givins relayed the lieutenant-governor's instructions to Anderson: "I am commanded by him to request you to inform the Indians that if they again act in this manner H.E. [His Excellency] will consider them unfit to be entrusted with the management of their own affairs and will annul the directions he has given for that purposes which were to commence after the 31st march next, and further that the L.G.[lieutenant-governor] hereby authorizes you, should you find it necessary, to apply the civil authorities to put an end to similar acts of violence on the part of the Indians."[40]

The following month, Givins reassured the Chiefs by relaying that Anderson would be instructed to hand over all the property that belonged to them and allow them to do what they wanted with the mill. Anderson reported on April 8 that the property transfer was complete.[41]

Chief Assance also claimed the Severn River sawmill under exclusive Chippewa control. Just five days before the outbreak of the 1837 Upper Canada Rebellion, Assance rejected leasing the sawmill to John Cathew, despite the threat of a lawsuit for damages. Anderson suspected Assance's reason for ensuring control over the gristmill and sawmill was to secure flour for his people over the winter, especially crucial since they had not planted crops.[42]

Peter Jones visited the Narrows and Coldwater on July 24 and 25, 1837, several months after the land had been ceded. At the Narrows, the Chippewas still occupied their villages, but "I was sorry to perceive that these people have almost wholly neglected their planting. This is some of the fruits of His Excellency Sir F.B. Head's administration of Indian affairs." At Coldwater, he wrote: "The Coldwater settlement of Indians appears to be quite broken up, and the fields are growing over with weeds and bushes. Another exhibition of our Governor's measures with the Indians."[43]

In this context of dispossession and removal, the Mississaugas of the Credit sent Peter Jones to London in 1837 to meet with Lord Glenelg and deliver a petition directly to the Queen. They asked for a title deed for their land on the Credit and argued for Indigenous land rights generally. Acquiring secure title to reserves would prove to be the leading political concern of this generation of Anishinaabe Methodists and "a lifelong objective of Jones."[44]

17

Defending the Crown

Anishinaabe decisions about where to relocate and the resolution of issues concerning the mills at Coldwater were complicated by the outbreak of the rebellion in Upper Canada, led by William Lyon Mackenzie, in 1837.

Mackenzie had many supporters east and west of Yonge Street to the north of Toronto, especially settlers who came from the United States before the War of 1812, including families of German and Irish heritage.[1] Well-established farmers and artisans, they believed British immigrants were favoured by the government. They felt discriminated against and were angry about the long-running alien controversy, which relegated them to second-class status and labelled them "residents of dubious loyalty." Farmers resented that many Clergy Reserve road allowances had yet to be cleared, impeding travel, while they were required to clear their own before receiving the deeds to their land.[2] Reformers resented and criticized the power of the Family Compact; they accused its members (including the Robinsons) of lining their own pockets, advancing friends, and controlling government through the appointed Executive Council. When reform by the elected Legislative Assembly appeared to be blocked, some turned to more radical action.

Daniel Stong sided with Mackenzie in the uprising when it broke out on December 4.[3] The related family of Joseph Shepard had close connections to Mackenzie. Shepard was Mackenzie's close friend and nominated him several times for election in York County. Although Shepard died a few months before the rebellion, all four of his sons participated. His farm was used as a staging area for the seven hundred to eight hundred farmers who, on December 7, went south to Montgomery's Tavern on Yonge Street with the intent to march south to Toronto (York was renamed and incorporated as a city in 1834) to seize a government arms cache.

Shepard's wife, Catherine Fisher, daughter of Jacob Fisher Sr. and aunt of Elizabeth Fisher Stong, tied strips of cloth around their arms to identify them to one another.[4] Before the rebellion, the Shepard boys went four or five times to their uncle Jake Fisher's farm in Vaughan to drill with muskets. A family mill—"an old structure a short distance in the rear of Gibson's farm, known as Shepard's mill"—had long been "a secret rendezvous for the radicals of the neighbourhood."[5]

One thousand militia sent from Toronto quickly put down the initial uprising and arrested some of the ringleaders. Mackenzie escaped to Buffalo, New York. An unconfirmed story suggests Daniel Stong was arrested and held in jail while Elizabeth Fisher Stong cared for their eight children.[6] Her relatives, Thomas and Michael Shepard, were captured at the home of the Silverthorne family in Etobicoke.[7] Although they were sent to Kingston to await deportation to Van Diemen's Land (Tasmania), they made a daring escape from Fort Henry to the United States. Their brothers, Joseph Shepard II and Jacob, were imprisoned on December 11 and released on May 12.[8] Mackenzie's good friend John Cummer was also arrested but released, while Samuel Cummer was drafted into the government's forces and locked up all night.[9] MacKenzie's printing press was apparently hidden in a dried-up well on Joshua Cummer's farm. Although two rebel leaders were hanged, Daniel Stong and Elizabeth Fisher's relations were all released. Everyone but Mackenzie received a general pardon in 1845.

Chippewa and Mississauga settlements to the north of Toronto were well located to help the Crown defend against the rebels, particularly since the loyalty of settlers in the Home District was uncertain, the militia was depleted, and Bond Head had sent regular troops to put down the Lower Canada rebellion.[10] Superintendent Anderson sent twenty-one warriors under Assance to Holland Landing, and militia captain Gerald Alley led an unknown number of Chippewas out to Yonge Street in the first days of the rebellion. Runners contacted other warriors in their hunting grounds, and on December 10, twenty Potawatomi warriors under Waukai joined them. On December 12, six warriors arrived from the Narrows under Chief Nainigishkung; thirteen more arrived the next day, followed by twelve Potawatomi under Chief Waubekan. In total, ninety Anishinaabek served at Holland Landing.[11] Because of the warriors' stereotyped reputation for ferocity, their presence suppressed rebel activity far more easily than the regular militia would have, especially since the militia's loyalty was not assured.[12]

Given the recent upheaval and protest over the surrender of their lands, why did the Chippewas and Mississaugas support the government? Anishinaabe involvement may have reflected broader tensions with farmers and ongoing efforts to secure government support. Chiefs and warriors may have felt obliged to heed the Indian agent's call or to honour their alliance with the Crown, despite the Crown's frequent failure to uphold its side of the relationship.

There could also be a practical motive. Because of changes to government present giving, most Indigenous men had no working guns by 1837. They needed to hunt to provide food, particularly since their fields had not been sown the previous summer.[13] Warriors who joined in the government's defence were issued guns and were promised they could keep them as well as clothing and rations after their service.

They were also willing to defend the government—or at least the Crown—"to preclude the possibility of annexation by the United States and the imposition of a massive removal policy similar to the one that was underway south of the border." Although the uprising was put down within days, American incursions into Upper Canada by rebel supporters led to fears of an invasion in the spring of 1838. Successful American attacks were mounted at Point Pelee in Lake Erie and on islands in the Detroit and Niagara Rivers; there were also pirate raids along the St. Clair frontier. It was feared that the Americans would try a reverse attack by landing at Penetanguishene and marching south to link up with rebels at Lloydtown and Newmarket.[14] The Chippewas and Mississaugas likely hoped their demonstrated loyalty would support their assertions that the government was obligated to assist them and treat them generously.[15]

During the rebellion, the government downplayed ongoing conflict over ownership of the mills for fear of alienating the Anishinaabek, whose loyalty was an open question. Local militia leaders recognized the necessity of maintaining an alliance with the Chippewas, so it was only during periods when the threat of insurrection and American invasion subsided that the thorny issue was raised. The Anishinaabek's Methodist supporters, hoping that the government's reliance on Indigenous warriors might make it more receptive, demanded that Lord Glenelg, secretary of the Colonies, issue title deeds. Samuel Peters Jarvis, the new chief superintendent of the Indian Department, was strongly opposed.[16]

As the likelihood of an American invasion faded, the Indian Department approved a rental proposal for the Coldwater mill and its surrounding land from two settlers, Miles Stennett and Mr. Barret. Lease terms were drafted without consulting the Chippewas. Chief Assance told Stennett the mills had not been given up and asked him to leave. Stennett claimed someone named Fan-gai-win-e-ne (likely Taugaiwinini, the Potaganesee speaker) incited the Chippewas to set fire to the mills rather than hand them over. The mills were damaged and some of the surrounding buildings dismantled. The Indian Department threatened that Assance would be held financially accountable. White settlers from five surrounding townships petitioned Jarvis to not allow the Anishinaabek to keep the mill.[17]

Nothing came of this confrontation because in November 1838 there were renewed fears of a US invasion, and the Chippewas were again needed to defend the colony. All the Indigenous Nations south of the Severn were organized into militia units. Captain Alley was ordered to gather all the Chiefs and warriors from Lakes Huron and Simcoe, and Saugeen at Holland Landing, where they'd be outfitted and supplied with ammunition and provisions. Nearly 170 warriors were placed under the command of Alley, Andrew Borland, and Lieutenant Eli Beman. Warriors from the Credit and Six Nations were also called out, and many warriors served at posts throughout the province in November and December 1838 and into January 1839.[18]

I've heard of gatherings in Holland Landing for the Rebellion. There's a list of our men who were there. I think it was 147 or so Anishinaabe men who were at

Pay list of Chiefs and Warriors from Chippewas of Lakes Huron and Simcoe at Holland Landing, 1839 | National Archives of Great Britain, PRO War Office, 13/3693, folio 601

Holland Landing trying to stop all these angry people from overthrowing the government.

—Ben Cousineau, Chippewas of Rama[19]

We look at a militia role document from the Rebellion of 1837. And who's there? The whole New Credit band list. Well, not New Credit, pardon me. The Credit River people are on there.

—Darin Wybenga, Mississaugas of the Credit[20]

When the threat of invasion receded, Jarvis summoned Chiefs Musquakie and Assance to Toronto to discuss the mills. The warriors at Holland Landing had not yet been disbanded. While in Toronto, Assance made no promise to hand over the mills, and Alley suggested the matter be dropped because the Chippewas' military support was too valuable to lose. Alley told Jarvis: "I well know the disposition of J. Aisance . . . I have not the slightest power to change the determination of John Aisance or his band in this local affair—His answer has been repeatedly given in a similar way, and I am obliged to confess that, I should fear the result of strong measures at this critical moment."[21]

However, Assance was eventually brought together with Stennett in Toronto, and Jarvis somehow extracted a Doodem signature from Assance on a document affirming Stennett and Barret's possession of the Coldwater mill and outbuildings, through unknown means.[22] Assance, Musquakie, and other Chiefs of Rama, Coldwater, and Snake Island insisted the Chippewas had not given up ownership.[23]

In January 1839, the government disbanded Indigenous military units at Holland Landing, and rations continued only until the month's end. Losing military employment in the middle of winter was deeply distressing to the warriors and worried their commanders. Alley was concerned they'd be hunting in townships that were disloyal.[24] Andrew Borland wrote to Alley:

> Since your absence the Indians have been Complaining most bitterly that they should be called out for so short a time Comming many of them a long distance to serve their Queen & Country & their pay to be stoped at so early period it is going to leave them destitute of means to return to their places from whence they started, they say if their great Mother sends them off in this way, their familys must starve, before they can reach their Hunting grounds, & not only that, but calling them out at that Season of the year, has destroy the means of their making a living for the remaining part of the Winter, notwithstanding those dificultys they are always ready to serve their great Mother when called upon, but they hope their father at Toronto will make some further provision for them.[25]

To make matters worse, Jarvis tried to make the warriors return the weapons they had been issued, an extremely unpopular move, as they needed the guns to hunt. In the face of rising discontent, Jarvis was forced to abandon this policy. Indigenous groups were thus able to leverage the 1837 uprising to secure new weapons at a critical time, while also fighting against possible US annexation and the threat of a removal policy similar to that experienced by Indigenous peoples south of the border.[26]

As historian Rhonda Telford notes, "On a per capita basis, many more Native people defended the province than did peoples of other origins . . . The Chippewas and Mississaugas played a significant and unique role in the defence of the Home District, one of the most troubled with pockets of rebel activity."[27]

Where to Go?

Bond Head's removal policy, unpopular with the Colonial Office, was abandoned after Bond Head was recalled to Britain in early 1838. Notwithstanding the Chippewas' demonstration of loyalty, the surrender of the Coldwater-Narrows Reserve was allowed to stand, and the Chippewas had to leave their homes. Anishinaabe scholar Darrel Manitowabi wrote in 2007, "For 170 years the Anishinaabeg have refuted the validity of this claim."[28]

In June 1838, Jarvis, the newly appointed chief superintendent of Indian affairs, wrote to the secretary of George Arthur, the new lieutenant-governor, to report that the majority of the Chippewas of the Coldwater-Narrows Reserve did not want to go to Manitoulin Island. Instead, they hoped to relocate as near as possible to their villages:

> With this view the tribe has proposed to purchase about 1000 acres of land on the east side of Lake Simcoe in the Township of Rama, for the accommodation of the principal Chief "Yellow Head," and his followers, the remainder under "John Assance" the Second Chief removing to the mouth of the River Severn where they already possess a tract of Land and Saw Mill.
>
> By this arrangement the Public High Way between the Narrows and Cold Water will cease to pass through an Indian Settlement, which I am of opinion will very soon become the residences of Industrious Farmers.[29]

In 1839, white settlers petitioned the government to remove the Chippewas. They quickly bought up the land and acquired the houses and barns of the former Narrows Village.

> *They'd cleaned it up, and they'd started growing stuff, and they were doing so good that the government took it all back off them and gave it to the settlers. Because it was a good place to grow stuff, "Natives shouldn't be living on that. It's too good for them."*
>
> —Andrew Big Canoe, Chippewas of Georgina Island[30]

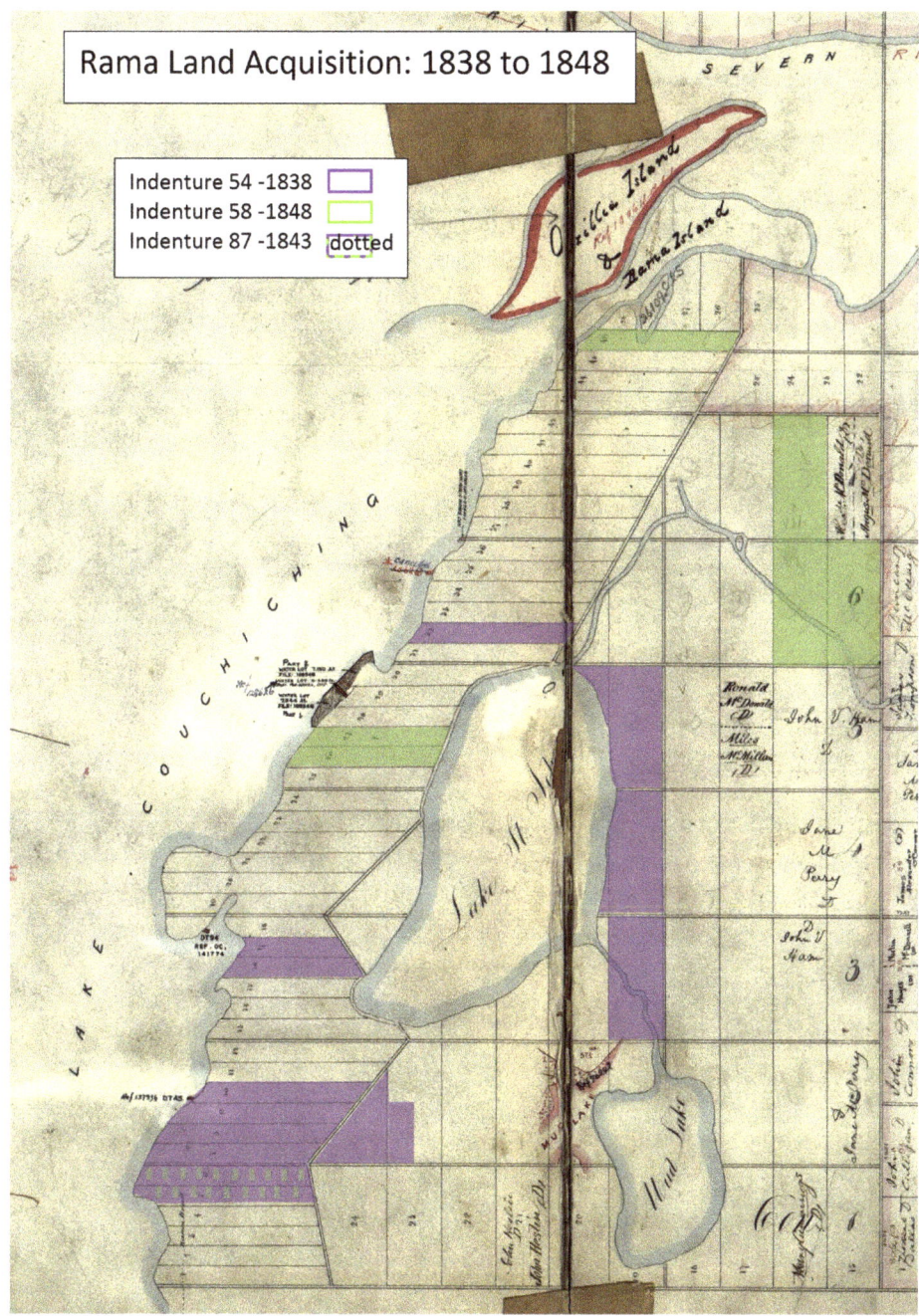

Extract of plan of Rama Township, 1856. Coloured annotations by Laurie Leclair show lots purchased for the Chippewas of Rama Reserve. The red outlined island is not part of the reserve | Ontario Archives, RG1-100-0-0-2359

Titus Hibbert Ware, *Indian Village at Rama, Lake Couchiching*, 1844 | Toronto Public Library, PICTURES-R-211

With their portion of the annuities being shared with the bands led by Assance and Snake, Musquakie's people purchased 1,600 acres in Rama Township on the east side of Lake Couchiching across the lake from their former village and moved there in the summer of 1839.³¹ The land consisted of several farms separated by land owned by speculators. The farms had been cleared but abandoned by white settlers. The soil was rocky or swampy, and the speculators had refused to cooperate in building a road. The purchase is part of contemporary oral memory.

Once that 10,000 acres between the Narrow and Coldwater was surrendered, we had no land now. The rest of our 3 million acres in the area was surrendered in 1816 and 1818. So, from there, we are basically homeless. We're squatters. And we kind of move to the Narrows. Some go to Chief Island. And a couple of years later, we start to . . . actually, Chief Yellowhead buys up land in Rama Township, which was basically abandoned farmland from the non-Indigenous War of 1812 veterans.

—Ben Cousineau, Chippewas of Rama³²

The guy we buy the land from is the guy that led the petition to get us off the Coldwater-Narrows Reservation. There was a petition signed by fifty prominent, well-to-do, connected British Anglicans. But meanwhile, he owns all this land here in Rama Township that's not been assigned to various soldiers or has been collected back. He's got this piece of land for sale. And Rama is one of the only three reservations in all of Canada that supposedly went and bought our own land. And then they deemed that we were children, and we didn't really deserve to own it. We'd bought and paid for it.

—Mark Douglas, Chippewas of Rama[33]

They wanted the good farmland. That's why they sent us out here to farm rocks.

—Sherry Lawson, Chippewas of Rama[34]

On the biggest farm, the Indian Department constructed twelve houses (housing two families each), barns, and a schoolhouse, and it distributed farm implements and tools. By 1839, 184 Chippewas and one of the Methodist missionaries from Narrows had moved to the new reserve. Musquakie's people rebuilt their lives and community and became known as the Chippewas of Rama.

Coldwater Mill Museum | Photo by Victoria Freeman

17 | Defending the Crown

Mnjikaning is our traditional name. We changed in 2010 from Mnjikaning back to Rama. There is a split in the community, and I think it goes back to religion, where people didn't like the word "Mnjikaning" because it was, in their words, too hard to say, too hard to spell, and they didn't understand the meaning of it. When, if you read a bit of history or understand any language, you know that the word is important to us. And not just us, but across Indigenous peoples in Ontario.

—Ben Cousineau, Chippewas of Rama[35]

In 1840, a new Methodist missionary, the Reverend Sylvester Hurlburt, wrote of the legacy of the move:

After they had laboured on these lands, under great disadvantages, for some years, and then to be driven out unceremoniously as they were, or rather forced to surrender them, could not but have an unfavourable effect. To see white men, who are strangers in the country, come into the possession of their houses and lands, without, as yet, their getting any remuneration, and themselves obliged to seek a habitation elsewhere must cause feeling, deep feeling, and though a small portion of land has been granted in another place, but as they have no title for it, dissatisfaction is still felt and fears are entertained that the same act of injustice may be repeated whenever the cupidity of white men may lead them to covet their present location.[36]

Although Assance's people stayed at Coldwater a bit longer and the Chief wanted to settle at the mouth of the Severn River, where they had land and a sawmill, many members of the band moved to Beausoleil Island in Georgian Bay and later to Christian Island, where the land was better for farming.[37] Today, they are known as Beausoleil First Nation. After the Chippewas relocated to Beausoleil, Miles Stennett took over the Coldwater mill, but it's unclear if the Chippewas received payments.

In 1845, Musquakie complained that they hadn't received payments for three years.[38] In 1849, the Chippewas sold the Coldwater gristmill to prominent businessman and mill owner George Copeland (who also took over the Coldwater sawmill). Copeland hired Jacob Gill's son John to operate it and John's brother Joseph to manufacture flour barrels and casks. The mill went through various owners and renovations, ceasing operations in 1994. Today, it's a museum.

Chief Snake's Band moved back to their islands on Lake Simcoe, where they had lived before moving to the Narrows. Today, they are known as the Chippewas of Georgina Island. A few others moved to the Saugeen Tract and Manitoulin Island.

So our people lived on Snake Island, and that was after our people were expelled and tricked out of our land at Coldwater.

—Kory Snache, Chippewas of Rama[39]

In 1991, a land claim was launched by the Chippewa Tri-Council and Chippewas of Nawash with reference to the cession of the Coldwater-Narrows Reserve. The Coldwater-Narrows claim concerned "the alleged surrender of the reserve in 1836 and the subsequent sale of those lands. The basis of the claim is that the alleged 1836 surrender of the reserve was invalid because it was conducted improperly and that the land was then sold below its value and in an untimely fashion."[40] The $307 million Coldwater-Narrows Land Claim Settlement Agreement was accepted by First Nations in 2012.

18

Surviving, Rebuilding, Adapting, Resisting

In March 1838, Peter Jones finally met with Lord Glenelg to press the British government for title deeds to Indigenous lands. He arrived in London the same month Lieutenant-Governor Bond Head was recalled from Toronto in the wake of the rebellion. With Glenelg's support, Jones took his petition directly to Queen Victoria in September.

He offered her Wampum then "proceeded to give her the meaning of the wampum; and told her that the white wampum signified the loyal and good feeling which prevails amongst the Indians toward Her Majesty and Her Government; but that the black wampum was designed to tell Her Majesty that their hearts were troubled on account of their having no title-deeds for their lands; and that they had sent their petition and wampum that Her Majesty might be pleased to take out all the black wampum, so that the string might be all white."[1]

The petition read, in part:

> We are the descendants of the original inhabitants of the soil, who formerly possessed this, their native country, in peace and harmony long before the French, the ancient enemies of your people, came over the great waters and settled upon our territories . . . Our people have begun to improve their farms; they wish to sell the produce at market and buy goods from the white people, but they are afraid to clear much ground, because they are told by evil-minded persons that their farms can be taken away from them at any time . . . We know that our people in times past have sold lands to our late father the king, but we never sold our lands at the Credit.[2]

To Jones' great joy, Queen Victoria approved Glenelg's recommendation to grant title deeds.

But the victory was illusory. The Mississaugas lost their most important ally when Glenelg resigned in February 1839. In Upper Canada, the new lieutenant-governor, George Arthur, ignored the question of title deeds, and no one from the Colonial Office insisted that he issue them. Jones continued to press, meeting Lord Sydenham (Charles Poulett Thomson), the new governor general of British North America, but nothing came of this meeting.[3]

Two years after Indigenous warriors had defended the Crown, Sydenham remarked: "He (the Indians) occupies valuable land, unprofitably to himself and injurious to the country, and adds nothing either to the wealth, the industry, or the defence of the Province."[4] Such sentiments did not augur well for British-Indigenous relations in the middle decades of the nineteenth century.

Farmland in Canada West was now in short supply. Non-Indigenous squatters continued to move onto Indigenous lands, and the poaching of game, fish, and timber from Indigenous lands was a serious problem. According to testimony submitted to an 1839 inquiry into the Indian Department, Chief Superintendent Jarvis "was not particularly upset to see local game disappear as he felt this would force the Indians to turn increasingly to agriculture for their livelihood."[5]

Although Indigenous people protested, the 1839 Crown Lands Protection Act, supposedly passed to protect Indigenous lands, made the government the guardian of Indian reserves. Rather than restoring authority to Indigenous communities, the legislation made "Indians" minors or wards of the Crown.[6]

By the 1840s, approximately 10,000 Anishinaabek and Haudenosaunee constituted a tiny minority in a colony of 450,000 settlers. This demographic imbalance only worsened over the next decades.[7] Extensive deforestation, an expanding road network, the building of railways, and industrial development transformed the landscape and increased the economic and political domination of Toronto over its hinterland.

Indigenous peoples were keenly aware of changing power dynamics and the importance of maintaining good relations with the British government. In the United States, thousands of Cherokees had died in 1838 when forced to trek more than 1,600 kilometres to Oklahoma on the "Trail of Tears"; disputes between settlers and Indigenous peoples over land had led to open warfare, with significant loss of life.

Given this reality, local First Nations adopted a variety of strategies to safeguard their lands, communities, and governance.

An Inter-Nation Council at the Credit, 1840

In 1840, the Mississaugas and Chippewas once again turned to their alliance with the Six Nations in the hope of gaining greater political leverage to protect their lands and governance. The minutes of a significant nine-day Council held at the Credit River that year provide a snapshot of their concerns: How could reserve lands and hunting territories be protected? Did it make more sense to move to one Indigenous territory or retain the small reserves they already had? How best to manage relations with the Crown? Tensions between old ways and new ways and between Christians and non-Christians shaped decisions about how to organize and run Councils, the bedrock of traditional governance systems: "It was stated that our fathers never recognized a presiding Chief in their Councils, but as we are imitating the good ways of the White people, it was thought proper to appoint a Chairman."

These words were recorded by Peter Jones, the appointed secretary, in English.

Twenty-seven Anishinaabe Chiefs and warriors attended, including John Assance; Musquakie, Thomas Nanigishkung, Negenaunaquot / Big Shilling, and Joseph Snake from the Lake Simcoe area; Joseph Sawyer and Peter Jones from the Mississaugas of the Credit; and Chiefs Elliot and Johnson from the Mississaugas of Balsam Lake (later Mississaugas of Scugog Island). Christianity was front and centre. Each day opened with hymn singing and praying. On Sunday, Jones preached in Anishinaabemowin to "a large congregation of his Indian brethren."[8] The Council also approved the use of band funds to reprint and expand Peter Jones's translated hymn book.

Items on the agenda included "to thank the British Government for giving them presents and to pray that they may still be continued"; to renew the title deed applications; to gauge the Council's opinion on the establishment of a "colony" or "a Great Council Fire somewhere"; and to discuss the possibility of a central "manual labour school." The Chiefs also wanted to consider "the propriety of petitioning the Queen to allow the Seat of Govt to continue at Toronto." Kingston had been chosen as capital of the new United Province of Canada, guaranteeing even less access to colonial administrators.

The new chief superintendent of Indian Affairs, Samuel Peters Jarvis, was invited to attend on the second day. Jarvis smoked the ceremonial pipe tomahawk that had been presented to Peter Jones in 1838 by Sir Augustus D'Este, Queen

Peter Jones, in regalia, photographed in Edinburgh, Scotland, in 1845, by Hill & Adamson. Jones holds a pipe tomahawk given to him by Sir Augustus d'Este, cousin of Queen Victoria, in 1838. The pipe had been ceremonially smoked at the 1840 Council at the Credit | National Galleries of Scotland, Edinburgh

Victoria's cousin and a significant leader of the Aborigines Protection Society. Jarvis "solemnly assured the Council that the British Govt had no intention of discontinuing the presents nor

18 | Surviving, Rebuilding, Adapting, Resisting

would they ever violate such a breach of faith as was made between the Indian Tribes and the Govt."

But Jarvis was "entirely opposed to the Indians receiving title Deeds and . . . his opposition arose from the good will he had to the Indians, as he knew if the Indians had deeds many of them would soon dispose of their lands."[9]

The Credit Chiefs later clarified that they were not seeking title deeds for individuals to hold plots of land in fee simple: "Our prayer to her Majesty's Govt. has been for the obtaining of a Govt. Document securing the lands to our Tribe and their posterity for ever."[10]

Jarvis offered the Chiefs a cosmetic alternative to the title deeds promised by Queen Victoria: "A map of the Reserve with a full description of it, and the names of Indians to whom it belongs, and the said map to contain the Seal of the province and the governor's signature." Given that the government had engineered the loss of most Indigenous land, this was hardly a guarantee of tenure into the future. But the government's philosophy of protective control through the Crown Lands Protection Act had already eliminated the possibility of the Mississaugas obtaining a title deed.[11]

In the government's eyes, Jarvis confirmed, the Anishinaabek were no longer considered allies but subjects. Though in true bureaucratic fashion, he claimed the matter was "under consideration." He was equally noncommittal about extending the reserve at Saugeen to create an "Indian colony." The government in fact refused to return the Saugeen lands surrendered under duress in the 1836 cession encouraged by Sir Francis Bond Head. Jarvis supported the idea of a manual-labour school, which would promote assimilation and teach farming skills to make Indigenous people less reliant on the government. Peter Jones also championed the proposal but for different reasons.

On the sixth day, fifteen Haudenosaunee Chiefs arrived to renew their peace and friendship treaty with the Anishinaabek and to work together to protect their sovereignty and lands. Of the Haudenosaunee Chiefs, only Mohawk Chief Sakayengwaraton (The Haze That Rises from the Ground in an Autumn Morning and Vanishes As the Day Advances) / John Smoke Johnson and Onandaga Chief Skanawiti (Beyond the River) / John Buck are named in the minutes.[12]

Chief Johnson told the Council "that the interests of all the Indians were one: that they had always supported the British Government, as they were strongly attached to it, and if that attachment should be lessened, it would not be their fault, but the fault of the government, in not keeping faith with the Indians." He called for all Indian tribes to unite to obtain titles to their lands, as "the government and the white people were taking away their lands by fair promises."[13]

As part of the treaty renewal, Buck and Musquakie each gave readings of the Dish with One Spoon and the Eternal Council Fires Wampums, which recorded the history and principles of the alliance between their peoples. Designated Wampum Keepers were trained from childhood to take on this important responsibility, and it was customary for both parties to an agreement to review the meaning of the Wampum symbols together to ensure their understandings were consonant. However, there appears to have been a significant disagreement between the Haudenosaunee and Anishinaabe interpretations of a key Wampum symbol—the Dish with One or Many Spoons—that may have derailed their joint action on land titles.

Buck, the Haudenosaunee Wampum Keeper, described the Dish with One Spoon agreement as

> the first Treaty made between the Six Nations and the Ojebways [Anishinaabek] . . . The belt was in the form of a dish or bowl in the centre, which the Chief said represented that the Ojebways and the Six Nations were all to eat out of the same dish; that is, to have all their game in common. In the centre of the bowl were a few white Wampums, which represented a beaver's tail, the favourite dish of the Ojebways. At this Council the treaty of friendship was formed, and agreement was made for ever after to call each other BROTHERS. This treaty of friendship was made so strong that if a tree fell across their arms it could not separate them or cause them to unloose their hold.[14]

But according to Musquakie's reading of the Eternal Council Fires Wampum—which the Haudenosaunee had given to the Anishinaabek as part of the same peace process to signal recognition of Anishinaabe Council Fires (i.e., seats of governance) over much of central Ontario—the sharing of resources was qualified. According to Musquakie, the Anishinaabek had placed a bowl with many ladles, including a ladle for the Six Nations, at the Narrows between Lakes Simcoe and Couchiching. While Buck related that the dish and ladle at Mnjikaning represented "abundance of game and food," Musquakie described it as a limited sharing: "At the Narrows our fathers placed a dish with ladles around it, and a ladle for the Six Nations, who said to the Ojebways that the dish or bowl should never be emptied, but he [Musquakie] was sorry to say that it had already been emptied, not by the Six Nations on the Grand River, but by the [Kahnawà:ke Mohawks] residing near Montreal."[15]

According to Musquakie, a dish had also been placed at the Credit, but he explained that "the right of hunting on the north side of the Lake was secured to the Ojebways, and the Six Nations were not to hunt here only when they come to smoke the pipe of peace with their Ojbeway brethren."[16] It's not clear if this hunting provision applied only when the Haudenosaunee came to attend treaty renewal Councils or if it was meant to last as long as they maintained peace with the Anishinaabek.

These interpretive differences persist to this day and figure in legal arguments over rights to consultation and resources in the Toronto region.[17] Because the Dish with One Spoon agreement was between First Nations and did not involve the Crown, its current legal status in relation to Ontario resources is unclear.

Despite these apparent differences in treaty interpretation, the historical alliance between the Haudenosaunee and Anishinaabek symbolized by the Dish with One Spoon was renewed in 1840—for the fifth time. Chief John Smoke Johnson called for another joint Council to be hosted by the Haudenosaunee in the future. However, the Six Nations were not signatories to the 1840 Council's petition to the lieutenant-governor requesting that he "secure to us and to our children, as soon as convenient, the lands on which we reside, as expressed in Lord Glenelg's dispatches."[18] The Anishinaabek and Six Nations did not work closely together over the next decades, although they did collaborate occasionally, notably in meetings of what in 1870 became the "Great Council Fire"—the Grand General Indian Council of Ontario.

Trying to Find Consensus and Maintain Unity

Even among the Anishinaabek, internal divisions hindered launching a coordinated campaign to lobby for title deeds or the return of the Saugeen Tract.

In the months following the 1840 Council, the Methodist church split into two bitterly antagonistic factions. Peter Jones sided with the "Canadian" (Episcopal) Methodists because of his loyalty to his close friend Egerton Ryerson. The Credit Village followed him, as did the Methodist Anishinaabek at Lake Simcoe (Rama), Mud Lake (Curve Lake), Saugeen, and Munceytown. Chief Paudash of Rice Lake, John Sunday at Alderville, and the mission at St. Clair joined the opposing faction, the "British" (Wesleyan) Methodists. The split ruptured decades-old relationships between Indigenous converts, missionaries, mission villages, and settler church groups.

Denominational rivalry between Catholics (especially after Jesuit missionaries returned to Canada in the 1840s), Anglicans, Baptists, Mormons, and others also strained relations between formerly close communities. John Assance's people at Beausoleil Island embraced Catholicism. Chief Musquakie of Rama joined the Church of England, although most of his people remained Methodists. Some converts became disillusioned with Christianity and returned to traditional beliefs.

Increasingly separated from each other by large areas of European settlement, each First Nation had to develop strategies for survival, depending on its history, culture, and local circumstances. Communities had to navigate internal differences between Christian converts of various denominations who were struggling for dominance and differences between Christians and traditionalists. These groups disagreed on whether Indigenous people should give up their cultural practices and beliefs or join Canadian society and, if so, on what terms. As the colonial government pressured communities to abandon traditional forms of governance, disputes erupted between community members who wanted elected forms of governance and those who preferred existing structures and practices, such as the Clan-based leadership and consensus decision-making practised by the Haudenosaunee Confederacy. At the Credit Village, majority voting rather than consensus or Clan-based political organization took precedence.[19]

As important as governance was, most Indigenous communities focused on rebuilding their communities after being forced to relocate to smaller reserves. Although Peter Jones, Assance, Musquakie, John Sunday, and others had spoken at the 1840 Council of the necessity of farming, many people lost their enthusiasm as they saw their people increasingly marginalized and impoverished while settlers took over their resources and flourished.

For those from the fertile Coldwater-Narrows Reserve, the new communities of Rama, Georgina Island, and Beausoleil were comparatively isolated from one another on marginal land. By 1842, the Chippewas had cleared 300 acres at Rama, built twenty houses, raised four barns, and were selling produce to local settlers, but it was profoundly discouraging to have to start all over again. Hunting and gathering on their family territories in Muskoka were an important source of food and helped maintain cultural continuity. Some men worked as hired hands on settler farms, in logging, or as fishing guides. Women made and sold crafts, such as baskets and moccasins, and bartered surplus fish or farm produce.[20]

Assance's people left Coldwater in 1842 for Beausoleil Island in Matchedash Bay. In 1846, Andrew Borland and his son John were contracted to build log houses for the 266 Chippewas who had moved there, but the soil proved too sandy to farm. In 1856, they moved to Christian Island in Georgian Bay.

Jessie Big Sail, n.d. | Chippewas of Georgina Island Historical Photo Collection

Similarly, Chief Snake's people returned from the Coldwater settlement to Snake Island and later moved to Georgina Island in southern Lake Simcoe. By 1844, they were farming 150 acres but continued to hunt along the Holland River.

They stopped viewing the whole lake as their home. They just viewed their little island as their sanctuary, kind of.

—Matthew Stevens, Chippewas of Georgina Island[21]

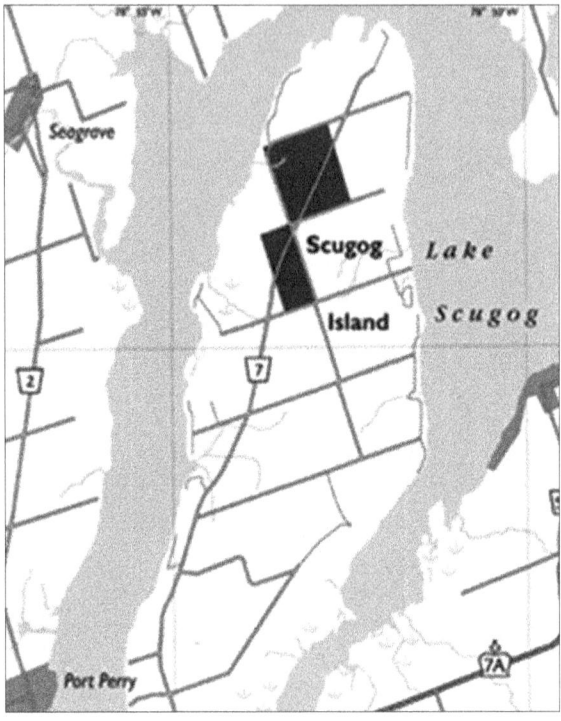

Mississaugas of Scugog Island Reserve, 1844 | Courtesy of Lake Scugog Historical Society

By 1843, the Mississaugas under Chief Jacob Crane, who had moved from Lake Scugog to Mud Lake in 1830 and to Balsam Lake in 1836, were being encouraged by the government to move yet again and take up subsistence farming. Because the land at Balsam Lake was rocky and unproductive, they wanted to return to their traditional territories at Lake Scugog. But their former camping grounds had been taken over by settlers (and would later become the town

of Port Perry). The only land available was 800 landlocked acres on Scugog Island. Most of their land had been taken from them without compensation, and now they were being required to purchase a reserve with their own money.[22]

The Mississaugas of the Credit were likewise facing relocation. Their village now included two sawmills, two carpenters, a shoemaker, a hospital building, two stores, a blacksmith, a school, a chapel, and a mission house. They were majority shareholders in the Credit Harbour Company, which shipped timber and crops from the area to ports around Lake Ontario.

> *We built our own schooner out of our own funds, the* Credit Chief . . . *And we used it to ship goods around Lake Ontario. It seemed to be a losing proposition, from what I understand at the time. But it was still a good try as far as I'm concerned.*
>
> —Darin Wybenga, Mississaugas of the Credit[23]

Many band members could read and write, and a significant number worked as missionaries, interpreters, and schoolmasters at the Credit or elsewhere. By any measure, they had become "civilized" on terms the British understood. Yet they knew their land and all they had built could all be taken away from them at any time.

In 1840, they requested good farmland elsewhere, citing poor soil at the Credit, the need for additional land, and the "evil example of nearby whites." They were running out of timber for firewood and salmon, which had once been so abundant. By 1846, *Smith's Gazetteer* reported that because of "the great number of mills which have been erected on the river during the last four years, the fishing is destroyed, the salmon being unable to make their way over the dams."[24]

The Credit Mississaugas had hoped to move to the fertile lands of the Saugeen Tract, but when the most fertile portion was surrendered in 1836, most decided to look elsewhere. (Three families, including Nahnebahwequay and her husband and David Sawyer, did relocate there on the belief that others would soon join them.) Chiefs Peter Jones and Joseph Sawyer reluctantly decided to move the band to a tract of rich agricultural land near Munceytown (close to present-day London), where Peter Jones had become resident missionary in 1841.

Although the Credit band approved the decision to relocate to Munceytown, a group of families led by the Herkimer brothers refused to move, rekindling a power struggle between the "progressives" (the Jones party) and the "moderates" (the Herkimers and their followers). Superintendent Jarvis supported the Herkimer faction and refused to allow the move. Jarvis was strongly disliked by the Credit Chiefs. Joseph Sawyer and John Jones described his behaviour as "uncourteous and repulsive."[25] Reluctantly, in 1844, the band abandoned its plan to move to Munceytown and renewed its search for a new location. The following year, Jones wrote: "The Indian territories have been taken away till our possessions are now so small that you would almost require a magnifying glass to see them. We are surrounded on all sides by white settlers, still encroaching on us."[26]

At Six Nations, Haudenosaunee lands had likewise been whittled away through 999-year mortgages, conditional surrenders, illegal surrenders, life leases, and squatters who simply built houses and cleared farms illegally.[27] White residents living in Brantford gained title to much of the Mohawk village. In 1835, the government ratified many illegal transactions after the fact.

Chief Superintendent Jarvis recommended that Haudenosaunee land could be better protected if the Mohawk, Cayuga, Seneca, Oneida, Onondaga, Tuscarora villages along the Grand River were consolidated into one area and the rest of the Haldimand Tract sold off, with the proceeds going to the Haudenosaunee. Although many Haudenosaunee contested his proposal, ten months after the 1840 Council, Upper Canada passed an Order-in-Council drastically reducing Haudenosaunee lands. While some, such as Chief John Smoke Johnson, agreed to the measure, others strongly opposed it. This fundamental political difference over land policy divided Haudenosaunee families and communities for decades.[28] The loss of most of the original Haudenosaunee land holdings and the size of the original grant under the Haldimand Proclamation are now under litigation between Six Nations of the Grand River and the federal and provincial governments.

And, through the passage of time and the ill dealings of the Crown, we're left with less than 5 per cent of the [Haldimand] tract.

—Phil Monture, Six Nations of the Grand River[29]

Settler Self-Government and Responsibility for "Indian" Affairs

The union of Upper and Lower Canada in 1841 into the Province of Canada (Canada West and Canada East, now Ontario and Quebec) increased local settler self-government. The governor general rather than the British Colonial Office administered Indian Affairs, although the British government did not formally cede control of Indian Affairs (and its financing) until 1860. The Crown's role in offering Indigenous people protection against settler interests was significantly reduced, and the status of Indigenous peoples as allies was downplayed, although colonial officials gave lip service to the alliance when useful. Six Nations historian Keith Jamieson captures this shift: "After 1841, the long-term impact of the transition of power from Britain to Canada proved devastating for the Six Nations of the Grand River community. The honoured relationship they enjoyed with the Crown was reinterpreted by the Province of Canada as one that relegated the Haudenosaunee as wards of the government, and their sovereign lands as reserves to which they would be restricted."[30]

Educating Colonial Officials amid Government Ineptitude

In 1841, Peter Jones tried another strategy to influence government policy. Under his Anishinaabe name, Kahkewaquonaby, he published "The Indian Nations: A Short Account of the Customs and Manners of the North American Indians, Particularly the Chippeway Nation," in the *Monthly Review Devoted to the Civil Government of the Canadas*.[31] He hoped that by educating British colonial officials and settlers about the history and culture of Anishinaabe peoples, settler governments would treat them in a more enlightened way. The article became the germ of *History of the Ojebway Indians: With Especial Reference to their Conversion to Christianity*, published posthumously in 1861 with additions and revisions by his British wife, Eliza. (The book was based on notes made over several decades until 1854–55, when he was too ill to continue.) Jones' published works offered readers valuable oral tradition from Elders as well as his own account, with numerous anecdotes of nineteenth-century Anishinaabe life viewed from a Christian perspective.

Despite Jones' efforts, the Indian Department continued to be unresponsive. It had the reputation of being "notoriously the worst and most inefficient department in the province."[32] An 1839 inquiry confirmed that until James Givins' long-deferred retirement in 1837, few records had been maintained. More information on Indigenous lands could be located in the Crown Lands Office and other departments than in the Indian Department. Although the duties of the chief superintendent and local agents had expanded since 1830, the department lacked central planning and clear roles for its officers. The inquiry reported on the "injudicious disposal of much valuable property and the disappearance of unaccounted funds."[33] Excessive, intrusive, and paternalistic bureaucracy was evident on many fronts, including the handling of annuity payments, which were not paid in cash unless requested by the Chief and approved by the chief superintendent. Instead, the chief superintendent unilaterally arranged the purchase of cattle, seeds, agricultural implements, and other items needed for farming. First Nations then had to apply to the local superintendent, who forwarded the request to the chief superintendent, who then directed the commissariat to transfer the supplies to a local depot.[34]

To make matters worse, Jarvis often did not act in the interests of Indigenous people. In 1843, Chiefs Joseph Sawyer and John Jones of the Mississaugas of the Credit reported to the governor general's secretary that, according to several Lake Simcoe Anishinaabek, Jarvis had fathered a child by a Snake Island woman.[35] The Chiefs also accused him of financial irresponsibility: since his appointment in 1837, there had been "no balance sheet furnished us . . . we do not know whether we get the full amount of our annuity, and the proceeds of the sale of our Reserves."[36] The Six Nations of the Grand River also contended that he misappropriated their funds while in office. In 1844, the Bagot Commission corroborated that Jarvis kept few, if any, accounts of band finances. In 1845, he was ordered to return the 4,000 pounds he had diverted from the people he was supposed to protect. He was then dismissed.[37]

19

From Civilization to Assimilation

Peter Jones had developed a close relationship with Methodist missionary Egerton Ryerson when they worked together to establish the church and bilingual school at the Credit Mission in 1826. The question of how best to educate Indigenous children to adapt to rapid change was a subject of ongoing mutual interest.

By 1841, Jones had identified irregular attendance as a problem, as parents took their children out of the day schools to travel with them to harvest food in various areas. After visiting the manual training schools for the Choctaw and Cherokee Nations in the United States, he became convinced that "the children must be taken for a season from their parents, and put to well-regulated Manual Labour Schools."[1] Other missionaries and colonial officials had come to the same conclusion. In an 1844 fundraising speech in London, England, Jones outlined his vision:

> Our contemplated plans are to establish two Schools; one for one hundred boys, the other for one hundred girls. The boys to be taught in connection with a common English education, the art of Farming and useful trades. The girls to be instructed in Reading and Writing, Domestic Economy, Sewing, Knitting, Spinning; so as to qualify them to become good wives and mothers. It is also our intention to select from each School the most promising boys and girls, with a view of giving them superior advantages; so as to qualify them for Missionaries and School teachers among their brethren.[2]

Initially, many Indigenous parents supported his proposals because they believed the schools would equip their children to navigate economic and social challenges and that Indigenous people would play a major role in their operation.[3]

Proposals for manual-labour schools were a major feature of the colonial government's 1844 Bagot Commission report—but for different reasons. The Bagot Commission, one of six commissions appointed to assess the government's handling of "Indian" affairs between 1828 and 1858, was convened by Governor General Charles Bagot and tasked with investigating the Indian Department and the purportedly slow progress of "Indian advancement." Its chief aim was reducing the department's expenditures "with a view to its diminishment and eventual extinction." But the commission affirmed the Crown's duty and responsibility to protect Indigenous peoples from insensitive local authorities and refuted Bond Head's removal policy.[4] According to the commissioners, there were no racial barriers to Indian advancement: the department needed to be reorganized, Indigenous people's lands and resources needed to be protected, and their children needed better education.

The 1844 final report documented conditions on reserves in Canada East and Canada West and advocated coercive strategies to speed up assimilation and end "dependence on the government." Indigenous children should be separated from their parents to expedite their assimilation by weaning them "from the habits and feelings of their ancestors."[5] Boarding schools with attached farms—now called Industrial Schools—were to be established to teach farming, trades, and domestic economy. The schools' farm crops would also reduce operating costs. The commissioners recommended the establishment of four Industrial Schools in partnership with the churches. Two existing schools (the Mohawk Institute at Brantford and the Methodist school at Rice Lake) would serve as models.[6]

Peter Jones was among those who made submissions to the Bagot Commission supporting the schools.[7] Although the proposed schools marked the beginning of the Indian Residential School system in Canada, Jones' vision differed from what the schools would become: he envisaged a system under Indigenous control that would help Indigenous people navigate the developing settler-colonial state.

The Bagot report's recommendation for schools was one of several recommendations promoting the assimilation of Indigenous peoples. It recommended reducing the annual presents promised in the 1764 Treaty of Niagara to affirm and maintain the Covenant Chain, the historic alliance of Indigenous peoples and the Crown. The report also recommended the preparation of band lists controlled by the government. People of mixed heritage ("half-breeds") would be deemed ineligible unless they were adopted by an Indigenous community. No Indigenous woman living with or married to a white man would receive presents nor would any child educated in an Industrial School.[8] Because of Indigenous opposition and the potential need for military allies during the Oregon border dispute, the government didn't end annual presents until 1858.

The Bagot Commission also proposed granting title deeds to Indigenous individuals for reserve land. Officials and missionaries believed title would encourage individual initiative, provide some legal standing for reserve lands and resources, and end Indigenous dependency on the government. But Indigenous leaders resisted the idea because it ran counter to the traditional practice of communal land ownership.[9] Temporarily shelved, the proposal would reappear in later legislation, such as the Gradual Civilization Act of 1857.

Although not all recommendations were implemented immediately, the Bagot Commission confirmed the overall direction of government policy. As historian John F. Leslie writes: "The Commissioners' report, intended originally as a blueprint to reduce operational costs and make Indian people less reliant on government, became, in practice, just another milestone in the evolution and development of a more costly, permanent, and expanded Indian department which would increasingly regulate and control the daily lives of Indian people in the Canadas."[10]

Peter Jones' 1842 testimony to the Bagot Commission affirmed Mississauga self-government and self-determination. He spoke of the 1830 Constitution of the Mississaugas of the Credit and emphasized the need to recognize their full civil and political rights, grant land title in perpetuity, and provide full financial transparency for annuities and land sales. However, only his views on education were taken up as both church and government officials now supported assimilation.[11]

The consequences of the Bagot Commission were profound. The position of chief superintendent was abolished in 1845 on account of financial mismanagement and the civil secretary ran the department until 1860. In 1851, the Imperial Parliament announced that diplomatic presents would cease in 1858, unilaterally ending the alliance relationship. In 1856, it ceased annual payments to support Indian Affairs. An annual transition grant of $3,000 was given until 1860, when responsibility for Indian Affairs was transferred fully to the colonial government of the Canadas.[12] These new arrangements accelerated the appropriation of Indigenous land and resources for government ends and the coercive push to assimilate Indigenous peoples.

The General Council of 1846

Although the Bagot Commission recommended manual-labour schools, it suggested no measures to fund them. Bagot's successor as governor general, Sir Charles Metcalfe, discontinued the supply of ammunition to several communities in a bid to find the money, but it wasn't enough.[13] Funding for the first two schools, at Alderville and Mount Elgin (Muncey), was then tied to a larger scheme to relocate First Nations in southern Ontario and get them to contribute a share of their annuities to the schools. For a time, this push coincided with First Nations' desire to relocate to one shared territory.

In 1845, while Peter Jones was in Britain to raise money for the schools, a General Council was held among the Anishinaabek. The Anishinaabek of Saugeen and Owen Sound invited the other communities to join them in creating a new homeland on what remained of the Saugeen Tract on the Bruce Peninsula, one of the last remaining unsurrendered territories in southern Ontario.

In 1846, the proposal was considered at a General Council at the Narrows, the developing settler town of Orillia. Called by Thomas Gummersall Anderson, former Indian agent of Coldwater and the Narrows and head of the Indian Department, the Council's purpose was to convince the Anishinaabek to abandon their small reserves and gather in three larger communities at Munceytown (near London), Alderville (near Belleville), and Owen Sound on Georgian Bay. Manual-labour schools would be built in each community, and those who relocated would receive deeds to the land.¹⁴ Conveniently, the move freed up yet more arable land for settlers.

> *Where the two lakes meet, where we were, that was a place of gathering and meeting. It was a place of healing and government meetings that took place there... The big meeting took place there... about the residential school system, whether our kids should be sent there, and runners were sent out from our community to all the other Native communities around to have their Chiefs come to that meeting.*
>
> —Sherry Lawson, Chippewas of Rama¹⁵

In return for deeds, the bands would commit one-quarter of their annuities for the next twenty to twenty-five years to support the schools. By then, Anderson claimed, "Some of your youth will be sufficiently enlightened to carry on a system of instruction among yourselves, and this proportion of your funds will no longer be required."¹⁶

Present at the Council were Anishinaabe Chiefs from the Credit, Scugog, Snake Island (Georgina), Rama, and Beausoleil and Mohawks from Tyendinaga but not Six Nations (presumably because they already had the Mohawk Institute).¹⁷ The Methodist missionaries included Peter Jones and John Sunday. Anderson opened the Council:

Brethren—For more than twenty years past, large sums of money have been spent by the Government, and your Missionaries have used their endeavours to divest you of Indian customs, and instruct you in the arts of civilized life, but it has not proved effectual. Though favourable alterations have taken place, and your condition has greatly improved, yet much remains to be done. And that you are not a better and happier people, and your civilization more advanced, is not the fault of the Government; neither can it be attributed to neglect on the part of your Missionaries; but it is because you do not feel, or know the value of education; you would not give up your idle roving habits, to enable your children to receive instruction. Therefore you remain poor, ignorant and miserable. It is found that you cannot govern yourselves. And if left to be guided by your own judgment, you will never be better off than you are at present; and your children will ever remain in ignorance. It has therefore been determined, that your children shall be sent to Schools, where they will forget their Indian habits, and be instructed in all the necessary arts of civilized life, and become one with your white brethren. In these Schools they will be well taken care of, be comfortably dressed, kept clean, and get plenty to eat. The adults will not be forced from their present locations.

They may remove, or remain, as they please; but their children must go.

Brethren—I wish seriously to impress upon your minds, that if you do not avail yourselves of this favourable opportunity of bringing you from darkness to light, it may be the last time you will have so good an offer. Remember that disgrace will attach to your character; and how justly future generations may reflect upon your names, if you at present neglect their best interest.

Brethren—For some years past, you have had the management of your own funds. Your money is gone; and you have nothing to shew for it. This is not satisfactory. Your money must in future be applied to purposes that will be of permanent benefit to your Tribes respectively.[18]

Anderson concluded: "The Government want to see Indian Doctors, they want to see Indian Lawyers, and Justices of the Peace; Indians of all Professions and Trades; and that you should be like the white people. This is what the Government wish to see among the Indians."[19]

Anderson and the missionaries—including Peter Jones—persuaded First Nations to commit one-quarter of their annuities to the schools, but Chief Musquakie objected to the removal plan:

> My mind has been engaged in considering the subject brought before me; and the events that have occurred before, especially in respect to the removal of my own people from this village before me [Orillia] where we were once before advised to remain settled as a religious people, and from which we were afterwards asked to remove to another place, where we now reside. And now I do not see what my young men are to subsist upon, not continuing to work the land; striving to settle here, in Orillia, and to be religious, and then required to remove; and now, when we are settled at Rama, before my young men have had time to make a fair trial there, being again required to remove to another place . . . I am not willing to leave my village, the place where my Forefathers lived, and where they made a great encampment; where they lived many generations; where they wished their children to live while the world should stand, and which the white man pointed out to me, and gave me for my settlement.[20]

Similarly, Chief Assance stated:

> You see this road here, my Chiefs, the Portage Road; the land on half of that road was given to me and my Tribe to live upon. We remained there scarcely seven years when our white Father asked us to give it back. Yet a little more I tell you, my Chiefs; you advised me to put up a Grist Mill. You told me that it would be a good thing for my Tribe. And you said to me, "you will derive a blessing from it." We are no longer owners of the Mill. You,

the white people, have it in use. But we do not know what use is made of it.²¹

Anderson challenged Assance's claims and suggested he had been reimbursed for the mill. Assance continued: "I do not wish to remove. I have already removed four times, and I am too old to remove again . . . The Scripture says, we are told it says, we must love one another; but now, if we give up our money for the benefit of the young, who will take care of the old people?"²²

Chief Snake also shared Musquakie's concerns: "I consider it a very good thing; but so many different Agents and Members of the Indian Department have thought differently, and when they have proposed one plan it has not continued long. This is another reason why I cannot consent."²³

The stark choice that Indigenous Nations faced was expressed by Tyendinaga Mohawk Chief Paulus Claus: "As there was a time when the Indians owned the whole of this continent, from the salt waters; but no sooner did the white men come, than the Indians were driven from their former homes, like the wild animals. We are now driven far from our former homes, into the woods. I cannot see the end of this, removing from one place to another, going still farther into the woods, unless we exert ourselves to conform to the ways of the white man."²⁴ Mississauga Chief Joseph Sawyer stated, "Suppose I have four dollars in my hand, I willingly give one dollar for the good of my children."²⁵

Anderson drafted a formal memorandum and requested a vote. All Chiefs but Musquakie, Assance, and Thomas Assance (sub-Chief of Beausoleil) voted yes.

And Yellowhead and Assance I think were the only two Chiefs who said no to the government. Because they said, basically, "We don't trust you. We don't want our children to go to these schools because you've done us wrong before, and we think you'll do it again." And they also refused to move to Manitoulin.

—Ben Cousineau, Chippewas of Rama²⁶

Anderson reiterated:

The project of removal did not originate with the Government. The idea was first suggested by some of the wisest and most intelligent of the Indian Chiefs. It must be clearly understood, that the Government will not force any Band or Tribe to remove; but those who do not must not complain, when hereafter they find that they are not as well off as those who have gone hand in hand with the Government, and who, I am convinced, will shortly be a subject of envy to those who shall not avail themselves of this plan, but prefer following the advice of interested individuals instead of that of the Government.²⁷

The following day, Musquakie and Assance changed their vote to yes, stating that their position had been based on a "misapprehension."[28] Although the Chiefs had the best intentions, the communities they represented would come to regret their decision.

> *In day two of the minutes from this meeting, Yellowhead is not there. And the government was really, basically, pissed off that Yellowhead had disrespected them and that he flat out said, "You guys are liars. I don't trust you" . . . The next day, Yellowhead isn't there, and someone speaking on his behalf says, "He's changed his mind. He's good now. He now approves of everything, except for the move. He's okay with manual labour schools, and it's all good" . . . But it [the minutes] just kind of assumes that it's legit and he's okay with it even though he's not there. And then a Nanigishkung who's there says, "I'll speak on behalf of my community. And I think it's okay" . . . The Yellowhead reign, I guess, if you will, of Chieftanship ends a few years after that. And from then on, it's Nanigishkung.*
>
> —Ben Cousineau, Chippewas of Rama[29]

Egerton Ryerson and Industrial Schools

In 1847, Egerton Ryerson, now superintendent for schools in Upper Canada, founded the Toronto Normal School, an institution for teacher training that attracted a number of Indigenous students—some of whom taught in on-reserve day schools.[30] That same year, following decisions made at the 1846 Orillia Council, the assistant superintendent of Indian affairs asked Ryerson to prepare a report on "the best method of establishing and conducting Industrial Schools for the benefit of the aboriginal Indian Tribes."

Referring now to the proposed boarding schools as "industrial schools," Ryerson described them as more than schools of manual labour, since they were also schools of learning and religion, where "industry" would be applied to mental and physical labour. Religious education would be "the animating and controlling spirit of each industrial school establishment." The students would learn "the English language, arithmetic, elementary geometry, or knowledge of forms, geography and the elements of general history, natural history and agricultural chemistry, writing, drawing and vocal music, book-keeping (especially in reference to farmers' accounts) religion and morals."

Boys would be trained to be farmers, with classroom lessons supporting that goal. The schools would operate year-round. Students would work eight to twelve hours a day and study for two to four hours in the summer. During planting and harvesting, classes might be cancelled for two or three weeks. During winter, classroom study time would increase while work would decrease. Religious organizations would run the schools, but the government would be responsible for hiring the superintendent, erecting the buildings, determining attendance, providing ongoing funding, and carrying out inspections.[31]

The Indian Department approved the construction of the schools at Alderville and Munceytown but abandoned the proposed school at Owen Sound. The Alnwick school expanded the Methodist school in Alderville and admitted students from central Ontario, including from Lake Huron, Lake Simcoe, Saugeen, Owen Sound, and Alnwick and Rice, Mud, and Scugog Lakes.[32] Mount Elgin, the school at Munceytown, near London, was completed in 1851 and drew students from southwestern Ontario, including New Credit.

Peter Jones was supposed to become the superintendent of Mount Elgin Industrial School. He moved to Munceytown in 1847 as the school was being constructed, but by the time it opened in 1851, he was too ill to accept the position. Both schools ended up being run by white missionaries with increasingly restricted input from Indigenous communities.

A system of resident agents supervised the schools and their model farms. They were to ensure that students learned either French or English as "nothing will so pave the way for the amalgamation of the Indian and white races, as the disuse among the former of their peculiar dialects."[33]

The schools were not a success. Communities objected to the way their children were treated

Announcement of the sale of the Credit Reserve | Library and Archives Canada, RG 10, vol. 458, p. 106

and withdrew them, resulting in low enrolment. The Truth and Reconciliation Commission noted:

> Residential schooling in the pre-Confederation era exhibited many of the problems that would characterize the system's entire history. Parents preferred to see

their children at home and were reluctant to send them to school. At the schools, children were lonely and frequently ran away. School life was hard and often unhealthy, and education focused largely on work and religion. Those children who completed their schooling often found that their ties to their home communities and cultures had been severed, but they had not been given the skills needed to succeed in the broader society. First Nations communities had agreed initially to provide funding to the schools, but they later withdrew their support, based on their experience with a system that was unresponsive to their wishes, disparaged their culture, and failed to deliver the promised economic benefits.[34]

Further Removals and Indigenous Mutual Aid

Despite support at the 1846 Council for the consolidation of Indigenous Nations in one location, it did not take place. The Credit Mississaugas supported the proposed move to Owen Sound as their best chance for a new homeland on good agricultural land. But several men visited the remaining Saugeen Tract and were deeply disappointed. Peter Jones reported: "There is quite a dissention amongst our people with regard to their removal to Owen Sound. Our young men who assisted in surveying the boundary line of our intended tract there have brought an evil report as to the quality of the soil. They say that the land is very rocky and that there is not more than one third of the whole tract fit for cultivation. In consequence of these tidings a large majority of our Tribe are reluctant to remove to that land."[35]

The move was called off.

Here we'd taken all this time to learn how to become farmers—and good farmers—and we're going to go to this tract of land in Saugeen that our people found was not conducive to agriculture. And so we went back and told Anderson, "We can't move there." But the word was "Sorry. Your lands are up for sale now. We thought you were going to move, so we've put the lands up for sale. You're going, whether you like it or not." We didn't know where we were going. We just knew we were going.

—Darin Wybenga, Mississaugas of the Credit[36]

When the Credit Mississaugas pulled out of the plan, the other communities followed, and the dream of an "Indian territory" was not realized.

Although not part of the Owen Sound relocation scheme, the Six Nations of the Grand River were also struggling with dispossession. In 1847, an Order-in-Council confirmed that George Martin's settlement near Brantford was outside of the land remaining to the Haudenosaunee, and the families living there would have to move. They refused. A mob from Brantford forcefully removed families from their homes, loaded them into carriages, and burned their homes and barns to the ground. George Martin's

Reduction of Six Nations lands and Mississauga relocation to New Credit. This map is for general information only. The size and exact boundaries of the original lands granted to the Six Nations through the 1784 Haldimand Proclamation vary in existing maps and are currently under litigation

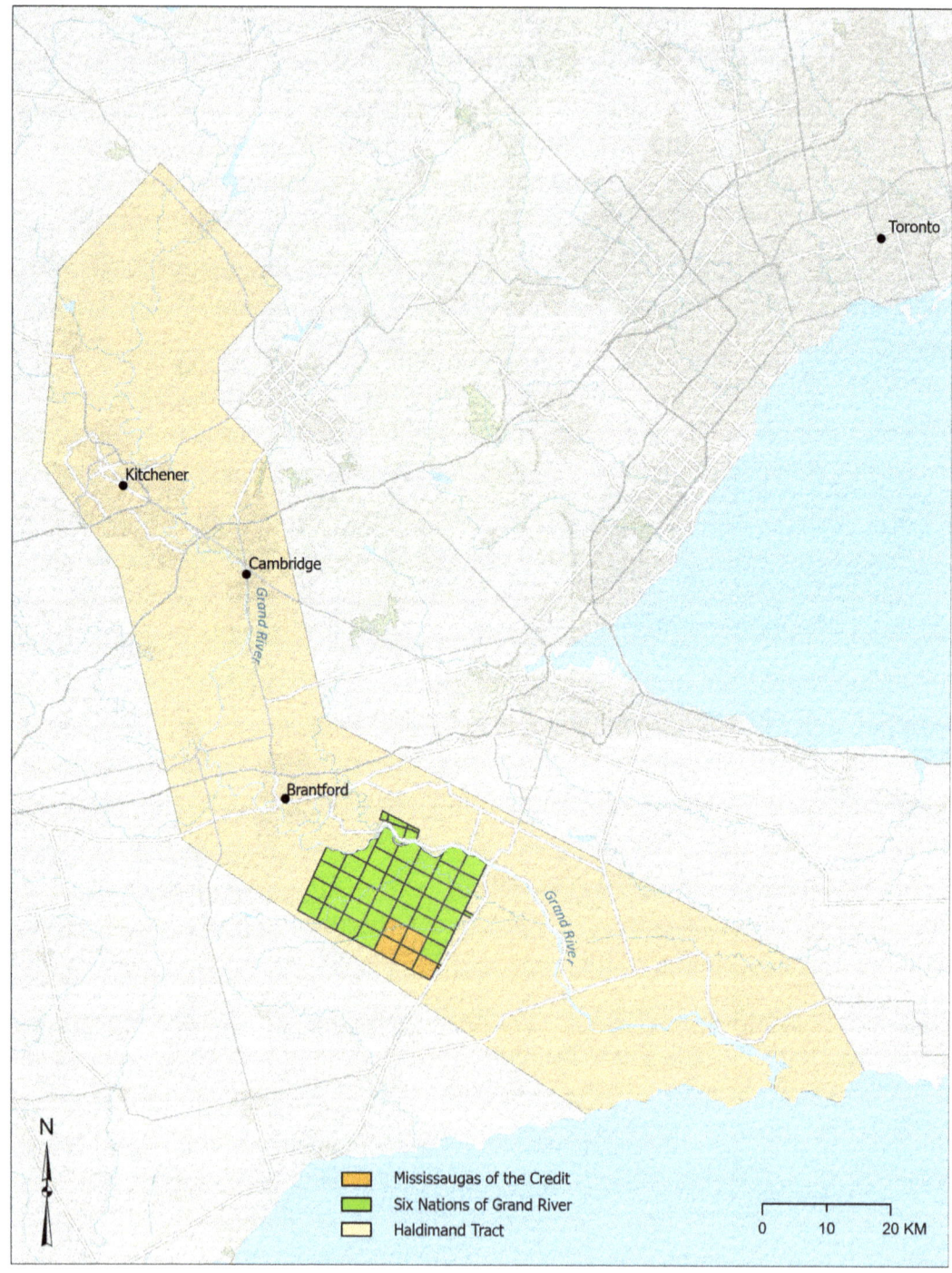

232

grandson Oronhyatekha (Dr. Peter Martin) was six years old at the time. Although the settlers' actions were reported, no action was taken to punish them or compensate the Haudenosaunee. After George Martin died in 1853, the lands were divided and leased to settlers. Even after the Haudenosaunee were confined to their much-reduced territory, squatters remained a problem.[37]

Given this much smaller territory, it is remarkable that the Haudenosaunee—not the government—came to the rescue of the Credit Mississaugas, especially given the sometimes difficult relationship between the two peoples. As Peter Jones related:

> Spring was advancing when preparations ought to have been made for planting, and we knew not whither to head our steps, or find a resting place . . . It is a remarkable fact, that about this time the Chiefs of the Six Nations, on the Grand River were holding a Council, who having heard of our situation took our case into consideration and unanimously agreed to offer us a portion of their tract; this was done without our knowledge or solicitation . . . It gave [the Six Nations] great pleasure to return us a similar kindness by giving us back a small portion from the large reserve they had received. Another reason was, that ever since they came to this country, they had lived in friendship with us.[38]

In 1847, the Haudenosaunee offered the Mississaugas land in the southernmost portion of their Reserve on the Haldimand Tract. In doing so, they were returning the gift of refuge originally extended by the Mississaugas in 1784, when the Mississaugas ceded the lands that became the Haldimand Tract to the Six Nations after the latter had been displaced from their homelands south of Lake Ontario by the American Revolution. This assistance was in keeping with the ethic of reciprocity ("gift for gift") and the responsibilities of allies under the Dish with One Spoon. Sadly, the Mississaugas of the Credit, a fishing people, would no longer have access to water, but they packed up their belongings to re-establish themselves on this land, which they called New Credit and where they live today.

> *We're the Mississaugas, water people. Moved here. No water. They lost their fisheries and everything. I would say that was a culture shock. For them to come here and have no water."*
>
> —Carolyn King, Mississaugas of the Credit[39]

A Mississaugas of the Credit publication also describes the move:

> Our ancestors left prosperous farms, and a village with homes furnished better than many of their settler neighbors, a hospital, mechanic's shops, a sawmill, and even a schooner. Upon the move to New Credit, some of our ancestors even had to make two trips back to their old village to walk all their domestic animals

to the new location. In short, our ancestors had prospered . . . There was a sense of optimism among our people, but also a sense of sorrow at leaving family members behind in the village graveyard.[40]

Every time I go across the Credit [River, on the QEW], I give a greeting to my ancestors.

—Garry Sault, Mississaugas of the Credit[41]

Peter Jones wrote in the *Christian Guardian* about their sorrow in leaving behind their Methodist co-religionists in the Toronto area, with whom they had formed relationships over two decades.[42] In part because of the increased social distance, the Methodist Church's advocacy for Indigenous legal issues declined over the next decade, as did the Methodists' support for the training of Indigenous teachers and the use of Indigenous languages in worship and education. As historian Neil Semple writes: "Notions of racial inferiority and the assumption that natives should not minister to their own emerged during the second half of the nineteenth century. Methodism thereby lost much of its original advantage over other churches."[43]

In 1903, after a dispute with the Haudenosaunee over their tenure, the Mississaugas purchased the land they had been offered in 1847 as well as an additional 1,200 acres from the Haudenosaunee. This land was set aside as a separate reserve (Indian Reserve 40A) by a federal Order-in-Council. However, the nature of the Mississaugas' title remains a matter of contention between the Six Nations and Mississaugas of the Credit.

The fundamental issue of Indigenous people's lack of legal ownership of their reserve lands has never been resolved. In Canadian law, reserve lands are Crown lands set aside for the use of Indigenous people.

We never achieved title to our lands at the [Credit] . . . It's much the same as today. We just get to live here [at New Credit] because the government says we get to live here.

—Darin Wybenga, Mississaugas of the Credit[44]

20

Black Wampum

The British Indian Department was created to maintain military and trading alliances with Indigenous peoples. After the War of 1812, when the need for allies receded, the department was tasked with "civilizing" and preparing Indigenous people to be peaceful, economically self-sufficient subjects who would give up most of their lands to settlers. But insatiable settler demand undermined the civilizational agenda: First Nations of the Toronto area and elsewhere were repeatedly uprooted, denied title to their lands or adequate compensation for them, cheated out of their band funds by corrupt department officials, and relegated to small isolated reserves where farming was difficult.

Although their way of life changed drastically, Indigenous peoples did not assimilate as intended but remained separate peoples, wary of settler intentions on the one hand and shunned and treated as second-class citizens by settlers on the other. When Indigenous populations stabilized and "temporary" reserves looked anything but, the imperial government wanted to rid itself of the financial burden that Indigenous peoples now represented without being accused by humanitarians of utterly abandoning them.

In the mid-1800s, several government inquiries investigated the administration of the Indian Department and why its civilization policy had not been as successful as anticipated. They examined expenses, policies and procedures, financial and reporting practices, the number of employees, and the expense of annual presents and considered whether the department should be disbanded and its responsibilities shifted to other administrative units. These issues became even more acute when the Imperial Parliament transferred authority over Indian affairs to the provincial government. Funding had always been in short supply and there had always been pressure to cut costs, but now the colony itself would be on the hook.

Between 1840 and 1860, when Indian Affairs was still under the control of the Imperial Parliament, an annual parliamentary grant covered the salaries and pensions of Indian agents, officers, and some missionaries and teachers. A smaller General Fund from interest, the sale of Indigenous lands, and fines for unlawfully cut timber paid for the small headquarters staff and a few other expenses. The

Land Fund, generated by sales of ceded Indian Lands, paid 10 per cent of the cost of operating the Crown Lands Department.

Until it was merged with other funds in 1860, the Six Nations Estate was a fourth source of income intended to pay for the management of that reserve. Finally, each community paid Chiefs, interpreters, missionaries, doctors, and schoolmasters from band funds accrued from the annuities paid in perpetuity for land cessions.[1]

Indigenous lands and band funds tempted administrators seeking new sources of revenue. Trustees misappropriated Haudenosaunee funds to finance numerous colonial infrastructure projects. For example, in 1846, the trustees transferred £200 to Simcoe District for unknown reasons and £4,412 to the City of Toronto. In 1846 and 1847, £2,900 of Haudenosaunee money was used to build roads in York County and does not appear to have been repaid. Significantly larger amounts were transferred to Public Works and towards the public debt. Most egregiously, in 1861 trustees informed the Confederacy Council that a significant proportion of its funds had been invested in the Grand River Navigation Company without its knowledge or consent and had been lost when the company declared bankruptcy.[2]

Historically, the Five Nations tract of land was basically bankrolling Canada at the beginning of Canada. And we have records that show that. And that's what we have before the courts today.

—Phil Montour, Six Nations of the Grand River[3]

On-reserve resources were another target. In 1850, Canada West empowered Crown land commissioners to grant licences for cutting timber on reserve lands and to fine trespassers (i.e., white settlers) for cutting illegally. Revenue from fines and licences would be directed to a fund to "benefit the Indians"; in practice, the money financed the Indian Department and was used to make small interest payments to bands. Timber sales became a significant source of revenue. The department insisted that all logs cut on Indian lands should be sold through the Indian agent, who administered the fund.[4]

As the end of the imperial grant approached, the Pennefather Commission in 1856 addressed the Indian Department's financing. Superintendent-General Richard Pennefather recommended that the department be restructured and subsumed within Provincial Crown Lands. The commissioner of Crown lands for the province of Canada would become the superintendent-general of Indian Affairs, a clear conflict of interest. The same official responsible for safeguarding Indigenous peoples' interests and upholding treaties would also be overseeing the disbursement of land and resources for settlers.

The government directed the department to replace imperial funding with increased sales of Indigenous land and resources but doing so would require expanded jurisdiction. At this time, the concept of protection shifted away from protecting Indigenous lands for the use of Indigenous peoples to protecting the government's ability to exclusively manage those lands and their fish, mineral, and timber wealth for government purposes. The role of Indian agents changed from distributing presents and annuities to administering local finances and band funds that were kept out of community control. They regulated reserve resource economies, including Indigenous resource use, increasing conflict with Indigenous leaders and communities.[5]

When Indian agents found it impossible to police Indigenous people's sales of their own timber, the solicitor general said they could be charged as trespassers on their own lands: "Cutting timber, staves or wood for any purpose upon Indian lands has been rendered unlawful . . . any persons whether *Indians* or others offending against the said statute will be prosecuted with rigor."[6]

Similarly, the Fishing Act of 1857 was "an undisguised effort to transfer the wealth of the aboriginal fisheries from the First Nations . . . to the department."[7] The act favoured non-Indigenous sports fisheries over Indigenous fisheries, imposed overseers and a licensing system, and regulated fishing seasons for various species. The Anishinaabek of Lakes Huron and Simcoe vigorously protested this legislation and reminded the government that "when we surrendered our lands to the Government we did not sign over all the game and the fish. Indians have always the privilege of hunting wherever they pleased."[8]

The Push to Break Up Reserves

The 1857 Gradual Civilization Act was an even more ambitious law meant to break up reserves to create individual citizens and end government financial obligations to Indigenous peoples. The Pennefather Commission's interim report had recommended individual land tenure to address the "problem" of communal land ownership and speed up assimilation. Following this logic, the legislation created a pathway for the removal of all legal distinctions between "Indians" and other residents of the colony, ending their special status as distinct peoples.[9] Indigenous men over the age of twenty-one, able to speak, read, and write in either English or French and "sufficiently advanced in the elementary branches of education and . . . of good moral character and free from debt," could apply to be enfranchised (given the rights of citizens, including the right to vote if they met property qualifications).[10] Once enfranchised, each man would receive a share of band annuities and a 50-acre allotment taken from reserve land. Individual bands retained some control over the process in that local council approval was required.

The legislation, by removing "all legal distinctions between Indians and Euro-Canadians actually established them."[11] It did so by defining who was an Indian. It stipulated that such a person could not be accorded the same rights and privileges enjoyed by Euro-Canadians until he passed certain tests, although, in fact, many settlers would not have been able to pass the tests. Ironically, the legislation codified the principle "that to be an Indian was not to be a citizen, and to be a citizen was not to be an Indian."[12]

Ominously, the act undermined the legal status of Indigenous women. Through the act, their status as "Indians" and membership in their communities now depended on their husbands' status. The wife, widow, and lineal descendants of an enfranchised man would be automatically enfranchised and no longer a member of their own or their husband's Nation, regardless of their wishes or ties to their birth community. However, if a widow or descendant of an enfranchised man married an "Indian," she would become a member of her husband's Nation or band and no longer enfranchised. The Gradual Civilization Act marked the beginning of a sustained attack on Indigenous women's rights that would persist for generations, with the repercussions still being felt today.

Because the act repudiated the historic treaty relationship, Indigenous reaction was overwhelmingly negative. In 1858, seventy-nine representatives from fifteen Indigenous communities met in Council at Six Nations and agreed to present the government with a petition and a string of Black wampum, a symbol of war or discord.[13] The legislation, in their view, was designed to break up reserves, communities, and even families and to absorb Indigenous people—as individuals—into mainstream society.[14] David Thorburn, superintendent of Six Nations, reported that the Chiefs were particularly concerned by provisions to dismantle reserves, which would threaten their existence as peoples: it was an attempt "to break them to pieces."[15] The Six Nations rejected the legislation because they believed the communal ownership of land was necessary to maintain their integrity as Nations.[16] The legislation also clearly threatened Indigenous sovereignty: by granting itself the authority to decide who was legally an Indian, the government threatened the ability of First Nations to determine their own membership and be self-governing.

The framers of the legislation wrongly assumed Indigenous men would jump at the opportunity to become British subjects with voting rights: over the next twenty years, only one Indigenous man chose to enfranchise.[17] In fact, a number of Indigenous people had abandoned the goal of "civilization" altogether. The Pennefather report described limited farming at Rama, for example. Many of the houses were derelict, and school was taught only half the time—surely a form of resistance. As the Chippewas had learned from bitter experience, if they farmed and improved their land, settlers only coveted it more.

The next summer, another Grand Council was convened at Rama to discuss the abrogation of Indigenous land and treaty rights, including hunting and fishing rights. Remarkably, the Chiefs chose a young Anishinaabe woman to travel to England to bring their land grievances to the attention of Queen Victoria and to inform her of the "peculiar and oppressive circumstances under which the Indians in British North America are placed."[18]

Nahnebahwequay

Nahnebahwequay (Upright or Standing Woman), also known as Catherine Sutton, was a Mississauga woman of the Eagle Doodem who had been raised at the Credit Mission and referred to Peter Jones (also of the Eagle Doodem) as her uncle. A protégé of Eliza Field, his British wife, she accompanied Field to England in 1837 at the age of thirteen. Peter Jones joined them as he embarked on a fundraising tour for missions and sought an audience with the Queen. After a year in England, Nahneebahwequay returned to the Credit Mission. In early 1839, she married Englishman William Sutton, a committed Methodist ally of the Mississaugas.

The Suttons lived at the Credit Village and raised their children as Mississaugas. They moved to the Saugeen territory in 1846, expecting other Mississaugas of the Credit to join them as part of the first relocation plan. But once the poor quality of the land was recognized, only the families of David Sawyer (son of Chief Joseph Sawyer) and Abner Elliott joined them. Most Mississaugas of the Credit moved to New Credit on the Haldimand Tract instead.

The Suttons' land tenure seemed secure. The Saugeen Anishinaabek had offered them 200 acres of reserve land, and Queen Victoria had made an Imperial Declaration in 1847 to confirm Anishinaabe ownership of the entire Saugeen Peninsula. Nahnebahwequay therefore joined the Nawash band in 1852–53, relinquishing her rights to annuities through the Mississaugas of the Credit.

A series of events and government rulings dispossessed the Suttons of their land. In 1854 the British, claiming they couldn't protect the land from squatters, pressured the Saugeen Anishinaabek to sign the Saugeen Peninsula Treaty (Treaty 72), which ceded 450,000 acres or three-quarters of their land base. Only five small reserves remained, one of which included

Photograph of Nahnebahwequay / Catharine Sutton, n.d. | Courtesy of Grey Roots Archival Collection, Owen Sound

the Suttons' land. In 1857, under more pressure, a small unofficial group went to Toronto and surrendered more land (the Owen Sound / Nawash Treaty 82), including the Sutton, Sawyer, and Elliott farms. The process did not follow the Royal Proclamation's requirement that surrenders needed majority consent at a public meeting on the territory in question. Nevertheless, the

Ann, daughter of Chief Joseph Snake, n.d. | Courtesy of Chippewas of Georgina Island Historical Photo Collection

government ruled the cession was valid. The Suttons no longer had title to their lands.

Nahnebahwequay protested this injustice. The government offered her the option to buy the land at half price but then rescinded the offer because Indians, as minors, could not purchase surrendered lands. In a further twist, the Indian Department refused to pay Nahnebahwequay or her children Nawash annuities because it no longer considered her an Indian. Indian agent William Bartlett informed her, "When an Indian woman marries a white man she is no longer considered a member of the Indian community, and if she be a participant in their monies, her name is erased from the list she must therefore follow the fortunes of her husband."[19]

Now legally deemed "white," Nahnebahwequay was denied reserve land under the Crown Lands Protection Act of 1839. Yet Eliza Field Jones, Peter Jones' wife, and Mary Holtby, the British second wife of John Jones, were legally "Indians": their children had status and rights to annuities, regardless of whether they spoke the language or knew anything about Anishinaabe culture. In addition, other Mississauga and Haudenosaunee women had married non-Indigenous men, but they and their children had not lost their status.[20]

The Gradual Civilization Act contradicted and undermined the role of women in their communities by only recognizing male political participation and land ownership in a system of private property. Before colonization, Anishinaabe and Haudenosaunee women held respected roles and exercised jurisdiction over some forms of property and aspects of governance. Anishinaabe women held responsibilities and rights over water, shoreline areas, and sugar bushes, which were economically important for wild rice and sugar production.[21] Because women kept their Doodem identity (passed down from their fathers) but joined their husband's families, and because all Anishinaabek had to marry outside their Clan, women frequently moved to other Anishinaabe communities. They developed social and familial connections and contributed to governance through the maintenance of Doodem relationships and alliances between communities.[22] Anishinaabe women also contributed to political decision-making through Women's Councils, which met alongside Men's Councils. The Chief woman, or Ogimaakwe, presented the results to the men. These advised on "matters of both peace and war." In some cases, women were signatories to treaties, as in the Between the Lakes Treaty of 1784.[23]

Haudenosaunee women, as members of a matrilineal society, likewise held central roles in politics and family law, especially since women were "holders of the land" under the Great Law of Peace and had rights and responsibilities over the large agricultural fields that supported Longhouse communities. Women cultivated the soil, headed their families (in partnership with the men), and selected *Royaners* (Hereditary Chiefs) from their Clan lineage. Clan mothers influenced men's decisions and could dehorn (depose) leaders who did not uphold their responsibilities. Since Clan identity was determined through the female line, national territories were also determined matrilineally.[24]

Indigenous women would be increasingly impacted by Victorian ideas of women's roles over the next decades. They would come to be regarded as the legal appendages of their husbands, as non-Indigenous women were regarded in law. Settler women did not gain the vote until after the First World War.

Perhaps because she was a thorn in his side, the Indian agent eventually offered Nahnebahwequay the opportunity to buy back her land at a reduced rate. But she needed to agree that the Nawash band's original grant of 200 acres to her was invalid and renounce her annuities from that band (and, hence, her Indian status). She refused on principle and was supported by a number of Anishinaabek. As Nahnebahwequay wrote in 1861, "Although I have been married 21 years, it was not until the last four years that the department has made this excuse for robbing me and my children of our birthright, which I inherited from my forefathers before the white man ever set his foot on our shores."

When the 1859 Council chose her to take their grievances to England, it was in recognition of her strength and eloquence in the face of injustice and her previous experience in England. The next spring, heavily pregnant, she travelled to London via New York. She was assisted by supportive Quakers and attacked by the Toronto *Globe* as an imposter. The newspaper tried to undermine her mission by claiming that Indians could buy land in the province and were well treated.[25]

In England, Nahnebahwequay addressed the Aborigines Protection Society, "gaining many sympathizers among our philanthropic men and women."[26] Through her Quaker connections, she met with the colonial secretary, the Duke of Newcastle, and secured an audience with Queen

William Armstrong, *Union Station (1858–1871), Waterfront, West of York St., Toronto, Ontario, 1859*. As the city industrialized, some Indigenous people took the train into Toronto to sell fish, baskets, brooms, and other items | Toronto Public Library, Canadian Documentary Art Collection, JRR291

Victoria. She gave birth to her sixth child three weeks later.[27]

During her audience, she raised the issue of the way she, David Sawyer, and Abner Elliott had been treated by the Indian Department and presented the Queen with a petition from the Nawash Nation. The Queen listened and referred the matter to Newcastle. Newcastle was instructed to investigate the situation during the Prince of Wales' upcoming royal tour, planned for later in the year. The public was informed that the duke had been "charged by her Majesty to enquire into the condition of her Indian subjects in this country, whose complaints have recently reached the Royal ear."[28]

Before leaving England, Nahnebahwequay gave a speech in Liverpool. The Aborigines Protection Society recorded her eloquent description of the failure of the civilization policy and the treatment of Indigenous people who tried to become farmers: "But how can the poor Indian be civilized? As soon as he makes his land valuable, he is driven further back . . . He is only clearing the land for the white men and making it valuable for the Indian department . . . And they know that the work they put on their land, that their children wont get the benefit of it . . . We should do to others as we should others to do to us."[29]

242   WHERE HISTORIES MEET

Catherine Sutton is my relation on my mother's side . . . Now you see where I get my uppity talk!

—Garry Sault, Mississaugas of the Credit[30]

Strategic Action during the 1860 Royal Tour

The Prince of Wales' visit provided an important opportunity for Indigenous peoples to draw attention to their ongoing presence and cultural persistence in a world that increasingly marginalized and erased them. By publicly demonstrating their loyalty to the Crown, they hoped to remind the Canadian public, colonial officials, and British royalty of the Crown's responsibilities as partners in a treaty relationship.

Although First Nations grievances were not reported in the press, they used several opportunities to present petitions and draw attention to the injustices they had endured. On Newcastle's arrival in Toronto, a delegation of Anishinaabe leaders greeted him and presented him with a petition dealing with nine issues, including the Sutton, Sawyer, Elliott land claims; the insecurity of title and the need for proper title deeds; the embezzlement or mismanagement of funds and the Indian Department's accountability to the legislature; and the loss of annuities when Indigenous women married white men.[31]

Towards the end of the tour, several hundred mostly Anishinaabe men and women, including at least eighty Chiefs, congregated at Sarnia, where they attended a reception for the prince. The following day, they presented a petition signed by "nearly every tribe and band of Canada":

> It began by asking Newcastle to undertake a thorough investigation of the conduct of the Indian Department. The petition then referred to specific grievances: the loss through fraud and carelessness of several hundred thousand dollars received in payment of lands; the loss of islands used as fishing stations and the government's imposition of new charges for fishing rights long guaranteed by treaties; the illegal sale of Indian lands without the permission of bands or compensation paid to them; the forcible confiscation of large tracts without adequate compensation, and government plans that would make possible the alienation of reserve lands without prior consent from bands.[32]

The petition stated that the department had been granted "authority to alienate our reserve lands, without obtaining our consent, and even against our will and remonstrance," a reference to the Gradual Civilization Act, which granted the superintendent-general the power to alienate up to 50 acres of reserve land for each man enfranchised.

The Sutton, Sawyer, and Elliott land claims were noticeably absent from this list of grievances. The Chiefs had refused to bring them forward, considering them private issues compared

Oronhyatekha in the ceremonial clothing he wore to meet the Prince of Wales in 1860 | Bodleian Library, Oxford University, c. 175, folio 366, Wikimedia Commons

to problems of a more general concern. During Nahnebahwequay's absence in England, some Anishinaabe Chiefs had also refused to support her trip and declined to endorse her petition, perhaps reflecting their ambivalence about the rights of Indigenous women and the influence of Victorian notions of womanhood.[33]

When the prince left Sarnia for Brantford, he was greeted by one thousand "painted and armed" Haudenosaunee warriors. A young Oronhyatekha, the grandson of George Martin, was chosen by the Haudenosaunee to deliver a short welcoming speech. Oronhyatekha also delivered a Six Nations petition that drew attention to the loss of much of their territory on the Haldimand Tract without any surrender or treaty and asked for greater control over their affairs, especially finances. With Henry Acland, the prince's protégé, Oronhyatekha raised the issue of the Queen no longer fulfilling the treaty promise of presents in perpetuity.[34]

The Mississaugas of the Credit met the prince in Hamilton. According to their Indian agent, James McLean, they wanted to discuss the treaty for their former lands on the Credit, for which they had not been paid, and their exclusive fishery on the river.[35]

Newcastle received at least twelve petitions from First Nations, but his investigation of Indigenous grievances, including those of Nahnebahwequay, Sawyer, and Elliott and the Six Nations, was superficial at best. As Nahnebahwequay wrote: "The Indian Department, with the Governor General at its head, are the parties complained of, and the Duke made his investigations

244   WHERE HISTORIES MEET

entirely through them; not a solitary friend of the injured party was allowed to be present to take part."[36] In another letter, she explained: "Had our friends been permitted to take part, they would have exhibited such an extensive state of wrongs and corruptions connected with the department, as would have astonished the public; but the department has had it all their own way."[37]

Although Newcastle had supported Nahnebahwequay in England, the political sands had shifted since then with the transfer of control of Indian Affairs from Britain to the Province of Canada. Newcastle and the British government did not want to interfere in what was now a Canadian matter.

In the end, Nahnebahwequay was unable to get her Indian status restored or purchase the farm she and her husband had worked so hard to create, although, in 1861, the Indian Department did allow her husband to purchase four lots from the original land granted to her, at the base price. For the rest of her life, she continued to advocate for Indigenous rights. She advised the Anishinaabek of Manitoulin Island regarding their land title when the government pressured them for more land cessions, and she called for protection of Indigenous fishing rights. She died in 1865.

I know about Catherine Sutton because we were researching her site up in Collingwood. She married out, right, and so she got taken off the rights list . . . She was an advocate. But she was Christianized.

—Carolyn King, Mississaugas of the Credit[38]

PART SIX:
New Strategies for Dark Times

21

The Indian Act and the Great Council Fire

The 1867 British North America Act created the Dominion of Canada as a nation of only two founding peoples, English and French: Indigenous Nations were not consulted or recognized as partners in Confederation. The BNA Act affected all First Nations, including those of the Toronto area, who had governed themselves for millennia.

Responsibility for Indigenous peoples formally passed from the British Crown to the government of Canada. Rather than confirming their status as allies, the BNA Act assigned responsibility for "Indians and Lands reserved for Indians" to the newly created federal government. Status Indians (those who had signed treaties or were otherwise recognized on band lists) became its legal wards, a dependent status similar to that of children. The British Crown essentially abdicated its duty to protect its Indigenous treaty partners from the interests of settlers, which had been affirmed in the Royal Proclamation of 1763. Federal government ministries often combined Indigenous affairs with other pro-development departments with competing agendas and did not serve Indigenous people's interests.

In a constitutional division of powers that bedevils Indigenous people to this day, the federal government was assigned responsibility for Indigenous peoples and their reserve lands, but the provinces were given jurisdiction over mining, agriculture, natural resources, and "Crown lands," which were ceded Traditional Territories upon which Indigenous peoples retained hunting, fishing, and, arguably, other rights. This division greatly impacted Mississauga and Chippewa lands in south-central Ontario, and First Nations' ability to exercise their rights to hunt and fish, as safeguarded in treaties.

Additional legislation increased government control over Indigenous lives and extended earlier legislation to the four provinces that constituted the new Dominion of Canada: Ontario, Quebec, Nova Scotia, and New Brunswick. The 1968 Indian Lands Act consolidated previous legislation such as the 1839 Crown Lands Act and transferred authority for the management of Indian lands to the federal government.[1] It defined who could be legally designated an "Indian" and "entitled to hold, use or enjoy the lands and other immoveable property" of a band. "Indians" were people of Indian blood who belonged to a "Tribe" and their descendants. Any woman who married an Indian acquired Indian status—even if she was non-Indigenous.[2]

They say Indian Affairs was put in place to look after the interests and look after the First Nations. But that never was the case. Their case was always to get rid of their Indian problem.

—Margaret Sault, Mississaugas of the Credit[3]

Over the next decades, Indigenous peoples experienced a massive legal and political transformation in their relationship with the federal government: a unilateral "constitutional change," in the words of historian John Milloy. Up until at least 1860, "Indian tribes were, de facto, self-governing. They had exclusive control over their population, land, and finances." A military alliance had served Britain well from 1793 to the War of 1812, and even after that, Britain continued to engage in Indigenous treaty-making processes that recognized Indigenous peoples as self-governing. But from Confederation onward, the federal government moved away from its historical nation-to-nation relationship with self-governing Nations in alliance with the Crown. "Federal control of on-reserve governmental systems became the essence of Canadian-Indigenous constitutional relations."[4]

These alarming developments galvanized Indigenous political leaders in Ontario—and from all the Indigenous communities near Toronto—to respond collectively.

Resisting Enfranchisement

The 1869 Gradual Enfranchisement Act revived and broadened the geographic scope of the 1857 Gradual Civilization Act.[5] The government hoped to eliminate reserves as sites of government responsibility by promoting individual land tenure through individual "location tickets" and regular Canadian citizenship.[6]

Under the act, an Indigenous man could become a full citizen and owner of an allotment of land by renouncing his Indian status, including his right to live on the reserve and receive annuity payments and other "special privileges." No longer a ward of the government, he'd acquire all the rights and privileges of Canadian citizenship, including the vote. The legislation reflected Victorian patriarchal attitudes: Indigenous women married to men who gave up their Indian status (or who had never had that status) automatically lost their status and their right to live on a reserve (as did all their descendants). The act confirmed that an Indigenous person couldn't be a Canadian citizen and Status Indian. It limited annuity payments to those with at least "one-quarter" Indian blood, and it stipulated that inheritance passed through the male line only, regardless of Indigenous custom. (Among the Haudenosaunee, for example, Clan membership is passed down through the female line.)

In a further violation of Indigenous self-determination, the 1869 act gave the government the power to impose elected governance on reserves on the order of the governor general. It also restricted the legislative powers of the elected Chief and "band" council. Band councils were limited to quasi-municipal responsibilities such as creating and maintaining schools, public buildings, roads, bridges, ditches and fences and framing rules on public health, public behaviour (such as drunkenness), or cattle trespassing. Although Hereditary or Life Chiefs were allowed to retain their position until they died or resigned, the government could remove them for "dishonesty, intemperance, immorality, or incompetency," a broad provision that gave the Department of Indian Affairs the power to replace troublesome traditional leaders.[7] In a departure from the 1857 Gradual Civilization Act, enfranchisement decisions were now made solely by the governor-general-in-council on the recommendation of the superintendent-general of Indian Affairs. Band consent was no longer required. The Department of Indian Affairs was also given exclusive jurisdiction over valuable natural resources on reserves.

By these means, the government hoped to solve the department's financial problems and undermine Indigenous peoples' resistance to government appropriation of on-reserve resources such as timber.[8]

The Grand General Council of Ontario

The 1869 Enfranchisement Act triggered "an immediate, coordinated, and broad-based response."[9] Meeting at a Grand Council called by Six Nations in 1870, Indigenous Nations founded the Grand General Indian Council of Ontario, Canada's first "pan-Indigenous" political organization. The inaugural meeting attracted nearly fifty Haudenosaunee delegates; thirty-six Anishinaabe delegates from thirteen communities, including Rama, Scugog Island, New Credit, Beausoleil (which moved to Christian Island in 1856), and Georgina Island; and representatives from Munsee-Delaware communities.

The Council minutes were recorded in English, but most business was conducted in Indigenous languages, with considerable translation going on between Haudenosaunee, Lenape, and Anishinaabe delegates. The attendees agreed to meet every two years on different reserves to review and coordinate responses to proposed and already-enacted government legislation and to counter government incursions on their sovereignty. They affirmed their own historical forms of governance and sought to define their relationship with Canada and its laws on their own terms.

The 1870 gathering built on inter-Nation gatherings held in 1840 and 1858 in response to government actions. It rekindled and regularized the process of meeting in Council and drew on the long-standing if sometimes challenging treaty relationship between the Anishinaabek and the Haudenosaunee.[10] There were family and political connections among the delegates at all three councils, and some delegates from previous councils continued to play key roles, such as John Smoke Johnson, the Mohawk Pine Tree Chief.

Johnson opened the 1870 Council with a reading of historic Wampum Belts. He explained that the meeting was grounded in Indigenous law and required the reactivation of nation-to-nation

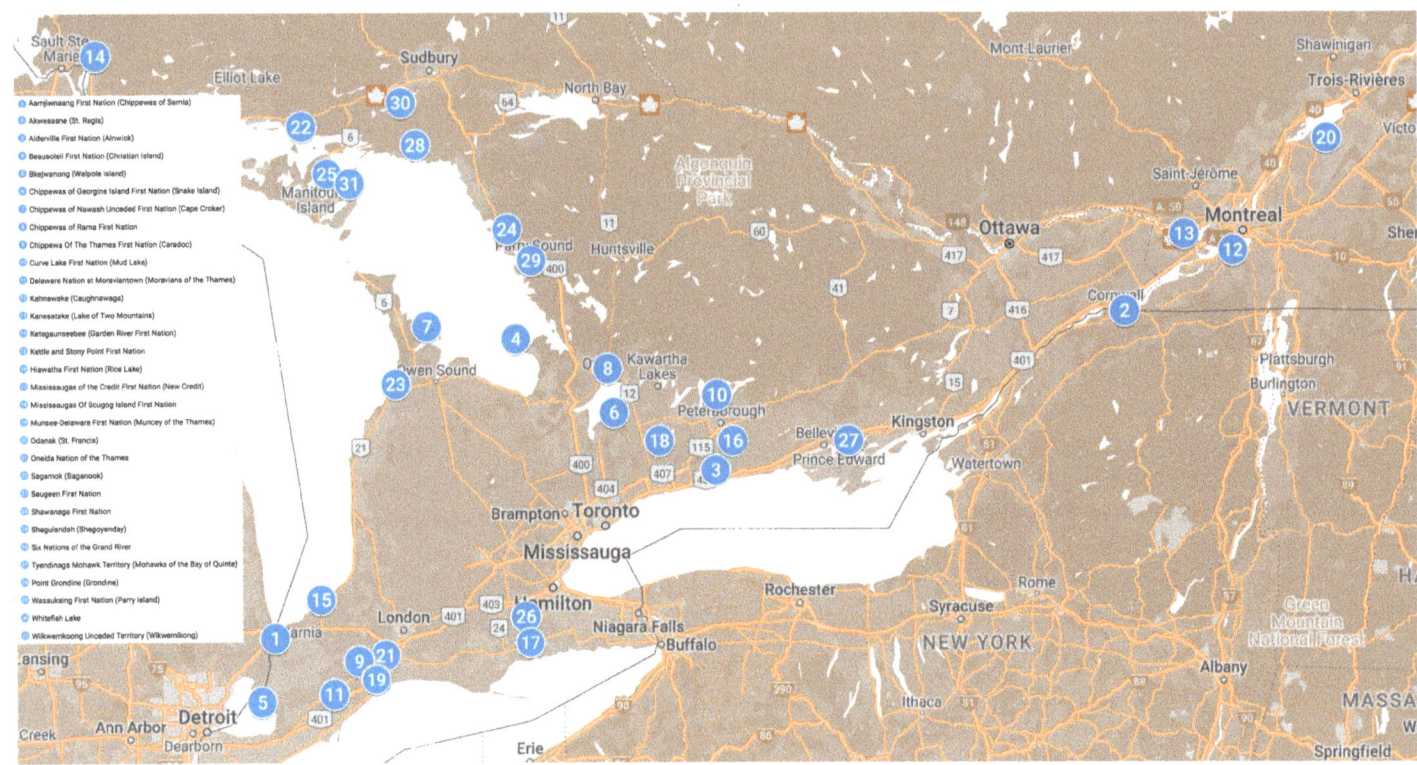

Participating communities at the Grand General Council, 1870–1906 | Murdoch, "Act to Control"

alliances among First Nations and with the Crown. He referred to the long history of alliance between the Haudenosaunee and Anishinaabek represented in the Dish with One Spoon and reminded delegates that "the policy of their forefathers was, when they were unanimous, they were stronger."[11] Johnson reminded delegates that the basis of the Covenant Chain alliance with the British had been noninterference in each other's internal affairs—a principle that went back to the early seventeenth-century Two Row Wampum agreement with the Dutch.

Delegates agreed that Wampum Belts should be present at all future gatherings as an expression of sovereignty, but cultural change was already apparent. A Christianized, Western-educated Anishinaabe Chief questioned the need for the lengthy Wampum readings and the opening Condolence Ceremony.[12]

Two months before the Grand Council, a delegation of Six Nations Chiefs had visited Ottawa to meet with Joseph Howe, who was the secretary of state and superintendent-general of Indian Affairs. They reminded him of the government's duty as their ally and brought out and explained the Wampum Belts to him.

Johnson, who had been one of the delegates to Ottawa, reported at the 1870 Council: "Mr. Howe asked them, what parts of the Indian Acts they objected to, they replied, the whole Act, which, they were not consulted in reference to it. Mr. Howe, on hearing the Act not agreeable to the Six Nations, asked, if they did not want any laws for their guidance and government, to which they answered, The Six Nations had already rules and regulations under which they had ever acted."[13]

The Council reviewed the 1869 Enfranchisement Act section by section and unanimously rejected almost all its provisions. Notably, the one exception was a clause dealing with liquor restrictions on reserve, which the delegates voted to keep. Delegates rejected the authority of the superintendent-general to grant location tickets and control inheritance; the one-quarter blood quantum requirement for annuity payments; the removal of women's Indian status if they married non-band members; and the imposition of elections.[14] In their petition to the governor general, the delegates clearly articulated their vision for government conduct: "The Council demands that proper consultation with the Indian people should be had, when any Act of Parliament is proposed which may affect them, and not left to subordinates who have no true knowledge of Indian advancements or requirements."[15]

Delegates called for restoration of their resource rights: exemption from game and fishery laws and band control over timber. They voted to go to the House of Commons to "press for justice when the Indian Bill was being read" and for "a liberal provision . . . to allow four natives in the House of Commons in Ottawa to represent the different tribes."[16] As historian Chandra Murdoch comments, "These motions demonstrate a radically different imaginary of what governance should look like in relation to the settler government than had been presented in the Act of 1869. They demanded that their sovereignty over their own communities be recognized, as it had been through historic alliance relationships."[17]

Consulting or Co-opting Indigenous Leadership

Indigenous resistance forced the government to consult with selected Indigenous leaders between 1869 and 1885 to make its legislation more palatable to local communities.[18] They chose leaders sympathetic to the idea of enfranchisement and influential at the Grand General Council. Through this dialogue, certain Anishinaabe and Haudenosaunee leaders expressed their opinions on what the Crown-Indigenous relationship should look like. The government also learned of community responses to their laws through petitions, correspondence, and Council minutes.

For example, David Laird, the superintendent-general of Indian Affairs, invited some members of the Grand General Council to consult on the Indian Act before it was passed in 1876. Prime Minister Sir John A. Macdonald asked Dr. Peter Edmond Jones, the son of Mississauga missionary Peter Jones, to rewrite it—though he disregarded most of Jones' suggestions.

The government also asked Oronhyatehka, also known as Dr. Peter Martin and another Grand Council member, for feedback. Oronhyatehka didn't represent a specific community, but he was the grandson of Chief George Martin and nephew of Chief John Smoke Johnson, and he had served as chairman of the Grand General Council, held at Sarnia in 1872. Oronhyatekha sent the Council's suggested amendments to Laird and commented: "When last in Ottawa, I had the honour to mention the subject in conversation with you, and you were good enough to request me to put the subject matter in writing."[19]

The 1876 Indian Act

Despite the Grand Council's efforts, sections of the 1869 act reappeared in the 1876 Indian Act, although the Council's recommendations on two important issues, locations and enfranchisement, were adopted. The Indian Act consolidated all previous legislation relating to Indigenous peoples and through numerous amendments extended government control over almost all aspects of Indigenous peoples' lives across Canada, including property, resources, governance, relationships, and education. As Murdoch notes, it "inaugurated a deeply repressive and enduring nexus of law that has since affected generation after generation of Indigenous people in Canada."[20]

The government confirmed its power to define who was a Status Indian (who could live on a reserve and receive annuities and who was forced to leave). While few men chose to enfranchise, generations of Indigenous women who married non-Indigenous men or Non-Status Indigenous men lost their status, as did their children and descendants. The number of Indigenous people entitled to treaty rights dwindled along with their political clout.

Through the act and its numerous subsequent amendments, the government was given the power to remove traditional governments and impose Indian agent–controlled elected band councils, to ban traditional spiritual ceremonies, to control Indigenous education, and to force children into church-run, state-funded schools. Indian agents gained increased powers to control day-to-day life on a reserve, including the movement of people, the sale of crops, and inheritance. Through these policies, which simultaneously segregated Indigenous peoples and attempted to assimilate them, Canada aimed to "peacefully" eradicate First Nations and, with them, treaty obligations or claims to land. As Duncan Campbell Scott, the deputy superintendent-general of Indian affairs, would infamously articulate in 1920, government policy would "continue until there is not a single Indian in Canada that has not been absorbed into the body politic, and there is no Indian question, and no Indian Department."[21]

The Indian Act greatly harmed Indigenous peoples and Nations and diminished Canadians' understanding of themselves as inheritors of ongoing treaty responsibilities. It reflected an era of hardening racial prejudice against Indigenous peoples. As the British Empire faced revolts and "rebellions" across the globe, so-called scientific racism claimed that the different "races" had significant biological differences arising from separate creations by God and that the British nation and the white race were superior to all others. Scientific racism justified coercive government policies, which generations of Indigenous peoples were forced to endure. Although some of the Indian Act's most draconian sections were repealed in 1951, the Indian Act still constrains many aspects of Indigenous life and governance.

The Grand General Council's Response

Surprisingly, the Grand General Council met at Saugeen in July 1876 and formally approved the Indian Act.[22] This Council was attended by Anishinaabe delegates only, and they expressed differing perspectives on the aims and usefulness of the law, its impact on their relationship with the Crown, and how it accorded with the future they envisaged for their communities. The Council emphasized that participating communities had the autonomy to engage with the law to suit their needs.

Chandra Murdoch suggests that Anishinaabe leaders approved the act because they believed they had gained new powers. Two years previously, the Grand Council had endorsed a proposal by Dr. Peter Edmund Jones that local bands should control enfranchisement decisions and that enfranchisees should retain "their rights to participate in the annuities and interest money, and rents and councils of the Tribe, band or body to which they belong."[23]

As Murdoch points out, "Jones' emphasis on maintaining annuity payments and participation in the political life of the Band suggest a very different vision than the assimilationist goals of the state." Delegates saw enfranchisement as "gaining a right to participate in settler government and society without losing their connection to, or authority over . . . their own communities. Their vision for increased political participation, while retaining and strengthening their own communities, can perhaps best be understood as akin to an idea of 'dual citizenship.' Rather than having to lose their own authority and communities through subjecthood and incorporation into the Canadian body politic, this would be retained, and their interest in enfranchisement was to further advance community prosperity as they understood this."[24]

Jones' proposals for the continuation of annuities and other benefits for enfranchised men were not included in the Indian Act. But band approval of enfranchisement applications was—a significant improvement over the 1869 law. It appears that many delegates accepted less palatable sections of the Indian Act because the government had partially accepted the change to the enfranchisement legislation advocated for at the 1874 Grand Council. This was interpreted by many leaders as proof that the government could be persuaded to alter legislation in the future through input presented at the Grand General Council.

Christianity, particularly Methodism, was also a factor in the Council's response. Christian leaders had previously influenced British and settler laws by engaging with government officials, and several, such as Peter Jones, had gained access to the highest levels of British and settler power. This appeared to be an effective strategy. Anishinaabe leaders connected to the Methodist Church, going back to the efforts of Peter Jones and John Sunday in the 1830s, had been active in efforts to secure land title to reserves. As Murdoch notes, the older generation of Anishinaabek had been accepted as equals within the Methodist Church, and their sons had been "educated in the institutions brought into being in part by their fathers' efforts."[25]

Many prominent voices within the Grand General Council had received Christian educations and engaged with settler politics through missionary networks. They had witnessed great changes in their communities during their lifetimes and had become leaders in their communities because of their ability to navigate both worlds. Several, such as Dr. Peter Edmund Jones, who became the first Indigenous doctor in Canada, served as models of successful adaptation to new social realities. These leaders supported the government project of Christianization, residential schooling (prior to the large-scale expansion of coercive state and church-run schools), and assimilation because, in their view, it had helped them and their communities.[26] Although they had firsthand experience of the negative impacts of racism and expanding settlement, these leaders were also influenced by British concepts of property and gendered and patriarchal aspects of Victorian Christianity.[27] They sought to protect their communities' interests, as they understood them, within the worldview they had accepted or inherited.

Notably, the Methodist community at the Credit River had adopted ideas of electoral governance through Peter Jones' written legal code of 1830, and support for elections on reserves was later taken up by the Methodist Conference.[28] Opposition to enfranchisement—and Anishinaabe support for it—was a key reason the Haudenosaunee did not attend some Grand General Councils and withdrew permanently in 1884. The Six Nations of the Grand River maintained a consistent position, first articulated at the 1858 and 1870 Councils: they did not want enfranchisement because it threatened their sovereignty as a Nation.

According to Mohawk historian Susan Hill, the Six Nations were in turmoil following the loss of Haldimand Tract land in the 1840s; families were "dealing with their third (or more) removal in less than seventy years."[29] The Confederacy Council was determined to protect their remaining lands. Asserting their right to self-determination, the Council developed "policies and procedures to address land issues in key areas including inheritance, marriage disputes, annuity payments, adoption, enfranchisement, band transfers, leases and sales, 'national parks,' and communal property."³⁰ These were all areas of jurisdiction that the Indian Act sought to control. The Council considered enfranchisement a serious threat to their lands and governance.

Most Haudenosaunee leaders shared this view, but it was not unanimous. According to historian Sally Weaver, "reformer" and "conservative" factions of the Grand River Council could not agree on an approach to government legislation. For example, reformers such as Oronhyatekha were supportive or neutral in their assessment of the 1869 enfranchisement provisions, while the Confederacy Chiefs rejected them outright.³¹ Although Oronhyatekha was willing to consider enfranchisement (and applied for enfranchisement himself, in 1872, though did not go through with it), he emphasized that such policies should not be imposed: "Should you recommend to the Government in any further Act to adopt any of the suggestions of the Indians such provisions would certainly be more likely to be carried out into practical effect by them as having been recommended by the Indians themselves."³²

In 1876, Haudenosaunee Chiefs presented a petition to the governor general against the Grand General Council's approval of the Indian Act; they protested the superintendent-generals' powers over their "lands, moneys, and properties without first obtaining the consent of the chiefs of the Six Nations." They asserted that the Indian Act would "in time deprive [them] of [their] liberties, rights and privileges which we now enjoy under the Treaty between Great Britain and the Six Nations Indians."³³

Women's Rights and the Grand General Council

When the Grand General Council first discussed the proposed legislation, the all-male delegates rejected women losing their status as "unjust in depriving a woman of her birthright." Six Nations opposed the principle of patrilineal descent because it broke with Haudenosaunee law.³⁴

The Grand Council, however, reversed its position and approved the proposed status legislation in 1874 when most Six Nations delegates were not in attendance. The Anishinaabe delegates were focused on other enfranchisement issues and may not have wanted to jeopardize reaching a consensus. As historian Norman Shields points out, "There is a measure of irony in that fact given that most people who surrendered their status over the following one hundred years did so involuntarily through the operation of section 6 [women marrying out]" and almost no Indigenous men chose to enfranchise.³⁵ Peggy Blair, a lawyer, noted in 2005, "Between 1958 and 1968 alone, more than 100,000 women and children lost their Indian status as a result of these provisions."³⁶ The repercussions of this loss of status over more than a century are still widely felt today, even though status has been restored for some.³⁷

When they did attend the Council, Haudenosaunee delegates consistently opposed the loss of status. Anishinaabe delegates were more ambivalent, in part because patrilineal descent was the norm for passing on Clan identity in their societies. According to Shields, Anishinaabe leaders were concerned about losing more land if Indigenous women married white men or

Chiefs of the Six Nations at Brantford, Canada, explaining their Wampum Belts to Horatio Hale, September 14, 1871. *Second from left*: Mohawk Chief George H.M. Johnson (Dyonhehgon), government interpreter and son of John Smoke Johnson; John Buck (Skanawiti), Onondaga Chief, Hereditary Keeper of the Wampum; John Smoke Johnson (Sakayenkwaraton), Mohawk Chief, speaker of the Council *(standing)* | Six Nations Legacy Consortium Collection, Six Nations Public Library Collection SNPL000088v00i, Creative Commons License CC BY-NC-ND 4.0

"non-treaty Indians," such as Potawatomi men from the United States who had neither annuities nor a land base in Canada.[38]

The 1876 Indian Act transformed the political, social, and material well-being of Indigenous women by excluding them from band governance and instituting unequal marriage and property laws. Yet despite their legal marginalization, Indigenous women still played a central role in maintaining Indigenous nationhood. They developed strategies to protect their homes and families and maintain their livelihoods, sometimes by acting against the Indian Act, sometimes by claiming rights through its provisions. They hired lawyers and appealed to Indian Affairs to overturn unjust decisions by band councils and Indian agents alike.[39]

The Grand General Council and the Indian Act after 1876

The Indian Act was amended almost yearly, and the Grand Council was kept busy responding to its many changes. Because Indigenous leaders either opposed the law or tried to alter it to better respond to their communities' needs, and Indian agents struggled to impose unpopular laws on reserves, the act was continually strengthened. In fact, subsequent legislation and the increasingly repressive means of enforcement evolved through a series of jurisdictional struggles between Ottawa, Indian agents on the ground, and Indigenous leaders.[40] But despite intense government coercion, many aspects of self-governance continued.

The Grand General Council debated the 1884 Indian Advancement Act, which extended government control over band governance, and the 1885 Franchise Act, which gave Indigenous men the right to vote federally (until it was repealed in 1898). Dr. Peter Edmund Jones was especially prominent in attempting to provide constructive feedback to the government. Attendees expressed a great diversity of perspectives on the political issues of the day, and some communities rejected the Council's decisions or developed alternative forms of political organization, such as the United Bands movement.[41]

Most of the Grand General Council's recommendations after 1876 were ignored.[42] Nonetheless, the Councils provided a forum for communities to share their views and come to a broader understanding of the implications of federal legislation. Nations built and maintained social and political relationships beyond their isolated communities and honed leadership and consensus-building skills. Ultimately, as Chandra Murdoch argues, "the federal government was simply not willing to respect these leaders' insistences that they knew what was best for their communities under the extreme paternalism of the law."[43]

In the twentieth century, the Grand General Council eventually evolved into the Union of Ontario Indians, which became the administrative arm of the Anishinabek Nation, a reconstituted government for thirty-nine Anishinaabe First Nations, including the Chippewas of Rama, Chippewas of Georgina Island, Beausoleil First Nation, and Mississaugas of Scugog Island. The same principle of organization—a Council of

Chiefs—is evident in the Assembly of First Nations, a national advocacy organization representing more than six hundred First Nations.

> *Union of Ontario Indians—my dad helped start that. He was honoured for it one night in Rama. They had a . . . They took us all up, the whole family, and they honoured him for being one of the members that started the Union of Ontario Indians.*
>
> —Albert Big Canoe, Chippewas of Georgina Island[44]

After withdrawing from the Grand General Council, the Six Nations deepened ties with other Haudenosaunee communities, such as Kahnawà:ke, Akwesasne, and Tyendinaga. They convened their own Grand Councils in support of hereditary governance and against the Indian Act system. The Six Nations also pressed for recognition of their sovereignty through other channels, such as educating settlers about Haudenosaunee laws and their system of government. Chief John Smoke Johnson worked with anthropologist Horatio Hale to record Haudenosaunee laws. Seth Newhouse (a delegate to the Grand General Council in 1882) and John A. Gibson prepared a written version of the Great Law of Peace.[45] As their relationship with the federal government deteriorated, the Haudenosaunee directed petitions and diplomacy towards the governor general as the true representative of the British Crown.[46]

In 1923, the Haudenosaunee attempted to have their sovereignty recognized internationally by appealing to the League of Nations, the precursor of the United Nations, but were blocked by Great Britain (and Canada).[47] The following year, the government coercively installed a band council against the wishes of a significant segment of the community and the Hereditary Chiefs, though elective governance was favoured by the progressive faction. Despite this, the Hereditary Council of the Haudenosaunee Confederacy persists to this day, along with the band council at Six Nations.

> *The biggest thing I would like to see happen is the split between the traditional government and the elective form of government to be healed, because that's a negative on all of our people. That's a big challenge. It's a very big challenge. Our generation and three generations before us have inherited that divide. It's not by our doing, but we've got to step up and take care of it. That's an internal issue. But, to me, that's one of the biggest challenges we're going to face.*
>
> —Phil Monture, Six Nations of the Grand River[48]

In assessing and proposing changes to legislation, the Grand General Council of Ontario (and those who left it) asserted and modelled what the Canadian Supreme Court has partially recognized as a "duty to consult and accommodate"—something all First Nations in the Toronto area still calling for. Articulated more fully, the principle is the right to free, prior, and informed consent—that is, Indigenous peoples can accept or reject projects affecting them or their territories. This right is enshrined, along with the more general right of self-determination, in the United Nations Declaration on the Rights of Indigenous Peoples, adopted by the UN General Assembly in 2007. The declaration was officially supported without qualification by Canada in 2016, and implementing legislation was passed in 2021.

> *We want to get out of the Indian Act and really become self-determined of our destiny as we move forward.*
>
> —Phil Monture, Six Nations of the Grand River[49]

Mohawk Institute for the Education of Indian Youth

In the post-Confederation era, the government's expansion of the residential school system propelled an assimilative assault on Indigenous individuals, families, and communities. The harms to Indigenous people included physical, sexual, emotional, and spiritual abuse, loss of language and culture, alienation from families and communities, poor health, and early death. Widespread trauma resulted and continues to impact Indigenous people intergenerationally. In 2007, the Indian Residential Schools Settlement Agreement, the largest class-action settlement in Canadian history, was negotiated by the Government of Canada, the churches who ran the schools, the Assembly of First Nations, and other Indigenous organizations. It resulted in a formal apology by the government of Canada, payments to survivors, commemorative activities, healing measures, and the establishment of the Truth and Reconciliation Commission. Shown here is the Mohawk Institute in Brantford in the 1880s. See also pages 274-275 | *Souvenir of Brantford, Ontario* (Brantford: J.R. Salmond, 1890), courtesy of Toronto Public Library

22

After 1876

The Indian Act led to perhaps the most difficult and repressive era of Indigenous-settler relations: it challenged Indigenous self-determination and self-government, and it reduced the power of traditional governance systems and Hereditary Chiefs, replacing them with a band council system monitored by Indian agents and the deputy superintendent-general of Indian affairs. Residential Schools caused untold damage to individuals, families, communities, cultures, and Nations.

I can remember my mom and my uncle and that they never practised any of the Native way. No ceremonies. Nothing like that. I think because maybe then they were told they couldn't. Not speaking their language. We were told we couldn't speak our language at school. That's why I can't speak it fluently.

—Leona Charles, Mississaugas of Scugog Island[1]

At the time, the teacher here taught us Grade 9, and then he left . . . And Dad heard about Mohawk Institute. "My god," he said. "That would be a great place." He didn't realize, at that point in history, what it was. Andrew only stayed a week, and he left. He ran away. I don't know how he got home. I stayed. I knew how to milk cows so that had me in the . . . they had their own little dairy . . . I was there two weeks, and then Dad came and got me. I guess Andrew must have told him what was going on.

—Albert Big Canoe, Chippewas of Georgina Island.[2]

All my brothers and my sisters were in residential school. My baby sister and I, we escaped it. When my mother moved to St. Catharines, she went and applied for welfare, and the welfare

Yet Indigenous peoples continued to be self-determining to the best of their ability in a radically changed environment. They worked hard to protect their families, communities, and lands. They adapted some aspects of settler culture for their own use. They tried to constructively engage with governments for the benefit of Indigenous peoples and others. They passed core cultural knowledge, values, and practices on to their children and grandchildren, even if they did so surreptitiously or didn't necessarily label them Indigenous.

Interviewee Leona Charles, Mississaugas of Scugog Island First Nation | Courtesy of Leona Charles

They used to spear fish. They used to trap muskrat and all that. I remember cleaning it! . . . Just down the road there. They would do it at night. Because I guess it must have been against the law. They would sneak it home. Especially muskelunge. And they would clean it up right there and get rid of all the evidence. We'd eat it up right now!

—Leona Charles, Mississaugas of Scugog Island[4]

people said, "We don't have to take care of these children. They gave them to the residential schools. It's better," they said. So, away they went.

—Garry Sault, Mississaugas of the Credit[3]

There were a few different families that would still practise Smudging Ceremony in secret. They would hide it from the Indian agent and from their children.

—Vicki Snache, Chippewas of Rama[5]

My mum ... would always hang out with the medicine people next door. And we'd have to go help them collect the medicines. We don't even think about it. We always made dandelion wine. We made poultice out of mallow ... I remember I stepped on a nail in the barnyard, and I got an infected foot ... We called it pennyleaf because it was round, but its science name is mallow. And they'd just boil it up, put it on a cloth, and put it on my foot.

—Carolyn King, Mississaugas of the Credit[6]

Although Indigenous people had few income-generating options, they made and sold traditional items such as ash baskets, brooms, moccasins, and quillwork and hired themselves out as hunting guides, as labourers in lumber camps or farms, and as domestic workers in settler homes. Some moved to Toronto or other cities for employment opportunities or found new ways to advance their own and their community's interests.

The older ladies still made baskets, picked sweetgrass, worked with quills, dyed them and made all the Native crafts and traditional foods. They grew the native corn, and then we'd take it all off in the fall and put it in jars. And then she'd do a lot to prepare it for soups and meals.

—Susan Hoeg, Chippewas of Georgina Island[7]

I know my late grandmother, she used to visit and travel to Georgina Island. And Christian Island, too, was mentioned. And Rama, of course, and Curve Lake.

—Pat LeSaux, Mississaugas of Scugog Island[8]

In this context, the activities of the Grand General Council of Ontario and Haudenosaunee Grand Councils represented one stream of ongoing collective action. Oronhyatekha (Dr. Peter Martin) and Dr. Peter Edmund Jones represented another: Western-educated individuals and cultural brokers who engaged with mainstream Canada and its elites to educate, advocate, and advance Indigenous interests as they understood them. Neither were traditional leaders: Oronhyatekha spent much of his life off-reserve and was never elected Chief; Jones was of mixed heritage, grew up off-reserve in settler society, and only returned to serve New Credit as an adult. As they gained access to power and privilege, they were sometimes mistrusted by Indigenous peoples who lived most of their lives on reserve. Both had significant connections to Toronto and broke barriers that largely prevented Indigenous peoples from participating in all but the lowest rungs of settler society. They challenged racist stereotypes of what Indigenous people were capable of, creating new possibilities for Indigenous lives.

Epidemic Diseases and the Myth of the "Vanishing Indian"

Peter Edmund Jones and Oronhyatekha began their public careers as the first and second Western-trained Indigenous medical doctors in Canada. In pursuing careers in medicine, they addressed one of the deepest traumas of colonization—the severe loss of life resulting from European epidemic diseases and the deterioration of Indigenous peoples' physical and mental health. The two men countered the prevalent belief that Indigenous people could not adapt to modernity and were doomed to sicken and die out.

Because Indigenous peoples had no immunity to European diseases or experience treating them, all members of a group became infected at once, with catastrophic results. In the post-contact period, wave after wave of epidemics swept through Indigenous communities, leaving weakened survivors of one disease more vulnerable to the next and everyday life severely disrupted. Data is scarce, but scholars' estimates of the death rate for all of North America vary from 25 per cent to upwards of 90 per cent.[9] In the 1790s, epidemics killed over one-third of the Mississaugas of the Credit, greatly weakening the community and reducing their numbers from 500 in the 1780s to 350 in 1798.[10] Smallpox killed many north of Toronto as well, as Lieutenant-Governor Simcoe discovered on his trip up the Humber in 1793.[11]

In the 1830s and 1840s, many at the Credit Village felt the health impacts of taking on the new settler lifestyle. In 1834, the village was struck by ague, or malarial fever, from mosquitoes in marshlands in the Credit River Valley. Widespread land clearing and disturbance had extended the northern range of malaria-carrying *Anopheles* mosquitoes to North America.[12] The move from semi-nomadic life in wigwams to crowded cabins in permanent villages also spread tuberculosis.

Peter Jones noted that child and infant mortality was very high: "It is painful for me to relate, that of all the children that have been born among those tribes with which I am acquainted, more than one half die before even reaching the period of youth."[13] He recorded the loss of many Indigenous youth and young adults: Joseph Quinepeno, grandson of Chief Quinepenon, in 1828, at the age of age twelve; Sahgahgewgahbahweh (John Summerfield), who studied at the Cazenovia Seminary in New York State and published his *Sketch of Grammar of the Chippeway Language* (1824) at the age of twenty and died at the Credit of tuberculosis in 1836; and William Wilson, "an Indian pupil of superior abilities," who attended Upper Canada College and the Methodist Upper Canadian College at Cobourg where he studied the classics, wrote poetry, and headed his class but contracted smallpox and died around 1838.[14]

The scale of loss in the first decades at the Credit Village was immense. Bunch and Polly Sunego lost all but three of many children to disease, and one of the survivors subsequently drowned in the millrace at the Credit River. Only Nahnebahwequay (Catherine Sutton) and her sister Mary lived to adulthood. The lives of the first wife of Peter Jones' brother John and her five children were cut short. In the mid-1830s,

David Sawyer lost seven relatives: his mother, her two sisters, his mother-in-law, his brother, his only sister, and his only child. In one year in the 1840s, the community lost twenty people or roughly 10 per cent of the entire band, mostly from measles.[15] In 1847, on the same day, Peter Jones lost his Mohawk half-brother, Joseph Oneida Jones, to smallpox and Joseph's Mississauga wife, Catherine Jackson Jones, to tuberculosis. Peter Jones' brother John died later that year.

By the mid-nineteenth century, the cumulative effects of unprecedented illness, death, and disruption had resulted in heartbreak and profound intergenerational trauma.[16] With the loss of so many Elders, who were repositories of cultural knowledge and tradition and respected sources of insight and judgment based on experience, communities were destabilized and weakened when they were most at risk. The loss of infants and children made it harder to maintain hope for the future. Some Indigenous people came to believe their Nations would die off, a belief that reduced their resiliency. Settlers interpreted the high death rate as evidence of inferiority and as evidence it was God's will that the land should be taken over by settlers. Trauma and cultural and physical dislocation led to social breakdown.

Many Indigenous people came to believe they were being punished for their "sins." When the 1832 cholera epidemic killed settlers in York and spread to Bluejay's people on the Humber, Peter Jones recorded in his journal: "Tuesday [July] 24th—Heard of the sudden death of some of the wicked Indians at the Humber by cholera. An awful warning to drunkards and obstinate sinners."[17]

Epidemics undermined confidence in traditional healing practices and the worldviews and knowledge systems that supported and guided them. Some Indigenous people questioned the validity of their own culture and became open to adopting new cultural forms such as Christianity—especially given that non-Indigenous people suffered less harm from infectious diseases and were thriving.

Although the trope of the "vanishing Indian" was based, in part, on ongoing high death rates, it was also a convenient settler justification for taking over Indigenous land. German visitor Johan Georg Kohl expressed this trope after he visited Toronto in 1855, noting that Indigenous people

> were numerous when the English founded here the town of York, and there are still people in Toronto who remember the fleets of bark canoes and little skiffs, in which the Indians used to bring fish and other things to sell to the inhabitants . . . But the Indians have now vanished like the morning mist, and nothing remains to recall even their memory, but the well sounding name they invented for this locality—the sonorous Toronto.[18]

Peter Jones and others challenged this belief: "I cannot suppose for a moment that the Supreme Disposer has decreed that the doom of the red man is to fall and gradually disappear, like the mighty wilderness, before the axe of the European settler. Some persons may affect to ascribe this waste of life to a divine decree, in order to screen themselves from the terrible responsibility which rests upon their souls."[19]

By countering the physical reality of poor Indigenous health and internalized beliefs that Indigenous peoples were doomed to die out, Oronhyatekha and Peter Edmund Jones offered hope for a better future. They recognized that Indigenous peoples had expertise in various kinds of healing and a huge body of traditional knowledge regarding medicinal plants, which they incorporated to some degree into their practices.

Indigenous plant knowledge represents, among other things, the continuity and validity of oral tradition, the value of Indigenous knowledge, and the deep connections of Indigenous peoples to the land. Acquired over millennia by observation and trial and error, Indigenous medicine was in many ways more scientific than the bleeding, blistering, and purging practices advocated by nineteenth-century Western medicine.[20] Even though Peter Jones recommended jettisoning many Indigenous customs and adopting white ways, he maintained his great respect for Indigenous medicines and prescribed them, including to his British wife, who suffered from migraine headaches and bouts of the flu.[21]

In *History of the Ojebway Indians*, Jones notes, "I have known instances of persons who had been given up by regular physicians, being restored to health by the simple administration of Indian medicines; and many of the white people, who have great confidence in their beneficial effects, will travel miles to place themselves under the care of an Indian doctor."[22] In late 1855, when Jones himself lay dying, he stayed for several weeks at the home of Egerton Ryerson in Toronto, where the best Western-trained doctors were consulted to no avail. The Reverend G. Osborne recounted in the introduction to Jones' posthumously published *History*: "When the Indians of the New Credit came, much sorrow filled their hearts to see their best earthly friend so low, that they proposed, at their own expense, to dispatch a messenger to Rice Lake for a noted Indian doctor."[23] (Jones died before the medicine man could be consulted.)

Indigenous knowledge of midwifery and plant medicines was sought out by settlers and continued to be used and passed on in Indigenous communities. As the number of medicine men (*powwows*) decreased because of persecution or Christian conversion, traditional healing knowledge was increasingly carried by women.[24] For example, Sarah Tekarihogen, the Mohawk wife of Augustus Jones, taught her daughter Catherine Jones Russell traditional healing and plant medicines. A descendant recalled Catherine's response when a young man fell and dislocated his shoulder: "Grandmother Catherine took off her shoe, put her foot against his ribs then pulled his shoulder into place. She then reached into her bag, took out a ball of yarn and placed it firmly in his armpit before bandaging the arm to his side; the shoulder healed perfectly."[25]

Elder and interviewee Susan Hoeg | Photo by Kim Big Canoe, courtesy of Chippewas of Georgina Island First Nation

My own great-grandmother was a midwife and a medicine woman. She was well known in the community for delivering babies and being that person who was always helping out all over the place. Even dressing dead people and getting them ready for a funeral. I have heard of her—other people have told me about her doing that . . . Her name was Anne Sandy Nanigishking.

—Emerson Benson Nanigishkung, Chippewas of Rama[26]

A settler writing in the 1860s recounted injuring his arm with an axe and it not healing until two women from Rama visited his camp: "One woman saw my arm in a sling and asked to see the wound and after seeing it she went off into the woods and soon returned munching bark or something like it and presently, after fully masticating the material, she placed the stuff in poultice form and it proved most efficacious and soon healed the wound. Those Indians, two families, the Yorks and Antoines, still reside in Rama Indian Village."[27]

My grandfather used to go back to Snake Island every year to get his medicines, his roots. But he never took me with him, so I don't know just where he went. But he always went back to Snake Island. And I remember him always leaving tobacco. And then, over here, there are certain spots where the heart medicine . . . I think they called it Wiikenh. And he always had that by his bed. He'd chew on it.

—Susan Hoeg, Chippewas of Georgina Island[28]

Dr. Peter Edmund Jones, 1898. Jones is wearing buckskin regalia inherited from his father and holding the tomahawk pipe given to his father by Sir Augustus d'Este | Wikimedia Commons

My mother knew lots of medicines. We'd be driving along the road, and she'd say, "Stop! Stop!" So we'd stop, and she'd say, "See those purple flowers out there in the field?" Yeah, there's a bull out there. "Ah, he's okay. Go out there and get it."

—Garry Sault, Mississaugas of the Credit[29]

While Peter Jones was a strong proponent of Indigenous plant medicines, he also supported requests by Indigenous communities for medical assistance from Western doctors. He called for a Western-trained doctor to be stationed near every reserve and welcomed vaccination against smallpox. "The English Government," he wrote in *History*, "have from time to time sent medical gentlemen to vaccinate the Indians; and this, under the blessing of God, has tended much to check the progress of that loathsome and often fatal distemper."[30] However, in the early nineteenth century, medical assistance was scarce even in new European settlements. William Roe, fur trader and postmaster of Newmarket, "had learned a few simple remedies from an Army surgeon and was widely sought after by settlers and Indians who fell ill."[31]

Recognizing the need for Indigenous Western-trained doctors, Peter Jones had asked Dr. John Rolph, founder of the Toronto School of Medicine, to help train them. The first Mississauga medical student was Francis Wilson, Peter Jones' half-brother Wahbunoo (Morning Light), son of Tubenahneequay and Mesquacosy. With Egerton Ryerson's assistance, Wilson was admitted to Upper Canada College in 1837 and then to Toronto's King's College, both of which waived tuition fees. Unfortunately, while on the hospital ward in his first year, Wilson contracted smallpox and died.[32]

Given Peter Jones' interest in herbal medicines and commitment to Western education, it's perhaps no surprise that his son became the first Indigenous medical doctor in Canada.

Elder Garry Sault, grandson of healer Peter Sault | Courtesy of Mississaugas of the Credit First Nation

Western-Trained Doctors

As a child, Peter Edmund Jones suffered from polio. He also revered his father, who died when he was twelve. He grew up at the Muncey Mission near London, where his father was stationed in the 1840s as a resident Methodist missionary, and later in Brantford, where he attended the Brantford Grammar School. He then attended medical school at the University of Toronto and at what is now Queen's University. He received his medical degree in 1866, one year before Oronhyatekha.[33] Notably, Jones asked that his Indigenous name, Kahkewaquonaby (the same as his father's), be put on the graduation list.[34]

His thesis topic was the "Indian medicine man." Given that much medical literature was dismissive of Indigenous peoples and their "pagan" medical practices, this was a courageous choice.[35] Unfortunately, the thesis has not survived, so whether he condoned or condemned Indigenous healing practices is unknown. But given that he later sold Indigenous medicines, he likely had a more balanced view than his non-Indigenous contemporaries. Raised mainly in a non-Indigenous environment, he had helped his mother edit his late father's diaries and manuscripts, which included details of treatments learned from Indigenous healers.[36]

Jones began practising medicine in Hagersville, on the edge of the New Credit Reserve, in 1868 or 1869, but he struggled financially because the white community had several doctors, and he likely faced racial prejudice. Indigenous patients couldn't afford his fees and were required to see the doctor appointed by the New Credit band council and approved by the Department of Indian Affairs.[37] To support his family, Jones sold medicines (as did many physicians of the time), likely including medicinal plants harvested by Indigenous herbalists. Jones' partner and salesman was his cousin Frank G.H. Wilson, son of the Francis Wilson who had died

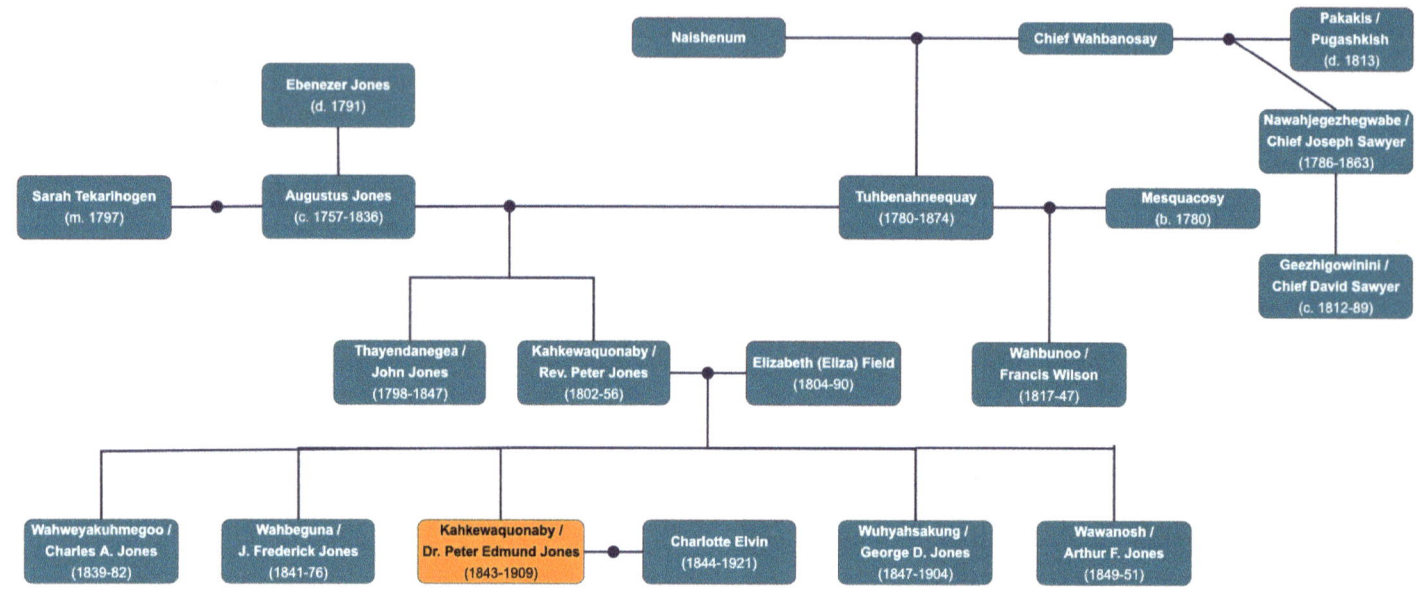

Dr. Peter Edmund Jones' family tree | Victoria Freeman and Ludia (Eun Seon) Bae

in medical school.[38] Other Credit Mississaugas became known as herbalists, including Maung-wudaus / George Henry, and Peter Salt / Sault, grandfather of Mississauga Elder Garry Sault, a respected traditionalist.[39]

> *Peter Sault was a third-degree Mide [member of the Midewewin or Grand Medicine Society of the Anishinaabek]. He really knew his medicines well. And he sent medicines from a shop on Dundas Street [in Toronto], and he shipped them all over the world. He cured so many people that, when he died, they put "Doctor" in front of his name.*
>
> —Garry Sault, Mississaugas of the Credit[40]

Some members of the New Credit Reserve did not recognize Peter Edmund Jones as Indigenous because his mother was a white woman, his father was of mixed Mississauga-British heritage,

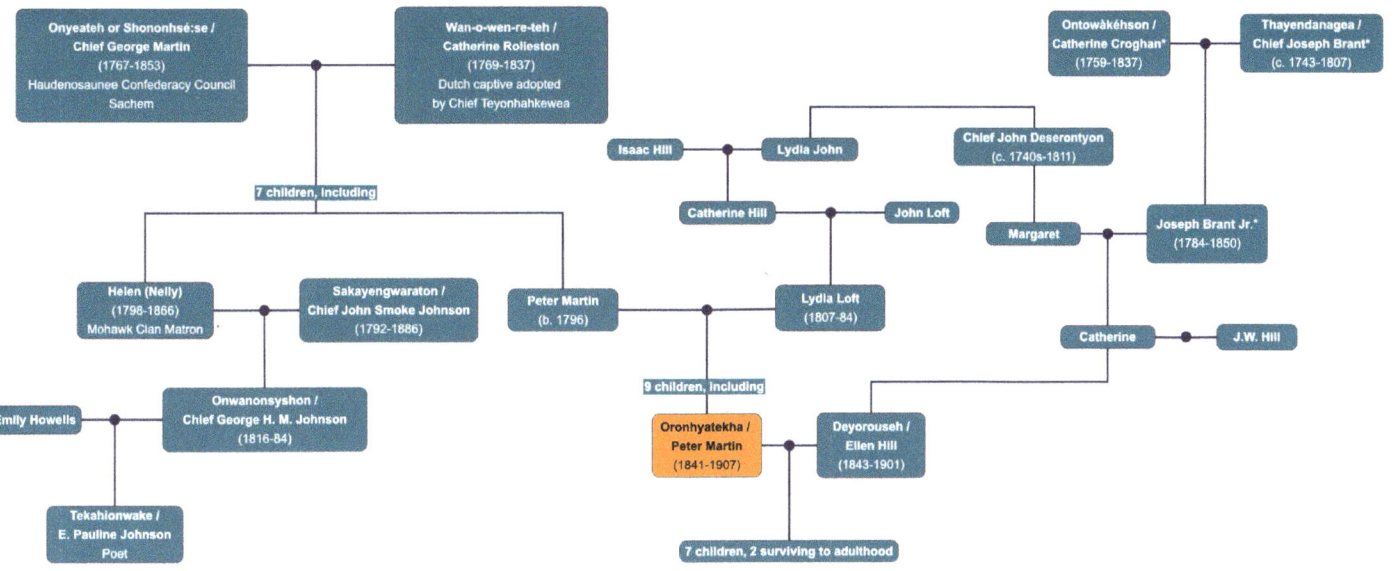

Dr. Oronhyatekha's family tree | Victoria Freeman and Ludia (Eun Seon) Bae, based on familysearch.org records and family tree in Jamieson and Hamilton, *Dr. Oronhyatekha*

and he was married to a white woman. But over time, he deepened his ties with the community. He visited his grandmother Tuhbenahneequay often and gained recognition and acceptance from a majority of the residents. Realizing he would never support his family from his practice in Hagersville, Jones began using his Anishinaabe name, Kahkewaquonaby (the same as his father's), improved his Anishinaabemowin, and became involved in New Credit band affairs (he was still a band member).

When Chief George King, the first Chief elected under the Gradual Enfranchisement Act of 1869, passed away in 1874, Jones was elected Chief by a margin of one vote—the beginning of his long career in politics. He served as Head Chief from 1874 to 1877 and again from 1880 until 1886. In 1875, the official doctor at New Credit asked to be relieved of his duties, and the band council chose Jones to succeed him. When his appointment was approved by Ottawa, he became the second Status Indian to become a band physician. Two years earlier, John A. Macdonald had appointed Dr. Oronhyatekha of Six Nations medical consultant to the Mohawks of the Bay of Quinte.[41]

Martin's Corner School, n.d. | Courtesy of Woodland Cultural Centre

Mohawk Institute for the Education of Indian Youth, Brantford, Ontario, c. 1880s | *Souvenir of Brantford, Ontario* (Brantford: J.R. Salmond, 1890), courtesy of Toronto Public Library | See page 262 for enlargement of photograph

Oronhyatekha (Burning Cloud) was born in 1841 on the territory of the Six Nations of Grand River. His father, also Peter Martin, was a veteran of the War of 1812, and his mother was from Tyendinaga. His maternal great-grandmother was a sister of John Deseronto, the Mohawk leader who led Haudenosaunee Loyalists to Tyendinaga on the Bay of Quinte in 1784, the same year that Joseph Brant led others, including his paternal grandfather, George Martin, to the Haldimand Tract on the Grand River. His aunt Helen on his father's side was a Clan Mother and the wife of John Smoke Johnson, the respected Pine Tree (i.e., nonhereditary) Chief. Their son, Oronhyatekha's cousin George Henry Martin Johnson, was also a Chief.

Oronhyatekha spent his early years in Martin's Corner, the settlement overlooking the Mohawk village (now Brantford) established by his grandfather George Martin. He attended Martin's Corner School, where he learned to speak and read English. Oronhyatekha was six years old when a mob from Brantford attacked the community.

In 1851, at the age of ten, Oronhyatekha was enrolled at the Mohawk Institute, an industrial school established by the New England Company on the Mohawk Village's farmlands at the request of John Brant, son of Joseph Brant. The Six Nations financially supported the school's construction, because the Mohawks considered education in the English language and Western traditions essential for success.[42] The Mohawk Institute became a boarding school four years after it was established and developed an aggressive assimilation agenda under its principal, the Reverend Abraham Nelles, an Anglican missionary. Oronhyatekha graduated before the school forbade the speaking of Indigenous languages, but the school was still a difficult environment. He ran away at least three times and received a whipping each time.[43] He was trained to be a shoemaker and apprenticed briefly after graduation.

Luckily, a visiting phrenologist (a now debunked type of practitioner who claimed to read character from the shape of one's skull) deemed Oronhyatekha suitable for further education. Oronhyatekha had a remarkable memory and was ambitious. After some academic preparation, he gained admission to Kenyon College in Ohio and obtained excellent grades.[44]

In 1860, the Chiefs of the Six Nations Council chose him to deliver the welcoming address to the Prince of Wales, later Edward VII, a turning point in his life.[45] It was later claimed that the prince was so impressed by Oronhyatekha that he invited him to study at Oxford University in England. The invitation likely came from Henry Wentworth Acland, a regius professor of medicine who accompanied the prince to North America and who became Oronhyatekha's lifelong friend and supporter.[46]

Oronhyatekha did attend Oxford in 1860 and was likely the first Indigenous person to study there. However, he left after one month because of funding and other difficulties. He had not asked the Indian Department or the New England Company (which ran the Mohawk Institute) for permission to leave Grand River. Although gifted, his ambitions were repeatedly thwarted by rumours that he had fathered an illegitimate child while at Kenyon College (never substantiated). His detractors used the rumour to deny him funding and block his advancement. The Reverend Nelles became his particular nemesis.[47] Daniel Wilson, who would teach English and history to Oronhyatekha at University College, Toronto, later noted that his strength and self-reliance made missionaries uncomfortable. The Indian Department treated Indigenous people like children, Wilson said, so if individuals showed independence, as Oronhyatekha did, they were considered rebellious troublemakers.[48]

In 1864, Oronhyatekha entered the University of Toronto, where he received a bachelor's degree in medicine in 1866. He obtained his medical degree from the Toronto School of Medicine in 1867, one year after Dr. Peter Edmund Jones. Although Wilson attempted to have him appointed to Grand River or the Indian Department, he was disqualified because officials raised the old charge of immorality against him.[49]

He practised medicine not far from Tyendinaga, where he conducted "a booming practice" with the Mohawks after advertising "Indian cures and herbal medicines" and where he mentored his brother-in-law George Hill, who also trained as a doctor.[50] He moved his practice to Stratford in 1870 and to London, Ontario, in 1874.

Political Activism

Peter Edmund Jones and Oronhyatekha became prominent figures who took an active role in politics and community issues.

Soon after being elected, Chief Jones pursued a land claim for the Mississaugas' lands at Credit River, Oakville, and Bronte Creek. The Crown Lands Department had sold the lands before obtaining a legal surrender from the band. The proceeds went to general revenues for the Province of Upper Canada rather than to the Mississaugas. Jones drew on his father's records of band finances to prove this injustice. A judgment favoured the band in 1884, but financial compensation became a political football. The payment, deposited in the band's account, was cancelled in 1894 by Duncan Campbell Scott, departmental accountant for Indian Affairs. For the rest of his life, Jones fought in vain for a just settlement.[51]

Beginning in 1874, Jones served as a New Credit delegate to the Grand General Indian Council of Ontario and played a leading role in its examinations of legislation. As Chief, he hosted the 1882 Grand Council at New Credit, one of the Council's most successful meetings, attended by more than a hundred delegates from twenty-one First Nations, including thirty-six from Six Nations, as well as three thousand guests, including government officials and non-Indigenous visitors from Toronto.[52]

An advocate of elective government, Jones believed First Nations should enjoy the same civil rights as other British subjects, including the right to vote in Canadian elections. But he argued that they should not have to give up their Indian status and band membership, as required in legislation such as the Gradual Civilization Act.[53]

In 1882, at Jones' instigation, the Mississaugas of New Credit adopted their own system of municipal-style regulations, building on the 1830 Constitution that his father had developed for the Credit Village.[54] New Credit also became the only band in Ontario to support the Indian Advancement Act of 1884. The legislation was strongly opposed by most First Nations, including the Six Nations. Although it increased band power over public health, policing, and taxation, it made the Indian agent chairman of the band council with broad powers to direct its functioning.[55]

Jones, a Conservative Party supporter, corresponded with John A. Macdonald (prime minister and superintendent-general of Indian Affairs) to suggest ways to improve the Indian Act. After meeting with Macdonald in 1886, Jones was asked to review the law and suggest amendments. Jones sent a detailed, annotated, and revised version of the legislation in 1887. His most significant change was a clause requiring a majority of electors to approve any important decision taken by a band council. As historian Chandra Murdoch notes, "By adding this clause, he fundamentally reorganizes the decision-making power of the electoral council away from the government model of council being responsible to Indian agents and back to greater directly democratic control that more closely resembles his father's legal code."⁵⁶

Peter Jones . . . was a very interesting man, but I found his son, the doctor, Peter Edmund Jones, was even more political—very.

—Margaret Sault, Mississaugas of the Credit⁵⁷

Unfortunately, Jones' amendments were not adopted. In the closing decades of the nineteenth century, band councils were restricted while the power of Indian agents expanded.⁵⁸ At New Credit, this oppression was mitigated because Jones was named the first Indian agent for New Credit in 1887, a position he held for a decade.

Oronhyatekha likewise sent petitions and letters to Macdonald (who became a friend) and the Department of Indian Affairs in the 1870s. His relationship with Six Nations was complex. He did not live there for most of his adult life, and his band membership was at various times revoked, switched to his wife's community of Tyendinaga, or reinstated. But he had sufficient standing among the Haudenosaunee and the broader Indigenous population of Ontario to be elected chairman of the Grand General Indian Council in 1872. In 1874, he was nominated to run again, but he came in second. Disagreements at this Council led most of the Haudenosaunee to withdraw, possibly including Oronhyatekha. He does not appear to have played a role in the Grand Council after this time.

In 1885, however, either on his own initiative or at Macdonald's request, Oronhyatekha visited several reserves to explain the Electoral Franchise Act to residents.⁵⁹ The act allowed Status Indian men who lived in central and eastern Canada and who met certain property qualifications to vote in federal elections. The legislation was an improvement in that it allowed individuals to maintain their Indian status and the rights associated with it. However, the act was controversial among Indigenous people and Canadian voters. The Laurier Liberal government rescinded the provisions in 1898. The right to vote would only be reinstated—and extended to Indigenous women—in 1960. Many Indigenous people still choose not to vote—particularly Haudenosaunee who assert their sovereignty as a Nation and as allies (rather than citizens) of Canada.

Seeking Fraternity

Oronhyatekha and Peter Edmund Jones joined fraternal organizations to advance their careers and social causes. Freemasonry, which began in England in 1711 and expanded throughout the British Empire, came to Upper Canada with the British soldiers who fought in the American Revolution. Several top Indian Department officials, including Sir John Johnson and John Butler, were masons, as was Joseph Brant.⁶⁰

Freemasonry appealed to some Indigenous men because of its language of universal brotherhood. Masons maintained that all men proceeded from the same common stock and belonged to the same universal human family.⁶¹ Freemasonry's

Joseph Brant / Thayendanegea's Masonic certificate, ink on paper, 1776 | Royal Ontario Museum, ROM2015_14693_1

emphasis on brotherhood and reciprocity largely continued even after it had been superseded elsewhere by virulently racist tropes.[62]

Oronhyatekha, like numerous Haudenosaunee, became a Freemason. He joined in Toronto when he was in medical school and served in several high masonic offices in southern Ontario.[63] Jones possibly secured his position as Indian agent of New Credit through his connections with Hamilton mason Thomas White, minister of the interior and superintendent-general of Indian affairs.[64]

Oronhyatekha and Jones joined other fraternal organizations, including temperance organizations and the Orange Order. In 1878, Oronhyatekha joined the Independent Order of Foresters (IOF), which provided "fraternity plus insurance." In the latter half of the nineteenth century, as more people moved into cities, were injured doing factory work, or were recent immigrants without family in Canada, societies such as the IOF assumed a role formerly performed by extended kin networks. At first, Oronhyatekha was told an "Indian" could not be a member because the order was only open to "white males": "That was enough for me; I had to get in."[65] Given his previous fraternal activity, his standing within the community, and his status among Orangemen (only Orangemen were admitted to the IOF), he was granted "special dispensation."[66]

The IOF became the perfect vehicle for his energy and talents. Soon, he was travelling the province at his own expense to advocate for fraternalism in small communities. In 1880, he was elected the first supreme chief ranger of a reformed

IOF and transformed it into the most successful fraternal insurance organization in Canada, which expanded across North America and overseas. By the time of his death in 1907, the IOF had transformed from an organization with a debt of $4,000 into one that "had accumulated over 10 million dollars in funds and had over one quarter of a million members throughout the world."[67]

During his long tenure as chief ranger, Oronhyatekha introduced an old-age pension benefit, created a retirement home for IOF employees, and built a home for orphans on lands he donated. Under his leadership, the IOF's world headquarters was established in Toronto in 1889, and he attended to the construction of the monumental Temple Building on the northwest corner of Bay and Richmond. When it opened in 1898, it was the tallest building in the British Empire. Along with the construction of City Hall at Bay and Queen, it sparked the development of a new financial district along Bay Street.[68]

By 1905, Oronhyatekha had been re-elected by acclamation as supreme chief ranger for twenty-five years. Under his leadership, more than one hundred thousand recipients received more than $20 million in benefits and insurance money, a record of financial assistance unmatched by any other public or private institution at the time.[69] When he died and his body lay in state at Massey Hall, an estimated ten thousand people paid their respects. Today, Foresters Financial, based in Don Mills, is the direct descendant of the fraternal organization Oronhyatekha built and proudly features him on its website. It provides insurance and other benefits to more than

Dr. Oronhyatekha, n.d. | Courtesy of Deseronto Archives

The Temple Building, northwest corner of Bay and Richmond Streets, Toronto, 1902. Old City Hall can be seen on the right | Photo by F.W. Micklethwaite, Wikimedia Commons

a million members in Canada, the United States, and the United Kingdom.

Public Educators

Oronhyatekha and Peter Edmund Jones engaged with the mainstream media and general public to educate Canadians about Indigenous peoples and Indigenous issues. For example, in 1875, they were involved in an exchange with two bigoted white writers who disparaged Indigenous people in letters to the Toronto *Daily Mail*.[70] Oronhyatekha used his sharp wit to satirize racist attitudes and stereotypes and became known for his eloquence and debating skills. In many public forums, he used his elevated social position to educate non-Indigenous people about Indigenous capabilities and culture. He contributed papers on the Mohawk language to the proceedings of the Canadian Institute.[71] At an 1885 American temperance conference, he made this statement: "I am an Indian, and of all the blessings I enjoy upon this earth, the fact that I am an Indian is the one I appreciate the most."[72] His public achievements contradicted stereotypes of Indian backwardness or lack of "civilization," and his Indigenous heritage served as a source of fascination for the public.[73]

But he was often seen as a remarkable exception to his race: "Canadians who believed in typical nineteenth-century native stereotypes interpreted his success as a result of assimilation; his attendance at residential school and other white educational institutions, his medical degree, residence in urban Toronto, his leadership of a Western-style business, and even his professional attire could be seen in opposition to his native birth. Whatever 'Indian-ness' remained was simply exotic, quaint, or entertaining."[74] Further, even the many Canadians who accepted him as the head of the IOF did not necessarily believe in the equality of Indigenous peoples.

Jones took another route to support the development of Indigenous communities and educate the public. In 1885, shortly after the North-West Resistance led by Louis Riel was forcibly put down and settler Canadian attitudes to both the Métis and First Nations hardened into intense racial prejudice, Jones launched a groundbreaking project to counteract stereotypes: a national newspaper *The Indian*. The first newspaper published by an Indigenous person in Canada, it was "devoted to the Aborigines of North America and especially to the Indians of Canada."[75] *The Indian*'s first issue appeared on December 30, 1885, and was distributed to reserves across Canada. Subsequent issues were published almost every two weeks through 1886.[76]

The Indian featured reports from reserves, explanations of legal decisions and government legislation affecting Indigenous people, reprinted House of Commons debates on Indian Affairs and reports on education, and news of colonial violence in the American West, among many other topics. Jones, then secretary of the Grand General Council of Ontario, also used the paper to solicit public input on issues to be discussed in Council.[77] In the first issue, he printed the minutes of the 1846 Council at Orillia, where his father had played a prominent role in gaining

Crowds paying their respects at Oronhyatekha's funeral procession in downtown Toronto, *Canadian Courier*, March 16, 1907 | Courtesy of Heritage Canadiana

Indigenous support for industrial schooling; he also sought opinions on successful models for day schools and advertised early residential schools.[78] He included biographies of the Anishinaabe missionaries of his father's generation and other Indigenous leaders, emphasizing their political involvement. Those memorialized included Joseph Brant, the Reverend Peter Jones, John Sunday, and Haudenosaunee Chief George H.M. Johnson, the son of John Smoke Johnson.

Jones sought contributions from Western-educated Indigenous people, but few, if any, Indigenous writers appeared in its pages—not even Oronhyatekha. Brief notices of news from

Masthead and related copy from *The Indian Newspaper*, December 30, 1885 | Toronto Reference Library, 923985

DEC. 30, 1886.

THE INDIAN.

THE INDIAN.

—A PAPER DEVOTED TO—

The Aborigines of North America,

—AND ESPECIALLY TO—

THE INDIANS OF CANADA.

SUBSCRIPTION $1.50 A YEAR IN ADVANCE

Will be published by THE INDIAN Publishing Company, of Hagersville, and for the present will be issued Fortnightly, and until further notice.

ADVERTISING RATES.

A limited number of advertisements will be received at the rate of $4.00 per inch per annum solid measure. Contracts for shorter periods at proportionate rates. Special contracts with large advertisers at a reduction of 10 to 20 per cent. off above rates.

The Indian Publishing Co.

Head Chief Kah-ke-wa-quo-na-by,
(DR. P. E. JONES)   Managing Editor.

BIRTHS, MARRIAGES AND DEATHS.

Insertions under this head for Indians will be 25 cents. For other than Indians 75 cents each insertion

MARRIAGES.

REAP—BIRD—On 25th. Nov. 1885, Mr. Wm. Reap Interpreter for the New England Society, to Miss Bella Bird of Kanyeageh Parsonage, Grand River Reserve.

DEATHS.

MARTIN—On 17thDec. 1885, Mr. Adam Martin a well educated and useful member of the Six Nation, a preacher and a great support of the church upon the Reserve.

THE MARKET REPORTS.

FISH MARKET.

Reported by J. Leckie.

We earnestly solicit correspondence from educated Indians, Trustees and School Teachers, with regard to the successful management of Indian Day Schools.

With this number we send subscription lists to all the principal bands of Indians. The special inducements for Indians to subscribe are as liberal as they possibly could be made. And we trust every family which contains a reading member will take this paper.

Subscriptions must invariably be *paid in advance*, and as the first issue will be limited to 5,000 copies it may be found necessary to discontinue promptly the mailing of papers to unpaid subscribers. In all future orders the cash must accompany the name of subscriber.

We also expect our local reporters will get their work in and that we shall have many items of interest from the various reserves. To our reporters we could say that although you may think the news you send is not of much consequence, still when it is distributed to outside bands who are more or less acquainted with your people then this becomes of great importance.

NEWS OF THE WORLD.

Mr. Justice Morrison died on Dec. 6th, at his residence, in North Toronto, after a lingering illness.

A special to *The Mail*, reports the alarming

various reserves might have been written by missionaries or Indian agents. Instead, Jones featured articles on local history and archaeology by Henry Scadding, Daniel Wilson, David Boyle, and other Toronto intellectuals, a measure of his standing among the leading cultural figures of the city.

Despite Jones' efforts, the paper attracted few Indigenous readers. "A cultural gulf" of education and privilege separated Jones from most Indigenous people, including other Mississaugas, many of whom judged him to be too white.⁷⁹ Furthermore, his strong support in *The Indian* for voting and elected band councils differed sharply with the political positions of the Haudenosaunee and many Anishinaabek. Jones' vision of an Indigenous-owned and -controlled newspaper was groundbreaking, but *The Indian* ceased publication in December 1886, after just twenty-four issues.

Preserving Indigenous Cultural Heritage

Oronhyatekha and Peter Edmund Jones also promoted Indigenous cultural preservation through collecting and archaeology. In part, they were emulating other Victorian collectors, but they were also affirming their peoples' deep ties to the land. Jones collected Indigenous "relics" and conducted archaeological excavations. He amassed the largest private collection in the province, much of which was donated to the Canadian Institute or the Smithsonian Institution in Washington.⁸⁰ Oronhyatekha also acquired a large collection of historical artifacts, many relating to Indigenous history, and curios from his travels around the world on behalf of the IOF. In 1902, he opened the Oronhyatekha Historical Rooms and Library in the Temple Building. The collection featured at least thirty-four cases with approximately two thousand items. It became one of the founding collections of the Royal Ontario Museum. Through these two men's efforts, many items were preserved for future generations and

A silver gorget gifted by the British Crown to an Indigenous warrior, indicating alliance with Britain in the War of 1812 | Royal Ontario Museum, Oronhyatekha Collection, ©ROM 911.3.209

did not simply disappear into private collections (although the relationship between Indigenous peoples and museums has also been fraught, with repatriation now on the agenda in many cases).⁸¹

A significant number of artifacts in Oronhyatekha's collection represented Great Lakes

Indigenous peoples and many were related to the War of 1812. Many could be read, curator Trudi Nicks has argued, "as symbolic of nation-to-nation meetings, agreements, or alliances," which was especially salient at a time when the federal government no longer recognized the sovereignty of Indigenous peoples and regarded them as subjects rather than allies of the Crown. As reminders of this history and evidence of their sovereign status, these items carry a message through time that is being reasserted today.[82]

Conclusion: Confronting History, (Re)making History

It's a powerful history that we have.

—Phil Monture, Six Nations of the Grand River[1]

How is this history remembered by local First Nations? How is it used? What is its power? The Knowledge Keepers, community activists, and Elders of the five First Nations interviewed for the Changing the Narrative project provide crucial perspectives on their communities' histories and the shared history of Indigenous peoples and settlers in the Toronto area.

Elder Garry Sault of the Mississaugas of the Credit expressed a basic truth about the colonial encounter: "Our leaders did their best. But they [the settlers] wanted our land more than our friendship."[2]

Ben Cousineau of Chippewas of Rama eloquently summarized how dramatically things changed for Anishinaabek:

> You were born in 1800. There is no Canada. You still have your original name. You're speaking just one language. You don't know much of church, and then, for someone born in Rama here, by the time it's 1840. You've seen yourself relocated to a reserve. The reserve's been taken away. You've now had religion forced on you. You've had Western education forced on you ... You have an Indian agent running your life by the time you die. Your kids are being taken away to school. You've been told that being Anishinaabe, being Indian, is wrong your whole life. Your own parent never experienced any of that at all. It's mind-boggling how quickly it changed ... And when you flip it to the pioneer perspective. That's the most exciting time in Canadian history. That's when they're opening everything up. The railway is here, everything's awesome. Screw England. We're going to this new, beautiful place where there is no coal, and

Elder and interviewee Margaret Sault. Sault is a long-time historical researcher for the Mississaugas of the Credit and, as of 2024, the organizer of thirteen Mississaugas of the Credit Historical Gatherings. Elders, scholars, community members, and others share and learn at these gatherings | Courtesy of Mississaugas of the Credit First Nation

we can breathe in the air. And they are excited for a new beginning, and they are given land in Muskoka, which they hold onto for a few generations, and now their grandkids live there and sell it for millions. But it's completely different histories, although at the same time period.[3]

Chief Kelly LaRocca of the Mississaugas of Scugog Island spoke of the need for people to understand "that when we talk about colonization, it's such a huge word with all kinds of bits and pieces and parts with tons of baggage that they just yawn and want to close their eyes. But it's real. The colonial experience is real."[4] Cousineau also emphasized that this history is not an abstraction:

> Now we talk about them as if they are these events that happened to this nameless, faceless group of people. But there are people who lived through all these things . . . And there's this underlying story of strength, I guess, where, despite everything, our ancestors—our grandmothers and grandfathers—survived all of that. And the result is that we still have

Elder and interviewee Sherry Lawson, Chippewas of Rama, storyteller and the author of several books | Photo by Victoria Freeman

The late Elder and former Chief Andrew Big Canoe with his grandson | Photo by Kim Big Canoe, courtesy of Chippewas of Georgina Island

some language, and we're trying to bring it back. We still have our culture. We still have a unique way of being . . . That doesn't happen without all that strength and stubbornness. It's not a completely defeatist history. There is resilience there.[5]

Mark Douglas also spoke of this resilience: "Wherever they went they adapted to where they were. And one of the worst places that that happened was Rama. We got moved over and over and over until . . . Okay. There's this really bad

Lauri Hoeg with the land acknowledgement plaque outside East Gwillimbury Civic Centre | Courtesy Lauri Hoeg

piece of land. It's rocky, swampy and no good for anything. But yet, we settled. We adapted."[6]

Matthew Stevens of Chippewas of Georgina Island reflected on the nineteenth and early twentieth centuries as a time of profound loss: "It's like the dark time. It's like the last hundred years that we existed in, people were really coping with the traumas." He noted the impact of trauma on the transmission of knowledge: "My grandma's generation and my grandpa, they would have had access to stories that their parents and grandparents would have had. But there was an interruption of that. And I think that's mainly because of the effects of how life was."[7]

Former Mississauga Chief Carolyn King spoke of trying to educate Torontonians when the Mississaugas were invited to help celebrate Toronto's 150th birthday in 1984:

> They asked our Chief of the day, which was Maurice LaForme . . . And he said, "No. We've got nothing to celebrate." And they kept calling. So I said to Maurice, "They really want you to go, and they said you can say whatever you want." And he said, "No. I'm not going. But it seems that you would like to go. You can go in my place" . . . So they call me up to speak after [Lieutenant-Governor] Jackman . . . And I just said, "I bring a message from the community and from the Chief. In war, there are winners and losers, and

there are survivors on each side. We are the survivors on the losing side. So as you celebrate, think of us.[8]

Although some things have improved since then, Stevens spoke of how the structural inequities created through the process of colonization are still present in his home community of Georgina Island: "So when I go home and I see the owner of DeBoers building a multi-million-dollar cottage . . . but we don't have adequate housing for our own, it's really . . . it's hard not to be upset. It's hard not to be angry with that."[9]

According to Ben Cousineau, there are many opportunities for the recovery of Indigenous knowledge and traditional practices because of the interconnections between communities: "Whereas there are things that maybe we lost, another community held on to. And those things are exchanged in ceremony and gatherings and stuff. And then, collectively, we all learn from each other again. So I think everything is still there."[10] Albert Big Canoe echoed this: "Well, it's certainly come back. We have the Powwows now. And they do ceremonies now. My sister herself, she was buried Native style. Because she was never a Christian."[11]

Rhonda Coppaway of Mississaugas of Scugog Island described a recent water ceremony held at Scugog to celebrate finally having clean drinking water: "So they had various drummers and dancers come in, and I'm going to get choked up here, and I don't normally get choked up. But I watched our children in their regalia, and they were so proud, and they danced and they danced. And we never had that growing up. We were ashamed. But I thought, here's little Scugog taking that step forward once again. Our children are so proud, and they're not going to know those things."[12]

Vicki Snache of Chippewas of Rama commented, "We had society. We had governance. We had all of these ways of being that were so rich. And only now that we are able to start practising our culture and our language and all of that again, only now are we scratching the surface of that beautiful richness of who we once were." She noted that even within a community, knowledge is being shared: "But each family is unique, and there are a lot of Knowledge Keepers in our community, various types of knowledge, whether it be medicine or ceremony or harvesting, fishing, crafting. Some family groups are known more for that than others." She also spoke of the recovery of identity and family: "A lot of people have been displaced through various mechanisms throughout history, and now they are coming home and relearning who they are."[13]

Kory Snache spoke of the challenges of bringing people together: "Within our communities, there are communities within communities. And I think that's a big thing that even our own people need to own up to and outsiders need to understand, too, I guess. That there are traditionalists, there are Christians, there are harvesters, nonharvesters, people with their status coming back, there are all these different communities. So each one kind of had their say."[14]

Phil Monture of Six Nations said that despite efforts to change historical gender relations, "The women are strong here. Very strong. We have the cultural side of it, and we're blessed that we still

Artwork created by research committee member Lauri Hoeg for the land acknowledgement plaque outside East Gwillimbury Civic Centre | Courtesy of Lauri Hoeg

have the Longhouse in which the ceremonies are kept. That teaching continues. The respect that goes with it. The ceremonies. The language part of it is coming back. Many of our generations were forbidden from speaking it."[15]

Lauri Hoeg of Georgina Island noted the persistence of the connection to the land, despite historical attempts to eradicate it: "The one thing that didn't get lost, really, is your connection to the fish and the water and the land. We've been doing that forever, and we're doing it now. We're still fishing."[16]

Others spoke of the persistence of Indigenous worldviews:

> The worldview, it still exists today, in that we're a part of Creation, and the world isn't ours. We're just a part of it. It's not ours to dictate and manipulate. We're all connected to each other and to the land and everything else within it. The belief and the teaching that everything has a spirit—that still exists today. It really contradicts with the Western and the Christianized view of things. We don't

believe that we are better than everything else and that we're apart from nature and that Mother Earth is here to serve us. It's kind of the other way around. So that worldview still exists.[17]

People say, "Just give me a book already." I don't have a Bible or a Torah or Koran. I just don't have that stuff, but you're walking on it. You're walking on our book. That's where you're living. And that's kind of how I'll put it to them, and they're like, "Oh!" And I'll say, "That's how our people have come to have a host or set of beliefs. By the doing of and the engaging in activities with land, and its beings. And by "beings," I mean anything with energy, whether it's water or rocks or trees and animals or whatever.

—Kelly LaRocca, Mississaugas of Scugog[18]

Cousineau noted that over the past five to ten years, Rama has experienced a revitalization "where the cultural teachings that make us Anishinaabe, those things that may be unique to Anishinaabe, are coming back again. And it's probably because of a lot of hard work from a few individuals. And more and more community acceptance and openness to those things that probably their grandparents were told were wrong."[19]

What can non-Indigenous people learn from this history? Vicki Snache hoped that non-Indigenous people would reflect on their own history and "come to a real understanding of who they are" so they can come to terms with that history and find ways to move forward: "How did they come to get here? What were the things that they did that caused them to believe the things that they believed at the time that they did those things? That caused them to create the laws that were created and the way that they were created?"[20]

Albert Big Canoe commented that he heard a lot of non-Indigenous people saying that Indigenous people had been conquered: "I say, 'You conquered us? When? What war was it and when?' And they look at you. They haven't got a clue what you're talking about. There's a lot of stuff that the non-Native people don't know."[21]

Leona Charles of Mississaugas of Scugog Island also commented on the lack of knowledge of non-Indigenous people in the region:

They need to learn a lot. I'll tell you that. Our culture and that? They have to learn that we are around, close by, even though they don't think so. We are. We are still here, as they say. Because I know at our PowWow and especially our Sunrise [Ceremony] people start coming. And they live like 2 miles down the road. And they said, "We didn't even know you were here. We didn't know this was a reserve. And in the Sunrise Ceremony, the one guy started crying. He said, "This is so beautiful. I never knew. I'll be back." They didn't know. But they could learn a lot or understand a lot about how and why we do things.[22]

Research committee member Tayler Hill, assistant director, Lands and Resources Department, Six Nations of the Grand River. Hill organized several friendship walks along the Haldimand Tract in September 2023 to build relationships and raise awareness about the Haldimand Proclamation and the loss and reclamation of Six Nations lands | Courtesy of the *Wellington Advertiser*

Several interviewees commented on the difficulties of confronting this history, for Indigenous and non-Indigenous people alike, and on how best to teach it to children: "It's hard to look at that history because it's dark. It's very dark. And it's not easy. Sometimes, we forget how hard it is to look at. Not just from a non-Native perspective but from our own perspective. It opens up triggers. So I would be looking at the good things for the children. Although not forgetting that [difficult] piece but focusing on all the wonderful ways in which we are . . . We have all of those things that make us rich. And those things can be shared."[23]

Ben Cousineau noted that there is now more public acknowledgement of this history. "There's this really awful history, which only in the past, like, ten years has really entered public consciousness. A lot of bad things were done to a lot of good people. The reason why was racial, ethnic, religious sense of superiority. Now, Canada at least says they did the wrong things."[24]

Matthew Stevens stressed that both the positive and negative aspects of the historical relationship between settlers and Indigenous peoples should be acknowledged: "Because the relationship wasn't . . . always negative. It wasn't always just constantly cowboys and Indians fighting. That wasn't the case. There was enough examples and experience of positive relations, positive, mutually beneficial agreements that did work for a time."[25] Similarly, Vicki Snache commented: "I

Former Chief Carolyn King of the Mississaugas of the Credit. King is the initiator of the Moccasin Identifier Project, which promotes public awareness of significant cultural historical sites and the ancestral presence of Indigenous communities through educational activities, including stenciling images of moccasins in public places | Courtesy of Moccasin Identifier™

William B. Davis Trail, Trillium Park, Toronto. The moccasins chiselled on rock reinscribe the ancestors' footprints at the waterfront and remind us of our treaty relationships to the land and to each other | Courtesy of Moccasin Identifier™

Conclusion | Confronting History, (Re)making History

think the pioneers did bring some really interesting, amazing knowledge to us. It's not to say that that stuff isn't real either."[26]

Kory Snache agreed: "I think the biggest thing is letting them know that there was a positive coexistence based on mutual agreement and understanding. And honouring those agreements. That's the biggest thing. Saying that there was a positive relationship. It wasn't all negative. And letting them know that out of a lot of both peoples' control, mainly government policy, it became sour. And that there is an opportunity to regain those ties again, to rebuild something great. I think those are the biggest things. There's an opportunity there for a renewed nation-to-nation relationship."[27]

Others spoke of the need for newcomers to understand the true nature of the treaties. Kory Snache said: "I think the biggest concept is the idea that land title and ownership is not solely Canada's. I think that needs to be understood. That Indigenous people still exist in the area and that there are fiduciary obligations to Indigenous people because of treaties and because of agreements."[28]

Phil Monture emphasized that peace, friendship, and respect were at the core of the treaties that Haudenosaunee entered into: "Those are always the foundation for our treaties. And I think the children need to know that those are their treaties too. They should share that part—the principle of peace, friendship and respect—and move forward. The commitment for the environment—all living things—that part is missing."[29]

Carolyn King added: "They need to understand what is an agreement and what's a promise. And not all promises are written down." She added, "The treaty is a colonial document, the government's document of the day, that allows you to come and live here. And it is still relevant. That's what you need to understand. And that's why our people still talk about it."[30]

Phil Monture spoke of his decades-long battle to have the rights of Six Nations recognized. "My battle has been with Canada, and the struggles have been to get justice for our land rights. We've been in litigation with Canada and Ontario since 1995. And it's very active right now as we speak. Our community is preparing for taking control of our own destiny on what injustices have occurred, for more land and preparing to address our housing crisis, get safe and clean drinking water to our community members."[31]

Several Knowledge Keepers spoke of aspects of Traditional Knowledge that were suppressed in the nineteenth century that are needed now. Matthew Stevens spoke of how "the Anishinaabe people, especially the—we'll call them Historic or Ancient Ones—they had mastered the way humans are supposed to live within this territory and this ecosystem. So anything that could be reimplemented from the way that they lived will help all life in this area."[32]

Lauri Hoeg spoke of the irony of being an Indigenous trustee advising settler educators about how to introduce land-based learning into their curriculums: "They took our people, historically, off the land and put them into classrooms, and now everybody's . . . studying soil in a textbook

... And the soil is outside, on the ground." Now, she noted, "They're trying to figure out, a hundred years later, how to get [students] back out of the classroom and back onto the land to learn from the land, which Indigenous people have been doing forever!"[33]

The fact that the research leading to this book originated in a critique of Black Creek Pioneer Village highlights that stories can either challenge or perpetuate colonial relations. They can either further understanding and build bridges, or they can be used to avoid difficult truths. Renaming this heritage site "The Village at Black Creek" marks a complex, inclusive moment of change for Indigenous peoples and settlers in the Toronto area. The name change was protested by some Torontonians.[34] But inclusiveness was welcomed by others. As Cousineau noted:

> It's easy to think that, as Anishinaabe, or even First Nations in general in Canada, these problems and things that we face are unique to us. But if you talk to people from . . . especially immigrants, they've gone through similar things at the hands of, I guess, colonial nations. They've been persecuted. They've had their languages taken. They've had their cultural ways removed completely off the face of the earth. They've been told who they are is wrong and so on. And I suspect that a lot of Toronto can find some commonalities with the stories of First Nations in Canada. Especially the immigrants. Fleeing whatever they're fleeing in their home country. There are a lot of similarities.[35]

The process of uncovering buried and suppressed histories is not something that can be accomplished on the first attempt. Kelly LaRocca recognizes that developing historical understanding is an iterative process: "There's this historical write-up in the casino from when the casino first opened. And I just cringe. I'm like, 'I know that's not right anymore.' We've learned more since that time. And I think that's really it. History . . . it's not like it's etched in some stone. It's a living, breathing entity that changes with the more work you do."[36]

Together, the participants in the Changing the Narrative project did some of that work. They—and I—have shared what we know or have learned about the living histories of this region in the hope of a better future for all.

Chief Kelly LaRocca in regalia at the 2023 Mississaugas of Scugog Powwow | Courtesy of Ang Tek Gie and Kelly LaRocca

Acknowledgements

Given the wide-ranging nature of this study and the extensive collaboration that made it possible, acknowledging my debt to others is especially important. *Where Histories Meet* was not written in isolation but with the help of a team of scholars and Indigenous Knowledge Keepers. Its publication would simply not have come about without the advocacy, support, encouragement, and energy of Jennifer Bonnell, head of the public history program at York University and the originator and academic lead of the Changing the Narrative project. It also depended upon the openness and support of Allison White, curator, and Wendy Rowney, senior manager, Community Outreach and Education, of The Village at Black Creek, and the willingness of their employer, Toronto and Region Conservation Authority to address this challenge. I often leaned on co-investigator Alan Corbiere, also of York's Department of History. His deep knowledge of Anishinaabe history, culture, and language and Indigenous research protocols guided me; his sense of humour kept me afloat.

I have thoroughly enjoyed working with Marcel Fortin, former head of the Map and Data Library (now associate chief librarian, data services, digital scholarship, and information technologies) at the University of Toronto, and his research assistant, Cheney Gao, who created twenty-one beautiful maps that appear in this book. I also want to acknowledge and thank the following research assistants for their timely and invaluable help: Eon Seon (Ludia) Bae for formatting the relationship charts and securing image permissions; Helena Cairns and Rosaria Moretti-Lawrie for work on image permissions; Johannes Chan for compiling the bibliography, formatting the endnotes, and researching milling in the Toronto area; and Olivia White and Morag Hegg for their review of selected published primary and secondary sources. I also want to thank my partner, Mark Fawcett, and Jennifer Bonnell for their timely help in acquiring high resolution images.

I have been extremely fortunate to have been guided by the First Nations research committee of the Changing the Narrative project. I am grateful to Ben Cousineau (Chippewas of Rama), Lauri Hoeg (Chippewas of Georgina Island), Marcie Sandy and Tayler Hill (Six Nations of the Grand River), Matthew Stevens (Mississaugas of Scugog Island), and Darin Wybenga (Mississaugas of the Credit) for their research suggestions, helpful comments on drafts of the research report, and willingness to work with me to find appropriate wording where there were differences of historical interpretation. I also thank

Keith Jamieson of Six Nations for his help with Six Nations genealogy, Robin Vanstone of Six Nations for her initial participation, and Mary-Anne Hoggarth for representing Mississaugas of Scugog Island more recently.

I have been guided more generally by the words of the Elders and Knowledge Keepers whom Alan Corbiere and I interviewed: Albert Big Canoe, the late Andrew Big Canoe, Leona Charles, Rhonda Coppaway, Ben Cousineau, Mark Douglas, Lauri Hoeg, Susan Hoeg, Carolyn King, Kelly LaRocca, Sherry Lawson, Pat LeSaux, Phil Monture, the late Emerson Benson Nanigishkung, Garry Sault, Margaret Sault, Kory Snache, Vicki Snache, Matthew Stevens, and Darin Wybenga. I have learned so much from their generous sharing of their experience, knowledge, and wisdom.

As this work is a survey of the history of a broad geographic area and period, I relied on the scholarship of many historians. I would like to acknowledge my indebtedness to Donald B. Smith for his groundbreaking work on the Mississaugas of the Credit and express my profound gratitude for his support of my initial forays into historical scholarship many years ago. I am also indebted to Chandra Murdoch, whose 2023 dissertation on the Grand General Indian Council filled in important gaps in the scholarship on Indigenous political organizing in the second half of the nineteenth century. I am grateful to Fred Blair, Ray Borland, Laurie Leclair, and David Town for generously sharing their knowledge and sources.

I would like to acknowledge Jesse Thistle and Martha Steigman for the short film *kiskisiwin|remembering*, which powerfully articulates why the settler-colonial narrative of Toronto history, as represented at Black Creek Pioneer Village, needed to change, and I thank Ruth Howard and Ange Loft, former artistic director and associate artistic director of Jumblies Theatre, for many years of artistic collaboration focused on the Indigenous history of Toronto. *Where Histories Meet* also draws on my own unpublished 2010 PhD dissertation on the historical memory of the Indigenous and colonial past of Toronto and the research for *A Treaty Guide for Torontonians* (2021), which I co-authored with Ange Loft, Martha Stiegman, and Jill Carter.

I am grateful to the funders who made this research possible. The Changing the Narrative project was funded by the Social Sciences and Humanities Research Council (Insight Development Grant, 2020, and Connections Grant, 2023); York University's Faculty of Liberal Arts and Professional Studies' minor grants programs; the University of Toronto Libraries' Chief Librarian Innovation Award; and Toronto and Region Conservation Authority, via a grant from the Federal Economic Development Agency for Southern Ontario. This book is a reworked version of the archival research report I prepared for that project.

I want to particularly thank Brian Scrivener, Helen Hajnoczky, Alison Cobra, and Melina Cusano for their patience in helping me birth this book. I give special thanks to copy editor Lesley Erickson: a pleasure to work with you again!

And lastly, a huge thank you to my ever-patient family and friends, who put up with me as I laboured for several years on this project while supposedly retired.

Selected Bibliography

ARCHIVAL COLLECTIONS

Archives of Ontario
    Crown Land Records, RG 1–2
E.J. Pratt Library, Victoria University Library, University of Toronto, Special Collections and Rare Books
    Donald B. Smith Fonds
    Peter Jones Collection
Library and Archives Canada
    Department of Indian Affairs, RG 10
Toronto Reference Library
    Baldwin Collection
    John Ross Robertson Collection
United Church of Canada Archives
    Methodist Church (Canada) Missionary Society Fonds

INTERVIEWS

Big Canoe, Albert, interview by Alan Corbiere and Victoria Freeman, Chippewas of Georgina Island First Nation, December 17, 2022

Big Canoe, Andrew, interview by Alan Corbiere and Victoria Freeman, Chippewas of Georgina Island First Nation, December 17, 2022

Charles, Leona, interview by Allan Corbiere and Victoria Freeman, Mississaugas of Scugog Island First Nation, July 7, 2022

Coppaway, Rhonda, virtual interview by Alan Corbiere and Victoria Freeman, October 20, 2022.

Cousineau, Ben, interview by Alan Corbiere and Victoria Freeman, Chippewas of Rama First Nation, July 6, 2022

Douglas, Mark, interview by Alan Corbiere, Chippewas of Rama First Nation, November 24, 2022

Hoeg, Lauri, interview by Alan Corbiere and Victoria Freeman, Chippewas of Georgina Island First Nation, December 17, 2022

Hoeg, Susan, interview by Alan Corbiere and Victoria Freeman, Chippewas of Georgina Island First Nation, December 17, 2022

King, Carolyn, virtual interview by Victoria Freeman, October 10, 2022

LaRocca, Kelly, virtual interview by Alan Corbiere and Victoria Freeman, October 20, 2022

Lawson, Sherry, interview by Alan Corbiere and Victoria Freeman, Chippewas of Rama First Nation, July 6, 2022

LeSaux, Pat, interview by Allan Corbiere and Victoria Freeman, Mississaugas of Scugog Island First Nation, July 7, 2022

Monture, Phil, virtual interview by Alan Corbiere and Victoria Freeman, November 15, 2022

Nanigishkung, Emerson Benson, interview by Alan Corbiere and Victoria Freeman, Chippewas of Rama First Nation, July 6, 2022

Sault, Garry, virtual interview by Alan Corbiere and Victoria Freeman, September 13, 2022

Sault, Margaret, virtual interview by Alan Corbiere and Victoria Freeman, September 2, 2022

Snache, Kory, virtual interview by Alan Corbiere and Victoria Freeman, September 21, 2022

Snache, Vicki, interview by Alan Corbiere and Victoria Freeman, Chippewas of Rama First Nation, July 6, 2022

Stevens, Matthew, virtual interview by Alan Corbiere and Victoria Freeman, October 6, 2022

Wybenga, Darin, virtual interview by Alan Corbiere and Victoria Freeman, August 24, 2022

OTHER SOURCES

Aborigines Protection Society. *Report of the Indians of Upper Canada, 1839*. Toronto: Canadiana House, 1968.

Archives of Ontario and Ontario Black History Society. "Sophia Burthen Pooley: Part of the Family?" *Enslaved Africans in Upper Canada* (online exhibit). https://www.archives.gov.on.ca/en/explore/online/slavery/sophia_pooley.aspx.

Baldwin, Henry, ed. *Minutes of the General Council of Indian Chiefs and Principal Men, Held at Orillia, Lake Simcoe Narrows, on Thursday, the 30th, and Friday, the 31st July, 1846, on the Proposed Removal of the Smaller Communities, and the Establishment of Manual Labour Schools*. Montreal: Canada Gazette Office, 1846.

Bennett, Matthew R., David Bustos, Jeffrey S. Pigati, et al. "Evidence of Humans in North America during the Last Glacial Maximum." *Science* 373, no. 6562 (2021): 1528–31.

Berchem, F.R. *The Yonge Street Story, 1793–1860: An Account from Letters, Diaries and Newspapers.* Toronto: Dundurn, 1996.

Binnema, Theodore, and Kevin Hutchings. "The Emigrant and the Noble Savage: Sir Francis Bond Head's Romantic Approach to Aboriginal Policy in Upper Canada, 1836–1838." *Journal of Canadian Studies* 39, no. 1 (2005): 115–38.

Birch, Jennifer, and Ronald F. Williamson. "Navigating Ancestral Landscapes in the Northern Iroquoian World." *Journal of Anthropological Archaeology* 39 (2015): 139–50.

Blair, Fred. "Orillia's Early Settlers, Part 4: Andrew Borland." Orillia Museum of Art and History. Facebook, February 18, 2021. https://www.facebook.com/orilliamuseum/photos/a.252204871475152/4357061550989443/?type=3.

Blair, Peggy. "Fact Sheet: Rights of Aboriginal Women On and Off Reserve." Scow Institute, 2005.

Blake, V.B. *Credit Valley Conservation Report, 1956.* Toronto: Department of Planning and Development, 1956.

Bohaker, Heidi. *Doodem and Council Fire: Anishinaabe Governance through Alliance.* Toronto: University of Toronto Press, 2020.

Bonnell, Jennifer. *Reclaiming the Don: An Environmental History of Toronto's Don River Valley.* Toronto: University of Toronto Press, 2014.

Burkholder, Mabel. "Palatine Settlements in York County." *Papers and Records: Ontario Historical Society* 37 (1945): 81–96.

Carroll, John. *Case and His Contemporaries.* Vol. 3. Toronto: Wesleyan Conference Office, 1871.

Carter, Robert Terence. *Stories of Newmarket: An Old Ontario Town.* Toronto: Dundurn Press, 2011.

Child, Brenda. *Holding Our World Together: Ojibwe Women and the Survival of Community.* New York: Penguin, 2012.

Constable, Jean M. *Stong Roots and Branches.* Peel Family Histories. Toronto, 2001.

Corbiere, Alan. "Anishinaabeg in the War of 1812: More Than Tecumseh and His Indians." *Active History*, September 10, 2014. http://activehistory.ca/2014/09/anishnaabeg-in-the-war-of-1812-more-than-tecumseh-and-his-indians/.

Corbiere, Alan. "Mookomaanish: The Damn Knife (Odaawaa Chief and Warrior)." *Active History*, October 8, 2014. https://activehistory.ca/2014/10/mookomaanish-the-damn-knife-odaawaa-chief-and-warrior.

Corbiere, Alan Ojiig. "Anishinaabe Treaty-Making in the 18th- and 19th-Century Northern Great Lakes: From Shared Meanings to Epistemological Chasms." PhD diss., York University, 2019.

Craig, Gerald M. *Upper Canada: The Formative Years, 1784–1841*. Toronto: McClelland and Stewart, 1963.

Cumberland, Barlow, and Oronhyatekha. *Catalogue and Notes of the Oronhyatekha Historical Collection*. Toronto: Supreme Court/Independent Order of Foresters, 1904.

Cummer, Wellington Willson, and Clyde Lottridge Cummer. *Cummer Memoranda: A Record of the Progenitors and Descendants of Jacob Cummer*. Cleveland: O.S. Hubbell, 1911.

Day, Alfred T. "The Legacy of John Stewart and the Wyandot." Methodist Mission Bicentennial series, 2019. https://www.umc.org/en/content/the-legacy-of-john-stewart-and-the-wyandot.

Dean, William G., and Geoffrey J. Matthews. *Economic Atlas of Ontario*. Toronto: University of Toronto Press, 1969.

Elbourne, Elizabeth. "The Sin of the Settler: The 1835–36 Select Committee on Aborigines and Debates over Virtue and Conquest in the Early Nineteenth-Century British White Settler Empire." *Journal of Colonialism and Colonial History* 4, no. 3 (2003): https://dx.doi.org/10.1353/cch.2004.0003.

Firth, Edith, ed. *The Town a York, 1793–1815: A Collection of Documents*. Toronto: Champlain Society / University of Toronto Press, 1962.

Freeman, Victoria. "'Toronto Has No History!' Indigeneity, Settler Colonialism, and Historical Memory in Canada's Largest City." PhD diss., University of Toronto, 2010.

General Council. *The General Council of the Six Nations and Delegates from Different Bands in Western and Eastern Canada, June 10, 1870*. Hamilton: Spectator Office, 1870.

Gillis, Peter R. "Rivers of Sawdust: The Battle over Industrial Pollution in Canada, 1865–1903." *Journal of Canadian Studies* 21, no. 1 (1986): 84–103.

Goldenberg, Susan. "Historic Stong Family." North York Historical Society, January 20, 2014. https://nyhs.ca/historic-stong-family/.

Hart, Patricia. *Pioneering in North York: A History of the Borough*. Toronto: General Publishing, 1968.

Henry, Alexander. *Travels and Adventures in Canada and the Indian Territories between the Years 1760 and 1776 in Two Parts*. New York: I. Riley, 1809.

Hill, Susan. *The Clay We Are Made Of: Haudenosaunee Land Tenure on the Grand River*. Winnipeg: University of Manitoba Press, 2017.

Holmes, Joan, and Associates. "The Coldwater Treaty: Draft Historical Report." Specific Claims INAC Report, 1993.

Holmes, Joan, and Associates. "Coldwater-Narrows Surrender of 1836: Report about Additional Research Findings." In *Chippewa Tri-Council Inquiry: Coldwater-Narrows Reservation Surrender Claim*. Ottawa: Indian Claims Commission, 2020.

Hughes, Alun. "Augustus Jones: The Life and Loves of a Pioneer Surveyor." *Association of Canadian Map Libraries and Archives Bulletin*, no. 111 (Spring/Summer 2001): 3–12.

Hunter, F. *A History of Simcoe County*. 2 vols. Barrie, ON: County Council, 1909.

Indian Claims Commission. *Mississaugas of the New Credit First Nation Inquiry: Toronto Purchase Claim*. Ottawa: Indian Claims Commission, 2003.

Indian Treaties and Surrenders from 1680 to 1890. Vol. 1. Ottawa: Brown Chamberlain Printers, 1891.

Jacobs, Dean M., and Victor P. Lytwyn. "Naagan Get Bezhig Emkwaan: A Dish with One Spoon Reconsidered." *Ontario History* 112, no. 2 (2020): 191–210.

Jamieson, Keith, and Michelle Hamilton. *Dr. Oronhyatekha: Security, Justice, and Equality*. Toronto: Dundurn, 2016.

Jezierski, John V., ed. and trans. "A 1751 Journal of Abbé François Picquet." *New York Historical Society Quarterly* 44, no. 4 (1970). 361–81.

Johnson, J.K., and Bruce G. Wilson, eds. *Historical Essays on Upper Canada: New Perspectives*. Montreal/Kingston: McGill-Queen's University Press, 2014.

Johnson, Leo A. "The Mississauga-Lake Ontario Land Surrender of 1805." *Ontario History* 83, no. 3, (1990).

Johnson, William. *The Papers of Sir William Johnson*. Vol. 8, edited by Alexander C. Flick. Vol. 11, edited by Milton W. Hamilton. Albany: University of the State of New York, 1921, 1933.

Johnston, Charles M. *The Valley of the Six Nations: A Collection of Documents*. Toronto: University of Toronto Press, 1964.

Jones, Peter. *History of the Ojebway Indians: With Especial Reference to Their Conversion to Christianity*. London: A.W. Bennett, 1861.

Jones, Peter. *Life and Journals of Kah-Ke-Wa-Quo-Na-By (Rev. Peter Jones), Wesleyan Missionary*. Toronto: A. Green, 1860.

Keane, David, and Colin Read, eds. *Old Ontario: Essays in Honour of J.M.S. Careless*. Toronto: Dundurn Press, 1990.

Kohl, Johann Georg. *Travels in Canada and through the States of New York and Pennsylvania*. Vol. 2. London: George Manwaring, 1861.

Korpan, Roxanne L. "Scriptural Relations: Colonial Formations of Anishaabemowin Bibles in Nineteenth-Century Canada." *Material Religion* 17, no. 2 (2021): 147–76.

Leclerc, Laurie. "Rama First Nation Land Acquisitions, 1838–1848." *Mzinigan, Our Heritage Place*, Chippewas of Rama First Nation, Dagwaagi/Fall 2022, 6–10. https://issuu.com/bencousineau/docs/mzinigan_fall_2022.

Leslie, John F. *Commissions of Inquiry into Indian Affairs in the Canadas, 1828–1858: Evolving a Corporate Memory for the Indian Department*. Ottawa: Treaties and Historical Research Centre, Indian Affairs and Northern Development Branch, 1985.

Leslie, John F. *The Report of the Pennefather Commission: Indian Conditions and Administration in the Canadas in the 1850s*. Ottawa: Treaties and Historical Research Centre, 1983.

Lesser, Gloria. "William Berczy's Portraits of Joseph Brant." *National Gallery of Canada Annual Bulletin* 6 (1982–83): 1–8.

Lizars, Kathleen. *The Valley of the Humber, 1615–1913*. Toronto: William Briggs, 1913.

Loft, Ange, Victoria Freeman, Martha Stiegman, and Jill Carter. *A Treaty Guide for Torontonians*. 2nd ed. Toronto: Art Metropole, 2022.

Macdonell, Alexander. "Diary of Gov. Simcoe's Journey from Humber Bay to Matchetache Bay, 1793." Extract from *Transactions of the Canadian Institute, 1890*. https://gutenberg.ca/ebooks/macdonella-simcoe/macdonella-simcoe-00-h.html.

Magrath, James. "Report of the State of the Indians on the River Credit." In *Authentic Letters from Upper Canada*, edited by Thomas William Magrath. Dublin: William Curry, 1833.

Manitowabi, Darrel. "From Fish Weirs to Casino: Negotiating Neoliberalism at Mnjikaning." PhD diss., University of Toronto, 2007.

Methodist Episcopal Church, Canada Conference, Missionary Society. *First Annual Report of the Canada Conference Missionary Society, Auxiliary to the Missionary Society of the Methodist Episcopal Church*. Kingston, ON: Hugh C. Thomson, 1825.

Methodist Episcopal Church, Canada Conference, Missionary Society. *Second Annual Report of the Canada Conference Missionary Society, Auxiliary to the Missionary Society of the Methodist Episcopal Church*. St. Catharines, ON: Hiram Leavensworth, 1826.

Methodist Episcopal Church, Canada Conference, Missionary Society, *Third Annual Report of the Canada Conference Missionary Society, Auxiliary to the Missionary Society of the Methodist Episcopal Church*. York: Society at the Office of the Colonal Advocate, William Lyon MacKenzie, 1827.

Miedema, Gary. "When the Rivers Really Ran: Water-Powered Industry in Toronto." In *HtO: Toronto's Water from Lake Iroquois to Lost Rivers to Low-Flow Toilets*, edited by Wayne Reeves and Christina Palassio. Toronto: Coach House, 2008.

Mika, Nick. *The Village at Black Creek: Toronto's Living History Village*. Toronto: Natural Heritage, 2000.

Milloy, John S. "The Early Indian Acts: Developmental Strategy and Constitutional Change." In *Sweet Promises: A Reader on Indian-White Relations in Canada*, edited by J.R. Miller. Toronto: University of Toronto Press, 1991.

Milloy, John S. "The Era of Civilization: British Policy for the Indians of Canada, 1830–1860." PhD diss., Oxford University, 1978.

Mitchell, William W. "Worshipful Brother Joseph Brant." *Historical Record of the Brant Masonic District, 1855–2020*. Brant Masonic District, 2020. https://www.brantmasons.com/files/BMD—Historytothe19Nov2020-1.pdf.

Morris, James Lewis. *Indians of Ontario*. Toronto: Dept. of Lands and Forests, 1943.

Moses, John, with Donald Graves and Warren Sinclair. *A Sketch Account of Aboriginal Peoples in the Canadian Military*. Ottawa: Minister of National Defense Canada, 2004.

Mulvany, Charles Pelham, and Adam Graeme Mercer. *History of Toronto and County of York, Ontario*. Vol. 1. Toronto: C.B. Robinson, 1885.

Murdoch, Chandra. "Act to Control: The Grand General Indian Council, The Department of Indian Affairs, and the Struggle over the Indian Act in Ontario, 1850–1906." PhD diss. University of Toronto, 2023.

Murray, Florence, ed. *Muskoka and Haliburton, 1615–1875: A Collection of Documents*. Toronto: Champlain Society / University of Toronto Press, 1963.

Nicks, Trudy. "Dr. Oronhyatekha's History Lessons: Reading Museum Collections as Texts." In *Reading beyond Words: Contexts for Native History*, 2nd ed., edited by Jennifer S.H. Brown and Elizabeth Vibert. Toronto: University of Toronto Press, 2003.

Osborne, Alexander Campbell. *The Migration of Voyageurs from Drummond Island to Penetanguishene in 1828*. Reprinted from *Papers and Records of the Ontario Historical Society*, Vol. 3, 1901. https://www.canadiana.ca/view/oocihm.86771/1.

Playter, George. *The History of Methodism in Canada*. Vol. 1. Toronto: Wesleyan Printing Establishment, 1862.

Preston, David L. "'We Intend to Live Our Lifetime Together as Brothers': Palatine and Iroquois Communities in the Mohawk Valley." *New York History* 89, no. 2 (2009): 179–90.

Radforth, Ian. "Performance, Politics, and Representation: Aboriginal People and the 1860 Royal Tour of Canada," *Canadian Historical Review* 84, no. 1 (2001): 1–32.

Radforth, Ian. *Royal Spectacle: The 1860 Visit of the Prince of Wales to Canada and the United States*. Toronto: University of Toronto Press, 2004.

Reimer, Gwen. "British-Canada's Land Purchases, 1783–1788: A Strategic Perspective." *Ontario History* 111, no. 1 (2016): 36–72.

Reimer, Gwen, and Jean-Philippe Chartrand. *Historic Metis in Ontario: Georgian Bay*. Report submitted to the Native Affairs Unit, Ontario Ministry of Natural Resources, Praxis Research Associates, 2000.

Robinson, Percy J. *Toronto during the French Régime: A History of the Toronto Region from Brûlé to Simcoe, 1615–1793*. 2nd ed. Toronto: University of Toronto Press, 1965.

Russell, Peter. *The Correspondence of the Honourable Peter Russell*. Vol. 2. Edited by Ernest A. Cruikshank and Andrew F. Hunter. Toronto: Ontario Historical Society, 1932.

Ryerson, Egerton. "Report on Industrial Schools, 26 May 1847." *Statistics Respecting Indian Schools*. Ottawa: Government Printing Bureau, 1898.

———. *The Story of My Life*. Edited by J. George Hodgins. Toronto: William Briggs, 1883.

Sandberg, L.A., J. Johnson, R. Gualtieri, and L. Lesage. "Re-connecting with a Historical Site: On Narrative and the Huron-Wendat Ancestral Village at York University, Toronto." *Ontario History* 113, no. 1 (2021): 80–105.

Scadding, Henry. *Toronto of Old: Collections and Recollections Illustrative of the Early Settlement and Social Life of the Capital of Ontario*. Toronto: Willing and Williamson, 1878.

Schmalz, Peter S. *The Ojibwa of Southern Ontario*. Toronto: University of Toronto Press, 1991.

Semple, Neil. *The Lord's Dominion: The History of Canadian Methodism*. Montreal/Kingston: McGill-Queen's University Press, 1996.

Shadd, Adrienne, Afua Cooper, and Karolyn Smardz Frost. *The Underground Railroad: Next Stop, Toronto!* Toronto: Dundurn Press, 2005.

Sherwin, Allan. *Bridging Two Peoples: Chief Peter E. Jones, 1843–1909*. Waterloo, ON: Wilfrid Laurier University Press, 2012.

Shields, Norman. "The Grand General Indian Council of Ontario and Indian Status Legislation." In *Lines Drawn Upon the Water: First Nations and the Great Lakes Borders and Borderlands,* edited by Karl Hele. Waterloo: Wilfrid Laurier University Press, 2008.

Shields, Norman D. "Anishinabek Political Alliance in the Post-Confederation Period: The Grand General Indian Council of Ontario, 1870–1936." Master's thesis, Queen's University, 2001.

Simcoe, Elizabeth. *The Diary of Mrs. John Graves Simcoe, Wife of the First Lieutenant-Governor of the Province of Upper Canada, 1792–6, with Notes and Biography by J. Ross Robertson*. Toronto: W. Briggs, 1911.

———. "Sketch Map of Upper Canada Showing the Routes Lt. Gov Simcoe Took on Journeys between March 1793 and September 1795." Archives of Ontario, F 47-5-1-0-37.

Simcoe, John Graves. *The Correspondence of Lieut. Governor John Graves Simcoe, with Allied Documents Related to the Government of Upper Canada*. Vol. 1, *1789–1793*. Edited by E.A. Cruikshank. Toronto: Ontario Historical Society, 1923.

Simcoe, John Graves. *The Correspondence of Lieut. Governor John Graves Simcoe, with Allied Documents Related to the Government of Upper Canada*. Vol. 2. *1793–1794*. Edited by E.A. Cruikshank. Toronto: Ontario Historical Society, 1923.

Sims, Catherine A. "Algonkian-British Relations in the Upper Great Lakes Region: Gathering to Give and to Receive Presents, 1815–1843." PhD diss., University of Western Ontario, 1992.

Sims, Catherine A. "Exploring Ojibwa History through Documentary Sources: An Outline of the Life of Chief John Assance." In *Gin Das Winan: Documenting Aboriginal History in Ontario—A Symposium at Bkejwanong, Walpole Island First Nation, September 23, 1994*, edited by Dale Standen and David McNab. Toronto: Champlain Society / University of Toronto Press, 1994.

Six Nations Lands and Resources Department. *Land Rights: A Global Solution for the Six Nations of the Grand River*. Ohsweken, ON: Six Nations Lands and Resources Department, 2020.

Six Nations Legacy Consortium. "Pledge of the Crown Wampum Belt." http://images.ourontario.ca/Partners/SixNPL/SixNPL002690749pf_0001.pdf.

Smith, Donald B. *Sacred Feathers the Reverend Peter Jones (Kahkewaquonaby) and the Mississauga Indians*. 2nd ed. Toronto: University of Toronto Press, 2013.

Smith, Donald B. *Mississauga Portraits: Ojibwe Voices from Nineteenth-Century Canada*. Toronto: University of Toronto Press, 2013.

Smith, William H. *The Canadian Gazetteer Comprising Statistical and General Information*.Toronto: H. Rowsell, 1846.

Société littéraire et historique de Québec. *Collection de mémoires et de relations sur l'histoire ancienne du Canada*. Vol. 8. Quebec: Société littéraire et historique de Québec, 1840.

Standen, Dale, and David McNab, eds. *Gin Das Winan: Documenting Aboriginal History in Ontario—A Symposium at Bkejwanong, Walpole Island First Nation*. Occasional Papers, Vol. 2. Toronto: Champlain Society / University of Toronto Press, 1996.

Surtees, Robert J. *Indian Land Surrenders in Ontario, 1763–1867*. Ottawa: Indian and Northern Affairs Canada, Research Branch, Corporate Policy, 1984.

Surtees, Robert J. "Land Cessions, 1763–1830." In *Aboriginal Ontario: Historical Perspectives on the First Nations*, edited by Edward S. Rogers and Donald B. Smith. Toronto: Dundurn Press, 1994.

Taylor, Alan. "The Late Loyalists: Northern Reflections of the Early American Republic." *Journal of the Early Republic* 27, no. 1 (2007): 1–34.

Telford, Rhonda. "The Anishinabe Presentation of Their Fishing Rights to the Duke of Newcastle and the Prince of Wales." *Papers of the Thirtieth Algonquian Conference*, edited by David H. Pentland. Winnipeg: University of Manitoba, 1999.

Telford, Rhonda. "The Central Anishinabe and the Rebellion, 1830–1840." In *Actes du trente-deuxième congrès des algonquinistes*, edited by John D. Nichols. Winnipeg: University of Manitoba, 2001.

Tiro, Karim M. "A Sorry Tale: Natives, Settlers, and the Salmon of Lake Ontario, 1780–1900." *Historical Journal* 59, no. 4 (2016): 1001–1025.

Town, David. *Orillia's Civil War*. Orillia: Orillia Museum of Art and History, 2017.

Town, David. *Yellowhead's Revolt*. Orillia: Impression House, 2020.

Trewhella, Ethel Willson. "The Yonge Street Quakers: The Story of 'The Friends' in the Early Days of York County, Ontario." *Canadian Quaker History Journal* 76 (2011): 52–66.

Truth and Reconciliation Commission of Canada. *Canada's Residential Schools: The History, Part 1, Origins to 1939: The Final Report of the Truth and Reconciliation Commission of Canada, Volume 1*. Montreal/Kingston: McGill-Queen's University Press, 2016.

Walters, Mark D. "'According to the Old Customs of Our Nation': Aboriginal Self-Government on the Credit River Mississauga Reserve, 18226–1847." *Ottawa Law Review* 30, no. 1 (1998–99): 1–45.

Walters, Mark D. "How to Read Aboriginal Legal Texts from Upper Canada." *Journal of the Canadian Historical Association* 14, no. 1 (2003): 93–116.

Weaver, Sally. "The Iroquois: The Consolidation of the Grand River Reserve in the Mid-nineteenth Century, 1847–1875." In *Aboriginal Ontario*, edited by Edward S. Rogers and Donald B. Smith. Toronto: Dundurn Press, 1994.

Wesley-Esquimaux, Cynthia C. "The Coldwater Narrows Reservation," ca. 1991. *Chippewa Tri-Council Coldwater-Narrows Reservation Claim: Compilation of Documents*, edited by Indian Claims Commission, 1996. https://iportal.usask.ca/docs/ICC_CD/Chippewas%20Tri-Council/open.pdf.

Whetung, Madeleine. "(En)gendering Shoreline Law: Nishnaabeg Relational Politics along the Trent Severn Waterway." *Global Environmental Politics* 19, no. 3 (2019): 16–32.

Williams, Paul, and Curtis Nelson. "Kaswentha." Paper prepared for the Research Program of the Royal Commission on Aboriginal Peoples, January 1995. https://publications.gc.ca/collections/collection_2022/bcp-pco/Z1-1991-1-41-114-eng.pdf.

Williamson, Ronald F., Peter L. Storck, Danielle A. Macdonald, et al. "New Insights into Early Paleoindian (Gainey) Associations with Proboscideans and Canids in the Niagara Peninsula, Southern Ontario, Canada." *Journal of Archaeological Science: Reports* 47, no. 103785 (2023): 1–12.

Winks, Robin W., and George Eliot Clarke. *Blacks in Canada: A History*. Montreal/Kingston: McGill-Queen's University Press, 2021.

Wood, J. David. *Making Ontario: Agricultural Colonization and Landscape Re-creation before the Railway*. Montreal/Kingston: McGill-Queen's University Press, 2000.

Wybenga, Darin. *Historical Tidbits: Mississaugas of the Credit First Nation*. Pillar 5 Committee, Mississaugas of the Credit First Nation Chief and Council, 2019.

Map Credits

P. XI Map by Marcel Fortin, University of Toronto Libraries, based on data from Toronto and Region Conservation Authority; Historical Hydrography, Tremaine's York County Historical Map, 1860, Ontario County Map Project, University of Toronto Libraries; Indigenous and Northern Affairs Canada

P. 16 Map by Marcel Fortin, University of Toronto Libraries, based on data from Toronto Region Conservation Authority; Historical Hydrography, Tremaine's York County Historical Map, 1860, Ontario County Map Project, University of Toronto Libraries; proposed route on the Holland River by Marcel Fortin

P. 29 Map by Cheney Gao, University of Toronto Libraries, with source material from Nick Adams, "Iroquois Settlement at Fort Frontenac in the Seventeenth and Early Eighteenth Centuries," *Ontario Archaeology* 46 (1986): 7, and "First Nations of Simcoe County: A History," Innisfil Library digital project

P. 30 Map by Marcel Fortin, University of Toronto Libraries, from Toronto Region Conservation Authority SubWatersheds

P. 31 Map by Marcel Fortin, University of Toronto Libraries, from Toronto Carrying Place Trails and Villages, courtesy of the Toronto Region Conservation Authority; Historical Hydrography, Tremaine's York County Historical Map, 1860, Ontario County Map Project, University of Toronto Libraries

P. 33 Map by Marcel Fortin, University of Toronto Libraries, based on a map by Mississaugas of the Credit First Nation

P. 34 Map by Cheney Gao, University of Toronto Libraries, based on research by Alan Corbiere

P. 38 Map by Marcel Fortin and Cheney Gao, University of Toronto Libraries, based on a map by Alan Corbiere and "Minutes of a General Council Held at the River Credit, 16 January 1840," Library and Archives Canada, RG 10, Paudash Papers, vol. 1011, part B: 60–92

P. 43 Map by Cheney Gao, University of Toronto Libraries, and Victoria Freeman, based on Robinson, *Toronto during the French Regime*

P. 53 Map by Marcel Fortin and Cheney Gao, University of Toronto Libraries, from Ontario Hydrography Network, Land Information Ontario; Treaties, Land Information Ontario and from Morris, *Indians of Ontario*

P. 75 Map by Darin Wybenga, Mississaugas of the Credit First Nation

P. 84 Map by Cheney Gao, University of Toronto Libraries, based on Hart, *Pioneering in North York*

P. 94 Map by Cheney Gao and Marcel Fortin, University of Toronto Libraries, and Victoria Freeman, from Moses, with Graves and Sinclair, *A Sketch Account of Aboriginal Peoples in the Canadian Military*; and "Indigenous Contributions to the War of 1812," Crown-Indigenous Relations and Northern Affairs Canada online exhibit, 2012

p. 100   Map by Marcel Fortin, University of Toronto Libraries, from Land Information Ontario, derived from Morris, *Indians of Ontario*

p. 101   Map by Cheney Gao and Marcel Fortin, University of Toronto Libraries, from Mississaugas of the Credit First Nation; Land Information Ontario, derived from Morris, *Indians of Ontario*

p. 108   Map by Cheney Gao, University of Toronto Libraries, adapted from Geo. W. Luesby, "Detail map showing the overland and shortened routes of the fur trade through Newmarket," in Richard MacLeod, "Legend of Newmarket's Trading Tree, true or not, recalls town's fur trade beginnings," *Newmarkettoday.ca*, Oct. 3, 2020

p. 122   Map by Marcel Fortin, University of Toronto Libraries, from "Trails, TRCA, Historical Mills, Streams and Rivers," Tremaine's York County Historical Map, 1860, digitized by Marcel Fortin

p. 124   Map by Cheney Gao, University of Toronto Libraries, from Historical Hydrography, Tremaine's York County Historical Map, 1860, Ontario County Map Project, University of Toronto Libraries, and La Société d'histoire de Toronto, with the Society of Heritage Associates, Mississaugas of the New Credit First Nation, and the Rousseau Project – Le Project Rousseau, "Toronto Historical Park – A Shared Path for a Shared Past"

p. 146   Map by Cheney Gao, University of Toronto Libraries, and Victoria Freeman, from Jones, *Life and Journals of Kah-Ke-Wa-Quo-Na-By*

p. 154   Map created by Marcel Fortin, University of Toronto Libraries, from Jones, *Life and Journals of Kah-Ke-Wa-Quo-Na-By*

p. 166   Compiled by W. Woitowich, 1994, original at Chippewas of Rama Public Library, courtesy of Chippewas of Rama First Nation

p. 170   Map by Marcel Fortin and Cheney Gao, University of Toronto Libraries

p. 175   Map by David and Leslie Town

p. 232   Map by Cheney Gao and Marcel Fortin, University of Toronto Libraries. From Land Information Ontario and Morris, James Lewis. *Indians of Ontario*. Toronto: Dept. of Lands and Forests, 1943. See https://www.arcgis.com/home/item.html?id=e146cfcf24694366b52fa304d74d2722

Notes

Introduction: Where Histories Meet

1. Sherry Lawson, interview by Alan Corbiere and Victoria Freeman, Chippewas of Rama First Nation, July 6, 2022.
2. Before the pandemic, attendance was approximately 160,000 visitors a year.
3. See Martha Stiegman and Jesse Thistle, dirs., *kiskisiwin|remembering*, National Screen Institute, 2016, https://nsi-canada.ca/film/kiskisiwin-remembering/.
4. The village has also reached out to other groups excluded from previous historical interpretations.
5. Kelly LaRocca, virtual interview by Alan Corbiere and Victoria Freeman, October 20, 2022.
6. Darin Wybenga, virtual interview by Alan Corbiere and Victoria Freeman, August 24, 2022.
7. Garry Sault, virtual interview by Alan Corbiere and Victoria Freeman, September 13, 2022.
8. Margaret Sault, virtual interview by Alan Corbiere and Victoria Freeman, September 2, 2022.
9. Rhonda Coppaway, virtual interview by Alan Corbiere and Victoria Freeman, October 20, 2022.
10. Carolyn King, virtual interview by Victoria Freeman, October 10, 2022.
11. Margaret Sault interview.
12. Kory Snache, virtual interview by Alan Corbiere and Victoria Freeman, September 21, 2022.
13. Carolyn King interview.
14. Vicki Snache, interview by Alan Corbiere and Victoria Freeman, Chippewas of Rama First Nation, July 6, 2022.
15. Alan Corbiere, "Oral History Interview Report: Mississaugas of the Credit," draft report, Changing the Narrative: Black Creek Pioneer Village Project, October 1, 2023, referring to Bruce Granville Miller's *Oral History on Trial: Recognizing Aboriginal Narratives in the Courts* (Vancouver: UBC Press, 2011), 51.
16. Any comments made in reference to Six Nations Haldimand Treaty (Haldimand Tract) and 1701 Nanfan Treaty Lands are "without prejudice" to *Six Nations of the Grand River Band of Indians v The Attorney General of Canada and His Majesty the King in Right of Ontario*, Court No. CV-18-594281-0000 current litigation.
17. Ben Cousineau, interview by Alan Corbiere and Victoria Freeman, Chippewas of Rama First Nation, July 6, 2022.
18. The spellings of these ethnonyms are taken from Ange Loft, Victoria Freeman, Martha Stiegman, and Jill Carter, *A Treaty Guide for Torontonians*. 2nd ed. (Toronto: Art Metropole, 2022).

Chapter 1: Toronto's Indigenous Name

1. Elizabeth Simcoe, *The Diary of Mrs. John Graves Simcoe, Wife of the First Lieutenant-Governor of the Province of Upper Canada, 1792–6, with Notes and Biography by J. Ross Robertson* (Toronto: W. Briggs, 1911), 187–88. Elizabeth Simcoe originally identifies the man as "Great Sail" and in a later diary entry as "Canise." These could be two names for the same person or son and father; the lieutenant-governor encountered a Great Sail and visited the family of the recently deceased Canise on his journey to Matchedash Bay. It is not clear which Canise or Great Sail is the subject of the portrait of a Chief sketched by Elizabeth Simcoe (see page 21).
2. Henry Scadding and John Charles Dent, eds., *Toronto, Past and Present, Historical and Descriptive: A Memorial Volume for the Semi-centennial of 1884* (Toronto: Hunter, Rose, 1884), 132.

3   Another possible translation of the Mohawk word is "The place where we sunk our canoes." The Wendat word "Tonrontonkh" (Land of plenty) has also been suggested, but recent linguistic research does not appear to support this theory.

4   Mark Douglas, interview by Alan Corbiere, Chippewas of Rama First Nation, November 24, 2022.

5   Kory Snache, virtual interview by Alan Corbiere and Victoria Freeman, September 21, 2022.

6   Andrew Big Canoe, interview by Alan Corbiere and Victoria Freeman, Chippewas of Georgina Island First Nation, December 17, 2022.

7   Alexander Henry, *Travels and Adventures in Canada and the Indian Territories between the Years 1760 and 1776 in Two Parts* (New York: I. Riley, 1809), 179–80.

8   Percy J. Robinson, *Toronto during the French Régime: A History of the Toronto Region from Brûlé to Simcoe, 1615–1793*, 2nd ed. (Toronto: University of Toronto Press, 1965), 150.

9   Donald B. Smith, *Sacred Feathers: The Reverend Peter Jones (Kahkewaquonaby) and the Mississauga Indians*, 2nd ed. (Toronto: University of Toronto Press, 2013), 255.

10 Margaret Sault, virtual interview by Alan Corbiere and Victoria Freeman, September 2, 2022.

11 Alexander Macdonell, "Diary of Lieutenant-Governor Simcoe's Journey from Humber Bay to Matchedash Bay in 1793 by Alexander Macdonell, Sheriff of the Home District," in Simcoe Papers, 2:70–72.

12 Simcoe, The Diary of Mrs. John Graves Simcoe, 196.

13 Simcoe, The Diary of Mrs. John Graves Simcoe, 196.

14 Emerson Benson Nanigishkung, interview by Alan Corbiere and Victoria Freeman, Chippewas of Rama First Nation, July 6, 2022.

Chapter 2: Deep Time in the Humber River Watershed

1   Fossilized footprints at White Sands National Park in New Mexico have been dated to between 21,000 and 23,000 years ago. See Matthew R. Bennett et al., "Evidence of Humans in North America during the Last Glacial Maximum," *Science* 373, no. 6562 (2021): 1528–31; cited in University of Arizona, news release, September 23, 2021, https://news.arizona.edu/story/earliest-evidence-human-activity-found-americas. Ancient lithic tools discovered in Chile suggest the presence of humans about 30,000 years ago, but some archaeologists do not accept these results. Archaeologist Lauriane Bourgeon has confirmed that extinct horse bones apparently worked by humans at the Bluefish Caves site in Yukon are about 24,000 years old. See CBC Docs, "New Discoveries Challenge Our Understanding of When the First People Arrived in North America," February 9, 2023, https://www.cbc.ca/documentaries/the-nature-of-things/new-discoveries-challenge-our-understanding-of-when-the-first-people-arrived-in-north-america-1.6733497. However, Indigenous archaeologist Paulette Steeves argues that the Americas may have been settled approximately 130,000 years ago. See Paulette F.C. Steeves, *The Indigenous Paleolithic of the Western Hemisphere* (Lincoln: University of Nebraska Press, 2021).

2   These comments on the global context of Indigenous presence in the Americas are adapted from a lecture by Sean Kheraj of York University.

3   "BCE" stands for "before the Common Era" and is used rather than "Before Christ" to indicate religious neutrality.

4   Kate McCullough, "Discovery of Blood on Mastodon Tools First of Its Kind in Ontario," *Hamilton Spectator*, December 31, 2022, https://www.thespec.com/news/hamilton-region/2022/12/31/discovery-of-mastodon-blood-on-ice-age-tools-first-of-its-kind-in-ontario.html. For further information, contact Archaeological Services. See also Ronald F. Williamson et al., "New Insights into Early Paleoindian (Gainey) Associations with Proboscideans and Canids in the Niagara Peninsula, Southern Ontario, Canada," *Journal of Archaeological Science: Reports* 47, no. 103785 (2023): 8, figure 5; and Stephen C. Lougheed and Natalie Morrill, "Quaternary History of Eastern Ontario: Impacts of Physical Landscape and Biota," Opinion Natural History: Physical and Biotic Environment at Queen's University Biological Station, https://opinicon.wordpress.com/physical-environment/quaternary/.

5   In 2022, research by McMaster University's Collaborative Archaeologies, Decolonized Foodways project and the Office of Lands and Resources for Six Nations of the Grand River Elected Council found earlier evidence of corn in pottery from this general area, according to Tayler Hill of Six Nations Lands and Resources, but this research has not yet been published.

6   Vicki Snache, interview by Alan Corbiere and Victoria Freeman, Chippewas of Rama First Nation, July 6, 2022.

7   Ben Cousineau, interview by Alan Corbiere and Victoria Freeman, Chippewas of Rama First Nation, July 6, 2022.

8   L.A. Sandberg et al., "Re-connecting with a Historical Site: On Narrative and the Huron-Wendat Ancestral Village at York University, Toronto," *Ontario History* 113, no. 1 (2021): 80–105. See also L.A. Sandberg, "Looking for the Huron-Wendat at York University?" Alternative Campus Tour, York University, August 12, 2021, https://alternativecampustour.info.yorku.ca/2021/08/looking-for-the-huron-wendat-at-york-university-l-anders-sandberg/; Lanna Crucefix, "The Parsons Site," ASI Heritage, https://asiheritage.ca/publication/the-parsons-site/; and Claire van Nierop, "Revisiting the Parsons Site," ASI Heritage, https://asiheritage.ca/revisiting-the-parsons-site/.

9   For more information on this pivotal moment in the region's Indigenous history, see Bruce Trigger, *Children of Aetaentsic: A History of the Huron People to 1660* (Montreal/Kingston: McGill-Queen's University Press, 1988); Georges Sioui, *Huron-Wendat: The Heritage of the Circle*, trans. Jane Brierley (Vancouver: UBC Press, 2000); and Kathryn Magee Labelle, *Dispersed but Not Destroyed: A History of the Seventeenth-Century Wendat People* (Vancouver: UBC Press, 2013).

10 See François Vachon de Belmont, "Histoire de l'eau-de-vie en Canada," in *Collection de mémoires et de relations sur l'histoire ancienne du Canada*, ed. Société littéraire et historique de Québec, vol. 8 (Québec: Impr. de W. Cowan, 1840).

11 Darin Wybenga, virtual interview by Alan Corbiere and Victoria Freeman, August 24, 2022.

12 The Six Nations of the Grand River maintain that they had a continued presence on the north shore of Lake Ontario after 1700 and that the Nanfan Deed recognized this. The Misssissaugas of the Credit and other Anishinaabek maintain that the Nanfan Deed is not a valid treaty and does not serve as the basis for Six Nations rights in Ontario. To complicate matters, the Nanfan Deed has been recognized as a treaty in two lower Ontario Court decisions (*R v Ireland and Jamieson* [1991] and *R v Barberstock* [2003], while the federal government's position is ambiguous. The Ministry of Indigenous-Crown Relations' online article "Treaties of Peace and Neutrality (1701–1760)" mentions the Nanfan Deed (referred to as the Albany Deed of 1701) only once: "In some cases, First Nations agreed to sell lands of the Great Lakes to the British in exchange for their protection and the continued right to hunt and fish, as in the 1701 Albany Deed": https://www.rcaanc-cirnac.gc.ca/eng/1360866174787/1544619566736. The Haudenosaunee do not agree that their intention was to sell the land. As of this writing, the Mississaugas of the Credit First Nation have been granted intervenor status in a key case brought forward by the Six Nations against the provincial and federal governments regarding lands granted through the Haldimand Proclamation in 1784. They intend to contest the validity and use of the Nanfan Deed to buttress Six Nations claims to land rights in Ontario. This may be a protracted legal struggle, possibly with appeals to higher courts.

13 Carolyn King, virtual interview by Victoria Freeman, October 10, 2022.

14 Phil Monture, virtual interview by Alan Corbiere and Victoria Freeman, November 15, 2022.

15 For a general introduction to the Dish with One Spoon, see Ange Loft et al., *A Treaty Guide for Torontonians*, 2nd ed. (Toronto: Art Metropole, 2022), 51–58. For discussion of the disputed meanings, see Dean M. Jacobs and Victor P. Lytwyn, "Naagan Get Bezhig Emkwaan: A Dish with One Spoon Reconsidered," *Ontario History* 112, no. 2 (2020): 191–210. For its interpretation in 1840, see page 215.

16 "Minutes of a General Council Held at the Credit River, 16 January 1840," Library and Archives Canada, Paudash Papers, RG 10, vol. 1011, Part B: 60–92.

17 Kory Snache, virtual interview by Alan Corbiere and Victoria Freeman, September 21, 2022.

18 Monture interview.

Chapter 3: Trade and Colonial Rivalries

1   V.B. Blake, *Credit Valley Conservation Report 1956* (Toronto: Dept. of Planning and Development, 1956), 6, https://cvc.ca/wp-content/uploads/2011/08/1956REPT.pdf.

2   Louis Antoine, comte de Bougainville, "Mémoire de Bougainville sur l'état de la Nouvelle-France à l'époque de la guerre de Sept ans (1757)," *Documents inédits sur l'histoire de la marine et des colonies: Revue maritime et coloniale* (1861): 582, https://www.canadiana.ca/view/oocihm.28049/23?r=0&s=1.

3   These were the people of Akwesasne, Kahnawà:ke, Kanesetake, and Oswegatchie. See D. Peter MacLeod, *The Canadian Iroquois and the Seven Years' War* (Toronto/Oxford: Dundurn Press / Canadian War Museum, 1996).

4   Darin Wybenga, virtual interview by Alan Corbiere and Victoria Freeman, August 24, 2022.

5   "At a Conference with the Toughkinaioinan Indians on Saturday at Niagara, 28 July 1764," in *The Papers of Sir*

William Johnson, vol. 11, ed. Milton W. Hamilton (Albany: University of the State of New York, 1921), 307–8. For a reading of the Covenant Chain and Twenty-Four Nations Wampum Belts eighty-eight years after the Treaty of Niagara, see "Petition from J.B. Assikinawk, October 10, 1851," Library and Archives Canada (LAC), RG 10, Indian Affairs Superintendency Records, Northern (Manitowaning), Superintendence Correspondence (Manitoulin Island), 1851–55, vol. 613: 440–43. The original Belts have not survived but early drawings of them were reproduced in A.F. Hunter, "Wampum Records of the Ottawas," *Annual Archaeological Report 1901: Being Part of an Appendix to the Report of the Minister of Education Ontario*, (Toronto: K. L. Cameron, 1902), 53. See Fig. 25, Belt No. 1 and Fig. 26, Belt No. 2.

6 See Ferral Wade to William Johnson, September 22, 1771, *The Papers of Sir William Johnson*, Alexander C. Flick, ed., vol. 8 (Albany: University of the State of New York, 1933), 270–76.

7 Toronto, "Baby Point Heritage Conservation Plan," https://www.toronto.ca/city-government/planning-development/planning-studies-initiatives/baby-point-heritage-conservation-district-study/study-finding/history-and-evolution. See John Clarke, "James Baby," *Dictionary of Canadian Biography*, vol. 6, University of Toronto / Université Laval, 2003, http://www.biographi.ca/en/bio/baby_james_6E.html.

8 Civil Secretary's Letter Books, Upper Canada, April 2, 1830, LAC, RG7-G16-C, vol. 23:2, reel C-10,792.

9 Robinson, Percy J., *Toronto during the French Regime: A History of the Toronto Region from Brûlé to Simcoe, 1615–1793*, 2nd ed. (Toronto: University of Toronto Press, 1965), 210.

10 F.R. Berchem, *The Yonge Street Story, 1793–1860: An Account from Letters, Diaries and Newspapers* (Toronto: Dundurn, 1996), 79. According to Kenneth Kidd, "War of 1812: The Story of Joseph Shepard Who Risked His Life in Battle of York," *Toronto Star*, April 20, 2013, accessed February 23, 2023, https://www.thestar.com/news/insight/2013/04/20/war_of_1812_the_story_of_joseph_shepard_who_risked_his_life_in_battle_of_york.html, the newspaper obituary for one of his sons, Joseph Jr., said that Shepard Sr. set himself up as a fur trader near the Toronto Carrying Place as early as 1775.

11 See page 85, "The Fishers and Related Families."

12 Ferral Wade to William Johnson, September 22, 1771, *Papers of Sir William Johnson*, vol. 8, 271.

13 See translated quote from François Vachon de Belmont, "Histoire de l'eau-de-vie en Canada," in Bruce West, *Toronto* (Toronto: Doubleday Canada, 1967), 7. Original in *Collection de mémoires et de relations sur l'histoire ancienne du Canada*, vol. 8 (Québec: Société littéraire et historique de Québec, 1840).

14 John V. Jezierski, ed., "A 1751 Journal of Abbé François Picquet," *New-York Historical Society Quarterly* 44, no. 4 (1970): 369, and discussion of alcohol traders in Robinson, *Toronto during the French Regime*, 120–21, 146–49, and Peter S. Schmalz, *The Ojibwa of Southern Ontario* (Toronto: University of Toronto Press, 1991), 87–89, 95–96.

15 Ferral Wade to William Johnson, September 22, 1771, *Papers of Sir William Johnson*, vol. 8, 272; and Schmalz, *Ojibwa of Southern Ontario*, 87–89.

Chapter 4: Early British Treaties

1 Darin Wybenga, virtual interview by Alan Corbiere and Victoria Freeman, August 24, 2022.

2 Phil Monture, virtual interview by Alan Corbiere and Victoria Freeman, November 15, 2022.

3 "A Six Nations' Meeting with the Mississaugas, May 22, 1784," PRO, CO 42, vol. 46:224–5, reproduced in *The Valley of the Six Nations: A Collection of Documents on the Indian Lands of the Grand River*, ed. Charles M. Johnson, Ontario Series, vol. 7 (Toronto: Chaplain Society, 1964), 45. At the beginning of this speech, Pokquan says, "We the Mississagas are not the Owners of all that Land laying between the three Lakes, but we have agreed, and are willing to transfer our right of Soil & property to the King our Father, for the use of His people, and our Brethren the Six Nations." According to the Haudenosaunee, this statement means the Mississaugas recognized that the Haudenosaunee retained rights to lands north of Lake Ontario. In contrast, Anishinaabek interpret Pokquan as saying that some of the lands in question were under the jurisdiction of other Anishinaabek, not the Mississaugas.

4 The Six Nations do not consider this agreement a treaty because, in their view, the Mississaugas merely relinquished their interest in the land while the Haudenosaunee maintained their rights to it, recognized through the Nanfan Deed of 1701. This interpretation is contested by the Mississaugas, who note that it's a treaty within the meaning of section 35 of the Constitution Act, 1982. It was included and superseded in the Between the Lakes Treaty

of 1792, which addressed problems with the original treaty boundaries (the land had not yet been fully surveyed in 1784). As noted, the Mississaugas of the Credit intend to challenge the legal status of the Nanfan Deed in a major Six Nations court case over Haldimand Tract lands, in which the Mississaugas have been granted intervenor status. In addition, there are disputed claims of treaty rights to the northern section of the lands granted through the Haldimand Proclamation of 1784. These lands were severed from the Haldimand Tract by the Simcoe Patent of 1793 (a move that was never accepted by the Six Nations). Six Nations says that this area is also covered by the Nanfan Deed / Treaty, while the Mississaugas of the Credit say it's their treaty land under the Ajetance Treaty (Treaty 19) of 1818. This issue may also be determined through litigation.

5   The Six Nations regard the Haldimand Proclamation and Deed as a treaty and their lands along the Grand River as treaty lands. The status of the Haldimand Proclamation and Deed is before the courts and will be determined through litigation.

6   "A Census of the Six Nations on the Grand River, 1785," Library and Archives Canada (LAC), Haldimand Papers, B 103, 457, in Johnston, *Valley of the Six Nations*, 52. In 1787, it was reported that Mississauga Chief Wabakinine led 506 people at the Head of the Lake: "Return of the Missisagay Nation of Indians Assembled at the Head of the Bay De Quinte . . . September 23, 1787," LAC, RG 10, vol. 1834, p. 197, reel C-1224.

7   Gwen Reimer, "British-Canada's Land Purchases, 1783–1788: A Strategic Perspective," *Ontario History* 111, no. 1 (2016): 36–72, https://doi.org/10.7202/1059965ar.

8   Margaret Sault, virtual interview by Alan Corbiere and Victoria Freeman, September 2, 2022.

9   John Butler was a Loyalist military officer who raised a regiment known as Butler's Rangers, which fought alongside Britain's Indigenous allies, including Joseph Brant, during the American Revolution. He was a senior official in the Indian Department of Upper Canada.

10 "List of Gifts Given to the Mississaugas: Memorandum of Bales and Boxes Brought from Cataraque Brought by Mr. Lines to Toronto and Delivered to Colonel Butler," in Percy Robinson, *Toronto during the French Regime: A History of the Toronto Region from Brûlé to Simcoe, 1615–1793*, 2nd ed. (Toronto: University of Toronto Press, 1965), 251.

11 Reimer, "British-Canada's Land Purchases," 62–70.

12 Darin Wybenga interview.

13 Kory Snache, virtual interview by Alan Corbiere and Victoria Freeman, September 21, 2022.

14 Joseph Brant, quoted in Patrick C.T. White, ed., *Lord Selkirk's Diary, 1803–4: A Journal of His Travels in British North America and the Northeastern United States* (Toronto: Champlain Society, 1958), 153.

15 Lord Dorchester to Lieutenant-Governor John Graves Simcoe, January 27, 1794, in *Simcoe Papers*, 2:138.

Chapter 5: Turning Indigenous Territory into Private Property

1   Historical geographer R. Gentilcore, quoted in Donald B. Smith, "Augustus Jones," *Dictionary of Canadian Biography*, vol. 7, University of Toronto / Université Laval, 2003, 2024, http://www.biographi.ca/en/bio/jones_augustus_7E.html.

2   Darin Wybenga, virtual interview by Alan Corbiere and Victoria Freeman, August 24, 2022.

3   In "Yellow Head's Answer to the President's Request, 22 May 1798," he states: "If you white people forget your transactions with us, we do not. The Lands you have just now shew to us belongs to you; We have nothing to do with it; We have sold it to our Great Father the King, as was well paid for it. Therefore make your mind at easy. There may be some of our young people who do not think so; They may tell your people that the Land is ours, but you must not open your ears to them, but take them by the arm and put them out of your houses": *The Correspondence of the Honourable Peter Russell*, ed. Ernest A. Cruikshank and Andrew F. Hunter (Toronto: Ontario Historical Society, 1932), 2:161.

4   In May 1921, the Mississaugas of Rice, Scugog, and Mud Lakes, through the law firm O'Connor and Moore, wrote to the superintendent-general of Indian affairs (Charles Stewart) claiming that no confirmatory surrender had been executed for the "lands comprising the Townships of Uxbridge, Reach, Scott, Brock, Thorah, Georgina, and North Gwilliambury." At the Williams Treaties hearings in 1923, four Chippewa and Mississauga witnesses testified that the townships south of Lake Simcoe had never been surrendered. See Gwen Reimer, "British-Canada's Land Purchases, 1783–1788: A Strategic Perspective," *Ontario History* 111, no. 1 (2016): 60–61, https://doi.org/10.7202/1059965ar.

5   Peter Jones, July 9, 1852, "Rev. P. Jones Missionary Tour to Lakes Huron and Superior," *Christian Guardian*, August 25, 1852.

6   Naishenum is listed as Tubenahneequay's mother in the New Credit Indian Mission book.

7   Joseph Brant, quoted in Patrick C.T. White, ed., *Lord Selkirk's Diary, 1803–4: A Journal of His Travels in British North America and the Northeastern United States* (Toronto: Champlain Society, 1958), 153.

8   Elizabeth Simcoe, *The Diary of Mrs. John Graves Simcoe, Wife of the First Lieutenant-Governor of the Province of Upper Canada, 1792–6, with Notes and Biography by J. Ross Robertson* (Toronto: W. Briggs, 1911), 141.

9   According to Six Nations Lands and Resources Department research, these were considered life leases and a condition of the leases was that they were not to be sold to non-family members.

10 For example, he was granted 999-year leases, signed by Brant (who was given a limited power of attorney for Six Nations in 1796), for 4,800 acres in Cayuga Township and for 1,200 acres in Brantford Township. Both grants were for the nominal annual rent of one peppercorn. Brant later overstepped his authority in 1798 by nominating purchasers for lands in Blocks 5 and 6 not included in the original power of attorney.

11 "C 33 Resolutions of a Six Nations' Council at the Onondaga Village, March 1, 1809," Library and Archives Canada, Indian Affairs, Records and Correspondence of the Deputy Superintendent-General, vol. 27, 511–.], reprinted in Charles M. Johnston, *The Valley of the Six Nations: A Collection of Documents* (Toronto: University of Toronto Press, 1964), 112. A trustee report was completed by Six Nations Trustees, Dunn, Hepburn and Markland in 1835. The report found very few leases confirmed. Augustus Jones' lease was not on the list. Six Nations in Council questioned these transactions in 1811, 1819, 1833, and 1835. LAC, RG 10, Department of Indian Affairs, vol. 103, 41–45.

12 The situation was further complicated by additional land transactions after Brant's death, made in his name.

13 This reason for Jones' retirement is suggested in Alun Hughes, "Augustus Jones: The Life and Loves of a Pioneer Surveyor," *Association of Canadian Map Libraries and Archives Bulletin*, no. 111 (Spring/Summer 2001): 10–11.

Chapter 6: Indigenous-Settler Encounters

1   For details of the murder and trial, see "State of Case the King vs Charles McCuen for Murder Committed on the Body of Waipykanine an Indian Chief," in *The Town of York, 1793–1815: A Collection of Documents of Early Toronto*, edited by Edith Firth (Toronto: Champlain Society / University of Toronto Press, 1962), 84–85; and Peter Russell to J.G. Simcoe, September 28, 1796, in *The Correspondence of the Honourable Peter Russell*, ed. Ernest A. Cruikshank and Andrew F. Hunter (Toronto: Ontario Historical Society, 1932), 1:50 (henceforth *Russell Correspondence*).

2   Peter Russell to J.G. Simcoe, September 28, 1796, *Russell Correspondence*, 1:50.

3   Augustus Jones to D.W. Smith, Saltfleet, March 11, 1797, AO, Surveyor's Letters, 28:137; and Peter Russell to Robert Prescott, April 18, 1797, *Russell Correspondence*, 1:165.

4   Donald B. Smith, "The Dispossession of the Mississauga Indians," in *Historical Essays on Upper Canada: New Perspectives*, ed. J.K. Johnson and Bruce G. Wilson (Montreal/Kingston: McGill-Queen's University Press, 2014), 37.

5   Duke of Portland to Peter Russell, September 11, 1797, *Russell Correspondence*, 1:277–78.

6   Duke of Portland to Peter Russell, November 4, 1797, *Russell Correspondence*, 2:3.

7   Enclosed in Peter Russell to Robert Prescott, August 9, 1798, *Russell Correspondence*, 2:233.

8   Enclosed in Russell to Prescott, *Russell Correspondence*, 2:233.

9   Leo A. Johnson, "The Mississauga–Lake Ontario Land Surrender of 1805," *Ontario History* 82, no. 3 (1990): 244.

10 Charles M. Johnston, *The Valley of the Six Nations: A Collection of Documents* (Toronto: University of Toronto Press, 1964), xliv, xlviii–xlix.

11 Margaret Sault, virtual interview by Alan Corbiere and Victoria Freeman, September 2, 2022.

12 For a detailed discussion of British strategy in the lead up to the 1805 "confirmation" of the Toronto Purchase, see Johnson, "Mississauga–Lake Ontario Land Surrender of 1805," and Indian Claims Commission (ICC), *Mississaugas of the New Credit First Nation Inquiry: Toronto Purchase Claim* (Ottawa: Indian Claims Commission, 2003), 2, 29–31.

13 Peter Russell to Robert Prescott, January 21, 1798, in *Russell Correspondence*, 2:68–69.

14 For details, see ICC, "Mississaugas of the New Credit First Nation Inquiry," 247–49.

15 The British apparently prepared two different maps, and when the Mississaugas could not remember the exact boundaries agreed to, the larger map was used. One of the government's critics, John Mills Jackson, alleged that the surveyor general had been dismissed because "he had shewn the Council their erroneous proceedings in a purchase of land from the Messessagua Indians, by necessarily shewing, in his official correspondence with them, how a false map had been procured, and the tribe thereby defrauded of seventeen thousand dollars": John Mills Jackson, "A View of the Political Situation of the Province of Upper Canada," pamphlet printed for W. Earle, London, 1809, 17. This discrepancy was a factor in the successful Toronto Purchase Special Claim of 2010, which awarded $145 million to the Mississaugas of the Credit.

16 See Mississaugas of the Credit First Nation, *Toronto Purchase Specific Claim: Arriving at an Agreement* (Hagersville, ON: Mississaugas of the Credit First Nation, 2001), https://mncfn.ca/wp-content/uploads/2017/04/MNCFN-Toronto-Purchase-Specific-Claim-Arriving-at-an-Agreement.pdf; ICC, "Mississaugas of the New Credit First Nation Inquiry"; Canada, "Canada and the Mississaugas of the New Credit First Nation Celebrate Historic Claim Settlement," news release, 2-3420, October 29, 2010, https://www.canada.ca/en/news/archive/2010/10/canada-mississaugas-new-credit-first-nation-celebrate-historic-claim-settlement.html.

17 "At a Meeting with the Mississagues at the River Credit," Lieutenant-Governor's Correspondence, August 1, 1805, Library and Archives Canada, RG 10, vol. 1, 295–96, reel C-10996.

18 Johnson, "Mississauga–Lake Ontario Land Surrender of 1805," 249.

19 Darin Wybenga, virtual interview by Alan Corbiere and Victoria Freeman, August 24, 2022.

Chapter 7: Settlers on Indigenous Lands

1 Sherry Lawson, interview by Alan Corbiere and Victoria Freeman, Chippewas of Rama First Nation, July 6, 2022.

2 See notice from *Upper Canada Gazette*, December 29, 1798, and Acting Surveyor General Upper Canada, July 15, 1794, in *Simcoe Papers*, 2:323.

3 Leo A. Johnson, "The Mississauga–Lake Ontario Land Surrender of 1805," *Ontario History* 82, no. 3 (1990): 233.

4 "Proclamation to Protect the Fishing Places and Burying Grounds of the Mississagas, December 14, 1797," *Upper Canada Gazette*, December 30, 1797.

5 Ben Cousineau, interview by Alan Corbiere and Victoria Freeman, Chippewas of Rama First Nation, July 6, 2022.

6 See, for example, "They are an unwarlike, idle, drunken, dirty tribe," versus "I have often observed (but never had more reason to do so than to-day) that when the Indians speak, their air and action is more like that of Roman or Greek orators than of Modern nations. They have a great deal of impressive action, and look like the figures painted by the Old Masters": Elizabeth Simcoe, *The Diary of Mrs. John Graves Simcoe, Wife of the First Lieutenant-Governor of the Province of Upper Canada, 1792–6, with Notes and Biography by J. Ross Robertson* (Toronto: W. Briggs, 1911), 115, 213.

7 Gwen Reimer and Jean-Philippe Chartrand, *Historic Metis in Ontario: Georgian Bay*, report by Praxis Research Associates submitted to the Native Affairs Unit, Ontario Ministry of Natural Resources, 2000), 59, referencing Don Whiteside, *An Annotated Bibliography of Articles in the Globe (Toronto), Related to Indians (Indians, Inuit and Half-Breeds) from Jan. 1, 1848 to Jan. 16, 1867* (Ottawa: Aboriginal Institute of Canada, 1980), 1–3. Although I am mindful of the current controversy over people of mixed heritage claiming Métis status in Ontario, *Historic Metis in Ontario* is a valuable study documenting the history of a specific group of people of mixed heritage who were descended from fur traders and Indigenous women and came from Drummond Island to the Penetanguishene area.

8 Kory Snache, virtual interview by Alan Corbiere and Victoria Freeman, September 21, 2022.

9 From the local magistrates, who issued the oath of allegiance and recommended newcomers for land grants, Surveyor General David W. Smith gathered data on the settlers, which he reported to the Executive Council in 1796. Of the 250 male immigrants who obtained land in Upper Canada between November 6, 1794, and December 31, 1795, about 71 per cent came from the United States, and 22 per cent from the British Isles. The Americans came mainly from New Jersey (54), New York (50), and Pennsylvania (29); smaller numbers came from New England (9) or the southern states (13). The majority were young men in their late teens or twenties (137); a smaller number were men in their thirties (59) or older (44). There were only two professionals, both low-paid teachers; 74 per cent were farmers, 18 per cent artisans, and 6 per cent labourers or sailors. Of the 719 male newcomers who took the oath of allegiance between 1794

and 1800 in the Home District, which included the Toronto area, 171 or 24 per cent made a mark instead of signing, which suggests an illiteracy rate three times higher than was the norm in the northern American states during the 1790s. Alan Taylor, "The Late Loyalists: Northern Reflections of the Early American Republic," *Journal of the Early Republic* 27, no. 1 (2007): 22n42: Upper Canada, Oaths of Allegiance, Home District, 1794–1800, Library and Archives Canada (LAC), RG 1, Executive Council Office, Province of Canada, reel E-11, vol. 16. For the second, smaller register, see Robert Kerr, Register, February 23, 1793, LAC, RG 1, vol. 11, reel E-11.

10 Lot 27 west of Yonge Street, according to F.R. Berchem, *The Yonge Street Story, 1793–1860: An Account from Letters, Diaries and Newspapers* (Toronto: Dundurn, 1996), 59.

11 Dean Snow, "Searching for Hendrick: Correction of a Historic Conflation," *New York History* 88, no. 3 (2007): 237.

12 David. L Preston, "'We Intend to Live Our Lifetime Together as Brothers': Palatine and Iroquois Communities in the Mohawk Valley," *New York History* 88, no. 2 (2008): 180.

13 Markham Berczy Settlers Association, "Berczy Settlers," https://markhamberczysettlers.ca/?page_id=14.

14 Apparently, the name "Markham" was given to the village and township by Palatine settlers "in honour of Capt William Markham, a young relative of William Penn, who arrived in Pennsylvania with a number of colonists in 1681, to conciliate the natives and clear the way for the arrival of the great benefactor and proprietor himself [i.e., Penn]": Mabel Burkholder, "Palatine Settlements in York County," *Papers and Records*, Ontario Historical Society 37 (1945): 81.

15 Gloria Lesser, "William Berczy's Portraits of Joseph Brant," *National Gallery of Canada Annual Bulletin* 6, 1982–83, 4, https://www.gallery.ca/bulletin/num6a/lesser4.html.

16 Preston, "'We Intend to Live," 188.

17 Nick Mika, *The Village at Black Creek: Toronto's Living History Village* (Toronto: Natural Heritage, 2000), 28.

18 Patricia Hart, *Pioneering in North York: A History of the Borough* (Toronto: General Publishing, 1968), 225–26.

19 "Searching for the Stongs," research paper held by Toronto Region Conservation Authority, author unknown, 22.

20 Wellington Willson Cummer and Clyde Lottridge Cummer, *Cummer Memoranda: A Record of the Progenitors and Descendants of Jacob Cummer* (Cleveland: O.S. Hubbell, 1911), 22, from oral family tradition handed down to Walter Harris from his mother, Mrs. Rebecca Cummer Harris, and related to the author of *Cummer Memoranda* in 1910.

21 Hart, *Pioneering in North York*, 167.

22 Catherine A. Sims, "Exploring Ojibwa History through Documentary Sources: An Outline of the Life of Chief John Assance," in *Gin Das Winan: Documenting Aboriginal History in Ontario—A Symposium at Bkejwanong, Walpole Island First Nation*, Occasional Papers vol. 2, ed. Dale Standen and David McNab (Toronto: Champlain Society, 1996), 36. For a more general discussion of the significance of presents, see Catherine A. Sims, "Algonkian-British Relations in the Upper Great Lakes Region: Gathering to Give and to Receive Presents, 1815–1843" (PhD diss., University of Western Ontario, 1992), 1–22.

23 See G. Elmore Reaman, *The Trail of the Black Walnut* (Toronto: McClelland and Stewart, 1957); and Arthur G. Dorland, *The Quakers in Canada: A History*, 2nd ed. (Toronto: Canadian Friends Historical Association / Ryerson Press, 1968).

24 Ethel Willson Trewhella, "Yonge Street Quakers: The story of 'The Friends' in the Early Days of York County, Ontario," originally published in 1937, republished in *Canadian Quaker History Journal* 76 (2011): 61.

25 Taylor, "Late Loyalists," 26.

26 Taylor, "Late Loyalists," 26.

27 Kory Snache interview. Snache is a member of Chippewas of Rama First Nation but can trace his lineage to Chief Joseph Snake of the Holland River/Georgina area.

28 Russell to the Duke of Portland, November 21, 1798, in *The Correspondence of the Honourable Peter Russell*, ed. Ernest A. Cruikshank and Andrew F. Hunter (Toronto: Ontario Historical Society, 1932), 2:317–18 (henceforth *Russell Correspondence*).

29 See James W. St. G. Walker, "Blacks as American Loyalists: The Slaves' War for Independence," *Historical Reflections / Réflexions Historiques* 2, no. 1 (1975): 51–67; and Robert L. Fraser, "Richard Pierpoint," in *Dictionary of Canadian Biography*, vol. 7, University of Toronto / Université Laval, 2003–, http://www.biographi.ca/en/bio/pierpoint_richard_7E.html. See also "The Long Family," Adrienne Shadd, Afua Cooper, and Karolyn Smardz Frost, *The Underground Railroad: Next Stop, Toronto!* (Toronto: Dundurn Press, 2005), 11.

30 Shadd et al., *Underground Railroad*, 15–16; and Robin W. Winks and George Eliot Clarke, *Blacks in Canada: A History*, 50th anniversary ed. (Montreal/Kingston: McGill-Queen's University Press, 2021), 26, 34, 53.

31 Shadd et al., *Underground Railroad*, 15.

32 Kory Snache interview.

Chapter 8: The War of 1812 and Its Aftermath

1. Janice Nickerson, York's Sacrifice: Militia Casualties of the War of 1812 (Toronto: Dundurn, 2012), 23.
2. Jean M. Constable, *Stong Roots and Branches*, Peel Family Histories (Toronto, 2001), 15; Susan Goldenberg, "Historic Stong Family," North York Historical Society, January 20, 2014, https://nyhs.ca/historic-stong-family/; and Clara Thomas Archives, York University, "Inventory of the Stong Family Fonds," http://archivesfa.library.yorku.ca/fonds/ON00370-f0000550.pdf. I have yet to locate an archival record of Daniel Stong's militia service.
3. "The Petition of Margaret Rousseau, of the Township of Ancaster," *Ninth Report of the Bureau of Archives for the Province of Ontario: The Journals of the Legislative Assembly of Upper Canada for the Years 1812, 1814, 1816, 1817, 1818* (Toronto: L.K. Cameron, 1913), 503.
4. Wendy Cameron, "Peter Robinson," *Dictionary of Canadian Biography* (*DCB*), vol. 7, University of Toronto / Université Laval, 2003–, http://www.biographi.ca/en/bio/robinson_peter_7E.html.
5. Fred Blair, "Andrew Borland, War of 1812 Veteran," *Orillia Museum of Art and History News*, June 9, 2021, https://www.orilliamuseum.org/andrew-borland-war-of-1812-veteran/.
6. Keith Jamieson and Michelle Hamilton, *Dr. Oronhyatekha: Security, Justice, and Equality* (Toronto: Dundurn, 2016), 43.
7. Phil Monture, virtual interview by Alan Corbiere and Victoria Freeman, November 15, 2022.
8. Quoted in Gerald Craig, *Upper Canada: The Formative Years* (Toronto: McClelland and Stewart, 1968), 72.
9. Darin Wybenga, virtual interview by Alan Corbiere and Victoria Freeman, August 24, 2022.
10. Emerson Benson Nanigishkung, interview by Alan Corbiere and Victoria Freeman, Chippewas of Rama First Nation, July 6, 2022.
11. Garry Sault, virtual interview by Alan Corbiere and Victoria Freeman, September 13, 2022.
12. Peter Jones, *Life and Journals of Kah-Ke-Wa-Quo-Na-By (Rev. Peter Jones), Wesleyan Missionary* (Toronto: A. Green, 1860), 5.
13. "Musquakie," *DCB*, vol. 9, http://www.biographi.ca/en/bio/musquakie_9E.html.
14. See Six Nations Legacy Consortium, "Pledge of the Crown Wampum Belt," http://images.ourontario.ca/Partners/SixNPL/SixNPL002690749pf_0001.pdf.
15. Catherine A. Sims, "Exploring Ojibwa History through Documentary Sources: An Outline of the Life of Chief John Assance," in *Gin Das Winan: Documenting Aboriginal History in Ontario—A Symposium at Bkejwanong, Walpole Island First Nation*, Occasional Papers vol. 2, ed. Dale Standen and David McNab (Toronto: Champlain Society, 1996), 38.
16. Quoted in Alan Corbiere, "Mookomaanish: The Damn Knife (Odaawaa Chief and Warrior)," *Active History*, October 8, 2014, https://activehistory.ca/2014/10/mookomaanish-the-damn-knife-odaawaa-chief-and-warrior/.
17. Alan Corbiere, "Anishinaabeg in the War of 1812: More Than Tecumseh and His Indians," *Active History*, September 10, 2014, http://activehistory.ca/2014/09/anishnaabeg-in-the-war-of-1812-more-than-tecumseh-and-his-indians/.
18. Peter Jones, *History of the Ojebway Indians: With Especial Reference to Their Conversion to Christianity* (London: A.W. Bennett, 1861), 209.
19. Ben Cousineau, interview by Alan Corbiere and Victoria Freeman, Chippewas of Rama First Nation, July 2022.
20. Duke of Portland to Peter Russell, November 5, 1798, in *The Correspondence of the Honourable Peter Russell*, ed. Ernest A. Cruikshank and Andrew F. Hunter (Toronto: Ontario Historical Society, 1932), 2:300 (henceforth *Russell Correspondence*).
21. Robert Surtees, "Land Cessions, 1763–1830," in *Aboriginal Ontario: Historical Perspectives on the First Nations*, ed. Edward S. Rogers and Donald B. Smith (Toronto: Dundurn), 112.
22. Craig, *Upper Canada*, 141; and Peter S. Schmalz, *The Ojibwa of Southern Ontario* (Toronto: University of Toronto Press, 1991), 136, 141.
23. Joseph Sawyer and John Jones to Sir John Colborne, River Credit, April 3, 1829, Library and Archives Canada (LAC), RG 10, Department of Indian Affairs, vol. 5:46, reel C-10997.
24. Sawyer and Jones to Colborne, April 3, 1829.
25. Darin Wybenga interview.
26. "Treaty No. 16," *Indian Treaties and Surrenders from 1680 to 1890*, vol. 1 (Ottawa: Brown Chamberlain Printers, 1891), 42–45.
27. Robert J. Surtees, *Indian Land Surrenders in Ontario, 1763–1867* (Ottawa: Indian and Northern Affairs Canada, Research Branch, Corporate Policy, 1984), 63–66.
28. Gwen Reimer, "British-Canada's Land Purchases, 1783–1788: A Strategic Perspective," *Ontario History* 111, no. 1 (2016): 69, https://doi.org/10.7202/1059965ar; and William G.

Dean and Geoffrey J. Matthews, *Economic Atlas of Ontario* (Toronto: University of Toronto Press, 1969), Plate 99, "Dates of the Original Township Surveys."

29 Ben Cousineau interview.

30 Emerson Benson Nanigishkung interview.

31 David Mills, *The Idea of Loyalty in Upper Canada, 1784–1850* (Montreal/Kingston: McGill-Queen's University Press, 1988), 35; and Craig, *Upper Canada*, 87.

32 George de Zwaan, "Elite and Society: Newmarket, Ontario 1857–1880" (master's thesis, Queen's University, 1980); "Paddy Town Was Newmarket's Little Ireland," *The Era*, March 16, 1983, 54; Cecil J. Houston, *Irish Emigration and Canadian Settlement: Patterns, Links, and Letters* (Toronto: University of Toronto Press, 1990), 188–208; and W. Perkins Bull, *From Macdonell to McGuigan: A History of the Growth of the Catholic Church in Upper Canada* (Toronto: Perkins Bull Foundation, 1939), referenced in M.W. Nicolson, "The Irish Experience in Ontario: Rural or Urban?" *Urban History Review / Revue d'histoire urbaine* 14, no. 1 (1985): 41.

33 Elizabeth Elbourne, "The Sin of the Settler: The 1835–36 Select Committee on Aborigines and Debates over Virtue and Conquest in the Early Nineteenth-Century British White Settler Empire," *Journal of Colonialism and Colonial History* 4, no. 3 (2003): https://dx.doi.org/10.1353/cch.2004.0003; and Theodore Binnema and Kevin Hutchings, "The Emigrant and the Noble Savage: Sir Francis Bond Head's Romantic Approach to Aboriginal Policy in Upper Canada, 1836–1838," *Journal of Canadian Studies* 39, no. 1 (2005): 115–38.

34 Daniel G. Hill, "Negroes in Toronto, 1793–1865," *Ontario History* 55 (1963): 74.

35 Adrienne Shadd, Afua Cooper, and Karolyn Smardz Frost, *The Underground Railroad: Next Stop, Toronto!* (Toronto: Dundurn Press, 2005), 18, 25; and J. David Wood, *Making Ontario: Agricultural Colonization and Landscape Recreation before the Railway* (Montreal/Kingston: McGill-Queen's University Press, 2000), 47–48.

36 In 1861, on the eve of the American Civil War, eighty-three people of African descent lived in Etobicoke. Northwest of Toronto, forty-one individuals of African descent lived in King Township in 1861. See Shadd et al., *Underground Railroad*, 47, 53, 57; and Michael Wayne, "The Black Population of Canada West on the Eve of the American Civil War: A Reassessment Based on the Manuscript Census of 1861," *Histoire sociale / Social History* 28, no. 56 (1995): 485.

37 See Jones, *Life and Journals*, 58, 395; Jones, *History of the Ojebway*, 219; and Donald B. Smith, *Sacred Feathers: The Reverend Peter Jones (Kahkewaquonaby) and the Mississauga Indians*, 2nd ed. (Toronto: University of Toronto Press, 2013), 207; and "Council Held at the River Credit," September 12, 1844, Council Minutes, 1835–48, LAC, RG 10, 1011, 206.

38 See Archives of Ontario and Ontario Black History Society, "Sophia Burthen Pooley: Part of the Family?," *Enslaved Africans in Upper Canada* (online exhibit), https://www.archives.gov.on.ca/en/explore/online/slavery/sophia_pooley.aspx. See also Ian Holryod, "Burlington Audience Hears Story of Slave Owned by Joseph Brant," *Burlington Post*, February 21, 2014, https://www.insidehalton.com/life/burlington-audience-hears-story-of-slave-owned-by-joseph-brant/article_48ea7498-ecf0-5bb6-8d36-ce191da3af5d.html.

39 See Bonita Lawrence and Zainab Amadahy, "Indigenous Peoples and Black People in Canada: Settlers or Allies?" in *Breaching the Colonial Contract: Anti-colonialism in the US and Canada*, (New York: Springer, 2009), 105–36.

Chapter 9: The Postwar Fur Trade along Yonge Street

1 Kory Snache, virtual interview by Alan Corbiere and Victoria Freeman, September 21, 2022.

2 Kory Snache interview.

3 Ben Cousineau, interview by Alan Corbiere and Victoria Freeman, Chippewas of Rama First Nation, July 6, 2022.

4 Edward Roe, "Roe Arrived after the War of 1812," *The Era* (Newmarket), June 4, 1975, https://www.uelac.org/events/2013-02-10-William-Roe.pdf.

5 Ray Borland, descendant of Andrew Borland, personal communication, July 25, 2022. See also Philip (Ray) Borland, "Andrew Borland 1795–1860: A Brief Historical Sketch," https://www.academia.edu/39820749/Andrew_Borland; and A.F. Hunter, *A History of Simcoe County*, vol. 1 (Barrie, ON: County Council, 1909), 24.

6 Charles Pelham Mulvany and Adam Graeme Mercer, *History of Toronto and County of York, Ontario*, vol. 1 (Toronto: C.B. Robinson, 1885), 181, https://www.canadiana.ca/view/oocihm.07392/1.

7 Canada Board of Registration and Statistics, Canada West Census, 1861, Library and Archives Canada (LAC), 13, https://central.bac-lac.gc.ca/.item/?app=Census1861&op=img&id=4108345_00211.

8 The 1797 date is given in Mary Garbutt, *Medonte, a Township Remembered* (Oro-Medonte: Oro-Medonte History

Committee, 2003), 252–52. However, the 1861 census lists Elizabeth Borland as fifty-five years, which would mean she was born in 1807 and married at age twelve.

9 David J. Wood, *Making Ontario: Agricultural Colonization and Landscape Recreation before the Railway* (Montreal/Kingston: McGill-Queen's University Press, 2000), 35; and Laura Peers and Jennifer S.H. Brown, "'There Is No End to Relationships among the Indians': Ojibwa Families and Kinship in Historical Perspective," *History of the Family* 4, no. 4 (1999): 536.

10 Gwen Reimer and Jean-Philippe Chartrand, *Historic Metis in Ontario: Georgian Bay,* report submitted to the Native Affairs Unit, Ontario Ministry of Natural Resources, Praxis Research Associates, 2000, 61.

11 Borland, personal communication.

12 Reimer and Chartrand, *Historic Metis in Ontario.*

13 Jean Baptiste Sylvestre's narrative, in Alexander Campbell Osborne, *The Migration of Voyageurs from Drummond Island to Penetanguishene in 1828,* Papers and Records of the Ontario Historical Society, vol. 3 (Ontario Historical Society, 1901), 22.

14 Mulvany and Mercer, *History of Toronto and County of York,* 1:181.

15 Peter Jones, *Life and Journals of Kah-Ke-Wa-Quo-Na-By (Rev. Peter Jones), Wesleyan Missionary* (Toronto: A. Green, 1860), 91, June 22, 1827. A.F. Hunter identifies "Bolen" with "Borland" in *A History of Simcoe County*, vol. 1, 20.

16 Borland, personal communication. The census lists Elizabeth Borland, widow of Andrew Borland, as "Indian" but her son John as "white." Canada Board of Registration and Statistics, Canada West Census, 1861, Medonte Township, 13, https://central.bac-lac.gc.ca/.item/?app=Census1861&op=img&id=4108345_00211. The 1901 census for Tay Township lists many Borlands as "Chippewa half-breeds."

17 Albert Big Canoe, interview by Alan Corbiere and Victoria Freeman, Chippewas of Georgina Island First Nation, December 17, 2022.

18 Mary O'Brien, *The Journals of Mary O'Brien, 1828–1838,* ed. Audrey S. Miller (Toronto: Macmillan, 1968), 59.

19 Wendy Cameron, "Peter Robinson," *Dictionary of Canadian Biography (DCB)*, vol. 7, University of Toronto / Université Laval, 2003–, http://www.biographi.ca/en/bio/robinson_peter_7E.html.

20 George Head, *Forest Scenes and Incidents, in the Wilds of North America* (London: J. Murray, 1829), 178–79.

21 Robert Terence Carter, *Stories of Newmarket: An Old Ontario Town* (Toronto: Dundurn, 2011), 42.

22 Julia Jarvis, "William Benjamin Robinson," in *DCB*, vol. 10, http://www.biographi.ca/en/bio/robinson_william_benjamin_10E.html.

23 See Nipissing First Nation, Robinson Huron Treaty Litigation Fund, https://www.robinsonhurontreaty1850.com; and Aya Dufour, "Collective or Individual? The Key Question behind Distributing $10B Robinson Huron Treaty Settlement," CBC News, April 24, 2024, https://www.cbc.ca/news/canada/sudbury/payments-robinson-huron-treaty-first-nations-northern-ontario-1.7186587.

24 Jones, *Life and Journals,* 167.

25 George F. Playter, *History of Methodism in Canada: With an Account of the Rise and Progress of the Work of God among the Canadian Indian Tribes, and Occasional Notices of the Civil Affairs of the Province* (Toronto: A. Green, 1862), 355.

26 Gerald Craig, *Upper Canada: The Formative Years* (Toronto: McClelland and Stewart, 1968), 107, 109.

Chapter 10: Deforestation, Farming, and Milling

1 David J. Wood, *Making Ontario: Agricultural Colonization and Landscape Re-creation before the Railway* (Montreal/Kingston: McGill-Queen's University Press, 2000), 163.

2 W.H Smith, *Canada: Past, Present, and Future,* vol. 1 (Toronto: Thomas Maclear, 1851), 273; and Wood, *Making Ontario,* xviii.

3 Alexander Macdonell, "Diary of Lieut. Governor Simcoe's Journey from Humber Bay to Matchedash Bay in 1793 by Alexander Macdonell, Sheriff of the Home District," in *Simcoe Papers*, 2:71.

4 Peter Jones, *History of the Ojebway Indians: With Especial Reference to Their Conversion to Christianity* (London: A.W. Bennett, 1861), 104.

5 William Cronon, *Changes in the Land: Indians, Colonists and the Ecology of New England* (New York: Hill and Wang, 2003), quoted in Wood, *Making Ontario,* 13.

6 Rhonda Telford, "The Central Anishinabe and the Rebellion, 1830–1840," in *Actes du trente-deuxième Congrès des Algonquinistes,* ed. John Nichols (Winnipeg: University of Manitoba, 2001), 569.

7 Andrew Big Canoe, interview by Alan Corbiere and Victoria Freeman, Chippewas of Georgina Island First Nation, December 17, 2022.

8   Wood, *Making Ontario*, 22, 27.

9   Wood, *Making Ontario*, 158.

10 Wood, *Making Ontario*, 158.

11 Ben Cousineau, interview by Alan Corbiere and Victoria Freeman, Chippewas of Rama First Nation, July 6, 2022.

12 William H. Smith, *The Canadian Gazetteer Comprising Statistical and General Information* (Toronto: H. Rowsell, 1846), 237.

13 Wood, *Making Ontario*, 19, quoting Anne Wilkinson, *Lions in the Way: A Discursive History of the Oslers* (Toronto: Macmillian, 1956), 59.

14 Chief Quenepenon, "Proceedings of a Meeting with the Mississagues at the River Credit, 1 August 1805," Library and Archives Canada (LAC), RG 10, Lieutenant-Governor's Correspondence, vol. 1, 294–95, reel C-10996.

15 Andrew Big Canoe interview.

16 Arthur Doughty, "Notes on History of Flour Milling in Canada," November 24, 1936, Marilyn and Charles Baillie Special Collections Centre, Toronto Reference Library, John Ross Robertson Manuscript Collection, folder for Alfred H. Bailey.

17 Wood, *Making Ontario*, 103; and City of Vaughan, "Importance of Mills," https://www.vaughan.ca/explore-vaughan/vaughans-history/importance-mills.

18 Gary Miedema, "When the Rivers Really Ran: Water-Powered Industry in Toronto," in *HtO: Toronto's Water from Lake Iroquois to Lost Rivers to Low-Flow Toilets*, ed. Wayne Reeves and Christina Palassio (Toronto: Coach House, 2008), 66–73.

19 Carolyn King, virtual interview by Victoria Freeman, October 10, 2022.

20 In 1808, John Schmidt (Smith) established a sawmill on Black Creek near Steeles Avenue. It was taken over by the Dalziel family. Smith's Edgeley mill (and another mill located on the property of his neighbour Richard Brown) remained in operation until the 1860s. Another sawmill on Black Creek operated on the Snider property east of Jane in 1851. The Fisher family ran a sawmill in 1820 and later a gristmill. John Dalziel's sawmill was the centre of Kaiserville, which had an adjacent blacksmith shop, carpenter's shop, and wagon shop. Jacob Stong, the son of Daniel Stong and Elizabeth Fisher Stong, erected a small sawmill where Black Creek crossed Jane Street in 1848. See Patricia Hart, *Pioneering in North York: A History of the Borough* (Toronto: General Publishing, 1968).

21 Karim M. Tiro, "A Sorry Tale: Natives, Settlers, and the Salmon of Lake Ontario, 1780–1900," *Historical Journal* 59, no. 4 (2016): 1005; and Kathleen Lizars, *The Valley of the Humber, 1615–1913* (Toronto: William Briggs, 1913), 118.

22 Augustus Jones, "Letter to Acting Surveyor-General D.W. Smith on July 7, 1796," Archives of Ontario (AO), microfilm, MS 7433.

23 Tiro, "A Sorry Tale," 1013–14; Gilbert Allardyce, "'The Vexed Question of Sawdust': River Pollution in Nineteenth-Century New Brunswick," *Dalhousie Review* 52, no. 2 (1972): 177–90; Peter R. Gillis, "Rivers of Sawdust: The Battle over Industrial Pollution in Canada, 1865–1903," *Journal of Canadian Studies* 21, no. 1 (1986): 84–103; and Jennifer Bonnell, *Reclaiming the Don: An Environmental History of Toronto's Don River Valley* (Toronto: University of Toronto Press, 2014), 21.

24 Tiro, "A Sorry Tale," 1013.

25 Speech of Chief Quinepenon, Upper Canada Civil Control, September 6, 1806, LAC, RG 10, Department of Indian Affairs, vol. 451.

26 Lizars, *The Valley of the Humber*, 126.

27 See Wood, *Making Ontario*, 46; and Tiro, "A Sorry Tale." See also Allardyce, "'The Vexed Question of Sawdust'; and Gillis, "Rivers of Sawdust."

28 F.R. Berchem, *The Yonge Street Story, 1793–1860: An Account from Letters, Diaries and Newspapers* (Toronto: Dundurn, 1996), 40.

29 City of Vaughan, "Thornhill," https://www.vaughan.ca/explore-vaughan/communities/thornhill.

30 Samuel Wilmot, "Diary of Samuel Wilmot," 1806, AO, microfilm, MS 7438.

31 V.B. Blake, *Credit Valley Conservation Report 1956* (Toronto: Dept. of Planning and Development, 1956), https://cvc.ca/wp-content/uploads/2011/08/1956REPT.pdf.

32 Peter Jones, *Life and Journals of Kah-Ke-Wa-Quo-Na-By (Rev. Peter Jones), Wesleyan Missionary* (Toronto: A. Green, 1860), 64, April 28, 1826.

33 Donald B. Smith, *Sacred Feathers: The Reverend Peter Jones (Kahkewaquonaby) and the Mississauga Indians*, 2nd ed. (Toronto: University of Toronto Press, 2013), 206; and Wood, *Making Ontario*, 102.

34 Donald B. Smith, *Mississauga Portraits: Ojibwe Voices from Nineteenth-Century Canada* (Toronto: University of Toronto Press, 2013), 12.

35 Tiro, "A Sorry Tale," 1002.

Chapter 11: Indigenous Christianity

1. Donald B. Smith, *Sacred Feathers: The Reverend Peter Jones (Kahkewaquonaby) and the Mississauga Indians*, 2nd ed. (Toronto: University of Toronto Press, 2013), 39.
2. Ben Cousineau, interview by Alan Corbiere and Victoria Freeman, Chippewas of Rama First Nation, July 6, 2022.
3. [William Warren Baldwin], "Thoughts on the Civilization of the Chippewa and Mississaga Tribes of Indians . . . ," c. 1819, Toronto Public Library, William Warren Baldwin Papers, 15.
4. Alfred T. Day, "The Legacy of John Stewart and the Wyandot," *Methodist Mission Bicentennial*, https://methodistmission200.org/about-the-bicentennial/the-legacy-of-john-stewart-and-the-wyandot/accessed.
5. Roxanne L. Korpan, "Scriptural Relations: Colonial Formations of Anishaabemowin Bibles in Nineteenth-Century Canada," *Material Religion* 17, no. 2 (2021): 149.
6. The Covenant Chain alliance between the English and Haudenosaunee was a successor to the early seventeenth-century alliance between the Dutch and the Mohawks. The English renewed the alliance when they took over Dutch-controlled territories in the colony of New York.
7. Smith, *Sacred Feathers*, 46.
8. George F. Playter, *History of Methodism in Canada: With an Account of the Rise and Progress of the Work of God among the Canadian Indian Tribes, and Occasional Notices of the Civil Affairs of the Province* (Toronto: A. Green, 1862), 355, 216.
9. See Susan Hill, *The Clay We Are Made Of: Haudenosaunee Land Tenure on the Grand River* (Winnipeg: University of Manitoba Press, 2017), 46–52.
10. Playter, *History of Methodism*, 216–17.
11. Playter, *History of Methodism*, 218.
12. Smith, *Sacred Feathers*, 62; Peter Jones, "Anecdote no. 33," in *Anecdote Book*, E.J. Pratt Library, Victoria University Library, University of Toronto, Peter Jones Collection.
13. Day, "The Legacy of John Stewart."
14. Smith, *Sacred Feathers*, 48.
15. Darin Wybenga, virtual interview by Alan Corbiere and Victoria Freeman, August 24, 2022.
16. Peter Jones, *Life and Journals of Kah-Ke-Wa-Quo-Na-By (Rev. Peter Jones), Wesleyan Missionary* (Toronto: A. Green, 1860), 8.
17. For a biography of David Sawyer that also includes information about Joseph Sawyer, see Conrad Vandusen, *The Indian Chief: An Account of the Labour, Losses, Suffering and Oppression of Ke-zig-ka-e-ne-ne (Avie Sawyer), a Chief of the Ojibeway Indians in Canada West* (London: William Nichols, 1867), https://www.canadiana.ca/view/ooc ihm.25329/4.
18. Playter, *History of Methodism*, 247.
19. Playter, *History of Methodism*, 268.
20. Methodist Episcopal Church, Canada Conference, Missionary Society, *First Annual Report of the Canada Conference Missionary Society, Auxiliary to the Missionary Society of the Methodist Episcopal Church* (Kingston, ON: Hugh C. Thomson, 1825), 14.
21. Jones, *Life and Journals*, 36–37.
22. Smith, *Sacred Feathers*, 70.
23. Smith, *Sacred Feathers*, 53.
24. Carolyn King, virtual interview by Victoria Freeman, October 10, 2022.
25. Smith, *Sacred Feathers*, 166.
26. See Elizabeth Elbourne, "The Sin of the Settler: The 1835–36 Select Committee on Aborigines and Debates over Virtue and Conquest in the Early Nineteenth-Century British White Settler Empire," *Journal of Colonialism and Colonial History* 4, no. 3 (2003): https://dx.doi.org/10.1353/cch.2004.0003; and Alan Lester and Fae Dussart, *Colonization and the Origins of Humanitarian Governance: Protecting Aborigines across the Nineteenth-Century British Empire* (Cambridge: Cambridge University Press, 2014).
27. Kahkewaqonaby to James Givins, Grand River, June 17, 1825, Library and Archives Canada (LAC), RG 10, Department of Indian Affairs, Chief George Paudash Papers, Letter Book, 1825–42, vol. 1011, 86203, reel T-1456.
28. Jones, *Life and Journals*, 37–38, July 12, 1825.
29. Jones, *Life and Journals*, 38.
30. Playter, *History of Methodism*, 251–52; and Jones, *Life and Journals*, 38–39.
31. Methodist Episcopal Church, Canada Conference, Missionary Society, "New Market Branch Missionary Society: Extract from the Letter of William Law, Secretary," *First Annual Report*, 20.

Chapter 12: Yonge Street Camp Meetings

1. George F. Playter, *History of Methodism in Canada: With an Account of the Rise and Progress of the Work of God among the Canadian Indian Tribes, and Occasional Notices of the*

2 Peter Jones, *Life and Journals of Kah-Ke-Wa-Quo-Na-By (Rev. Peter Jones), Wesleyan Missionary* (Toronto: A. Green, 1860), 70.
3 Jones, *Life and Journals*, 73.
4 Methodist Episcopal Church, *Second Annual Report of the Canada Conference Missionary Society, Auxiliary to the Missionary Society of the Methodist Episcopal Church* (St. Catharines, ON: Hiram Leavensworth, 1826), 16–17.
5 Jones, *Life and Journals,* 75.
6 Playter, *History of Methodism,* 284–28.
7 Playter, *History of Methodism,* 301–2.
8 Playter, *History of Methodism*, 303.
9 Jones, *Life and Journals*, 149, June 10, 1828.
10 Playter, *History of Methodism*, 350–51.
11 Jones, *Life and Journals*, 162, August 8, 1828.
12 Jones, *Life and Journals,* 349, July 4, 1832.
13 Letter of Egerton Ryerson, reprinted in Methodist Episcopal Church, *Second Annual Report*, 19.
14 Playter, *History of Methodism*, 353.
15 Jones, *Life and Journals,* 163–64, August 13 and 14, 1828.
16 Methodist Episcopal Church, *Second Annual Report*, 19–20.
17 Jones, *Life and Journals*, 93, November 18 and 19, 1827.
18 Jones, *Life and Journals,* 162, August 9, 1828.
19 Jones, *Life and Journals,* 164–65, August 14, 1828,.
20 Playter, *History of Methodism*, 353.
21 Kory Snache, virtual interview by Alan Corbiere and Victoria Freeman, September 21, 2022.
22 Donald B. Smith, *Sacred Feathers: The Reverend Peter Jones (Kahkewaquonaby) and the Mississauga Indians*, 2nd ed. (Toronto: University of Toronto Press, 2013), 76–77; and Donald B. Smith, *Mississauga Portraits: Ojibwe Voices from Nineteenth-Century Canada* (Toronto: University of Toronto Press, 2013), 52.
23 Albert Big Canoe, interview by Alan Corbiere and Victoria Freeman, Chippewas of Georgina Island First Nation, December 17, 2022.
24 Jones, *Life and Journals*, 81.
25 Peter Jones, *History of the Ojebway Indians: With Especial Reference to Their Conversion to Christianity* (London: A.W. Bennett, 1861), 174.
26 John Carroll, *Case and His Contemporaries,* vol. 3 (Toronto: Wesleyan Conference Office, 1871), 259.
27 Playter, *History of Methodism*, 261; and Methodist Episcopal Church, *First Annual Report.*
28 Darin Wybenga, "Education at the Credit River Mission," *Historical Tidbits: Mississaugas of the Credit First Nation,* Pillar 5 Committee, Mississaugas of the Credit First Nation Chief and Council, 2019.
29 Wybenga, "Education at the Credit River Mission."
30 Jones, *Life and Journals*, 112–13, February 22, 1828.
31 Methodist Episcopal Church, Canada Conference, Missionary Society, *Third Annual Report of the Canada Conference Missionary Society, Auxiliary to the Missionary Society of the Methodist Episcopal Church* (York: Society at the Office of the Colonal Advocate, William Lyon MacKenzie, 1827), 9.
32 Elizabeth Graham, *Medicine Man to Missionary: Missionaries as Agents of Change among the Indians of Southern Ontario, 1784–1867* (Toronto: Peter Martin Associates, 1975), 20–27.
33 Smith, *Mississauga Portraits*, 68; and Chandra Murdoch, "Act to Control: The Grand General Indian Council, the Department of Indian Affairs, and the Struggle over the Indian Act in Ontario, 1850–1906" (PhD diss., University of Toronto, 2023), 164.
34 Darin Wybenga, virtual interview by Alan Corbiere and Victoria Freeman, August 24, 2022.
35 Methodist Episcopal Church, *Third Annual Report*, 9.
36 Playter, *History of Methodism*, 323, 327.
37 Smith, *Sacred Feathers*, 78, quoting Peter Jones to Samuel Martin, River Credit Mission, January 18, 1830, E.J. Pratt Library, Victoria University Library, University of Toronto, Peter Jones Collection.
38 Kory Snache interview.
39 Albert Big Canoe interview.
40 Jones, *History*, 117.
41 Jones, *Life and Journals*, 269, January 27, 1830.
42 Jones, *Life and Journals*, 386.

Chapter 13: The Credit Mission

1 Methodist Episcopal Church, Canada Conference, Missionary Society, *Third Annual Report of the Canada Conference Missionary Society, Auxiliary to the Missionary*

2. *Society of the Methodist Episcopal Church,* (York: Society at the Office of the Colonial Advocate, William Lyon MacKenzie, 1827), 6-7.
2. George F. Playter, *History of Methodism in Canada: With an Account of the Rise and Progress of the Work of God among the Canadian Indian Tribes, and Occasional Notices of the Civil Affairs of the Province* (Toronto: A. Green, 1862), 303.
3. Darin Wybenga, virtual interview by Alan Corbiere and Victoria Freeman, August 24, 2022.
4. Playter, *History of Methodism,* 348.
5. Playter, *History of Methodism,* 349.
6. James Magrath, "Report of the State of the Indians on the River Credit," in *Authentic Letters from Upper Canada,* ed. Thomas William Magrath (Dublin: William Curry, 1833), 310-11.
7. Magrath, "Report," 312.
8. Donald B. Smith, *Sacred Feathers: The Reverend Peter Jones (Kahkewaquonaby) and the Mississauga Indians,* 2nd ed. (Toronto: University of Toronto Press, 2013), 157.
9. Robin Jarvis Brownlie, "First Nations Perspectives and Historical Thinking in Canada" (paper presented at the Canadian Historical Association, Saskatoon, May 2007, 8); and Maureen Konkle, *Writing Indian Nations: Indian Intellectuals and the Politics of Historiography, 1827-1863* (Chapel Hill: University of North Carolina Press, 2004), 40.
10. The code is reprinted in Elizabeth Graham, *Medicine Man to Missionary: Missionaries as Agents of Change among the Indians of Southern Ontario, 1784-1867* (Toronto: Peter Martin Associates, 1975), Appendix III, 107. See also Chandra Murdoch, "Act to Control: The Grand General Indian Council, the Department of Indian Affairs, and the Struggle over the Indian Act in Ontario, 1850-1906" (PhD diss., University of Toronto, 2023), 169-70.
11. Murdoch, "Act to Control," 169-70.
12. Murdoch, "Act to Control," 171; and Mark Walters, "How to Read Aboriginal Legal Texts from Upper Canada," *Journal of the Canadian Historical Association* 14, no. 1 (2003): 106.
13. Peter Jones, *Life and Journals of Kah-Ke-Wa-Quo-Na-By (Rev. Peter Jones), Wesleyan Missionary* (Toronto: A. Green, 1860), 70-71, August 21, 1826.
14. "James Ajetance, Peter Jones, Joseph Sawyer, John Jones, and 49 other Mississaugas of the River Credit to the House of Assembly of Upper Canada, January 31, 1829," Library and Archives Canada, RG 10, Department of Indian Affairs, vol. 1011, reel T-1456.
15. Tenth Parliament, "An Act, the Better to Protect the Mississaga Tribes Living on the Indian Reserve of the River Credit, in Their Exclusive Right of Fishing and Hunting Therein" *Statutes of His Majesty's Province of Upper Canada, Passed in the First Session of the Tenth Provincial Parliament* (York: Robert Stanton, 1829), 23, passed 20 March, 1829; and Karim M. Tiro, "A Sorry Tale: Natives, Settlers, and the Salmon of Lake Ontario, 1780-1900," *Historical Journal* 59, no. 4 (2016): 1018.
16. Jones, *Life and Journals,* 352, July 24, 1832.
17. William and Lawrence Herkimer were the grandsons of Johan Jost Herkimer of German Flatts, Herkimer County, New York, a Palatine German and Loyalist colonel who settled at Cataraqui (Kingston) in the mid-1780s. Their father was Johan's son Lawrence, a Rice Lake fur trader; their mother was Magiyakamigokua, a Mississauga woman. William, Lawrence, and their brother Jacob moved to the Credit River.
18. Smith, *Sacred Feathers,* 155-57.
19. Wybenga interview.
20. Smith, *Sacred Feathers,* 157.
21. Smith, *Sacred Feathers,* 158.
22. Darin Wybenga, "Rev. Peter Jones—*History of the Ojebway Indians,*" *Historical Tidbits: Mississaugas of the Credit First Nation,* Pillar 5 Committee, Mississaugas of the Credit First Nation Chief and Council, 2019.
23. Margaret Sault, virtual interview by Alan Corbiere and Victoria Freeman, September 2, 2022.

Chapter 14: The Coldwater and the Narrows Settlement

1. Vicki Snache, interview by Alan Corbiere and Victoria Freeman, Chippewas of Rama First Nation, July 6, 2022.
2. Henry Darling, "Report upon the Exact State of the Indian Department," July 24, 1828, enclosed in Earl of Dalhousie to Sir George Murray, Secretary of the State for the Colonies, October 27, 1828, *Parliamentary Papers,* 1834, vol. 617, ed. BCO, 22-35, excerpts published in Aborigines Protection Society, *Report of the Indians of Upper Canada, 1839* (Toronto: Canadiana House, 1968), henceforth *Report of the Indians, 1839.*
3. For discussion of the Darling report, see John F. Leslie, *Commissions of Inquiry into Indian Affairs in the Canadas, 1828-1858: Evolving a Corporate Memory for the Indian*

    Department (Ottawa: Treaties and Historical Research Centre, Indian Affairs and Northern Development Branch, 1985).

4 Darling, *Report of the Indians, 1839*, 6–8.

5 Kory Snache, virtual interview by Alan Corbiere and Victoria Freeman, September 21, 2022.

6 According to Margot Maddison-McFaydyen, a descendant. Personal communication with author, February 25, 2024.

7 Gwen Reimer, "British-Canada's Land Purchases, 1783–1788: A Strategic Perspective," *Ontario History* 111, no. 1 (2016): 64, https://doi.org/10.7202/1059965a.

8 *Simcoe Papers*, 2:72; and Reimer, "British-Canada's Land Purchases," 48.

9 Reimer, "British-Canada's Land Purchases," 49; and "Return of Indian Stores, March 22, 1788," Library and Archives Canada (LAC), RG 10, Department of Indian Affairs, vol. 1834, reel C-1224, 20. The return's cover page reads: "Return of Indian Stores given to Mississagay Nations of Indians as a payment for the Lands at Toronto & the communication to Lake Huron relinquished by them to the Crown."

10 Robert Surtees, "Land Cessions, 1763–1830," in *Aboriginal Ontario: Historical Perspectives on the First Nations*, ed. Edward S. Rogers and Donald B. Smith (Toronto: Dundurn), 107.

11 "Memorial Address of the Lake Huron and Simcoe Tribes," c. 1847–48, LAC, RG 10, vol. 123, file 6199–6202, cited in Reimer, "British-Canada's Land Purchases," 69; the cover page to this memorial reads: "Vide letter to CC Lands 1 February 1848." This memorial is also filed together with other returns dated 1847–48 containing "claims by Indians in Canada West to certain lands which they state have not been ceded to the Crown": Campbell to Commissioner of Crown Lands, February 1, 1848, LAC, RG 1–273-5-1-1, 8–9.

12 Indian Claims Commission (ICC), *Chippewa Tri-Council Inquiry: Beausoleil First Nation, Chippewas of Georgina Island First Nation, Chippewas of Mnjikaning (Rama) First Nation; Coldwater-Narrows Reservation Surrender Claim*, 2003, 8, https://publications.gc.ca/Collection/RC31-15-2003E.pdf (henceforth Chippewa Tri-Council Inquiry).

13 Much of my analysis draws on two key research reports, Cynthia C. Wesley-Esquimaux, "The Coldwater Narrows Reservation," c. 1991, and Joan Holmes and Associates, "The Coldwater Treaty Draft Historical Report," both prepared for Specific Claims INAC, March 1993, and revised October 1993. These reports and supporting documents can be found in the first two volumes of ICC, *Chippewa Tri-Council Coldwater-Narrows Reservation Claim: Compilation of Documents*, submitted for the Coldwater-Narrows Reserve land claim in 1996 and released in 2008. See University of Saskatchewan Indigenous Studies Portal, https://iportal.usask.ca/docs/ICC_CD/Chippewas%20Tri-Council/open.pdf.

14 Albert Big Canoe, interview by Alan Corbiere and Victoria Freeman, Chippewas of Georgina Island First Nation, December 17, 2022.

15 T.G. Anderson, Superintendent of Indian Affairs, Coldwater, to J. Givins, Chief Superintendent of Indian Affairs, April 25, 1830, LAC, RG 10, vol. 46, reel C-11014; Anderson to L. Mudge, Secretary of Lieutenant-Governor, Upper Canada, March 22, 1830, LAC, RG 10, vol. 5, reel C-10997–10998; and Anderson to Givins, May 3, 1830, LAC, RG 10, vol. 46, reel C-11014.

16 Chief Yellow Head, Speech, July 12, 1830, LAC, RG 10, vol. 46, reel C-11014, as reproduced in Holmes, "The Coldwater Treaty Draft Historical Report," 50.

17 Yellowhead, 1830, LAC, RG 10, vol. 5, 577–80, in Florence Murray, ed., *Muskoka and Haliburton, 1615–1875: A Collection of Documents* (Toronto: Champlain Society, 1963), 105–6.

18 ICC, *Chippewa Tri-Council Inquiry*, 12.

19 J. Colborne, Lieutenant-Governor of Upper Canada, to G. Murray, Secretary of State, October 14, 1830, "Aboriginal Tribes," *Parliamentary Papers*, Great Britain, House of Commons, 1834, vol. 617, 128, hereafter *Parliamentary Papers*.

20 Colborne to Baron Aylmer, Governor General of Canada, February 19, 1831, in "Aboriginal Tribes," *Parliamentary Papers*.

21 Anderson to Mudge, May 10, 1831, LAC, RG 10, vol. 47, reel C-11015; and Anderson to Givins, September 17, 1832, LAC, RG 10, vol. 51, reel C-11016–11017.

22 Anderson to Givins, October 4, 1832, LAC, RG 10, vol. 52, reel C-11017.

23 Anderson to Givins, February 20, 1832, LAC, RG 10, vol. 50, reel C-11016. Anderson also suggested that "it would also be an act of charity to allot a parcel of Land for the Half Breeds and enable them to form a settlement subject to the rules of this Establishment."

24 A.F. Hunter, *A History of Simcoe County* (Barrie, ON: County Council, 1909), 2:9, and Anderson to Givins, December 3, 1832, LAC, RG 10, vol. 52, reel C-11017.

25   Chief and Rev. Peter Jones to Viscount Goderich, Secretary of State, July 26, 1831, "Aboriginal Tribes," *Parliamentary Papers*.

26   See Fred Blair, "Orillia's Early Settlers, Part 4: Andrew Borland," Orillia Museum of Art and History, February 18, 2021, https://www.facebook.com/orilliamuseum/photos/a.252204871475152/4357061550989443/?type=3.

27   Wesley-Esquimaux, "The Coldwater Narrows Reservation," 25–27, 44–46.

28   Craig Heron, *Booze: A Distilled History* (Toronto: Between the Lines, 2013), 18, 42, 50–51.

29   Wesley-Esquimaux, "The Coldwater Narrows Reservation," 26.

30   Givins to Anderson, November 6, 1830, LAC, RG 10, vol. 499, reel C-13341–13342, as reproduced in Holmes, "The Coldwater Treaty Draft Historical Report," 60.

31   Anderson to Givins, January 24, 1831, LAC, RG 10, vol. 47, reel C-11015; and Wesley-Esquimaux, "The Coldwater Narrows Reservation," 43–44.

32   Anderson to Givins, December 4, 1830, LAC, RG 10, vol. 6, reel C-11014.

33   Givins to Anderson, December 18, 1830, LAC, RG 10, vol. 499, reel C-13341–13342.

34   Anderson to Givins, September 28, 1832, LAC, RG 10, vol. 51, reel C-11016–11017.

35   Anderson to Givins, November 20, 1832, LAC, RG 10, vol. 52, reel C-11017.

36   Givins to Anderson, December 5, 1832, LAC, RG 10, vol. 500, reel C-13341.

37   David Town, *Yellowhead's Revolt* (Orillia: Impression House, 2020), 30.

38   Quoted in Wesley-Esquimaux, "The Coldwater Narrows Reservation," 1991, 51. See also "Proceedings of an Inquiry into the Truth of Certain Statements, Made by Captain Anderson and Mr. G. Alley of the Indian Department . . . ," *Christian Guardian*, March 14, 1832, 70.

39   David Town, *Orillia's Civil War* (Orillia: Impression House, 2016), 32–33. See also "Proceedings of an Inquiry," 70.

40   Anderson to Givins, August 13, 1834, LAC, RG 10, vol. 56, reel C-11018–11019.

41   Anderson to Givins, August 13, 1834.

42   Town, *Yellowhead's Revolt*, 30–31.

43   Givins to Anderson, July 16, 1832, LAC, RG 10, vol. 499, reel C-13341–1342.

44   Chief John Aisence, Coldwater, July 24, 1832, LAC, RG 10, vol. 51, reel C-11016–11017; and Anderson to George Phillpotts, Captain, Royal Engineers, February 6, 1833, LAC, RG 10, vol. 53, reel C-11017–11018.

45   Aisence, July 24, 1832.

46   Phillpotts to Anderson, February 18, 1833, LAC, RG 10, vol. 53, reel C-11017–11018.

47   "Proceedings of an Indian Council Held at Coldwater, April 16, 1833," LAC, RG 10, vol. 54, reel C-11018.

48   Anderson to Phillpotts, February 6, 1833, LAC, RG 10, vol. 53, reel C-11017–11018.

49   Anderson to Givins, May 6, 1834, LAC, RG 10, vol. 55, reel C-11018.

50   Anderson to Givins, November 28 and December 27, 1834, LAC, RG 10, vol. 56, reel C-11018–11019; and Anderson to Givins, July 16, 1832, LAC, RG 10, vol. 51, reel C-11016–11017.

Chapter 15: "Progress," Setbacks, and Strategies for Self-Sufficiency

1   Cynthia C. Wesley-Esquimaux, "The Coldwater Narrows Reservation," c. 1991, in *Chippewa Tri-Council Coldwater-Narrows Reservation Claim: Compilation of Documents*, ed. Indian Claims Commission, 1996, 25–27, https://iportal.usask.ca/docs/ICC_CD/Chippewas%20Tri-Council/open.pdf.

2   Vicki Snache, interview by Alan Corbiere and Victoria Freeman, Chippewas of Rama First Nation, July 6, 2022.

3   T.G. Anderson, Superintendent of Indian Affairs, Coldwater, to J. Colborne, Lieutenant-Governor of Upper Canada, August 1, 1832, Library and Archives Canada (LAC), RG 10, Department of Indian Affairs, vol. 51, reel C-11016–11017.

4   *Chippewa Tri-Council Inquiry*, 13; and John Webster Grant, *Moon of Wintertime: Missionaries and the Indians of Canada in Encounter since 1534* (Toronto: University of Toronto Press, 1984), 84.

5   "Proceedings of an Indian Council Held at Coldwater, April 16, 1833," LAC, RG 10, vol. 54, reel C-11018.

6   Wesley-Esquimaux, "The Coldwater Narrows Reservation," 31.

7   Grant, *Moon of Wintertime*, 84–85.

8   Diary of Reverend G. Hallen, January to August 1835, Simcoe County Archives, Midhurst, ON, referenced in David

9 "Proceedings of an Indian Council."
10 "Proceedings of an Indian Council."
11 "Proceedings of an Indian Council."
12 "Proceedings of an Indian Council."
13 Anderson to [Major] Winniett, September 16, 1833, LAC, RG 10, vol. 54, reel C-11018.
14 Anderson to Givins, October 25, 1834, LAC, RG 10, vol. 56, reel C-11018–11019.
15 Chiefs John Aisence, John Jones, Pierre Ashagashe, and Naineishkung, January 5, 1835, LAC, RG 10, vol. 60, reel C-11020.
16 Anderson to Givins, January 5, 1835, LAC, RG 10, vol. 60, reel C-11020.
17 "In consequence of the very severe Frosts it became necessary to stop the Saw Mill in order that the Grist Mill might continue to Grind, therefore the rent could not be exacted, and the Indians being very desirous to get the Mill under their own management, it has been given up by Mr. G. Mitchell": Anderson to Givins, April 9, 1835, LAC, RG 10, vol. 57, reel C-11019.
18 Anderson to Colborne, September 24, 1835.
19 David Town, *Orillia's Civil War* (Orillia: Impression House, 2016), 42–43.
20 Wesley-Esquimaux, "The Coldwater Narrows Reservation," 71.

Chapter 16: The Quest for Secure Land Tenure

1 Chief and Rev. Peter Jones to Viscount Goodrich, Secretary of State, July 26, 1831, "Aboriginal Tribes," *Parliamentary Papers*, Great Britain, House of Commons, 1834, vol. 617, 128.
2 Peter Jones, *Life and Journals of Kah-Ke-Wa-Quo-Na-By (Rev. Peter Jones), Wesleyan Missionary* (Toronto: A. Green, 1860), 351.
3 John Colborne, Lieutenant-Governor of Upper Canada, to R. Hay, Colonial Secretary, December 15, 1831, "Aboriginal Tribes," *Parliamentary Papers*.
4 T.G. Anderson, Superintendent of Indian Affairs, Coldwater, to J. Givins, Chief Superintendent of Indian Affairs, January 29, 1832, Library and Archives Canada (LAC), RG 10, Department of Indian Affairs, vol. 50, reel C-11016.
5 Givins to Anderson, January 31, 1832, LAC, RG 10, vol. 499, reel C-13341–13342.
6 "Proceedings of an Indian Council held at Coldwater, September 16, 1833," LAC, RG 10, vol. 54, reel C-11018.
7 "Proceedings of an Indian Council."
8 Mississaugas of Scugog Island First Nation, "Origin and History," https://www.scugogfirstnation.com/Public/Origin-and-History. See also Grant Karcich, *Scugog Carrying Place: A Frontier Pathway* (Toronto: Dundurn, 2013), 152.
9 Joan Holmes and Associates, "Coldwater-Narrows Surrender of 1836: Report about Additional Research Findings," in *Chippewa Tri-Council Inquiry: Coldwater-Narrows Reservation Surrender Claim* (Ottawa: Indian Claims Commission, 2020), 21.
10 Joan Holmes and Associates, "Coldwater-Narrows Surrender," 21.
11 Chiefs John Aisence, John Jones, Pierre Ashagashe, and Peter Katakickwou to Francis Bond Head, Lieutenant-Governor of Upper Canada, August 19, 1836, LAC, RG 10, vol. 62, reel C-11021.
12 Givins to Anderson, October 6, 1836, LAC, RG 10, vol. 501, reel C-13342; and Rhonda Telford, "The Central Anishinabe and the Rebellion, 1830–1840," in *Actes du trente-deuxième congrès des algonquinistes,* ed. John D. Nichols (Winnipeg: University of Manitoba, 2001), 555.
13 *Chippewa Tri-Council Inquiry*, 19.
14 Anderson to Givins, November 30, 1835, LAC, RG 10, vol. 59, file 60240-42.
15 Bond Head to Lord Glenelg, Secretary of State for the Colonial Department, August 20, 1836, no. 32, in *British Parliamentary Papers: Correspondence, Returns and Other Papers Relating to Canada and to the Indian Problem Therein, 1839*, vol. 12 (Shannon: Irish University Press, [1969]).
16 Theodore Binnema and Kevin Hutchings, "The Emigrant and the Noble Savage: Sir Francis Bond Head's Romantic Approach to Aboriginal Policy in Upper Canada, 1836–1838," *Journal of Canadian Studies* 39, no. 1 (2005): 125.
17 Anna Brownell Jameson, *Winter Studies and Summer Rambles in Canada*, afterword by Clara Thomas (Toronto: McClelland and Stewart, 1990 [1838]), 339.
18 Bond Head to Lord Glenelg, August 20, 1836, in Joan Holmes and Associates, "The Coldwater Treaty: Draft Historical Report," Specific Claims INAC Report, 1993, 137–38.

19 Chiefs Aisence, Jones, Ashagashe, and Katakickwou to Francis Bond Head, August 19, 1836.

20 Givins to Chief Yellowhead, Narrows, October 6, 1836, LAC, RG 10, vol. 501, reel C-13342.

21 Givins to Anderson, October 26, 1836, LAC, RG 10, vol. 501, reel C-13342.

22 Chief Yellowhead to Givins, November 6, 1836, LAC, RG 10, vol. 63, reel C-11021.

23 Coldwater Agreement, November 26, 1836, *Indian Treaties and Surrenders from 1680 to 1890*, vol. 1 (Ottawa: Brown Chamberlain Printers, 1891), 117.

24 Bond Head to Lord Glenelg, August 15, 1837, "Correspondence Returns, and Other Papers Relating to Canada and to the Indian Problem Therein," *Parliamentary Papers*, Great Britain, House of Commons, 1839, vol. 323, 149–52.

25 Joan Holmes and Associates, "Coldwater-Narrows Surrender," 25.

26 Rama, Snake Island, and Coldwater Indians to Sir Charles Bagot, 1842, in Florence Murray, ed., *Muskoka and Haliburton, 1615–1875: A Collection of Documents* (Toronto: Champlain Society, 1963), 115–16.

27 Anderson to William Hepburn, December 17, 1836, LAC, RG 10, vol. 63, reel 62254–62257, quoted in Telford, "The Central Anishinabe and the Rebellion, 1830–1840," 556.

28 Andrew Big Canoe, interview by Alan Corbiere and Victoria Freeman, Chippewas of Georgina Island First Nation, December 17, 2022.

29 He did this by saying that whites would take the land anyway without any compensation whatsoever: James Evans, St. Clair, March 24, 1838, *Christian Guardian*, April 1838.

30 Eighty-one men to Lord Glenelg, April 10, 1837, LAC, RG 10, vol. 65, reel C-11022.

31 Resident and Ministers of the Wesleyan Methodist Church in Canada to Bond Head, June 24, 1837, LAC, RG 10, vol. 66, reel C-11022–11023.

32 Quoted in Binnema and Hutchings, "The Emigrant," 130.

33 Aborigines Protection Society to Earl of Durham, Governor General of Canada, April 3, 1838, *Report of the Indians of Upper Canada 1839* (Toronto: Canadiana House, 1968), 22–27.

34 Elizabeth Elbourne, "The Sin of the Settler: The 1835–36 Select Committee on Aborigines and Debates over Virtue and Conquest in the Early Nineteenth-Century British White Settler Empire," *Journal of Colonialism and Colonial History* 4, no. 3 (2003): https://dx.doi.org/10.1353/cch.2004.0003.

35 Great Britain and Aborigines Protection Society, *Report of the Parliamentary Select Committee on Aboriginal Tribes (British Settlement)* (London: W. Ball, A. Chambers, and Hatchard and Son, 1837), iv.

36 The report also argued for metropolitan oversight of Aboriginal affairs because colonial legislators faced an inevitable conflict of interest: duty of protection versus responding to their electors' desires: Elbourne, "Sin of the Settler," paras. 4, 15, 24, 26.

37 Elbourne, "Sin of the Settler," 66–68.

38 "Despatch on Indian Affairs-Missions," *Christian Guardian*, March 21, 1838, Victoria University Library, Donald B. Smith fonds, 2013.08, box 7, file 11.

39 Chandra Murdoch, "Act to Control: The Grand General Indian Council, the Department of Indian Affairs, and the Struggle over the Indian Act in Ontario, 1850–1906" (PhD diss., University of Toronto, 2023), 168; and John F. Leslie, *The Report of the Pennefather Commission: Indian Conditions and Administration in the Canadas in the 1850s* (Ottawa: Treaties and Historical Research Centre, 1983), 5.

40 Givins to Anderson, February 11, 1837, LAC, RG 10, vol. 501, reel C-13342.

41 *Chippewa Tri-Council Inquiry*, 26–27.

42 Telford, "The Central Anishinabe and the Rebellion," 558.

43 Jones, *Life and Journals*, 384, July 24–25, 1837.

44 Murdoch, "Act to Control," 167.

Chapter 17: Defending the Crown

1 Gerald Craig, *Upper Canada: The Formative Years* (Toronto: McClelland and Stewart, 1968), 212.

2 Scott Kennedy, with Jeanne Hopkins, *200 Years at St. John's York Mills: The Oldest Church in Toronto* (Toronto: Dundurn Press, 2016), 266.

3 Susan Goldenberg, "Historic Stong Family," North York Historical Society, January 20, 2014 https://nyhs.ca/historic-stong-family/.

4 Ronald J. Stagg, "Joseph Shephard," in *Dictionary of Canadian Biography* (*DCB*), vol. 7, University of Toronto / Université Laval, 2003–, http://www.biographi.ca/en/bio/shepard_joseph_7E.html.

5   J.C. Dent, *Story of the Upper Canadian Rebellion* (Toronto: C. Bleckett Robinson, 1885), 2:47; and Patricia Hart, *Pioneering in North York: A History of the Borough* (Toronto: General Publishing, 1968), 161–62.

6   "Black Creek Pioneer Village: Elizabeth (Fisher) Stong," Hiking the GTA, https://hikingthegta.com/tag/daniel-stong/#:~:text=In%20the%20rebellion%20of%201837,arrested%20and%20held%20in%20jail.

7   They, along with one other rebel, were setting fire to the Don Bridge when Montgomery's Tavern was burned.

8   Hart, *Pioneering in North York*, 162.

9   Wellington Willson Cummer and Clyde Lottridge Cummer, *Cummer Memoranda: A Record of the Progenitors and Descendants of Jacob Cummer* (Cleveland: O.S. Hubbell, 1911), 28–31.

10 T.G. Anderson, "Memo Shewing the Number of Indians Who Were Employed under My Direction in the Late Rebellion, between the 7th and 15th December 1837 Inclusive," June 26, 1838, Library and Archives Canada (LAC), RG 10, Department of Indian Affairs, vol. 68, file 64592-95; Gerald Alley, letter, December 10, 1837, LAC, RG 10, vol. 67, file 64191-92; Anderson to S.P. Jarvis, Chief Superintendent of Indian Affairs, December 14, 1837, LAC, vol. 124, file 69672; Alley to Jarvis, November 30, 1838, LAC, RG 10, vol. 124, file 69972-73, cited in Rhonda Telford, "The Central Anishinabe and the Rebellion, 1830–1840," in *Actes du trente-deuxième congrès des algonquinistes,* ed. John D. Nichols (Winnipeg: University of Manitoba, 2001), 561.

11 Telford, "The Central Anishinabe and the Rebellion," 560–61. A further 170 Rice Lake Mississaugas were summoned by militia captain Charly Anderson, their Indian agent, to go to Toronto by steamer, but their journey was aborted because they weren't needed.

12 Telford, "The Central Anishinabe and the Rebellion," 560, 562.

13 Telford, "The Central Anishinabe and the Rebellion," 551–52.

14 Telford, "The Central Anishinabe and the Rebellion," 562.

15 Telford, "The Central Anishinabe and the Rebellion," 552, 560.

16 Telford, "The Central Anishinabe and the Rebellion," 564.

17 Telford, "The Central Anishinabe and the Rebellion," 557.

18 Telford, "The Central Anishinabe and the Rebellion," 564–65.

19 Ben Cousineau, interview by Alan Corbiere and Victoria Freeman, Chippewas of Rama First Nation, July 6, 2022.

20 Darin Wybenga, virtual interview by Alan Corbiere and Victoria Freeman, August 24, 2022.

21 See Jarvis to Alley, December 5, 1838, LAC, RG 10, vol. 502, file 158–60; Alley to Jarvis, December 8, 1838, LAC, RG 10, vol. 69, file 65196; Jarvis to Alley, December 12, 1838, LAC, RG 10, vol. 502, file 170-71; and Alley to Jarvis, December 14, 1838, LAC, RG 10, vol. 124, file 69974-71.

22 Telford, "The Central Anishinabe and the Rebellion," 566.

23 Rama, Snake Island, and Coldwater Indians to Sir Charles Bagot, 1842, in Florence Murray, ed., *Muskoka and Haliburton, 1615–1875: A Collection of Documents* (Toronto: Champlain Society, 1963), 115–16.

24 Alley to Jarvis, January 24, 1839, LAC, RG 10, vol. 124, file 69943-44.

25 Andrew Borland to Alley, January 30, 1839, LAC, RG 10, vol. 124, file 172, quoted in Murray, *Muskoka and Haliburton*, 114.

26 Telford, "The Central Anishinabe and the Rebellion," 567–70.

27 Telford, "The Central Anishinabe and the Rebellion," 570.

28 Darrel Manitowabi, "From Fish Weirs to Casino: Negotiating Neoliberalism at Mnjikaning" (PhD diss., University of Toronto, 2007), 9.

29 Jarvis to John McAulay, Secretary to Lieutenant-Governor of Upper Canada, June 19, 1838, Department of Indian Affairs and Northern Development, Ontario, file 10-1-10.

30 Andrew Big Canoe, interview by Alan Corbiere and Victoria Freeman, Chippewas of Georgina Island First Nation, December 17, 2022.

31 See Laurie Leclerc, "Rama First Nation Land Acquisitions, 1838–1848," *Mzinigan, Our Heritage Place*, Chippewas of Rama First Nation, Dagwaagi/Fall 2022, 6–10. https://issuu.com/bencousineau/docs/mzinigan_fall_2022.

32 Ben Cousineau interview.

33 Mark Douglas, interview by Alan Corbiere, Chippewas of Rama First Nation, November 24, 2022.

34 Sherry Lawson, interview by Alan Corbiere and Victoria Freeman, Chippewas of Rama First Nation, July 6, 2022.

35 Ben Cousineau interview.

36 Quoted in Cynthia C. Wesley-Esquimaux, "The Coldwater Narrows Reservation," c. 1991, *Chippewa Tri-Council Coldwater-Narrows Reservation Claim: Compilation of Documents*, edited by Indian Claims Commission, 1996, https://iportal.usask.ca/docs/ICC_CD/Chippewas%20Tri-Council/open.pdf.146–47.

37 *Chippewa Tri-Council Inquiry*, 28.

38 "Chiefs John Aisance, Yellowhead, and Snake (written by T.G. Anderson, Deputy Superintendent General of Indian Affairs," memo, October 17, 1845, LAC, RG 10, vol. 268, reel C-12653.

39 Kory Snache, virtual interview by Alan Corbiere and Victoria Freeman, September 21, 2022.

40 Aboriginal Affairs and Northern Development Canada, "Fact Sheet: The Coldwater-Narrows Land Claim," May 20, 2011, http://specific-claims.bryan-schwartz.com/wp-content/uploads/docs/Fact_Sheet-The_Coldwater-Narrows%20Land%20Claim_2011.pdf.

Chapter 18: Surviving, Rebuilding, Adapting, Resisting

1 Peter Jones, *Life and Journals of Kah-Ke-Wa-Quo-Na-By (Rev. Peter Jones), Wesleyan Missionary* (Toronto: A. Green, 1860), 407.

2 "Petition to the Queen, from the Credit Indians, Praying to Have Their Lands Secured to Them," October 4, 1837, in Peter Jones, *History of the Ojebway Indians: With Especial Reference to Their Conversion to Christianity* (London: A.W. Bennett, 1861), 265–67.

3 Donald B. Smith, *Sacred Feathers: The Reverend Peter Jones (Kahkewaquonaby) and the Mississauga Indians*, 2nd ed. (Toronto: University of Toronto Press, 2013), 166, 175.

4 Sydenham to Lord John Russell, Colonial Secretary, July 22, 1841, Province of Canada, Journals of the Legislative Assembly, *Sessional Papers*, 1844–45, Appendix EEE, quoted in John F. Leslie, *Commissions of Inquiry into Indian Affairs in the Canadas, 1828–1858: Evolving a Corporate Memory for the Indian Department* (Ottawa: Treaties and Historical Research Centre, Indian Affairs and Northern Development Branch, 1985), 122. The interpretation in parentheses is Leslie's.

5 Macaulay Report, April 22, 1839, Library and Archives Canada (LAC), RG 10, Department of Indian Affairs, vol. 718, 28–29; and Leslie, *Commissions*, 83.

6 Donald B. Smith, *Mississauga Portraits: Ojibwe Voices from Nineteenth-Century Canada* (Toronto: University of Toronto Press, 2013), 77.

7 Smith, *Sacred Feathers*, 174

8 "Minutes of a General Council Held at the River Credit Commencing on January 16th 1840," LAC, RG 10, Paudash Papers, Council Minutes, 1835–48, vol. 1011, 77.

9 "Minutes of a General Council."

10 Joseph Sawyer, Peter Jones, and John Jones to Colonel S.P. Jarvis, Credit, February 24, 1842, LAC, RG 10, Letter Book, 1825–42, vol. 1011, 190.

11 Smith, *Mississauga Portraits*, 77.

12 Haudenosaunee names as spelled in Smith, *Sacred Feathers*, 174–76.

13 Jones, *History*, 120.

14 "Minutes of a General Council," 82.

15 "Minutes of a General Council," 86.

16 "Minutes of a General Council," 87.

17 For more on these interpretations and the use of the Dish with One Spoon in land acknowledgements, see Dean M. Jacobs and Victor P. Lytwyn, "Naagan Get Bezhig Emkwaan: A Dish with One Spoon Reconsidered," *Ontario History* 112, no. 2 (2020): 191–210.

18 Smith, *Sacred Feathers*, 176; and Jones, *History*, 126.

19 See Mark D. Walters "'According to the Old Customs of Our Nation': Aboriginal Self-Government on the Credit River Mississauga Reserve, 1826–1847," *Ottawa Law Review* 30, no. 1 (1998–99): 1–45.

20 Johann Georg Kohl, *Travels in Canada and through the States of New York and Pennsylvania*, vol. 2 (London: George Manwaring, 1861); and Indian and Northern Affairs Canada, *Indian Affairs Annual Reports, 1864–1990* (Ottawa: National Library of Canada / Indian and Northern Affairs Canada, 2004), referenced in Darrel Manitowabi, "From Fish Weirs to Casino: Negotiating Neoliberalism at Mnjikaning" (PhD diss., University of Toronto, 2007), 10.

21 Matthew Stevens, virtual interview by Alan Corbiere and Victoria Freeman, October 6, 2022.

22 Mississaugas of Scugog Island First Nation, "Origin and History," https://www.scugogfirstnation.com/Public/Origin-and-History.

23 Darin Wybenga, virtual interview by Alan Corbiere and Victoria Freeman, August 24, 2022.

24 William Henry Smith, *Smith's Canadian Gazetteer* (Toronto: H. Rowsell, 1846), 40.

25 Quoted in Smith, *Sacred Feathers*, 177.

26 Peter Jones, quoted in *The Banner*, August 15, 1845, cited in Smith, *Sacred Feathers*, 222.

27 For details, see Six Nations of the Grand River Lands and Resources Department, "Land Rights: A Global Solution for the Six Nations of the Grand River," https://www.sixnations.ca/LandsResources/SNLands-GlobalSolutions-FINALyr2020.pdf.

28 Keith Jamieson and Michelle Hamilton, *Dr. Oronhyatekha: Security, Justice, and Equality* (Toronto: Dundurn, 2016), 44.

29 Phil Monture, virtual interview by Alan Corbiere and Victoria Freeman, November 15, 2022.

30 Jamieson and Hamilton, *Dr. Oronhyatekha*, 38.

31 Chief Kahkewaquonaby, "The Indian Nations: A Short Account of the Customs and Manners of the North American Indians, Particularly the Chippeway Nation," *Monthly Review Devoted to the Civil Government of the Canadas* 1, no. 5 (1841): 318–26.

32 Macaulay Report, April 22, 1839, LAC, RG 10, vol. 718, 254, cited in Leslie, *Commissions*, 82n8.

33 Province of Canada, Journals of the Legislative Assembly, "Report of Committee No. 4, on Indian Department," *Sessional Papers*, 1847, App. T, App. no. 1, quoted in Leslie, *Commissions*, 83.

34 Leslie, *Commissions*, 85.

35 Smith, *Sacred Feathers*, 194.

36 "A Paper Talk of the River Credit Indians [Signed Joseph Sawyer, John Jones, Chiefs] Laid before the Governor General," LAC, RG 10, Port Credit, Entry Book, December 5, 1844, vol. 1011, 107, quoted in Smith, *Sacred Feathers*, 194.

37 Smith, *Sacred Feathers*, 194.

Chapter 19: From Civilization to Assimilation

1 Peter Jones, *Christian Guardian*, September 29, 1841, quoted in Truth and Reconciliation Commission of Canada (TRC), *Canada's Residential Schools: The History, Part 1, Origins to 1939: The Final Report of the Truth and Reconciliation Commission of Canada, Volume I* (Montreal/Kingston: McGill-Queen's University Press, 2016), 74.

2 Peter Jones, "An Address to the Christian Public of Great Britain and Ireland in Behalf of the Indian Youth of Upper Canada, 1845," December 26, 1844, quoted in Donald B. Smith, *Sacred Feathers: The Reverend Peter Jones (Kahkewaquonaby) and the Mississauga Indians*, 2nd ed. (Toronto: University of Toronto Press, 2013), 195.

3 TRC, *Final Report*, 71.

4 Province of Canada, Legislative Assembly, "Report on the Affairs of the Indians in Canada," by Charles Bagot, *Sessional Papers*, 1844–45 (hereafter Bagot Commission), App. EEE, sec. 3, "Present Mode of Conducting Indian Affairs, with Recommendations for Its Amendment"; and John F. Leslie, *Commissions of Inquiry into Indian Affairs in the Canadas, 1828–1858: Evolving a Corporate Memory for the Indian Department* (Ottawa: Treaties and Historical Research Centre, Indian Affairs and Northern Development Branch, 1985), 89, 90.

5 Province of Canada, Legislative Assembly, *Sessional Papers*, 1847, App. T, sec. 3, "Report on the Affairs of the Indians of Canada."

6 *Sessional Papers*, 1847, App. T, submissions 30 and 38, cited in Leslie, *Commissions*, 90.

7 Smith, *Sacred Feathers*, 183.

8 Province of Canada, Journals of the Legislative Assembly, *Sessional Papers*, 1847, parts 4 and 5, cited in Leslie, *Commissions*, 91.

9 Leslie, *Commissions*, 104–5.

10 Leslie, *Commissions*, 109.

11 Chandra Murdoch, "Act to Control: The Grand General Indian Council, the Department of Indian Affairs, and the Struggle over the Indian Act in Ontario, 1850–1906" (PhD diss., University of Toronto, 2023), 171–72.

12 Murdoch, "Act to Control," 50–51.

13 TRC, *Final Report*, 75.

14 TRC, *Final Report*, 75.

15 Sherry Lawson, interview by Alan Corbiere and Victoria Freeman, Chippewas of Rama First Nation, July 6, 2022.

16 TRC, *Final Report*, 75.

17 The school, which was founded by the New England Company (the Society for the Propagation of the Gospel in New England) in 1828 as a day school for boys, became a Residential School in 1831 and opened to girls in 1834.

18 Henry Baldwin, ed., *Minutes of the General Council of Indian Chiefs and Principal Men, Held at Orillia, Lake Simcoe Narrows, on Thursday, the 30th, and Friday, the 31st July, 1846, on the Proposed Removal of the Smaller Communities, and the Establishment of Manual Labour Schools* (Montreal: Canada Gazette Office, 1846), 6–7.

19 Baldwin, *Minutes*, 23.

20 Baldwin, *Minutes*, 20.

21 Baldwin, *Minutes*, 21.

22 Baldwin, *Minutes*, 21.
23 Baldwin, *Minutes*, 26–27.
24 Baldwin, *Minutes*, 22, quoted in TRC, *Final Report*, 76.
25 Baldwin, *Minutes*, 25, quoted in TRC, *Final Report*, 76.
26 Ben Cousineau, interview by Alan Corbiere and Victoria Freeman, Chippewas of Rama First Nation, July 6, 2022.
27 Baldwin, *Minutes*, 28.
28 Baldwin, *Minutes*, 32–33.
29 Ben Cousineau interview.
30 See "Toronto Normal School, 1847–1897: Jubilee Celebration (October 31st, November 1st and 2nd, 1897," referenced in Murdoch, "Act to Control," 166.
31 "Appendix A, Report of Dr. Ryerson on Industrial Schools," Library and Archives Canada (LAC), RG 10, Department of Indian Affairs, vol. 2952, file 202, 239; and Egerton Ryerson, "Report on Industrial Schools, May 26, 1847," in *Statistics Respecting Indian Schools* (Ottawa: Government Printing Bureau, 1898).
32 TRC, *Final Report*, 78.
33 Province of Canada, Legislative Assembly, *Sessional Papers*, 1858, App. 21, "Report of the Special Commissioners to Investigate Indian Affairs in Canada: Part 2, Industrial Schools at Alderville and Mount Elgin," quoted in Leslie, *Commissions*, 153.
34 TRC, *Final Report*, 64.
35 Peter Jones to George Vardon, Port Credit, January 21, 1847, LAC, RG 10, Entry Book, 1831–48, vol. 1011, quoted in Smith, *Sacred Feathers*, 210.
36 Darin Wybenga, virtual interview by Alan Corbiere and Victoria Freeman, August 24, 2022.
37 Keith Jamieson and Michelle Hamilton, *Dr. Oronhyatekha: Security, Justice, and Equality* (Toronto: Dundurn, 2016), 45–46.
38 Peter Jones, "The Removal of the River Credit Indians," *Christian Guardian*, January 12, 1848.
39 Carolyn King, virtual interview by Victoria Freeman, October 10, 2022.
40 Darin Wybenga, "January 1848—Eight Months after the Move from the River Credit," *Historical Tidbits: Mississaugas of the Credit First Nation*, Pillar 5 Committee, Mississaugas of the Credit First Nation Chief and Council, 2019.
41 Garry Sault, virtual interview by Alan Corbiere and Victoria Freeman, September 13, 2022.
42 Jones, "Removal," 1.
43 Neil Semple, *The Lord's Dominion: The History of Canadian Methodism* (Montreal/Kingston: McGill-Queen's University Press, 1996), 172.
44 Darin Wybenga interview.

Chapter 20: Black Wampum

1 Chandra Murdoch, "Act to Control: The Grand General Indian Council, the Department of Indian Affairs, and the Struggle over the Indian Act in Ontario, 1850–1906" (PhD diss., University of Toronto, 2023), 49–50, referencing J.E. Hodgetts, *Pioneer Public Service: An Administrative History of the United Canadas, 1841–1867* (Toronto: University of Toronto Press, 1955), 217–18. In 1839, the parliamentary grant was £20, 000 (£15,850 going to presents and £4,150 to salaries).
2 The Grand River Navigation Company was established in 1832 to build dams and locks to ship goods such as milled flour and lumber along the Grand River between Brantford and Lake Erie. "Without the knowledge of the Haudenosaunee," Keith Jamieson writes, "officials had funnelled large sums of their trust funds to buy company stock, and sold their lands to finance further investments": Keith Jamieson and Michelle Hamilton, *Dr. Oronhyatekha: Security, Justice, and Equality* (Toronto: Dundurn, 2016), 86; see also Six Nations of the Grand River, "Land Rights: A Global Solution for the Six Nations of the Grand River," https://www.sixnations.ca/LandsResources/SNLands-GlobalSolutions-FINALyr2020.pdf. Six Nations of the Grand River has been seeking a full accounting of these expenditures as there is no record of repayment or repayment with interest. A major lawsuit has been launched.
3 Phil Montour, virtual interview by Alan Corbiere and Victoria Freeman, November 15, 2024.
4 Murdoch, "Act to Control," 44, 57.
5 Murdoch, "Act to Control," 48–49.
6 Reverend P. Choné to Superintendent-General of Indian Affairs, August 15, 1862, Library and Archives Canada (LAC), RG 10, Department of Indian Affairs, vol. 292, file 195634–195637, reel C-12669, emphasis in original, according to Choné. Quoted in Murdoch, "Act to Control," 68.
7 Rhonda Telford, "The Anishinabe Presentation of Their Fishing Rights to the Duke of Newcastle and the Prince of Wales," *Papers of the Thirtieth Algonquian Conference*, ed.

8   David H. Pentland (Winnipeg: University of Manitoba, 1999), 386.

8   Quoted in Telford, "The Anishinabe Presentation," 387, found in LAC, RG 10, vol. 266.

9   *An Act to Encourage the Gradual Civilization of the Indian Tribes in This Province, and to Amend the Laws Respecting Indians*, S.C. 1857, c. 6, cited in John F. Leslie, *Commissions of Inquiry into Indian Affairs in the Canadas, 1828–1858: Evolving a Corporate Memory for the Indian Department* (Ottawa: Treaties and Historical Research Centre, Indian Affairs and Northern Development Branch, 1985), 140–41. Leslie points out that passage was backed by A.A. Dorion, J.A. Macdonald, G.E. Cartier, W.B. Robinson, and George Brown: *The Globe*, May 15, 1857.

10 Others who did not reach this standard but who were deemed to possess a satisfactory level of knowledge and intelligence were placed on three years' probation before becoming enfranchised.

11 John L. Tobias, "Protection, Civilization, Assimilation: An Outline History of Canada's Indian Policy," in *Sweet Promises: A Reader on Indian-White Relations in Canada*, ed. J.R. Miller (Toronto: University of Toronto Press, 1991), 130.

12 Tony Hall, "Native Limited Identities and Newcomer Metropolitanism in Upper Canada, 1814–1867," in *Old Ontario: Essays in Honour of J.M.S. Careless*, ed. David Keane and Colin Read (Toronto: Dundurn 1990), 161.

13 Murdoch, "Act to Control," 118.

14 Leslie, *Commissions*, 141.

15 David Thorburn to Richard Pennefather, October 13, 1858, LAC, RG 10, vol. 245, Civil Secretary's Office Correspondence, no. 11401–11600.

16 Thorburn to Pennefather, October 13, 1858.

17 J.S. Milloy, "The Era of Civilization: British Policy for the Indians of Canada, 1830–1860" (PhD diss., University of Oxford, 1978), 280.

18 Telford, "Anishinabe Presentation," 387.

19 Donald B. Smith, *Mississauga Portraits: Ojibwe Voices from Nineteenth-Century Canada* (Toronto: University of Toronto Press, 2013), 85.

20 Smith, *Mississauga Portraits*, 85–86.

21 Murdoch, "Act to Control," 215, drawing on Brenda Child, *Holding Our World Together: Ojibwe Women and the Survival of Community* (New York: Penguin, 2012); and Madeleine Whetung, "(En)gendering Shoreline Law: Nishnaabeg Relational Politics along the Trent Severn Waterway," *Global Environmental Politics* 19, no. 3 (2019): 16–32; and others.

22 Heidi Bohaker, *Doodem and Council Fire: Anishinaabe Governance through Alliance* (Toronto: University of Toronto Press), 79.

23 Historian Heidi Bohaker noted consultation with Women's Councils on three early treaties with the British between 1792 and 1796 as well as three women signatories to the 1784 Mississauga-Anishinaabe land cession providing land for displaced Haudenosaunee: *Doodem and Council Fire*, 141.

24 Susan Hill, *The Clay We Are Made Of: Haudenosaunee Land Tenure on the Grand River* (Winnipeg: University of Manitoba Press, 2017), 58, in Murdoch, "Act to Control," 217–18.

25 Smith, *Mississauga Portraits*, 89. See "Lo the Poor Indian," *The Globe*, March 16, 1860; "An Indian Woman among the Friends," *The Globe*, April 5, 1860; and "The Indian Imposter," *The Globe*, May 23, 1860.

26 "From Our London Correspondent," *The Globe*, July 7, 1860.

27 Smith, *Mississauga Portraits*, 90. See also Celia Haig-Brown, "Seeking Honest Justice in a Land of Strangers: Nahnebahwequa's Struggle for Land," *Journal of Canadian Studies* 36, no. 4 (2002): 143–70.

28 *The Globe*, September 1, 1860, quoted in Ian Radforth, "Performance, Politics, and Representation: Aboriginal People and the 1860 Royal Tour of Canada," *Canadian Historical Review* 84, no. 1 (2001): 18.

29 Smith, *Mississauga Portraits*, 91.

30 Garry Sault, virtual interview by Alan Corbiere and Victoria Freeman, September 13, 2022.

31 Telford, "Anishinabe Presentation," 391.

32 Ian Radforth, *Royal Spectacle: The 1860 Visit of the Prince of Wales to Canada and the United States* (Toronto: University of Toronto Press, 2004), 231. For the original petition, see "Points of Grievance Complained of at Sarnia, September 1860," LAC, RG 10, vol. 266, 163, 028-163, 378.

33 Smith, *Mississauga Portraits*, 91.

34 Jamieson and Hamilton, *Dr. Oronhyatekha*, 81, 85.

35 Telford, "Anishinabe Presentation," 393. James McLean to David Thorburn, September 15 and September 20, 1860, LAC, RG 10, vol. 842, 143–45.

36 Smith, *Mississauga Portraits*, 94.

37 Smith, *Mississauga Portraits*, 94.

38 Carolyn King, virtual interview by Victoria Freeman, October 10, 2022.

Chapter 21: The Indian Act and the Great Council Fire

1. *An Act Providing for the Organisation of the Department of the Secretary of State of Canada, and for the Management of Indian and Ordnance Lands*, S.C., 1868, c. 42.

2. Norman D. Shields, "Anishinabek Political Alliance in the Post-Confederation Period: The Grand General Indian Council of Ontario, 1870—1936" (master's thesis, Queen's University, 2001), 27-28.

3. Margaret Sault, virtual interview by Alan Corbiere and Victoria Freeman, September 2, 2022.

4. John S. Milloy, "The Early Indian Acts: Developmental Strategy and Constitutional Change," *Sweet Promises: A Reader on Indian-White Relations in Canada*, ed. J.R. Miller (Toronto: University of Toronto Press, 1991), 145–56. See also Chandra Murdoch, "Act to Control: The Grand General Indian Council, the Department of Indian Affairs, and the Struggle over the Indian Act in Ontario, 1850–1906" (PhD diss., University of Toronto, 2023), 95–96.

5. *Act for the Gradual Enfranchisement of Indians, the Better Management of Indian Affairs, and to Extend the Provisions of the Indian Lands Act*, S.C., 1869, c. 6.

6. Murdoch, "Act to Control," 90.

7. Murdoch, "Act to Control," 94.

8. Murdoch, "Act to Control," 89.

9. Murdoch, "Act to Control," 90.

10. Murdoch, "Act to Control," 102.

11. Murdoch, "Act to Control," 107.

12. Murdoch, "Act to Control," 109–10.

13. Minutes of the Six Nations in Council, April 26, 1870, Library and Archives Canada (LAC), RG 10, Department of Indian Affairs, vol. 347, 126–31, C-9590.

14. Murdoch, "Act to Control," 121.

15. *Copy of Petition to His Excellency Sir John Young, Governor General of Canada, the General Council of the Six Nations and Delegates from Different Bands in Western and Eastern Canada, June 10, 1870* (Hamilton: The Spectator Office, 1870), 27, quoted in Murdoch, "Act to Control," 122.

16. Murdoch, "Act to Control," 123.

17. Murdoch, "Act to Control," 123.

18. Murdoch, "Act to Control," 88–89.

19. Dr. Oronhyatekha to Minister of the Interior, June 11, 1872, LAC, RG 10, vol. 1934, file 3541.

20. Murdoch, "Act to Control," 3.

21. Duncan Campbell Scott, Deputy Superintendent-General of Indian Affairs, to the Special Parliamentary Committee of the House of Commons, *The Indian Problem*, 1920, LAC, RG 10, vol. 6810, file 470-2-3, vol. 7, 55 (L-3) and 63 (N-3).

22. While minutes of the meeting have not survived, there was a lengthy discussion about the Indian Act. The Council informed David Laird that it had approved the legislation sixty-six votes to one. The letter states that "J. Henry, Puhgwujenene, William Wawanosh, Lamorandiere, Waucaush, J.L. Kerby, Rev. H.P. Chase, Rev. J. Jacobs, J.B. Nanigishkung, Andrew Jacobs, D. Sawyer, Sumner, Mahsegeshig, Kabaosa, Wahbemama, Menace, J. Fisher, Paudauch etc. etc." participated: H.P. Chase to David Laird, July 12, 1876, LAC, RG 10, vol. 1994, file 6829, referenced in Murdoch, "Act to Control," 139.

23. Murdoch, "Act to Control," 23.

24. Murdoch, "Act to Control," 135.

25. Murdoch, "Act to Control," 165–66.

26. Murdoch, "Act to Control," 129.

27. Allan Sherwin, *Bridging Two Peoples: Chief Peter E. Jones, 1843-1909* (Waterloo, ON: Wilfrid Laurier University Press, 2012).

28. Murdoch, "Act to Control," 131, 167, 169, 172–73.

29. See Susan Hill, *The Clay We Are Made Of: Haudenosaunee Land Tenure on the Grand River* (Winnipeg: University of Manitoba Press, 2017), 188,

30. Hill, *Clay We Are Made Of,* 187, quoted in Murdoch, "Act to Control," 142.

31. Sally Weaver, "The Iroquois: The Consolidation of the Grand River Reserve in the Mid-Nineteenth Century, 1847–1875," in *Aboriginal Ontario: Historical Perspectives on the First Nations*, ed. Edward S. Rogers and Donald B. Smith (Toronto: Dundurn), 207–9.

32. Oronhyatekha to the Minister of the Interior, June [11?], 1872, LAC, RG 10, vol. 1943, file 3541.

33. "Six Nations Reserve: Petition from Several Indians Protesting the Indian Act of 1876," LAC, RG 10, vol. 2077, file 11,432, quoted in Keith D. Smith and Mary-Ellen Kelm, eds., *Talking Back to the Indian Act: Critical Readings in Settler-Colonial Histories* (Toronto: University of Toronto Press, 2018), 53–54.

34. *The General Council of the Six Nations, and Delegates from Different Bands in Western and Eastern Canada, June 10,*

35 Shields, "Anishinabek Political Alliance," 46.

36 Peggy Blair, "Fact Sheet: Rights of Aboriginal Women On and Off Reserve," Scow Institute, 2005.

37 See, for example, Assembly of First Nations, "What Is Bill C-31 and Bill C-3?," https://www.afn.ca/wp-content/uploads/2020/01/16-19-02-06-AFN-Fact-Sheet-Bill-C-31-Bill-C-3-final-revised.pdf.

38 Norman Shields "The Grand General Indian Council of Ontario and Indian Status Legislation," in *Lines Drawn upon the Water: First Nations and the Great Lakes Borders and Borderlands*, ed. Karl Hele (Waterloo: Wilfrid Laurier University Press, 2008), 209.

39 See Brenda J. Child, *Holding Our World Together: Ojibwe Women and the Survival of Community* (New York: Viking, 2012); and Murdoch, "Act to Control," 214–15.

40 Murdoch, "Act to Control," 2.

41 Murdoch, "Act to Control," 297.

42 Shields, "Anishinabek Political Alliance," 143.

43 Murdoch, "Act to Control," 305.

44 Albert Big Canoe, interview by Alan Corbiere and Victoria Freeman, Chippewas of Georgina Island First Nation, December 17, 2022.

45 Murdoch, "Act to Control," 142.

46 Hill, *Clay We Are Made Of*, 186; and Murdoch, "Act to Control," 142.

47 See Deskaheh, "The Redman's Appeal for Justice," 1923 https://www.sfu.ca/~palys/TheRedmansAppealForJustice1923.pdf; and Brian Titley, "The Six Nations Status Case," *A Narrow Vision: Duncan Campbell Scott and the Administration of Indian Affairs in Canada* (Vancouver: UBC Press, 1988), 110–44.

48 Phil Monture, virtual interview by Alan Corbiere and Victoria Freeman, November 15, 2022.

49 Phil Monture interview.

Chapter 22: After 1876

1 Leona Charles, interview by Allan Corbiere and Victoria Freeman, Mississaugas of Scugog Island First Nation, July 7, 2022.

2 Albert Big Canoe, interview by Alan Corbiere and Victoria Freeman, Chippewas of Georgina Island First Nation, December 17, 2022.

3 Garry Sault, virtual interview by Alan Corbiere and Victoria Freeman, September 13, 2022.

4 Leona Charles interview.

5 Vicki Snache, interview by Alan Corbiere and Victoria Freeman, Chippewas of Rama First Nation, July 6, 2022.

6 Carolyn King, virtual interview by Victoria Freeman, October 10, 2022.

7 Susan Hoeg, interview by Alan Corbiere and Victoria Freeman, Chippewas of Georgina Island First Nation, December 17, 2022.

8 Patricia Le Saux, interview by Alan Corbiere and Victoria Freeman, Mississaugas of Scugog Island First Nation, July 7, 2022.

9 The Royal Commission on Aboriginal Health accepted a figure of five hundred thousand for the number of Indigenous people in Canada in the late fifteenth century. On the death rate, see Michael R. Haines and Richard H. Steckel, *A Population History of North America* (Cambridge: Cambridge University Press, 2000), 12; Herbert C. Northcott and Donna Marie Wilson, *Dying and Death in Canada* (Toronto: University of Toronto Press, 2008), 25–27; and William G. Dean, Conrad Heidenreich, and Thomas McIlwraith, eds., *Concise Historical Atlas of Canada* (Toronto: University of Toronto Press, 1998), 2. Data specific to the Greater Toronto Area or southern Ontario region could not be located.

10 Donald B. Smith, *Sacred Feathers: The Reverend Peter Jones (Kahkewaquonaby) and the Mississauga Indians*, 2nd ed. (Toronto: University of Toronto Press, 2013), 30.

11 "Diary of Lieutenant-Governor Simcoe's Journey from Humber Bay to Matchedash Bay in 1793," by Alexander Macdonell, Sheriff of the Home District, *Simcoe Papers*, 2:73, cited in Smith, *Sacred Feathers*, 270. Smith also cites William Osgoode to Ellen Copley, Niagara, September 25, 1793, in A.R.M. Lower, ed., "Three Letters of William Osgoode: First Chief Justice of Upper Canada," *Ontario History* 57 (1965): 185; extract of a letter from Nathaniel Lines, Interpreter for the Indian Department, Kingston, October 17, 1796, Library and Archives Canada (LAC), RG 8, British Military and Naval Records, vol. 249, file 215; and Augustus Jones to D.W. Smith, Saltfleet, March 1797, Archives of Ontario, Surveyors' Letters 28, 131.

12 Smith, *Sacred Feathers*, 147; and Jennifer Bonnell, *Reclaiming the Don: An Environmental History of Toronto's Don River Valley* (Toronto: University of Toronto Press, 2014), 24–25.

13 Peter Jones, *History of the Ojebway Indians: With Especial Reference to Their Conversion to Christianity* (London: A.W. Bennett, 1861), 143.

14 Smith, *Sacred Feathers*, 160–61.

15 Smith, *Sacred Feathers*, 209.

16 See Cynthia Wesley-Esquimaux and Magdalena Smolewski, *Historic Trauma and Aboriginal Healing* (Ottawa: Aboriginal Healing Foundation, 2004).

17 Peter Jones, *Life and Journals of Kah-Ke-Wa-Quo-Na-By (Rev. Peter Jones), Wesleyan Missionary* (Toronto: A. Green, 1860), 352.

18 Johann Georg Kohl, *Travels in Canada and through the States of New York and Pennsylvania*, vol. 2 (London: George Manwaring, 1861), 14.

19 Jones, *History*, 29.

20 Allan Sherwin, *Bridging Two Peoples: Chief Peter E. Jones, 1843–1909* (Waterloo, ON: Wilfrid Laurier University Press, 2012), 155.

21 In fact, a box containing Peter Jones' herbs, along with a pharmacy scale, survived an 1838 shipwreck near Port Daniel, Quebec. These items were donated to the McCord Museum in Montreal. See Sherwin, *Bridging Two Peoples*, 23.

22 Jones, *History*, 153.

23 Jones, *History*, 16.

24 Sherwin, *Bridging Two Peoples*, 155–66.

25 Mrs. Rosanna Hoover to Wilma Jamieson, Thessalon, ON, September 16, 1959, cited in Sherwin, *Bridging Two Peoples*, 165.

26 Emerson Benson Nanigishkung, interview by Alan Corbiere and Victoria Freeman, Chippewas of Rama First Nation, July 6, 2022.

27 "Vernon B. Wadsworth's Reminiscences of Indians in Muskoka and Haliburton, 1860–4," in *Muskoka and Haliburton, 1615–1875: A Collection of Documents*, ed. Florence Murray, (Toronto: Champlain Society, 1963), 176–77.

28 Susan Hoeg interview.

29 Garry Sault interview.

30 Jones, *History*, 143.

31 Edward Roe, "Roe Arrived after War of 1812," *The Era* (Newmarket, ON), June 4, 1975, https://news.ourontario.ca/newmarket/page.asp?ID=2436443&po=13&n=600.

32 Sherwin, *Bridging Two Peoples*, 8.

33 Donald B. Smith, "Peter Edmund Jones," *Dictionary of Canadian Biography* (*DCB*), vol. 13, University of Toronto / Université Laval, 2003, http://www.biographi.ca/en/bio/jones_peter_edmund_13E.html.

34 Mikayla Wronko, "The Duality of Peter E. Jones: A Queen's Graduate and the First Indigenous Physician of Canada," *Queen's University Journal*, September 30, 2016, https://www.queensjournal.ca/story/2016-09-30/features/the-duality-of-peter-e-jones.

35 Sherwin, *Bridging Two Peoples*, 23.

36 Murdoch, "Act to Control," 22.

37 Murdoch, "Act to Control," 44.

38 "Frank, like his late father, was well educated and taught school for several years, but when the herbal medicine business lagged, he left the reserve to travel the world as an advance sales agent for the Royal Italian Circus and Menagerie": Murdoch, "Act to Control," 40.

39 On Maungwudaus, "Following each performance he presented himself as an experienced Aboriginal Medicine Man and sold packages containing a variety of herbal cures. His son, George Henry Jr., acquired his father's herbal recipes in due course": Sherwin, *Bridging Two Peoples*, 57. For more on Maungwudaus, see Donald B. Smith, *Mississauga Portraits: Ojibwe Voices from Nineteenth-Century Canada* (Toronto: University of Toronto Press, 2013), 126–63.

40 Garry Sault interview.

41 Sherwin, *Bridging Two Peoples*, 51.

42 Keith Jamieson and Michelle Hamilton, *Dr. Oronhyatekha: Security, Justice, and Equality* (Toronto: Dundurn, 2016), 49.

43 Jamieson and Hamilton, *Dr. Oronhyatekha*, 52.

44 Jamieson and Hamilton, *Dr. Oronhyatekha*, 63–64.

45 Oronhyatekha's speech reminded the prince that the Haudenosaunee had been allies of the British Crown for almost two hundred years and were joined together by the metaphorical Covenant Chain. But there was no time to deliver the speech. The *Brant Expositor* reported that all the speeches were submitted on paper in a ceremony that lasted about five minutes. See Jamieson and Hamilton, *Dr. Oronhyatekha*, 80–81.

46 Jamieson and Hamilton, *Dr. Oronhyatekha*, 86.

47 Nelles was a powerful figure on the reserve. His father and grandfather had served in the British Indian Department, and Joseph Brant had granted the Loyalist family land on the Haldimand Tract. Nelles was even entrusted by the Confederacy Council with communications with the British Crown. He remained headmaster of the Mohawk Institute until he retired in 1872. See Jamieson and Hamilton, *Dr. Oronhyatekha*, 50, 89, 92–93, 99–103.

48 Jamieson and Hamilton, *Dr. Oronhyatekha*, 103.

49 Jamieson and Hamilton, *Dr. Oronhyatekha*, 117.

50 Jamieson and Hamilton, *Dr. Oronhyatekha*, 121.

51 Sherwin, *Bridging Two Peoples*, 89–94, 153.

52 A big party was held to celebrate the opening of the New Credit Council House. The guests enjoyed a rich dinner, speeches by Haudenosaunee and Anishinaabe Chiefs, music by several reserve brass bands, and a war dance. See Norman D. Shields, "Anishinabek Political Alliance in the Post-Confederation Period: The Grand General Indian Council of Ontario, 1870—1936" (master's thesis, Queen's University, 2001), 63–66.

53 Shields, "Anishinabek Political Alliance," 53. See Mark D. Walters "'According to the Old Customs of Our Nation': Aboriginal Self-Government on the Credit River Mississauga Reserve, 1826–1847," *Ottawa Law Review* 30, no. 1 (1998–99): 1–45.

54 Shields, "Anishinabek Political Alliance," 77.

55 Malcolm Montgomery, "The Six Nations Indians and the Macdonald Franchise," *Ontario History* 57, no. 1 (1965): 13-25.

56 Murdoch, "Act to Control," 191–92.

57 Margaret Sault, virtual interview by Alan Corbiere and Victoria Freeman, September 2, 2022.

58 Murdoch, "Act to Control," 193.

59 Jamieson and Hamilton, *Dr. Oronhyatekha*, 158–59.

60 William W. Mitchell, "Worshipful Brother Joseph Brant," *Historical Record of the Brant Masonic District, 1855–2020*, 370–79, https://www.brantmasons.com/files/BMD—Historytothe19Nov2020-1.pdf; and Dr. G. Brett, "The Life and Masonic Career of Joseph Brant," *Papers of the Canadian Masonic Research Association,* vol. 1 (Cambridge, ON: Heritage Lodge No. 730, 1986), 273–80, https://archive.org/details/papersofcanadian01cana/page/274/mode/2up.

61 Jessica Harland-Jacobs, "All in the Family: Freemasonry and the British Empire in the Mid-nineteenth Century," *Journal of British Studies* 42, no. 4 (2003): 464.

62 Harland-Jacobs, "All in the Family," 477.

63 Sherwin, *Bridging Two Peoples*, 124.

64 Sherwin, *Bridging Two Peoples*, 123.

65 Oronyhatekha, *History of the Independent Order of Foresters* (Toronto, ON: Hunter, Rose, 1895), 58–59; and "Great I.O.F. Invitation," *Globe*, February 19, 1902, cited in Jamieson and Hamilton, *Dr. Oronhyatekha*, 180.

66 Gayle M. Comeau-Vasilopoulos, "Oronhyatekha," in *DCB*, vol. 13, http://www.biographi.ca/en/bio/oronhyatekha_13E.html.

67 Jamieson and Hamilton, *Dr. Oronhyatekha*, 161–62.

68 Jamieson and Hamilton, *Dr. Oronhyatekha*, 229, 231. Demolished in the 1960s, a piece of its facade is preserved at Guildwood Park in Scarborough.

69 Comeau-Vasilopoulos, "Oronhyatekha."

70 See R.A. Phipps, "Red Man vs White Man," *Toronto Daily Mail*, November 30, 1875; Oronhyatekha, "The Prohibition Question," *Toronto Daily Mail*, December 4, 1875; B.A., "Red Men vs. White Men," *Toronto Daily Mail*, December 8, 1875; P.E. Jones, "Red Man v White Man," *Toronto Daily Mail*, December 14, 1875; and Oronhyatekha, "Red Man v White Man," *Toronto Daily Mail*, December 14, 1875.

71 Jamieson and Hamilton, *Dr. Oronhyatekha*, 236.

72 Quoted in Jamieson and Hamilton, *Dr. Oronhyatekha*, 30.

73 Jamieson and Hamilton, *Dr. Oronhyatekha*, 198.

74 Jamieson and Hamilton, *Dr. Oronhyatekha*, 27–28.

75 George Copway was the first Indigenous person from Canada to produce a weekly newspaper—*Copway's American Indian*—but it was published in New York. See Penny Petrone, *Native Literature in Canada: From Oral Tradition to the Present* (Toronto: Oxford University Press, 1990), 45.

76 Copies of all twenty-four issues are held at the New Credit Public Library. They are also on microfilm at the Toronto Reference Library.

77 "The Grand General Council of Ontario," *The Indian* (Hagersville, ON), December 30, 1885; and Murdoch, "Act to Control," 188.

78 Murdoch, "Act to Control," 188–89; "The Indian Homes," *The Indian*, February 3, 1886; and *The Indian*, July 7, 1886.

79 Smith, "Peter Edmund Jones."

80 Sherwin, *Bridging Two Peoples*, 68–71.

81 See Michelle A. Hamilton, *Collections and Objections: Aboriginal Material Culture in Southern Ontario* (Montreal/Kingston: McGill-Queen's University Press, 2010).

82. Trudy Nicks, "Dr. Oronhyatekha's History Lessons: Reading Museum Collections as Texts," in *Reading beyond Words: Contexts for Native History*, 2nd ed., ed. Jennifer S.H. Brown and Elizabeth Vibert (Toronto: University of Toronto Press, 2003), 476.

Conclusion: Confronting History, Re(making) History

1. Phil Monture, virtual interview by Alan Corbiere and Victoria Freeman, November 15, 2022.
2. Garry Sault, virtual interview by Alan Corbiere and Victoria Freeman, September 13, 2022.
3. Ben Cousineau, interview by Alan Corbiere and Victoria Freeman, Chippewas of Rama First Nation, July 6, 2022.
4. Kelly LaRocca, virtual interview by Alan Corbiere and Victoria Freeman, October 20, 2022.
5. Ben Cousineau interview.
6. Mark Douglas, interview by Alan Corbiere, Chippewas of Rama First Nation, November 24, 2022.
7. Matthew Stevens, virtual interview by Alan Corbiere and Victoria Freeman, October 6, 2022.
8. Carolyn King, virtual interview by Victoria Freeman, October 10, 2020.
9. Matthew Stevens interview.
10. Ben Cousineau interview.
11. Kory Snache, virtual interview by Alan Corbiere and Victoria Freeman, September 21, 2022.
12. Rhonda Coppaway, virtual interview by Alan Corbiere and Victoria Freeman, October 20, 2022.
13. Vicki Snache, interview by Alan Corbiere and Victoria Freeman, Chippewas of Rama First Nation, July 6, 2022.
14. Kory Snache interview.
15. Phil Monture interview.
16. Lauri Hoeg, interview by Alan Corbiere and Victoria Freeman, December 17, 2022.
17. Ben Cousineau interview.
18. Kelly LaRocca interview.
19. Ben Cousineau interview.
20. Vicki Snache interview.
21. Albert Big Canoe, interview by Alan Corbiere and Victoria Freeman, Chippewas of Georgina Island First Nation, December 17, 2022.
22. Leona Charles, interview by Allan Corbiere and Victoria Freeman, Mississaugas of Scugog Island First Nation, July 7, 2022.
23. Vicki Snache interview.
24. Ben Cousineau interview.
25. Matthew Stevens interview.
26. Vicki Snache interview.
27. Kory Snache interview.
28. Kory Snache interview.
29. Phil Monture interview.
30. Carolyn King interview.
31. Phil Monture interview.
32. Matthew Stevens interview.
33. Lauri Hoeg interview.
34. See, for example, Jerry Agar, "AGAR: Exclusion Not the Solution to Achieving Inclusion," *Toronto Sun*, April 22, 2024, https://torontosun.com/opinion/columnists/agar-exclusion-not-the-solution-to-achieving-inclusion.
35. Ben Cousineau interview.
36. Kelly LaRocca interview.

Index

A

Aborigines Protection Society, 195, 213, 241
Acland, Henry, 244, 275
agriculture, 1–3, 23, 26, 54–55, 68, 74, 77, 79, 83, 87–88, 99, 104–105, 118–121, 123, 131–134, 138, 140, 149, 153, 157, 159–161, 165, 167, 169, 171–175, 177, 179, 181–182, 189, 196, 197, 199–200, 204, 206–208, 211–212, 214, 217–219, 221, 223–224, 229–231, 233, 235, 238, 241–242, 249, 265
    See also horticulture
Aitken, Alexander, 56
Ajetance Treaty (Treaty 19), 99, 103
Albany, New York, 35, 41
    See also fur trade
alcohol, 41, 44, 46–47, 109, 113, 123, 131, 137, 139–141, 144, 150, 163, 172–173, 179, 183, 195–196
    abstinence, 46, 113, 135, 137, 140, 153, 179, 278, 280
    See also fur trade; Methodism; slavery and slave trade
Alderville, 32, 56, 216, 225, 230
Alley, Gerald, 173–176, 181, 201, 203
alliances, 26, 28, 32, 35, 37, 39, 42, 44–45, 52, 56, 61, 67, 70–72, 95–96, 98–99, 105, 134, 140, 167, 189, 194, 196, 200–201, 212, 214–215, 220, 224, 233, 235, 241, 249–250, 252–253, 277, 283–284
    See also Covenant Chain Wampum; Dish with One Spoon Wampum; governance, Indigenous; Mississauga-Haudenosaunee alliance of the 1790s; presents; Treaty of Niagara; Wampum; Wendat (Huron)
Alnwick residential school, 230
American Revolution, 51, 79, 81, 88–89, 114, 189
Anderson, Elizabeth, 168
Anderson, Thomas Gummersall, 167–168, 171–177, 179–180, 182–184, 187–189, 191, 193–194, 197, 225–228, 231
Anglicans
    See Church of England
Anishinaabe(k), 7–9, 13–15, 17–18, 20, 22, 25–26, 32, 34–35, 37–39, 42, 44, 46, 52, 54, 61–62, 69–70, 86, 88, 95–96, 100, 103, 107, 111, 114, 117, 125–126, 134, 137, 139, 143, 145, 148–149, 155–156, 162–163, 165, 167–169, 173–174, 177, 180, 183, 187–188, 191, 196–197, 199–201, 204, 213–216, 220–221, 225–226, 237–241, 243–244, 251–253, 255–257, 259, 272, 283, 285, 291, 294–295, 297
    Great Flood re-creation story, 22
    See also Chippewas; Grand General Council of Ontario; Mississaugas of Scugog Island; Mississaugas of the Credit; Odaawaa; Ojibwe; oral tradition; Potawatomi (Bodewadmi)
annuities, 117, 176–177, 181, 206, 225–227, 237, 239–241, 243, 254–255, 259
Archeological discoveries, 24, 32
Ashanyoong
    See Lake Simcoe (Ashanyoong / Azhoonyaang)
Assance, John (Little Shell), 96, 102, 107, 117, 147–149, 167, 172, 174, 176–177, 180–181, 183, 188, 193, 196–197, 200–201, 203, 206, 208, 213, 216–217, 227–229
Assiginack, Jean-Baptiste, 180
Atherley Narrows
    See Narrows, the (Mnjikaning)
Attawandaron
    See Neutrals (Attawandaron)

B

Baby, Jacques Duperon, 44
Baby, James, 44
Bagot Commission, 221, 223–225
Bagot, Charles, 223
Balsam Lake, 107, 188–189, 213, 218
band administration
    band council, 250, 254, 259–260, 263, 271, 273, 276–277, 283
    band funds, 213, 235–237
    band lists, 203, 224, 249

band administration (*continued*)
    See also Gradual Civilization Act (1857); Indian Department / Indian Affairs Administration; Indian reserves; land rights and tenure
Battle of York, 96–97
Beausoleil First Nation, 19
Beausoleil Island, 169, 208, 216–217
Beaver Wars, 37
Beman, Eli, 171, 201
Beman, Elisha, 114–115, 127, 171
Benson Nanigishkung, Emerson, 21–23, 95, 103
Berczy, William, 81–83, 127
Big Canoe, Albert, 114, 149, 155, 169, 260, 263, 289, 291
Big Canoe, Andrew, 15, 120, 123, 194, 204, 287, 298
Big Shilling (Negenaunaquot), 149, 181, 213
Black Creek, 26, 30, 79, 84, 125, 297–298
Black Creek Pioneer Village
    See Village at Black Creek, The
Bluejay, 139, 162, 267
boats and ships, 15, 17–18, 47, 95, 112–115, 120, 123, 125, 127, 149–150, 155–156, 169, 183–184, 194, 204, 218, 233, 260, 263, 267, 269, 287, 289, 291, 298
    See also canoe; portages
Bodewadmi
    See Potawatomi (Bodewadmi)
Bond Head, Francis, 115, 189–191, 193–197, 204, 211, 214, 224
Bootaaganasiig
    See Potagunasees (Bootaaganasiig)
Borland & Roe, 109–111, 113, 173
Borland Family, 112–113
Borland, Andrew, 93, 109–113, 115, 173–174, 177, 184, 201, 203, 217, 298
Borland, Elizabeth, 111–112
Borland, John, 112
Brant, Christiana, 138
Brant, Joseph (Thayendanegea), 7, 51–52, 57, 66–68, 70–72, 79, 81–83, 99, 105, 134, 138, 274–275, 277–278, 281
    See also American Revolution; Freemasons; Haldimand Tract; Jones, Augustus; Mississaugas of the Credit; Six Nations of the Grand River
Brantford, 32, 66, 134, 219, 224, 231, 244, 258, 262, 271, 274
British and Foreign Bible Society, 133
British colonialism, 66, 76, 104–105, 117, 132, 140, 220, 255, 277, 279

    See also civilizational agenda; forts and trading posts; Indian Department / Indian Affairs administration; Indian policy; land cessions and agreements; settlers and settlement—British settlers; war and warfare
British North America Act, 249
British Wesleyan Methodists
    See Methodism—Wesleyan Methodists
Brock, Isaac, 93, 95
Buck, John (Skanawiti), 214–215, 258
Butler's Rangers, 79
Butler, John, 56, 79, 277
    See also Johnson-Butler treaties (1787–88)

C

Canada, 1, 23, 44, 51–52, 54, 89, 96, 98–99, 103, 105, 110, 134, 150, 167, 192–195, 207, 213, 216, 220, 224–225, 236, 243, 245, 249, 251, 253–254, 255–256, 259–261, 265–266, 270, 276–281, 284–285, 292, 294–295
    Confederation, 71, 249–250
    Province of, 213, 220, 236, 245
    See also Upper Canada
Canada West, 13, 212, 220, 224, 236
Canise / Kenease, 20–21, 54, 169
canoe, 17–18, 47, 95, 125, 150, 156, 267
    See also boats and ships; portages; Toronto Carrying-Place Trail; transportation
Carleton, Guy
    See Dorchester, Lord (Guy Carleton)
Catholics, 115, 133, 180, 216
    See also Odaawaa
Cayuga (Gayogo̱ho:nǫ), 9, 36, 134, 219
    See also Haudenosaunee Confederacy; Six Nations of the Grand River
Changing the Narrative project, 2, 285, 297–298
Charles, Leona, 263–264, 291
Cherokee Nation, 212, 223
Children of Peace
    See Quakers (Society of Friends); Willson, David
Chippewas, 1–2, 4, 6–9, 14–15, 21–22, 26, 39, 54, 57, 62, 69, 77–79, 87, 90, 95–99, 102–103, 105, 107, 109, 113–114, 120–121, 123, 126, 132–133, 149, 153, 155, 165–167, 169, 172–177, 179, 181–182, 184, 188–191, 193–194, 196–197, 200–209, 212, 217, 226, 228–229, 238, 240, 249, 259–260, 263–265, 269, 285, 287–289, 297

of Beausoleil First Nation, 19, 167, 169, 208, 216–217, 226, 251, 259

of Georgina Island, 2, 7, 15, 62, 114, 120, 123,126, 149,155, 165, 169, 194, 204, 217, 208, 240, 259–260, 263, 265, 269, 287–288, 297

of Lakes Huron and Simcoe, 54, 62, 79, 96, 99, 102–103, 107, 153, 167, 169, 202

of Rama, 1, 2, 4, 6–8, 14, 21-22, 26, 39, 57, 77–79, 87, 90, 95, 98, 103,107, 109, 121,132, 149, 155, 165,167, 169, 179, 184, 193, 203–209, 216–217, 226, 228–229, 251, 259–260, 264–265, 269, 285, 287, 289, 291, 297

Tri-Council, 189, 209

See also Anishinaabe(k); Assance, John (Little Shell); Beausoleil First Nation; Coldwater-Narrows Reserve; Grand General Council of Ontario; land cessions and agreements; land claims; Musquakie (William Yellowhead); Musquakie (Yellowhead); Rebellion of 1837; Snake, Joseph; War of 1812

Christian Guardian, 196, 234

Christian Island, 167, 208, 217, 251, 265

Christian names, 9, 149

Christianity, 3, 5, 7–9, 20, 28, 46, 63–64, 67–68, 111, 113, 131–141, 143–145, 147–153, 155–157, 160, 162–163, 165, 167, 174, 179, 196, 208, 212–213, 216–217, 220, 234, 251, 256, 265, 268, 289

See also Catholics; Church of England; clergy reserves; Indigenous Christianity; Methodism; missionaries; Quakers; religion

Church of England, 63, 99, 117–118, 133–134, 136, 143, 167, 179–180, 207, 216, 275

See also clergy reserves; missionaries; Strachan, John

Circle Wampum, 64

citizenship

See enfranchisement

civilizational agenda, 3, 8, 129, 131–134, 140,151, 160, 163, 165, 167, 189, 235

Clans, 36, 38–39, 62–63, 81, 114, 149, 167, 216–217, 241, 250, 257, 274

See also Doodems, 55, 73, 102, 125, 203, 238,

Claus, William, 72, 76, 96, 99

clergy reserves, 99, 143, 199

Cobeckenonk

See Humber River (Gebekanaang / Cobekhenonk)

Colborne, John, 113, 161, 167, 169, 172-174, 184, 187, 189

Colborne paddle steamer, 113, 184

Coldwater Road, 113, 169, 172–173, 175–176, 184, 189, 194

Coldwater Treaty, 193

Coldwater-Narrows Land Claim, 209

Coldwater-Narrows Reserve, 3, 165, 167–177, 179, 182–184, 189, 191, 193–194, 204, 207, 209, 217

See also Chippewas

Collins Purchase, 54, 57

Coppaway, Rhonda, 5, 289, 298

Corbiere, Alan, 2, 4, 6, 297–298

Cousineau, Ben, 4, 8, 26, 78, 98, 103, 109, 121, 132, 203, 206, 208, 228–229, 285–286, 289, 291–292, 295, 297–298

Covenant Chain, 44, 134, 224, 252

See also alliances

Covenant Chain Wampum, 44

Crane, Jacob, 109, 188

Crawford, Seth, 136, 138

Credit Chief, 214, 218

Credit Mission, 3, 7, 105, 127, 145, 151–153, 155–161, 163, 216, 223, 238–239, 266–267, 276

See also education; Field, Eliza; Herkimer, Lawrence (brother of William); Herkimer, William; Jones, John (Thayandenaged); Jones, Peter (Kahkewaquonaby / Desagondensta); Mississaugas of the Credit; Methodism; Nahnebahwequay (Sutton, Catherine); Ryerson, Egerton

Credit Mission legal code, 256, 276-7

Credit River, 3, 5, 35, 39, 99, 102, 127, 137, 141, 151, 153, 156–159, 165, 189, 203, 212, 256, 266, 276

See also Mississaugas of the Credit

Crown Lands Protection Act (1839), 212, 240

Cummer Mill, 83, 143, 145

Cummer, Elizabeth (Fisher), 3, 45, 83, 86, 143, 199–200

Cummer, Jacob, 83–84, 126, 143

Cummer, John, 84, 126, 143, 145,147, 200

Cummer, Joshua, 200

Curve Lake

See Mud Lake

D

D'Este, Augustus, 213, 270

Darling, Henry C., 165, 167

Davis, Thomas, 135–136, 138, 147, 150, 293

Davisville, 136–138

Detroit, 28, 44, 62, 88, 93, 95, 201

disclaimers, 8, 311n16

diplomacy, Indigenous
: *See* alliances; governance, Indigenous; presents
disease, 20, 28, 46–47, 76, 131–132, 195, 266–267, 270
: smallpox, 20, 28, 266–267, 270
: *See also* Credit Mission; Jones, Peter Edmund (Kahkewaquonaby); medicine, Indigenous; Oronhyatekha (Martin, Peter)
Dish with One Spoon Wampum, 17, 36–37, 39, 51, 214–216, 233, 252
dispossession
: *See* land rights and tenure—dispossession
Don River, 56, 59, 79, 82–83, 90, 126
Doodems, 36, 38, 55, 62–63, 73, 102, 125, 203, 238, 241
: *See also* Clans
Dorchester, Lord (Guy Carleton), 57, 191
Douglas, Mark, 14, 184, 207, 287, 298
Drummond Island, 112–113, 168

E

education, 67, 79, 109, 126, 133, 140, 149–153, 156–157, 159-160, 172, 179–180, 182–183, 223–227, 229–231, 234, 237, 254, 256, 262–263, 270–271, 274–275, 281–282, 285, 288, 294–295
: curriculum and teaching methods, 1, 4, 38, 46, 53, 72, 141, 151–153, 157, 159, 161, 183, 194, 214–215, 223, 229, 232, 251–252, 254, 269, 294, 297
: schools, 3, 66, 99, 113, 127, 133, 138, 144–145, 148–153, 156–157, 161, 172, 179–183, 189, 196, 213–214, 218, 223–231, 236, 238, 251, 254, 256, 263–264, 270–272, 274–275, 278, 280–281, 285
: teachers, 22, 36, 55, 67, 109, 134–135, 151–153, 156, 159, 172, 181, 223, 229, 234–236, 263, 280, 290–291, 294
: *See also* civilizational agenda; Credit Mission; industrial schools; Jones, John (Thayandenaged); manual-labour schools; Martin's Corner School; Mohawk Institute; Oxford University; residential schools; Ryerson, Egerton; schools; Toronto Normal School; Toronto School of Medicine; University of Toronto
enfranchisement, 237–238, 243, 250–251, 253–257, 273
: *See also* Gradual Enfranchisement Act (1869); Grand General Council of Ontario; Jones, Peter Edmund (Kahkewaquonaby)
environmental change, 1, 119, 123, 126, 127, 131,135, 188
: deforestation, 119, 120, 123, 125–126, 212
: habitat loss, 120, 182
: impact on wildlife, 46, 119–121, 228
: water levels, 46, 120, 125–126, 188
: water pollution, 125
: *See also* agriculture; milling; salmon
Eternal Council Fires or Yellowhead Wampum, 38–39, 214–215
Etobicoke, 61, 88, 93, 105, 200
Etobicoke Creek, 56, 76

F

Family Compact, 44, 114, 117, 199
farming
: *See* agriculture
Field, Eliza, 156, 220, 238, 240
First Nations, 2, 4, 6–9, 21, 28, 56, 61, 95, 116–117, 151–152, 166, 170, 173, 177, 193, 209, 212, 215, 221, 225, 227, 235, 237–238, 243–244, 249–250, 252, 254, 259–261, 276, 281, 285, 295, 297
: *See also individual names*
Fisher, Catherine, 45, 199
Fisher, Elizabeth
: *See* Cummer, Elizabeth (Fisher) *and also* Stong, Elizabeth (Fisher)
Fisher family, 68, 83, 84, 86
Fisher, Jacob (brother of Elizabeth [Fisher] Stong), 83–85
Fisher, Jacob, Jr., 83, 84
Fisher, Jacob, Sr., 84, 86, 199
Fisher, Jake, 199
Fisher, John, 86
fishing, 13–14, 23, 25, 35, 47, 55–57, 78, 80, 99, 102–103, 119, 121, 123, 125–126, 159–162, 172, 179, 182, 184, 188, 191, 212, 217, 219, 233, 236–238, 242–245, 249, 253, 264, 267, 289–290
Fishing Act of 1857, 237
: *See also* Narrows, the (Mnjikaning); salmon
Five Nations, 9, 32, 37, 40, 71–72, 95, 236
: *See also* Haudenosaunee Confederacy
Five Nations or Aienwatha / Hiawatha Wampum, 37
Fort Rouillé
: *See* Fort Toronto
Fort Toronto, 41–42
: *See also* fur trade
forts and trading posts, 17, 35, 41–43, 46, 61, 88, 93, 95–96, 105, 107, 110, 115-116

Francouer, Catherine Mathiasnockoue, 112
fraternal organizations, 277–279
   See also Freemasons; Independent Order of Foresters
Freemasons, 277–278
French colonialism and influence, 9, 13–14, 18, 26, 28, 32, 35, 37, 39, 41–43, 45–46, 72, 79–81, 87–88, 112, 115, 133–134, 147–148, 211, 230, 237, 249
   See also forts and trading posts; fur trade; Montreal; war and warfare
French royalists, 79–80, 87–88
fur trade, 18, 20, 28, 35, 37, 39, 41–46, 88, 93, 107–115, 118, 121, 149–150, 174, 215
fur traders, 17, 28, 41, 44–47, 64, 66, 93, 107, 109, 111–115, 133, 148–149, 163, 167–168, 184, 270
   See also Albany, New York; alcohol; alliances; Baby, Jacques Duperon; Borland, Andrew; Borland & Roe; Fort Toronto; Holland Landing; Humber River (Gebekanaang / Cobekhenonk); intermarriage; Magasin Royal; Montreal; Newmarket; Oswego; Quetton St. George, Laurent (Waubewayquon); Robinson, Peter; Robinson, William; Rousseau, Jean-Baptiste St. John; Rousseau, Jean-Bonaventure; Shepard, Joseph, Sr.; Wade, Ferral

G

Gabekanaang
   See Humber River (Gebekanaang / Cobekhenonk)
Ganetsekwyagon, 15, 35
   See also Seneca (Onödowa'ga)
Ganiodaio
   See Handsome Lake (Ganiodaio)
Gayogǫho:nǫ
   See Cayuga (Gayogǫho:nǫ)
gender roles, 156
   See also women
Georgina Island, 165, 208, 217, 251, 265, 289, 290
   See also Chippewas—of Georgina Island
German Flatts, 81
gift-giving
   See presents
Gill, Jacob, 110, 177, 183, 208
Givins, James, 70, 96, 102, 133, 140–141, 144, 147–148, 159, 161, 169, 174–176, 182, 187–188, 191, 193, 197, 220
Glenelg, Lord (Charles Grant), 140, 190, 196–197, 201, 211, 216

governance, Indigenous, 26, 38, 45, 63, 68, 118, 155, 160, 212, 215–217, 240, 250–251, 253, 255, 257, 259–260, 263, 289
   Council Fires, 38–39, 214–215
   General Councils, 138, 156, 160, 195, 212, 225-229, 251–257, 259–260, 265, 281
   hereditary chiefs, 63, 68, 195, 241, 251, 258, 260, 263, 274
   Men's Councils, 241
   Women's Councils, 241
   See also alliances; Anishinaabe(k); Clans; Credit Mission legal code; Haudenosaunee Confederacy; Grand General Council of Ontario; Great Law of Peace; sovereignty
Gradual Civilization Act (1857), 224, 237–238, 240, 243, 250–251, 276
Gradual Enfranchisement Act (1869), 250–251, 273
Grand General Council of Ontario, 251–257, 259–260, 265, 281, 298
   See also enfranchisement; Gradual Civilization Act (1857); Indian Act (1876); Jones, Peter Edmund (Kahkewaquonaby); Oronhyatekha (Martin, Peter); Six Nations of the Grand River; Union of Ontario Indians
Grand River, 7, 52, 61, 66, 80, 93, 95, 131, 133, 135–136, 138, 141, 153, 155, 187, 215, 219, 233, 236, 274–275
   See also Six Nations of the Grand River
Grand River Navigation Company, 236
Great Law of Peace, 5, 37, 260
Great Peace of Montreal (1701), 36–37
Great Sail, 20–21
"Gunshot Treaty", 56
   See also Johnson-Butler treaties (1787–88)
Gwillimbury (East and West), 87, 103, 288, 290

H

Haldimand Proclamation (1784), 52–53, 219, 232, 292
Haldimand Tract, 61, 67–68, 70, 72, 81, 83, 116, 134, 187, 219, 233, 239, 244, 256, 274, 292
   See also Brant, Joseph (Thayendanegea); Jones, Augustus; Six Nations of the Grand River; Tekarihogen, Henry
Hale, Horatio, 258, 260
Handsome Lake (Ganiodaio), 67, 134–135
harvesting and gathering, 5, 25, 35, 87, 107, 125, 156, 159, 179, 217, 223, 226, 229, 289

Haudenosaunee, 3, 6–9, 18, 20, 25–26, 28–29, 32, 35–37, 39–40, 42, 51–52, 61, 63–65, 67–68, 70–72, 81, 89, 93, 95–96, 98, 105, 125, 131, 134–135, 155–156, 212, 214–216, 219–220, 233–234, 236, 240–241, 244, 250–253, 257, 260, 265, 274, 277–278, 281, 283, 294
   See also agriculture; Haudenosaunee Confederacy; land rights and tenure; Mohawk (Kanien'keha:ka); Six Nations of the Grand River; Tyendinaga
Haudenosaunee Confederacy, 7, 9, 28, 36–37, 51, 63–64, 89, 93, 156, 216, 236, 256–257, 260
   Clan Mothers, 63, 81, 241
   Royaners (Hereditary Chiefs), 7, 63, 81, 93, 241, 257
   See also alliances; Cayuga (Gayogo̱ho:nǫ); Great Law of Peace; Mohawk (Kanien'keha:ka); Oneida (Onyota'a:ka); Onondaga (Onoñda'gega); Seneca (Onödowa'ga); Six Nations of the Grand River; treaties; Tuscarora (Skarù:re); Wampum
Head of the Lake Purchase (Treaty 14), 74, 76, 99, 127
Henry, Alexander, 17
Henry, Sarah
   See Tuhbenahneequay
Herkimer, Lawrence, Sr., 163
Herkimer, Lawrence, Jr., 95, 163, 219
Herkimer, William, 162–163, 219
Hill, Susan, 256, 265, 269, 298
Hill, Tayler, 292, 297
historical interpretation, 2, 7–8, 37, 215, 297
historical memory, 5, 298
   intergenerational transmission, 5–6, 37
   Wampum Keepers, 37, 214
   See also oral tradition; Wampum
History of the Ojebway Indians, 119, 220, 268
   See also Jones, Peter (Kahkewaquonaby / Desagondensta)
Hoeg, Lauri, 126, 265, 269, 288, 290, 294, 297–298
Holland Landing, 20, 22, 62–63, 87, 89, 103, 107–109, 113–116, 127, 147–148, 183–184, 200–203
Holland River, 18, 62, 87, 107, 110, 114, 165, 217
Home District, 61, 123, 180, 200
horticulture, 25, 134
housing, 26, 66, 99, 119, 123, 134–135, 140–141, 144, 147, 156–157, 159, 161, 169, 171–173, 176, 179, 181–182, 188, 196, 204, 207–208, 217, 219, 238, 266, 289, 294
Howe, Joseph, 253
humanitarianism, 104, 140, 165, 195, 235

Humber River (Gebekanaang / Cobekhenonk), 3, 14, 15, 18, 23, 26–28, 30–32, 35, 41–45, 56–57, 76, 79, 96, 107, 119, 124–127, 138, 140, 162–163, 266–267
   watershed, 3, 23, 26, 30, 61, 79
   See also Toronto Carrying-Place Trail
hunting, 3, 23, 25, 28, 32, 35, 47, 55–56, 99, 102–103, 107, 121, 131, 133–134, 152, 156, 159, 161, 166, 169, 179, 182–183, 187, 189, 191, 193, 200, 203–204, 212, 215, 217, 237–238, 249, 265
hunting territories, 32, 47, 107, 121, 152, 166, 200, 203, 212
Hurlburt, Sylvester, 208
Huron
   See Wendat (Huron) *and also* Lake Huron; Chippewas—of Lakes Huron and Simcoe
Huron-Wendat Nation, 16, 27–28
Huronia, 26, 28, 168

I

Immigration
   See settlers and settlement
Independent Order of Foresters, 278
Indian Act (1876), 2, 249, 253–255, 257, 259–261, 263, 276
Indian Department / Indian Affairs administration, 9, 46, 54, 56, 63, 66, 71–72, 78–79, 83, 89, 93, 96, 99, 165, 167–169, 174, 197, 201, 204, 207, 212–213, 219–221, 223, 225, 229–230, 235–236, 240, 242–245, 250–251, 253–254, 257, 259, 263, 271, 275–278, 281
   Indian agents, 66, 70, 133, 140–141, 144, 159, 167, 225, 235–237, 240–241, 244, 254, 259, 263–264, 276–278, 282, 285
   See also Anderson, Thomas Gummersall; Claus, William; Givins, James; Indian policy; Jarvis, Samuel Peters; Thorburn, David
Indian policy
   assimilation, 164–165, 214, 223–225, 235, 237, 254–256, 280
   Colonial Office, 104, 204, 211, 220
   Darling Report, 165
   Indian Advancement Act of 1884, 259, 276
   Indian status, 9, 212, 241, 245, 249–250, 253, 257, 277
   Pennefather Commission, 236–238
   See also Bagot Commission; Bond Head, Francis; civilizational agenda; Colborne, John; enfranchisement; Gradual Civilization Act (1857); Gradual Enfranchisement Act (1869); Indian Act (1876); Indian reserves; Johnson, John; land cessions

and agreements; Macdonald, John A.; Maitland, Peregrine; Metcalfe, Charles; Portland, Duke of (William Henry Cavendish-Bentinck); Russell, Peter; residential schools; Simcoe, John Graves; Sydenham, Lord (Charles Poulett Thomson)

Indian reserves, 3, 7, 21, 105, 112, 120, 127, 132, 158, 165, 167, 169–173, 175–176, 181–182, 184, 188–189, 191, 193, 204–207, 209, 212, 214, 217–218, 224, 229–231, 233–234, 236–237, 239–240, 243, 249–251, 253–254, 265, 270–272, 285, 291

Indigenous Christianity, 131–141, 179–180, 216, 256
  See also Methodism—Indigenous Methodism; Jones, Peter (Kahkewaquonaby / Desagondensta)

Indigenous spirituality
  medicine people, 5, 119, 148, 268, 271, 289, 291, 296
  spirit beings, 96, 139, 148
  worldview, 1, 22, 132, 137, 162, 256, 267, 290–291
  See also Handsome Lake (Ganiodaio); Indigenous Christianity

industrial schools, 224, 229
  See also residential schools

intermarriage, 3, 7, 42, 46, 61, 66, 109, 111, 114, 156, 239–240, 273

Iroquoian, 25–26

Iroquois
  See Haudenosaunee

J

Jameson, Anna, 190–191
Jarvis, Samuel Peters, 82–83, 116, 191, 193, 201, 203–204, 212–214, 219, 221
Jarvis, William, 83, 90, 116
Johnson, John Smoke (Sakayengwaraton), 97, 214, 219, 254, 258, 260, 274, 281
Johnson, John, 54–55, 58, 76, 89, 277
Johnson, William, 44–45
Johnson-Butler treaties (1787-88), 52, 54–57, 62, 74, 79
  See also "Gunshot Treaty"; land cessions and agreements—First "purchase" at Toronto
Jones, Augustus, 53, 61–69, 87, 99,125, 136, 138, 151, 268
  See also Brant, Joseph (Thayendanegea); Haldimand Tract; Jones, John (Thayendanged); Jones, Peter (Kahkewaquonaby / Desagondensta); Tekarihogen, Henry; Tekarihogen, Sarah; Tuhbenahneequay; Wahbanosay / Wabenose

Jones, Eliza
  See Field, Eliza
Jones, John (Thayendanaged), 63, 66, 99, 120, 138, 145, 159, 163, 219, 221, 240
Jones, Peter (Kahkewaquonaby / Desagondensta), 63, 68, 96, 99, 105, 113, 119–120, 127, 131, 136–140, 143, 145, 147–156, 160, 163–164, 179–180, 187, 195, 197, 211, 213–214, 216–217, 219–220, 223–227, 230–231, 234, 238–240, 254, 256, 266–268, 270, 281
  See also Credit Mission; Methodism; missionaries; Mississaugas of the Credit; petitions; Ryerson, Egerton; Victoria, Queen
Jones, Peter Edmund (Kahkewaquonaby), 255–256, 259, 265–266, 268, 270–272, 275, 277, 280, 283
  See also enfranchisement; Grand General Council of Ontario; Macdonald, John A.; New Credit

K

Kahkewahquonaby
  See Jones, Peter (Kahkewaquonaby / Desagondensta); Jones, Peter Edmund (Kahkewahquonaby)
Kaiser family, 83, 93
Kandoching, 156
Kanien'kehá:ka
  See Mohawk (Kanien'kehá:ka) and also Haudenosaunee Confederacy; Six Nations of the Grand River
Kenease
  See Canise / Kenease
Kinepinew
  See Quinepenon / Kinepinew (Golden Eagle)
King, Carolyn, 35, 125, 140, 233, 245, 265, 288, 293–294
Kingston, 46, 69, 78, 115, 200, 213
kiskisiwin | remembering (film), 2

L

Lake Couchiching, 13, 149, 184, 206
Lake Huron, 7, 15, 20, 35, 46, 54, 69, 79, 93, 95, 115, 143, 168–169, 190, 230
Lake Ontario, 13–14, 17, 20, 25, 28–29, 32, 35, 39, 41, 51–52, 56–57, 61–62, 69, 71, 76, 110, 125, 127, 153, 156, 218, 233
Lake Scugog, 35, 103, 147, 149, 187–188, 218
Lake Simcoe (Ashanyoong / Azhoonyaang), 13–15, 17–18, 20, 26, 28, 35, 54, 57, 62–63, 79–80, 82, 86, 99, 102–103, 105, 107, 109, 113, 115, 117, 123, 143, 145, 147, 150, 152–153, 155, 165, 167, 169, 179, 187–188, 201, 204, 208, 213, 216–217, 221, 230

land cessions and agreements, 52, 54, 57, 61–62, 74, 99, 102, 158, 168–169, 236, 245
    Ajetance Treaty (Treaty 19), 99, 103
    Between the Lakes Treaty (1784), 51–52, 241
    Coldwater Treaty, 193–194
    Collins Purchase, 54, 57
    First "purchase" at Toronto (1787), 52, 54–59, 62, 69, 71–72, 89
    Head of the Lake Purchase (Treaty 14), 74, 76, 99, 127
    Lake Simcoe Purchase (Treaty 16), 102, 105, 169
    Lake Simcoe-Nottawasaga (Treaty 18), 99, 102–103, 169
    Manitoulin Island (Treaty 45), 189, 191,
    Owen Sound Treaty (Treaty 82), 239
    Penetanguishene Purchase of 1798 (Treaty 5), 169
    Rice Lake Purchase of 1818 (Treaty 20), 103
    Saugeen Peninsula Treaty (Treaty 72), 239
    Saugeen Tract (Treaty 45 ½), 191–192, 194, 208, 219, 225, 231
    Toronto Purchase of 1805 (Treaty 13), 62–63, 73–76
    Treaty 22, 158
    Treaty 23, 158
    Williams Treaties, 62, 166, 169
    See also "Gunshot Treaty"; Haldimand Tract; Johnson-Butler treaties (1787–88)
land claims, 3, 6, 76, 209, 243, 276
    See also Chippewa—Tri-Council; Mississaugas of the Credit; Six Nations of the Grand River
land rights and tenure, 140, 187, 197, 237, 239, 294
    dispossession, 1, 74, 98, 102–103, 115, 132, 197, 231, 239
    fee simple, 68, 214
    location tickets, 250, 253
    Nanfan Deed (1701), 7, 32, 39
    settler encroachment (squatters), 6, 99, 147, 179, 188, 191, 206, 212, 219, 233, 239
    title deeds, 197, 201, 211, 213–214, 216, 224, 243
    See also Gradual Civilization Act (1857); Haldimand Tract; women
languages, Indigenous, 5, 9, 42, 47, 61, 78, 88, 96, 109–111, 134–135, 137, 140, 149, 151–152, 180, 196, 208, 213, 229, 234, 240, 251, 263, 266, 273, 275, 277, 280, 285, 287, 289–290, 295, 297
LaRocca, Kelly, 5, 286, 291, 295–296, 298
Lavallee, Celeste, 112
    See also Borland, John
Lavallee, Denis David, 112

Lawson, Sherry, 1, 77, 207, 226, 287, 298
Lines, Nathaniel, 57–58
literacy
    See education
logging, 119, 123, 127, 182, 217, 236
    See also environmental change—deforestation
London, England, 197, 211, 223, 241
London, Ontario, 219, 225, 230, 271, 276
Longhouse religion
    See Handsome Lake (Ganiodaio); Indigenous Spirituality
Lower Canada (Canada East / Quebec), 27–28, 77, 89, 112, 200, 220, 224, 249
Loyalists, 45, 51, 62, 68, 77, 79, 81, 89, 105, 115–117, 274

M

Macdonald, John A., 254, 273, 276–277
Mackenzie, William Lyon, 199–200
Magasin Royal, 41
See also fur trade
    Maitland, Peregrine, 133, 141, 144
Manitoulin Island, 189, 191, 194–195, 204, 208, 245
manual-labour schools, 223, 225, 229
    See also education; residential schools
Markham, 82–83
marriage, 35, 45, 61, 63–64, 67, 111–114, 159, 256, 259
    loss of status for marrying out, 237–238, 240–241, 245, 250, 253–254, 257
    See also intermarriage
Martin, George, 93, 231, 233, 244, 254, 274
Martin, George Henry, 134, 274
Martin, Peter
    See Oronhyatekha (Martin, Peter)
Martin's Corner School, 274
mastodon, 23–24
Matchedash, 17–18, 20, 52, 54, 57, 102, 153, 165, 167–169, 187, 217
Matchedash Tract, 102, 168–169
McLean, James, 127, 244
medicinal plants, 66, 265, 268–272
medicine, Indigenous, 66, 156, 266, 268–272
    medicine person / healer, 5, 119, 148, 265, 268–269, 271–272, 289, 291, 296
    See also medicinal plants
Mesquacosy, 63, 270
Metcalfe, Charles, 225

Methodism, 46, 64, 113, 117, 132–141, 143–144, 149–153, 155–157, 162–163, 167, 175, 179–180, 194–197, 216, 234, 256
  camp meetings, 3, 136, 143–147, 149, 179
  Episcopal Methodists, 64, 133, 138, 167, 179
  Indigenous Methodism, 113, 136–141, 143–149, 151, 153–155, 157, 161, 163, 179, 197, 213
  Newmarket Branch Missionary Society, 141
  Toronto Circuit, 155
  Wesleyan Methodists, 153, 155, 167, 194, 216
  Yonge Street Circuit, 143
  See also Crawford, Seth; Credit Mission; Indigenous Christianity; Jones, John (Thayandenaged); Jones, Peter (Kahkewaquonaby / Desagondensta); missionaries; Ryerson, Egerton; Sunday, John (Shawundais)
Michi Saagiig
  See Mississaugas
militia, 42, 81, 87, 93, 95, 98, 118, 200–201, 203
milling, 82–83, 109, 114–115, 119, 122–123, 125–127, 176, 181–182, 189, 196, 199, 201, 203, 219, 279, 297
  gristmills, 123, 126–127, 172, 176–177, 183, 196–197
  See also sawmills
missionaries, 3, 7, 105, 113, 117, 127, 132–133, 136, 139–141, 143, 145, 147, 149–160, 163, 167, 175, 179–180, 189, 194–196, 207–208, 216, 218–219, 223–224, 226–227, 230, 235–236, 238–239, 241, 254, 256, 271, 275, 281–282
  missionary societies, 147, 149, 153
  See also Catholics; Church of England; Credit Mission; Indigenous Christianity; Methodism
Mississauga-Haudenosaunee alliance of the 1790s, 71–72
Mississaugas, 2, 5–7, 9, 18, 20, 26, 31–33, 35, 37, 41–42, 44, 46, 51–52, 54–57, 59, 61–64, 68–74, 76–78, 80–81, 83, 95–97, 99, 101–103, 105, 109, 113, 117, 119, 121, 123, 125, 127, 131, 133, 136–141, 144–145, 147, 150, 152–153, 155–167, 169, 187–189, 192, 197, 200–201, 203–204, 211–214, 218–219, 225, 228, 231–234, 239–240, 243–245, 249–250, 254, 259, 263–267, 270–272, 276–277, 283, 285–286, 288–289, 291, 293, 296–298
Mississaugas of Scugog Island, 2, 5, 7, 35, 56, 103, 109, 153, 187–188, 213, 218, 226, 230, 251, 259, 263–265, 289, 291, 296–298
  See also Balsam Lake
Mississaugas of the Credit, 2, 5–7, 32, 35, 56, 61, 72, 74, 76, 101, 127, 131, 138, 140, 144, 152, 157, 159–160, 163, 167, 169, 187–188, 192, 197, 213, 218–219, 231, 233–234, 239, 244, 271–272, 285–286, 293, 297

Wabakinine, 52, 55–56, 69–71, 131
Wabbicommicot, 44
See also Anishinaabe(k); Credit Mission; Jones, Peter (Kahkewaquonaby / Desagondensta); Jones, Peter Edmund (Kahkewaquonaby) land cessions and agreements; land rights and tenure; Mississauga-Haudenosaunee alliance of the 1790s; New Credit; petitions; Pokquan; Pontiac's War; Sawyer, Joseph (Nawahjekezhegwabe); War of 1812
Mitchell, Andrew, 184
Mitchell, Elizabeth, 168
mixed heritage, 163, 224
  See also intermarriage
Mnjikaning
  See Narrows, the (Mnjikaning); Orillia; Tkaranto
Mohawk (Kanien'keha:ka), 9, 13, 28, 51–52, 57, 61, 63–64, 66, 81, 83, 89, 133–136, 138, 153, 187, 190, 214–215, 219, 224, 226, 228, 251, 256, 258, 262–263, 267–268, 273–275, 280
  See also Haudenosaunee Confederacy; Six Nations of the Grand River
Mohawk Chapel, 134
Mohawk Institute, 224, 262–263, 274–275
  See also residential schools
Mohawk Valley, 81
Montgomery's Tavern, 199
Monthly Review Devoted to the Civil Government of the Canadas, 220
Montreal, 28, 36–37, 39, 41, 107, 110, 118, 174, 215
Monture, Phil, 39–40, 51, 95, 219, 236, 260–261, 285, 289, 294, 298
Mount Elgin Industrial School, 230
  See also industrial schools; residential schools
Mud Lake, 56, 109, 188, 216, 218, 265
Munceytown, 216, 219, 225, 230
Munsee-Delaware, 153, 251
Murdoch, Chandra, 252, 254–255, 276, 298
Muskoka, 18, 20, 41, 107, 112, 217, 286
Musquakie (William Yellowhead), 38–39, 96, 102, 107, 117, 149, 167, 171–172, 174, 179, 181–183, 188–189, 191, 193, 203, 206–208, 213–217, 227–229
Musquakie (Yellowhead), 62, 96

Index   349

N

Nahnebahwequay (Sutton, Catherine), 219, 238–245, 266
Nainigishkung, 200
Nanaboozhoo, 22
Nanebeaujou, 45
Nanfan Deed (1701), 7, 32, 39
    See also Haudenosaunee; land claims; land rights and tenure
Nanigishking, Thomas, 95, 269
Nanigishkung, Emerson Benson, 21–23, 95, 103, 155, 181, 213, 229, 298
Narrows, the (Mnjikaning), 13–14, 17, 35, 39, 88, 105, 107, 110, 113, 153, 165, 167, 169–170, 172–175, 177, 179–180, 182–184, 188–189, 191, 193, 196–197, 204, 206, 208, 215, 225
    See also Orillia; Tkaronto
Nawahjekezhegwabe
    See Sawyer, Joseph (Nawahjekezhegwabe)
Nawash, 209, 239–242
Negenaunaquot
    See Big Shilling (Negenauanaquot)
Nehkik (Otter), 82–83
    See also Jarvis, Samuel Peters
Neolin, 139
Neutrals (Attawandaron), 25–26, 28
New Credit, 7, 163, 203, 230, 232–234, 239, 265, 268, 271–273, 276, 278
    See also Mississaugas of the Credit
New England Company, 274
New France, 18, 44, 81
    See also French colonialism and influence
New York City, 149
New York State (formerly Colony), 28, 51, 61, 81, 266
Newcastle, Duke of (Henry Pelham Fiennes Pelham-Clinton), 241–245
Newhouse, Seth, 260
Newmarket, 79, 104, 107–118, 121, 127, 141, 143, 155, 171, 201, 270
Niagara, 15, 17, 44, 61, 69, 81, 83, 88–89, 93, 95, 125, 127, 201, 224
Nimquasim, 69
North York Historical Society, 86
Norton, John, 95

O

Odaawaa (Ottawa), 9, 25, 180, 259, 273
    See also Anishinaabe(k)
Ohio Valley, 87, 189
Ojibwe, 9, 86, 180, 191
    See also Anishinaabe(k)
Old Sail, 20
Oneida (Onyota'a:ka), 9, 81, 153, 219
    See also Haudenosaunee Confederacy
Onödowa'ga
    See Seneca (Onödowa'ga)
Onoñda'gega
    See Onondaga (Onoñda'gega)
Onondaga (Onoñda'gega), 9, 214
    See also Haudenosaunee Confederacy
Ontario, 1, 7, 13–14, 28, 32–33, 52, 61 100, 103, 105, 116, 120–121, 208, 215 220, 225, 230, 249–250, 262, 274, 276–278, 283, 294, 298
    See also Canada West; Grand General Council of Ontario; Lake Ontario; Union of Ontario Indians; Upper Canada
Onyota'a:ka
    See Oneida (Onyota'a:ka)
oral tradition, 5, 32, 35, 37, 86, 220, 268
    See also historical memory; Wampum
Orillia, 3, 32, 169, 171, 175, 183, 193, 225, 227, 229, 281
    See also Narrows, the (Mnjikaning)
Oro Township, 105
Oronhyatekha (Martin, Peter), 93, 233, 244, 254, 257, 265–266, 268, 271, 273–281, 283
    See also fraternal organizations; Grand General Council of Ontario; Independent Order of Foresters; Mohawk Institute; Oxford University; Royal Tour of 1860; Temple Building
Oshawa, 7, 109
Oswego, 41–42
Ottawa (city), 253–254, 259, 273
Ottawa (Odaawaa)
    See Odaawaa (Ottawa)
Ottawa River, 41
Owen Sound, 225, 230–231, 239
Oxford University, 275
    See also Oronhyatekha (Martin, Peter)

P

Palatine Germans
    See settlers and settlement—German settlers
Parsons site, 26
Peace treaties, 83
    See also Dish with One Spoon Wampum; Great Peace of Montreal (1701); Treaty of Ghent; Treaty of Niagara; Treaty of Paris
Penetanguishene, 20, 26, 102–103, 105, 107, 112, 119, 147, 169, 171, 180, 184
Penetanguishene Purchase (Treaty 5), 169
Penn, William, 79, 83, 87
Pennefather Commission, 236–237
Pennefather, Richard, 236
Pennsylvania, 3, 66, 68, 81–83, 86–89, 110
Pennsylvania Germans
    See settlers and settlement—German settlers
Peterborough, 35, 109, 115, 153
petitions, 20, 161, 182, 189, 191, 194–197, 201, 204, 207, 211, 213, 216, 238, 242–244, 253, 257, 260, 277
Pierpoint, Richard, 89
Playter, George, 117, 138, 145, 147
Pledge of the Crown Wampum, 96
Pokquan, 51
Pontiac's War, 44
Port Credit, 127
Port Perry, 218
portages, 7, 14–15, 17–18, 20, 28, 35, 41, 54, 107, 109, 169, 172, 227
    See also canoe; Humber River (Gebekanaang / Cobekhenonk); Toronto Carrying-Place Trail; transportation
Portland, Duke of (William Henry Cavendish-Bentinck), 70–71
Potagunasees (Bootaaganasiig), 169, 172
Potawatomi (Bodewadmi), 9, 166, 200, 259
Powell, William Dummer, 116
presents, 20, 39, 45, 55–56, 69–72, 86, 95, 98–99, 131, 138, 140–141, 147–148, 159, 161, 165, 167–168, 174, 190, 213, 224–225, 235, 237, 244
    See also alcohol; alliances; fur trade
Prince of Wales (Albert Edward), 242–244, 275
Puhgashkis(h), 63, 96

Q

Quakers (Society of Friends), 79, 83, 87, 241
Quebec, 27–28, 77, 112, 220, 249
    See also Lower Canada (Canada East / Quebec)
Queen's Rangers, 62, 71, 88
Quetton St. George, Laurent (Waubewayquon), 88, 115
Quinepenon / Kinepinew (Golden Eagle), 76, 121, 125, 131, 266

R

railway, 212, 285
Rama, Chippewas of
    See Chippewas—of Rama
Rebellion of 1837, 197, 199–203, 211
reciprocity, 20, 45, 86, 233, 278
    See also presents
religion, 67, 121, 135, 148, 155, 157, 159, 208, 229, 231, 234, 285
    See also Christianity; Indigenous spirituality
removal policy, 167, 189–90, 195–197, 200, 204, 224, 227
    See also Bond Head, Francis
residential schools, 230, 256, 263–264, 280–281
    See also education; industrial schools; manual-labour schools; Mohawk Institute; Mount Elgin Industrial School
revitalization movements, 139
Rice Lake, 32, 103, 153, 163, 189, 216, 224, 268
Rice Lake Purchase (Treaty 20), 103
Robinson Huron Treaty, 117
Robinson Superior Treaty, 117
Robinson, Christopher, 114–115
Robinson, John Beverley, 116
Robinson, Peter, 93, 114–116, 127, 133, 184
Robinson, William, 114, 116–117, 193
Roe, William, 109–111, 113, 171, 173–174, 270
    See also Borland & Roe
Rogers, Timothy, 87
Rouge River, 15, 28, 35, 41
Rousseau, Jean-Baptiste St. John, 45, 93
Rousseau, Jean-Bonaventure, 45
Royal Proclamation of 1763, 67, 70, 189, 191, 239, 249
Royal Tour of 1860, 242–244
Russell, Peter, 69–70, 72, 78, 87, 89–90, 268
Ryerson, Egerton, 143–144, 149, 157, 159, 196, 216, 223, 229, 268, 270

S

Sakayengwaraton
   See Johnson, John Smoke (Sakayengwaraton)
salmon, 57, 80, 125, 127, 145, 161–162, 218–219
   See also fishing
Sandy, Marcie, 4, 297
Saugeen Ojibwe, 191
Saugeen Peninsula Treaty (Treaty 72), 239
Saugeen Tract, 191–192, 194, 208, 219, 225, 231
Saugeen Tract Treaty 45 ½, 191–192
Sault, Garry, 96, 234, 243, 264, 270–272, 285, 298
Sault, Margaret, 5–6, 18, 56, 72, 164, 250, 277, 286, 298
sawmills, 83, 123, 125, 127, 159, 172, 177, 182–183, 197, 208, 218, 233
Sawyer, David (Kezhegowinninne), 137, 219, 239, 242, 267
Sawyer, Joseph (Nawahjekezhegwabe), 149, 160, 213, 219, 221, 228, 239
Sayre, Esther, 114
Scarborough, 62, 83, 93
schools
   Seee education—schools
Scott, Duncan Campbell, 254, 276
Scugog Island, Mississaugas of, 2, 5, 7, 107, 187–189, 213, 218, 259, 263–264, 289, 291, 296–297
Seneca (Onödowa'ga), 9, 15, 26, 28, 31–32, 35, 41, 67, 116, 134, 219
   villages in Toronto area, 15, 28, 32, 35, 41, 46
   See also Haudenosaunee Confederacy; Six Nations of the Grand River
settlers and settlement, 1–3, 7–8, 13, 20–23, 45, 47, 51, 55, 59, 61–62, 64, 67–72, 74, 76–84, 87–90, 93, 95, 98–99, 103–105, 110–111, 113, 116–121, 123, 125–127, 131–134, 136, 139–141, 143, 152–153, 155–156, 159, 164–165, 167, 169, 171–173, 175–176, 179–184, 188–189, 191, 195–197, 199–201, 204, 206, 209, 211–212, 216–220, 224–227, 231, 233, 235–236, 238, 241, 249, 253, 255–256, 260, 263–270, 274, 276, 281, 285, 288, 292, 294–295, 298
   American settlers, 77–79, 103,118
   Black settlers, 79, 89–90, 105, 116
   British settlers, 77, 79, 89, 103–105, 117, 195, 199
   German settlers, 68, 79, 81–83, 89
   See also Loyalists
Seven Years War, 42
Shawundais
   See Sunday, John (Shawundais)
Shepard, Joseph, Sr. 45, 93, 199–200
Shepard, Joseph, Jr., 200
Simcoe, Elizabeth Posthuma, 13, 18, 29–21, 58–59, 66, 78
Simcoe, John Graves, 13, 18, 20, 57–58, 77, 83, 90, 114, 123, 165
Six Nations of the Grand River, 2, 4–5, 7–9, 32, 35, 39–40, 42, 45, 51–53, 63, 68, 70–72, 80, 95–97, 115, 153, 189, 201, 215–216, 219–220, 226, 231–234, 236, 238, 244, 251, 253, 256–258, 260–261, 273–275, 277, 285, 289, 292, 294, 297–298
   disclaimer, 8, 311n16
   See also American Revolution; Brant, Joseph (Thayendanegea); Buck, John (Skanawiti); Grand General Council of Ontario; Haldimand Proclamation; Haldimand Tract; Haudenosaunee; Haudenosaunee Confederacy; Indian Act (1876); Johnson, John Smoke (Sakayengwaraton); Martin, George; Mississauga-Haudenosaunee alliance of the 1790s; Mohawk Institute; Tekarihogen, Henry; War of 1812
Skanawiti
   See Buck, John (Skanawiti)
Skandatut, 26
slavery and slave trade, 44, 47, 89–90, 105, 115, 140, 196
   abolition, 90, 105
Smith, Donald B., 298
Snache, Kory, 14, 39, 57, 79, 87, 90, 107, 109, 149, 155, 167, 209, 289
Snache, Vicki, 6, 26, 165, 179, 264, 289, 291–292, 298
Snake Island, 121, 167, 193, 203, 209, 217, 221, 226, 269
Snake, Joseph, 144, 149, 165, 167, 174, 208, 213, 217, 228, 240
Snake, William, 113, 149
Snake, Ryerson, 149
Society for Converting and Civilizing the Indians, 181
Society of Friends
   See Quakers (Society of Friends)
sovereignty, 39, 132, 160, 179, 214, 220, 238, 252–253, 256, 260, 263, 277, 284
   See also governance, Indigenous
spirituality, Indigenous
   See Indigenous spirituality
squatters
   See land rights and tenure—settler encroachment
Squires, Philemon, 113, 174

Stennett, Miles, 201, 203, 208
Stevens, Matthew, 217, 288-289, 292, 294, 297-298
Stewart, John, 133
Stong, Daniel, 1, 3, 86, 93, 199-200
Stong, Elizabeth (Fisher), 3, 45, 85, 199-200
Strachan, John, 117, 140
Sunday, John (Shawundais), 143, 162, 213, 216-217, 226, 256, 281
surveying, 52, 56-57, 61-62, 66, 68, 127, 171, 231, 298
   See also Jones, Augustus
Sutton, Catherine
   See Nahnebahwequay (Sutton, Catherine)
Sutton, William, 239
Sydenham, Lord (Charles Poulett Thomson), 211-212
Sylvestre, Jean-Baptiste, 112-113

T

Tanikawabononkoua, 113
Taugaiwinini, 188, 201
teachers
   See education—teachers
Tecumseh, 95, 98, 139, 189
Teiaiagon, 15, 28, 32, 41, 46
   See also Seneca (Onödowa'ga)
Tekarihogen, Henry, 66-68, 134
Tekarihogen, Sarah, 63, 65-66, 136, 268
Telford, Rhonda, 204
Temple Building, 279-280, 283
Thayendanegea
   See Brant, Joseph (Thayendanegea)
Thayendenaged
   See Jones, John (Thayandenaged)
Thorburn, David, 238
Thornhill, 79, 82, 127
Tkaranto, 13
   See also Narrows, the (Mnjikaning)
Tobeco, James, 163
Toronto (city and region), 1-4, 7, 11, 13-14, 17 , 23-24, 26-28, 32, 37, 41-42, 44, 52, 54-59, 61-62, 68-69, 72, 76, 80, 86-89, 96, 99, 104-105, 107, 117, 120, 122, 127, 147, 149-150, 155, 168-169, 184, 190, 193-194, 196, 199-200, 203, 211-213, 215, 234-236, 239, 242-243, 249-250, 261, 265-268, 270-272, 275-276, 278-282, 285, 288, 293, 295, 297-298
   newspapers, 65, 89, 152, 241, 255, 280

   See also Fort Toronto; land cessions and agreements—First "purchase" at Toronto (1787); Toronto Carrying-Place Trail; Toronto Purchase of 1805; Temple Building; York; Yonge Street
Toronto and Region Conservation Authority, 1, 27, 85, 123, 297
Toronto Carrying-Place Trail, 11, 14-18, 20, 26, 28, 32, 35, 41-42, 54, 63, 76, 102, 107, 109, 165, 169, 172
Toronto Normal School, 229
Toronto Purchase Land Claim (2010), 76
Toronto Purchase of 1787
   See Johnson-Butler treaties (1787-88); land cessions and agreements—First "purchase" at Toronto (1787)
Toronto Purchase of 1805 (Treaty 13), 62-63, 73-76
   See also land cessions and agreements—First "purchase" at Toronto (1787); York
Toronto School of Medicine, 275
trade
   See fur trade
traditionalists, 67-68, 131, 135, 155, 162-163, 216, 272, 289
Trail of Tears, 212
transportation, 3, 7, 87, 105, 107, 109, 113
   See also canoe; boats and ships; Coldwater Road; portages; railway; Yonge Street
trauma, 5, 47, 131-132, 137, 266-267, 288
treaties, 6-7, 20, 32, 35, 37-40, 44, 51-52, 54, 56-57, 61-63, 74-76, 83, 95, 98-103, 105, 117, 121, 127, 131, 157-158, 161, 166, 169, 191-194, 214-215, 224, 238-239, 241, 243-244, 249-251, 254-255, 257, 259, 293-294, 298
   See also alliances; Haldimand Proclamation; land cessions and agreements; land rights: Nanfan Deed (1701); peace treaties; *names of individual treaties*
Treaty of Niagara, 15, 17, 44, 224
   See also alliances
treaty rights, 6, 32, 238, 254
Truth and Reconciliation Commission, 230
Tuhbenahneequay (Henry, Sarah), 63-64, 66, 137, 273
Tunkers, 87
Twenty-Four Nations Wampum, 44
Two Row Wampum, 252
Tyendinaga, 153, 226, 228, 260, 274, 277

U

Union of Ontario Indians, 260
United Bands Movement, 259
United Empire Loyalists, 79, 89
  See also Loyalists
United Nations Declaration on the Rights of Indigenous Peoples, 261
United States, 45, 51, 77, 79, 87, 105, 131–133, 152–153, 167, 189, 199–200, 212, 223, 259, 280
  See also American Revolution; Loyalists; Rebellion of 1837; Upper Canada; War of 1812
University of Toronto, 2, 80, 192, 271, 297–298
Upper Canada, 13, 18, 57, 61, 65, 69–70, 77, 80–81, 87, 89–90, 99, 103–105, 115, 117–119, 131, 133–134, 140, 143, 152–153, 164–165, 167, 169, 173, 187, 189, 195–196, 199, 211, 219, 229, 266, 270, 276–277
  administration, 76, 81–82, 99, 115–118, 131, 167, 199, 223, 225
  See also Canada West; clergy reserves; Indian department and Indian administration; Indian policy; Ontario; Russell, Peter; settlers and settlement; Simcoe, John Graves; slavery and slave trade
Upper Canada College, 266, 270
Upper Canada Rebellion
  See Rebellion of 1837

V

Vaughan, 83, 105, 123, 127, 199
Victoria, Queen, 211, 213–214, 238–239
  Imperial Declaration (1847), 239
  See also Jones, Peter (Kahkewaquonaby / Desagondensta); Nahnebahwequay (Sutton, Catherine)
Village at Black Creek, The (formerly Black Creek Pioneer Village), 1–5, 45, 84–85, 93, 123, 160, 295, 297

W

Wabakinine, 52, 55–56, 69–71, 131
Wabanip, 69, 71
Wabbicommicot, 44
Wade, Ferral, 45
Wahbanosay / Wabenose, 62–63, 96, 131, 140
Wampum, 7, 35–39, 44–45, 64, 71, 96, 148, 211, 214–215, 235, 238, 251–253, 258
  See also Circle Wampum; Covenant Chain Wampum; Dish with One Spoon Wampum; Eternal Council Fires or Yellowhead Wampum; Five Nations or Aienwatha / Hiawatha Wampum; Pledge of the Crown Wampum; Twenty-Four Nations Wampum; Two Row Wampum
war and warfare, 3, 6–7, 15, 32, 37, 39, 42, 44, 51, 57, 69, 78–79, 81, 83, 88–89, 93–99, 102–105, 109, 113–114, 127, 131–133, 135, 138, 189, 199, 202, 206, 235, 238, 241, 250, 274, 283–284, 288, 291, 294
  See also American Revolution; Beaver Wars; Pontiac's War; Seven Years War; War of 1812
War of 1812, 3, 79, 83, 89, 93–95, 97–99, 102–103, 105, 109, 113, 131, 199, 206, 235, 274, 283–284
  See also Battle of York
Wazhushk (muskrat), 22, 121, 264
Wendat (Huron), 3–4, 14, 18, 25–28, 31–32, 35
  See also Wyandot
Wesleyan Methodists
  See Methodism—Wesleyan Methodists
Western Alliance, 70
Whitchurch, 83, 87, 116
white supremacy, 105
wild rice, 23, 87, 188, 240
Williams Treaties, 62, 166, 169
Willson, David, 87
  See also Quakers (Society of Friends)
Windham settlement, 88
women, 8, 17, 46, 52, 66, 76, 78, 81, 89, 105, 111–112, 115–116, 127, 134, 145, 150, 156, 159, 168, 172, 217, 221, 224, 237–238, 240–241, 243–244, 249–250, 253–254, 257, 259, 268–269, 272–273, 277, 289
  See also gender roles; intermarriage; marriage—loss of status for marrying out; Nahnebahwequay (Sutton, Catherine)
Wyandot, 28, 70, 133
  See also Wendat (Huron)
Wybenga, Darin, 5–6, 32, 42, 51, 57, 62, 76, 95, 102, 137, 153, 159, 163, 203, 218, 231, 234, 297–298

Y

Yellowhead
    See Musquakie (Yellowhead); Musquakie (William Yellowhead)
Yellowhead Wampum
    See Eternal Council Fires Wampum
Yonge Street, 3, 18, 20, 62–63, 79, 82–83, 87–88, 103, 107, 115, 118, 126–127, 143, 145, 157, 171, 199–200
    camp meetings, 3, 143–147
    Circuit, 143
York, 13, 18, 20–21, 45–46, 49, 52, 57, 59, 61–63, 69-70, 78–79, 81–82, 88–90, 93, 95–98, 104–105, 107, 109–110, 113–116, 118, 121, 126, 131, 133, 141, 143–145,150, 152, 155–157, 160, 165, 171, 174, 188, , 236, 267
    County, 83, 86–87, 199, 236
    founding of, 18, 21
    militia, 93
    See also Battle of York; Toronto
York Bible Society, 133
York County, 83, 86–87, 199, 236
York, Duke of (Prince Frederick), 13
York University, 2, 26, 297–298

www.ingramcontent.com/pod-product-compliance
Lightning Source LLC
Chambersburg PA
CBHW061934290426
44113CB00025B/2912